S0-DSQ-641

DATE DUE

THE
PHILOSOPHY
OF
BEING

THE
PHILOSOPHY OF BEING

A SYNTHESIS OF METAPHYSICS

BY

Rt. Rev. LOUIS DE RAEYMAEKER, Ph.D., S.T.D.

Professor of Philosophy at Louvain University
President of the Institut Supérieur de Philosophie

TRANSLATED BY

Rev. EDMUND H. ZIEGELMEYER, S.J.

B. HERDER BOOK CO.
15 & 17 SOUTH BROADWAY, ST. LOUIS 2, MO.
AND
33 QUEEN SQUARE, LONDON, W. C.

CUM PERMISSU SUPERIORUM

This translation was made from the second revised French edition of *Philosophie de l'être. Essai de synthèse métaphysique,* published by L'Institut Supérieur de Philosophie de l'Université de Louvain in 1947.

IMPRIMI POTEST: Daniel H. Conway, S.J.

                                   Provincial, Missouri Province

NIHIL OBSTAT: John C. Baskett, A.M., S.T.L.

                                   Censor Librorum

IMPRIMATUR: ✝ Edwin V. O'Hara, D.D.

                                   Bishop of Kansas City

Library of Congress Catalog Card Number: 53-8704

9214

Reprinted 1957

Copyright 1954 by B. Herder Book Co.

PRINTED IN THE UNITED STATES OF AMERICA

by Vail-Ballou Press, Inc., Binghamton, New York

TRANSLATOR'S PREFACE

It has become standard strategy to introduce every new clash of arms on the field of metaphysics with an apology to the American reader. Such procedure seems to be an insult to our intelligence, just as if all we knew on this side of the Atlantic was the touch of Midas, the discovery of labor-saving devices, or the wangling of a college degree by means of a quarterback sneak.

Regrettably, positivism and pragmatism have had indeed a strangle hold on our philosophical speculation for decades, but at the same time we have had a few "lovers of the vision of Truth" who have made herculean efforts to rise above undigested facts and isolated phenomena. There are thinkers even here in America who, being in love with Wisdom, are not content with flitting over the surface of things, but burn with a desire to delve to their very roots, their essences, their ultimate causes. Positivists and pragmatists, to be sure, anathematize all such burrowing; while posing as trumpeters that summon us to the fray, they would have us cringe and cower behind a congeries of facts, or at best would grudgingly allow us to heap up a breastwork of laws and tables of invariable antecedents and consequents, seemingly a formidable rampart, but in reality a Maginot line.

Such rank empiricism, or more accurately sensism, would sound the death-knell for all science by outlawing the remotest vestiges of abstraction, which enables us to rise above the singular and to extract the universal; and sooner or later its unholy issue must inevitably be driven to intellectual bankruptcy and philosophical suicide. Centuries ago both Plato and Aristotle were shrewd enough to observe that we do not deserve to be called lovers of Wisdom until we begin to wonder; they saw, too, that this curiosity is not slaked until we have ferreted out the causes of the things that begot our wonder. To get to these causes we must transcend the physical, the realm of the senses; we must, painful as it may seem, hoist ourselves up to the very zenith of abstraction, there to contemplate being, as being. Until we reach that stratosphere, as it were, we are just so many cave men whose fetters prevent them from beholding anything more than flimsy shadows of genuine, bona fide reality.

Monsignor Raeymaeker's *Philosophy of Being* strikes off these shackles, so that we may "fly away from earth to Heaven," there to drink deep draughts of the intoxicating vision of Truth; but at the same time it keeps us in immediate, living contact with the reality which we ourselves are. It is thus a synthesis which succeeds in charting the one safe channel between the vortex of essentialism and the reefs of existentialism; and this feature most of all inspired our present endeavor to enable those not conversant with French to follow the Monsignor as he tries to pull all the loose skeins of metaphysics together. For he makes it possible for those enamored of Wisdom to get to being, but not to rest therein as in some abstract, specter-like notion; rather, he provokes us to keep on soaring ever higher and higher until we reach Being par excellence, subsistent Being, Wisdom personified, God Himself.

While not professedly a textbook, this synthesis can readily be adapted to the classroom. To the teacher, however, who has only three semester hours at his disposal, we suggest that he confine himself to the first four chapters of Part I, Chapter VI of Part II, and Chapters IX, XI and XII of Part III. Obviously, in an introductory course the lengthy historical inquiry into the origins of the real distinction between essence and existence, and the disquisition on the existence and nature of the creative Cause will have to be summarized rather rapidly. And yet it would be fatal to skim over the masterly concluding chapter which offers a panoramic vision of the whole problem, and once again drives home the Parthian shaft that the adequate explanation of finite, participated being can be found, not in another participated being or even in a whole galaxy of things contingent, but only in the inexhaustible source of infinite, absolute Perfection.

This preface would be incomplete and ungrateful, did it not acknowledge my indebtedness to my sister, Elfrieda Kay, for her encouragement, and above all to Ann Josephine Dixon, whose generosity and self-sacrifice in typing and retyping the manuscript made it possible for this translation to appear in print.

TABLE OF CONTENTS

THE
PHILOSOPHY
OF
BEING

CHAPTER I

INTRODUCTION

1. General and Special Metaphysics

MAN is a prey to a natural desire for knowledge;[1] he never grows weary of knowing. Even the needs of practical life urge him on to observe nature and to discover its laws; but more than this, he feels himself attracted towards knowledge for itself and he experiences a profound delight in acquiring and possessing purely theoretical knowledge. Down through the centuries men have transmitted philosophy and the sciences from generation to generation as a precious treasure, which they continually strive to increase more and more.

From the very dawn of philosophy the human mind has unhesitatingly grappled with the deepest problems, which concern the substance, the origin, and the destiny of the whole universe. Yet in the measure in which reflection became systematic and the methods of research more precise, men took into account the variety and the intricacies of the data, as well as the necessity of dividing up this work. Soon various branches of philosophy were distinguished, one from the other, and in the course of time a series of sciences, mathematical, experimental, and historical, was progressively set up as independent disciplines.[2]

In the course of this long evolution, men recognized more and more clearly that, for a problem to be solved perfectly, it had to be stated in precise terms. They saw the advantage of reducing the scope of particular inquiries and giving the preference to works that pursue immediate and limited but still well-defined objectives. The astonishing success of the empirical sciences in modern times resulted in good part from the minute observation of some ordinary and easily ac-

---

[1] Aristotle, *Metaph.*, Bk. I, chap. 1, *initio.*
[2] Cf. author's *Introduction à la philosophie*, 2nd ed., Louvain-Brussels, 1944, pp. 8–18.

3

cessible facts, from the methodical and exhaustive study of such questions which might appear, at first blush, to be concerned with details,
devoid of any importance.

Yet the vast problems of philosophy never lost their attraction. Is
it not remarkable to observe that in our day the development of the
natural sciences everywhere keeps step with a rebirth of interest in
metaphysics? Kant was quite right in saying that metaphysics responds to a natural and irradicable disposition of the human mind.[3]
Today as in the past, man feels the need of studying metaphysics,
that is, of seeking the fundamental principle of reality, taken in its
entirety; and in spite of the difficulties and disillusionments philosophers do not grow weary in pursuing the study of this problem.[4]

To Christian Wolff (1679–1754) we can trace the division of metaphysics into general and special, and this distinction rests on the following basis. We have a tendency to classify things according to their
resemblance; and thus it is that we group natural beings as living and
non-living, that we distinguish living things as plants and animals,
and among these latter we reserve a special place for man. The particular philosophical study of each of these groups belongs to special
metaphysics. We generally regard this latter as consisting of cosmology, which is devoted to the philosophy of the inorganic world (and
to this we often attach the study of vegetative life), and of rational
psychology, which is the philosophical study of corporeal living beings
and is especially the study of man.[5]

---

[3] Cf. *Critique of Pure Reason,* Introd. vi (tr. by Norman Kemp Smith, London, Macmillan and Co., 1929), pp. 55–58.

[4] We know that the origin of the word "metaphysics" attaches to the edition
of Aristotle's works which was prepared at Rome in the first century before our
era by Andronicus of Rhodes. He arranged the various works of the Stagyrite
according to the subjects there treated. He placed after the books of the physics
the fourteen books which he entitled "Ta meta ta (biblia) physica," i.e., the
books which come after the treatises on physics, and which contain principally
the studies relevant to what Aristotle calls "first philosophy." The formal object
of this latter, according to the Stagyrite, is "being and what of itself belongs to
being."

For the history of the works of Aristotle, cf. J. Bidez, *Un singulier naufrage
littéraire dans l'antiquité. A là recherche des épaves de l'Aristote perdu. (Collect.
Lebègue,* 3rd series, no. 36), Brussels, 1943.

[5] Following Aristotle's lead, the medieval Scholastics generally divided theoretical philosophy into three branches: physics, mathematics, and metaphysics.
This division is founded on what they agreed to call the three degrees of abstraction. According to this conception, physics studies nature from the point
of view of its sensible characters, subject to motion and time. As a matter of fact,
this physics therefore included all the questions that today are raised in cos-

In nature these groups of realities are by no means isolated. On the contrary, each one is bound up with the others, so as to form a whole. This fact seems to be true of all beings: they ought to constitute a single complexus. Hence we have good reason to study them under this relation: what is required that beings may be able to form this complete unity? To general metaphysics belongs the treatment of this problem; but Aristotle, who set himself to define this branch of philosophy, calls it "first or fundamental philosophy." [6]

2. *The Natural Tendency of Man towards Metaphysics*

Human experience is confined within narrow limits. Hence it does not seem possible to solve the problems of first philosophy by the simple processes of observation; and yet that is what philosophical empiricism would wish to do. It devotes itself to the empirical study of facts in order to draw from them the principles of a complete explanation of reality. But how would it be justified in extending beyond the domain of experience the field of application of the empirical laws? Really, there are no philosophers worthy of the name who confine themselves to a self-contained empiricism.

More numerous are the defenders of philosophical positivism. They think that in philosophy we cannot affirm or even deny anything with certitude about a subject which would go beyond the realm of experience. Kantianism is a form of philosophical positivism, at least as regards theoretical or speculative reason. It preaches a subjectivistic formalism, which forbids this theoretical reason to make any incursion into transphenomenal reality; but Kant did not rest satisfied with this agnosticism. He believed that he had discovered in practical

mology and psychology. Besides, we must observe that the distinction between the method of philosophy and that of the experimental sciences has been nicely drawn only in our own day, and that the "physics" of the ancients included empirical and experimental researches just as much as the philosophical study of the data.

[6] In the classification of the branches of philosophy proposed by Christian Wolff, theodicy is attached to "special" metaphysics, because just as cosmology and psychology, it is concerned with a particular domain of reality, which is, in this case, that of the divine Being. The medieval Scholastics, on the contrary, did not separate the study of God from that of general metaphysics, because philosophy can know God only as the Creator of the universe, as the principle of the complexus of beings, so that the philosophical study of God goes back precisely to that of the fundamental metaphysical problem. This is the reason why the Scholastics, as Aristotle, called "first philosophy" (natural) theology.

reason the means to get at the domain of the noumena, which had been irremediably closed to speculative philosophy.

Kant's procedure was imitated by many philosophers, for there are very few who resign themselves to ignoring completely what goes beyond phenomena. The defenders of Kantian agnosticism have quite frequently entered into the paths of irrationalism,—those of feeling, of action, or of some fundamental intuition—in order to discover a satisfactory explanation of reality.

It is an incontestable fact that the greatest philosophers of all times, e.g., Plato, Aristotle, Plotinus, Augustine, Thomas Aquinas, Duns Scotus, Descartes, Malebranche, Leibnitz, Spinoza, Berkeley, Kant, Fichte, Schelling, Hegel and so many others, have thought that it is in man's power by natural and philosophical means to get to the non-empirical principle of reality. If we give the meaning of "empirical" to the term "physical," we must say that these philosophers extol a metaphysical or transempirical explanation of the universe.[7] The greater number are defenders of an intellectual metaphysics; and yet in our day, a goodly number propose metaphysical theories, which are anti-intellectual and irrational.

3. The Reason of This Tendency

Whence does man derive this ineluctable tendency to place himself at the point of view of the whole complexus of things in order to seek for its explanation? The reason for this tendency is easily discovered; it derives from the nature of human knowledge. I know that I know, I feel that I know; in other words, I have consciousness that it is I who know. My acts of knowledge are, all of them, shot through and illumined internally by the presence of this conscious ego, which is the active principle and support of these acts. These latter are centered in the ego, and they are integrated in its conscious synthesis, a complicated synthesis which presents any number of aspects. It embraces elements which are arranged in many different ways and in a variety of relations; but it is always the omnipresent ego which is the nucleus of them and which everywhere projects the light of its consciousness.

---

[7] "It is called metaphysics, i.e., *transphysica,* because it comes to be studied after the physics by us, to whom it belongs to come to the knowledge of non-sensible things from the sensible." St. Thomas Aquinas, *In lib. Boethii De Trinitate,* q. 5, a. 1. Cf. Suarez, *Disputationes metaphysicae,* disp. I.

What is metaphysical in the sense of transempirical, is beyond the psychical fact as much as it is beyond the physical and sensible fact.

The sphere of knowledge stretches out through time; I knew yesterday, I know today. Yesterday and today are not synonymous terms;
and yet the ego which knew yesterday and knows today is fundamentally one and the same. We must indeed admit that this ego escapes from the clutches of the flow of time in the measure in which,
being conscious of itself, it recognizes itself, and in which it finds itself identically the same in divers moments of time, or again in the
measure in which it is the constant witness of the events that succeed
one another. For this reason I have the power to consider time as a
whole and in each of its elements; I grasp the interplay of the relations
which it implies. In fact, at the present moment I can recognize the
past as such (inasmuch as it is opposed to the present and the future),
the present as such (inasmuch as it is opposed to the future and the
past), and the future as such (inasmuch as it is opposed to the past
and the present). I am not immured in any one of the moments of
time and I do not disappear with them. When I consider time from a
non-temporal point of view I consider it as a whole, I can pass judgment on it. By thought I transcend the course of time; thus I can at
one and the same moment represent it to myself, make it present to
my mind, embrace it in a single glance, and in a sweeping panorama
get at it in all of its instants.

The same is true with our conscious grasp of space. I am here and
I am there; here and there are opposed to each other, just as yesterday and today. This difference does not prevent me from remaining
always the same, here, down there, and elsewhere. Wherever I am, my
consciousness bears witness to the persistent presence of one and the
same ego; in changing from one place to another, I do not change my
identity. To this extent I escape from the law of spatial dispersion of
matter, and, while being bodily in a determined place, I raise myself
up in spirit to a point of view that transcends all spatial relativity.
From this coign of vantage I survey space as a whole; I can analyze
it and grasp the relations which it embraces. In the nucleus of consciousness I conjure up, as it were, space as a whole, and spiritually
I get at the elements which compose it.

In a general way, objective knowledge implies the conscious relation between subject and object; I know this latter. The relation
depends on its terms and changes with them; if this object here is distinguished from that one there, the relation which binds the knowing subject to the first object is not that by which the subject is
related to the second object. Now, whereas knowledge, the conscious

activity of the ego, is unceasingly modified in reaching out to other objects, the ego completely preserves its fundamental unity. It transcends the particular point of view of each object, since it envelops them and penetrates all with its own peculiar light. It goes beyond them and rises above them, for it is in a position to compare them, to analyze them, to judge them. It frees itself from the relativity which is inherent in them, embracing them in the synthesis which is peculiar to itself.

It is, consequently, evident that in reality everything holds together, since everything can find a place in the transcendental apperception of the ego. The affinity of things is undeniable; everything is mutually related. We are not, then, surprised that from its very origin, philosophical reflection has been directed to this point, and that it has never ceased to hold on to it. What is the principle that explains universal unity? This is the chief problem of all philosophy; and in the solution of this problem of general metaphysics the fundamental disagreement of the various systems is brought to light.

PART I

MANIFESTATION OF BEING
AND OF
THE METAPHYSICAL PROBLEM

CHAPTER II

BEING. THE PROBLEM OF METAPHYSICS

1. *Apprehension of the Ego and the Non-ego*

THE choice of the basis of metaphysics is of capital importance. This basis ought to guarantee the very existence and the validity of metaphysics, while giving this science at the same time its formal object and a solid foundation. But if metaphysics is bound up with the study of a universal unity or of the totality of things, and if then, our inquiry ought to be concerned with the whole, how can we determine the choice of a point of departure?

Let us at once set down the fact with which we have decided to begin this inquiry. This remarkable fact presupposes that in our activity of knowing we are not entirely determined and that we can on occasion take the initiative and determine for ourselves the course of our inquiry. We have the power to undertake an inquiry into the validity of our convictions, to formulate doubts, to pose problems, to push this work always farther and farther, at the same time unceasingly raising up new difficulties, and all this in the hope of encountering and finally solving the most fundamental questions.

All this activity implies consciousness, which permits us to know and to follow our own intellectual activity. In fact, we are endowed with a mind able to reflect; we can turn back upon ourselves, enter into ourselves, recollect ourselves, recognize ourselves in the immanence of our actions. This fact, therefore, that it is in our power to act in the clarity of consciousness, suggests to us that we fix our attention on this movement of reflection, with a view to bringing it into fuller evidence, and to isolating sharply the course and the content of our conscious activity.

This path indeed is the one which a considerable number of great philosophers have followed, and we have good reason to emphasize this point. To give only a few examples: St. Augustine confronts the skeptics with this truth: "For if I am deceived, I exist." [1] Whoever doubts, he remarks, cannot doubt about his own doubt, since he has consciousness of it; at least that fact is beyond doubt and it must be held as certain. The system of Descartes is founded on the "Cogito, ergo sum." [2] St. Thomas finds in the movement of reflection proper to consciousness an adequate method for determining the validity of thought. He writes: "The intellect reflects upon its own act." [3] Kant's method, too, is quite analogous: by reflection he turns his attention to the subject to reassure himself of the nature and the conditions of human knowledge. [4]

We surely do not maintain that these philosophers agree fundamentally, or that it would be possible to reduce Augustinianism, Thomism, Cartesianism, and Kantianism to one and the same system. The divergence of their ideas flashes out in questions that are most important. We merely note that these thinkers direct their researches in the same direction, as soon as there is question of defending themselves against skepticism and of discovering the foundation of true and certain knowledge.

Although they struck out on the same path, how is it that they do not attain the same result? How does it happen that they propose systems which mutually exclude one another? Could it be that they got off the track somewhere along the road? This solution is not impossible; but here again we should not adopt too simple an explanation. The method indicated was not easy to handle, and the path to pursue was not accurately mapped out. Undoubtedly in our conscious life we attain to certitude that is solidly grounded; and on that general affirmation agreement could be established without too much difficulty. But as soon as we have to explore this terrain and determine its nature, enormous difficulties crop up, and the most diverse opinions come to light.

The reason for this difficulty is found in the complexity of our conscious life. [5] If we wish, for example, to determine the validity of the cognitive faculties, there can be no question of isolating these faculties and of emptying them of their content, in order thereafter to observe

---

[1] De Civitate Dei, Bk. XI, chap. 26.

[2] Cf. II Méditation (ed. Adam-Tannery, Vol. IX, Paris, 1904, p. 19); Discours de la Méthode Vol. VI, Paris, 1902, p. 32.

[3] De veritate, q. 1, a. 9.

[4] Critique of Pure Reason, preface to first edition (tr. by Norman Kemp Smith, London, Macmillan and Co., 1929) pp. 7–15.

[5] Cf. Fernand Van Steenberghen, Épistémologie, Louvain, 1945, pp. 51–142.

them at our leisure and at close range. To have consciousness of knowing is to have consciousness of knowing something; the term "knowledge" is a word without meaning if it designates a knowledge which
does not contain anything. Whoever reflects on the genuine facts of
knowledge, is concerned with the knowledge of this or that. The subject of knowledge is never conscious of himself before he passes over
to the act of knowledge; as long as his faculty is in pure potency to
know, he cannot have any consciousness of it. It is in his power to lay
hold of this faculty only in the immanent relation which binds it to
the object. Besides, we must note that the power of knowing is never
separated from the will or from the senses; these three, as it were,
compenetrate, imply and mutually influence one another. They form
together an active indissoluble unity. Consequently the analysis of
consciousness and the critical examination of knowledge are no simple
matter; they give rise to a host of divergent opinions and errors.

Let us try to ferret out the principal elements which compose the
structure of consciousness.

Consciousness implies always an experience, a coming into contact
with reality, and first of all an experience of self, a consciousness of
self that is lived. I feel myself living; I feel myself a really living being;
I have consciousness of being, of existing. This consciousness manifests to me the reality which I am. The consciousness which is lived
is not in a sphere foreign to life, no more than conscious life is outside existing reality and over and above it, and hostile to every category of being.[6] Quite the contrary. Consciousness of self is nothing
outside of the living ego, which feels itself living and which recognizes
itself in the direct perception of its active development. I lay hold of
myself from within, in the interior clarity which I call up within myself, thanks to the identity of the conscious ego and of the real, living
ego. I *am*, and precisely of this am I conscious. The knowledge which
I have of myself, does not consist originally in a schematic representation or in an abstract concept; but it is, first and foremost, the lived
perception of the living and existing reality which I am. And thus consciousness is chiefly an experience of real life, hence an ontological
perception, a consciousness of being.[7]

At the same time it is always the consciousness of my own self. The

---

[6] "It is by means of a fiction that idealism under its traditional form tries to
maintain on the margin of being a consciousness which posits it or denies it."
Gabr. Marcel, "Position et approches concrètes du mystère ontologique," in
Le monde cassé, Paris, 1933, p. 264.

[7] "The naive and even invincible impulse (*élan*) which is expressed by what

acts and the conscious states are characterized by their belonging to
the self. To see, to hear, to sense, to think, to wish: these do not exist;
what does exist is the ego: *I* see, *I* hear, *I* sense, *I* think, *I* will. Every
thought of which I am conscious is *my* thought; every sensation lived
is *my* sensation. Now this belonging to me is not an external addition;
there are no impersonal acts or states that would by a kind of over-
growth be grafted on to a subject. No living ego subsists outside of
its vital activity, and that vital activity contains nothing other than
the living ego. "I know" signifies only the ego knowing; "I will" means
the ego willing.

The source and the seat of these acts and states is the ego; there is
question then truly of an ego which moves and which manifests itself
in its immanent activity. There is question always of the same real,
living ego, which acts and is developed, and which in the uninterrupted flow of its activity crops out into consciousness. "Cogito" ("I
think") signifies the ego thinking, the ego which exists while thinking:
Cogito . . . sum; I am thinking.

Consequently, consciousness carries with it at one and the same
time and necessarily an apprehension of being and an apprehension

---

Spinoza calls the fundamental tendency of every being to persevere in being,
reveals itself and is brought to light in us not merely by the very instinct of
self-preservation, but by a native faith which even the suicide does not destroy.
Irresistibly, at the moment when a man seeks to destroy himself, he avows by
this desire of self-destruction the conviction which he has of his existence, and
not merely of his own existence but of the reality in conflict with himself. . . .

"In this sense, antecedently to all doctrine and every will, nihilism is not at
all possible. Being does not raise any question for him who is; and that which
not long ago they called the total presence of being to itself, eliminates the possibility of going out of the real, even if this be done by thought that is most
expert in critique, in negation, in destruction. . . .

"It would be to formulate a fictitious problem, denatured and by that very
fact insoluble, thus to pose the question: How do we get to being? We do not
have to depart from what is not, to come to what would be conceived as outside of him who seeks or outside of what is sought. Being is not if it is not already
wherever the enigma of its existence arises. We do not, therefore, have to go
out of ourselves in order to trap it in some way on its distant flight or in its
mysterious retreat, for we are in being, '*in eo sumus.*' We are in it and we are
of it; and this is why the fundamental vice from which derive so many antinomies
without solution, is precisely this conviction or, let us speak more accurately,
this mistaken spatial phantasm according to which the subject would have to
leap out of an abyss in order to traverse the vacuum which separates him from
reality. And this reality he would never reach, since he has already pretended as
if he himself were not a part of this reality." Maurice Blondel, *L'être et les êtres,*
Paris, 1935, pp. 8 f.

of the self, the consciousness of being and of being the self. It is the
immanent apprehension of the active identity of the real ego.[8]

My experience extends further than this lived apprehension of the
ego. I feel myself living in a world which surrounds me. On every side
I brush up against objects which are there, on the outside, and which
are distinct from myself; they form a non-ego.[9] For I do not perceive
them on the inside, as identified with my lived and immanent apprehension. I see plants, animals, mountains, and clouds; I am conscious
of seeing all those things but in no wise of being them. Nevertheless
that fact does not signify that I would be conscious of not being those
things. We must distinguish the fact of not having consciousness of
being such a thing, from that of having consciousness of not being
that thing. For the present we are limiting ourselves to emphasizing
that I have consciousness of identifying myself with certain data of
experience, whereas other data appear to me as being outside of this
consciousness of identity. Undoubtedly the perception of these data
is a manifestation of my activity of life, for this perception is nothing
other than the ego perceiving this; but I am forbidden to say in this
connection that these things are mine. If I should maintain that some
of these external things are mine, this assertion is true because of an
extrinsic relation which I have with them. I speak of my house, my
hat, my dog, because they belong to me; but precisely this relation of
ownership presupposes the real non-identity of the terms of the relation. It would be nonsense to say that I have the ownership of my
dreams, of my perceptions, or of my sensations, at least if we use
these words in their proper sense. There is question in this last case
of my conscious life, which always remains immanent in the fundamental unity of the ego.

A divergence of opinions obtains as to whether all these data (those
of the ego and of the non-ego, in the precise sense just now defined)
belong to one and the same profound reality; this question will be
examined later on. For the moment, let it suffice to note that there is
an evident distinction (whatever be its nature, superficial or profound) between the data presented as the constituents of the conscious ego and those that do not manifest themselves as such.

---

[8] On the consciousness which man has of himself, cf. N. Balthasar, *La
méthode en métaphysique*, Louvain, 1943, pp. 124 ff.

[9] Cf. L. Noel, *Le réalisme immédiat*, Louvain, 1938, pp. 97 ff.; "Le 'cogito'
thomiste."

The contact with my ego is a lived apprehension of the reality which I am; the contact with the world about me is never a lived apprehension of my real identity with these objects. In this sense we say that the first contact concerns my ego, the other concerns what is exterior to my ego, that is, the non-ego.

It would be futile to make here a complete inventory of what belongs to the ego and to the non-ego, or even to trace with precision the line of demarcation between these two domains. We may be satisfied to emphasize that there is given to us a lived apprehension, in which the living ego appears to consciousness; and that, moreover, in another form of experience, some things manifest themselves without our having the feeling that they constitute a moment of the conscious evolution of our ego.

The conscious ego finds itself face to face with the non-ego. This last surrounds the ego and opposes an insurmountable limit to it, for the lived apprehension is restricted to the ego and does not go beyond it; the non-ego remains a closed book to it. Consequently the ego, a conscious reality, feels itself limited. The non-ego, which is the extrinsic reason of this real limitation, belongs itself to the domain of reality. To the "I am" corresponds "That thing is"; the real comprehends the one and the other, *sum—est*.

A limit unites, just as it separates adjacent regions; it is the place where distinct sectors meet each other. Thus the ego and non-ego are related one to the other. The limited ego does not exist without its limit, nor does it exist without the non-ego which limits it. It is by its own nature an ego in the world, an ego surrounded by non-egos.

Further, conscious activity is naturally bound up with the activity of the senses. If this latter becomes defective, I lose consciousness. I can indeed pass from one or the other sense in particular, but not from all of them at once. Now the senses are oriented towards the external world and they put me in relation with the things that are outside of that lived apprehension of my ego. These things present themselves as belonging to the non-ego.

Similarly, my perception of the external world is conscious. I know that I perceive things, and later I will be able to recall them. The world does not become present to me without my perceiving myself as of it, without my being present to this activity of my senses. Consequently, the knowledge of the non-ego is naturally bound up with the consciousness of the ego, just as the consciousness of my ego is produced always within the framework of the perception of the non-ego.

What is the nature of the distinction between the ego and the non-ego? The question is of capital importance; for there is reason to believe that if the opposition of the two terms were only superficial, and if it were founded on the profound unity of their being, the problems to be faced would be very different from those which would be posed by the real and radical distinction of the ego and the non-ego.

The nature of this distinction evidently depends on the nature of the present terms. And as I lay hold of my self in the immediacy of a conscious identity, this clearly suggests that the first question should be about the nature of the ego, in as far as the present question demands.

On my activity I throw the light of consciousness: I feel myself living, acting; I live the actions which I perform. This activity appears to me as an irrepressible, constant and variegated tendency towards an expansion of life ever larger, of richer variety and more profound. It is penetrated with divers feelings, it is founded on them and enjoys them. Further, it carries with it knowledge under a variety of aspects, knowledge which is changed into reflex thought, seeking to comprehend and explain data, to foresee their results and to adapt its conduct accordingly.

Thought puts clarity and precision into action and by it we can discover the essential traits which characterize the conscious ego. The man who thinks and reflects, brings home to himself his own reality. He is not content with merely suffering impressions and drawing up a list of them. He observes data, delays with them, and examines their different aspects, with the intention of forming for himself a calm and objective opinion about their nature and their validity. To do this he expands his point of view; he directs his attention beyond each phenomenon in particular, in such a way as to distinguish different data, to mark down their respective limits, to determine their relations, in a word, to recognize the order of which they are the constituent parts.

It is indeed remarkable that every person acts in this same way in regard to his own ego. I reflect on my nature and I recognize its limits. To discover the meaning of life I turn my eyes on my own ego and on the non-ego; I reflect on what I am in myself and in the world, and thus I encompass in one single glance the ego and the non-ego. It is not by starting with a subjective experience that I estimate their validity; on the contrary I judge them from a point of view which transcends the one and the other, and which goes beyond their opposition and their relations. For the present there is no reason to define this point of view more accurately; it is the point of view of *being*, and there will be question of this later on. Nor need we now wonder about all that is implied by this power which permits me to lift myself up, so to speak, above my own ego. Here let it suffice to indicate in a general manner the direction which the natural movement of the human mind follows.

Thanks to reflection, I can somehow comprehend my life and pass judgment on the place which I occupy in the world, a judgment which corresponds to reality. The vital impulse which is developed under the light of this comprehensive thought goes by the name of will. If I happen to follow consciously this direction and not that other, it is because I have willed it; in other words, it is after reflection that I have thus decided. This choice is mine, in the most proper sense of the word; for there is question here of a deliberate and free will, of an autonomous decision, of a formal affirmation of independence.

A free decision rests on a thought that is firm; it results from a state of clear and reflex consciousness, and it has as its support reasons which we have understood and whose import we have weighed. But how does it happen that these reasons are not necessitating, that they are incapable of forcing our hand? We must observe first of all that the reasons which come into play in the choice of placing an action, are many in number; for every real situation is complicated and presents different aspects. For example, if I have a mind to give an alms, I have to choose the persons or the institutions which I wish to make the beneficiary of my mite. I can examine, one after the other, the reasons which militate for this side or that other; but it always remains in my power to examine all these motives, to compare them, to consider them in their complexity. It will be evident to me that one is distinct from the other, and that each one has its own value; that one is undoubtedly stronger than the other, but that no one motive is perfect to the point of annulling all the value of the others. Consequently, if I come to a decision while resting on such a motive, I do not fail on that account to see the value of the others, and I take into consideration the limits of the first motive. This motive does not blind me; it does not by sheer force extort my consent. Hence, I continue to recognize that the other motives could, strictly speaking, initiate a course of action, perhaps less good or even bad, but nonetheless human and rational, because founded on a motive that is known, that is, on a reason. It seems to me, then, that if my choice is made in this direction, it is without doubt because one or more reasons militate for this solution, but in the last analysis it is because I myself have decided that in the end I would give these reasons my preference, that they would be my motives for acting. Under the light of reflective thought I clearly perceive the situation in which I find myself; I understand it and dominate it, and as there is question of my own personal condition, I have dominion over my own self and I come to a decision as a master of the course of my actions: I am free. Consequently, a voluntary decision plunges its roots down into thought; it is reflection which is the measure of it. Freedom is an essential property of consciousness, a natural consequence of the lived apprehension of the ego.

It is quite understandable that the feeling of responsibility is so profoundly anchored in the heart of man; my decision belongs to me, to me alone, and to no other person. I carry all the responsibility of it, for its source is in me and nowhere else. In the measure in which the act of the will is free, it spurts out, as it were, from a personal decision; it is a self-determination of an ego whose activity is at once impulse and thought, power and light, that is, a life that is fully conscious.

We have observed above that the ego manifests itself in consciousness as a reality which feels itself living, which lives its own real activity, and that all that the ego implies is characterized undeniably as mine. Over against the ego there appears the non-ego, which I simply cannot perceive as mine; it is the other, the external world. The opposition becomes precise as soon as we observe that the conscious ego implies thought and free will; as a matter of fact, in the measure in which the ego exercises its liberty, it perceives itself and knows itself as detached from the non-ego. The ego itself makes decisions; it is not an integral part of a more extensive reality; it acts on its own account; it is sufficient unto itself; it is autonomous in its action, and on that account it is complete in itself. It is subsistent; it is one being.

The ego is limited by the non-ego; its liberty necessarily runs up against limits. That means, first of all, that the world in which my life unfolds itself, lies outside the clutches of my willing. It is not a free and conscious decree of my will which is responsible for the origin of this world, no more than I am the reason for its continuing in existence. External things are given to me as facts; they are posited before me as phenomena, whose objectivity I see myself forced to verify and allow.

Further, I cannot withdraw myself from the physical action of the world which surrounds me. It closely surrounds the flow of my life and makes its weight felt on all the forms of my activity. Consciousness, which is an intellectual and free life, awakens within the framework of sensible experience, from which it remains inseparable. This is tantamount to saying that consciousness presents likewise a sensible counterpart. In fact, I am conscious of seeing, of hearing etc., although the action of my senses belongs to the human body, which is subject to the determinism of the physical laws. The ego, which preserves its identity all through the course of life, and whose reality appears by that same token as withdrawn from the relativity of time and space, this ego informs and animates sense activity which is measured in time and space. It assimilates this activity of the senses to itself and penetrates it with its own light; the ego is a subject which feels itself seeing and hearing. And yet these operations do not for all of that lose their sensible and material character, so much so that the conscious ego finds itself really moving in a material world, and in the same measure it is subject to the necessitating law of matter.

The permanent identity of the ego bears witness to its indivisible unity. If it includes irreducible elements, these are united to the point of compenetrating one another and of each one's imprinting its own character on the whole ego. It is thus that the activity of the senses, just as intelligence, shares in the identity of consciousness; and on the other hand thought experiences in itself the repercussions of the material extension proper to the senses. Hence, this thought will never attain to a vision of the real, that is at the same time complete and crystal-clear; it will have to resign itself to plodding along the tedious and painful path of abstraction and of discursive reasoning in order to throw a bit of light on the data of experience. Never is the ego of the man in this world an exclusively thinking ego, for it is not in his power to strip himself of the complexus of his sensations. These latter, too, go to make up an opaque fringe, which clouds the vision of the mind and resists perfectly transparent intellection.

For these same reasons the will never succeeds in impressing on life, once and for all, a calm, well-regulated direction which definitively guarantees its entire destiny. For the will can assert itself only by means of instinctive tendencies, and it would have to be disengaged from these in order to impose its dominion upon them. Consequently, the ego has to wage an interior struggle and to make constant efforts to subdue and to utilize, as best it can, the powers of sentient life.

Consciousness, moreover, considered as the lived apprehension of the ego, is subject unceasingly to the influence of the varying conditions of corporeal existence. Health, sickness, sleep, old age, affect consciousness in different ways; sometimes they intensify, sometimes they diminish or even extinguish it. Even under the best conditions consciousness includes some obscure areas; the activity of the senses and of the imagination is full of things unknown. As regards tendencies and feelings, these conceal within themselves a number of mysteries; only in the operations of the intellect and free will does the ego really see and possess itself.

Furthermore, there is an internal factor which binds the will, and this is the reality of the ego itself. The act of consciousness confronts me with the reality which I am; it puts me face to face with a fact, a datum to be admitted. I have no consciousness of being the author of my being; in waking up to life I see myself thrown out into existence, in the midst of the world, and never would I have been able to change that fact. My being and my nature are not subject to my freedom; they condition my free activity, and in this sense they are an objective reality to which I must needs submit myself. The ego, therefore, is at one and the same time nature and liberty. Inasmuch as it is nature, it shares in the non-ego, in the *other*, and is subject to its law, and just by so much is its autonomy over nature diminished. Free will is limited in itself and carries dependence in its train. Human liberty cannot deploy its powers ad infinitum; everywhere it brushes up against resistance, in itself and in the external world.

Let us conclude: our consciousness asserts itself with undeniable force and evidence. It is first and foremost the lived apprehension of the ego which manifests its spiritual permanence and its autonomy in the exercise of thinking and willing. Sense life, completely organic as it is, does not extinguish this consciousness; on the contrary, it rests on it as on its support and finds its completion therein. Furthermore, as this sense activity belongs to the physical order, it lies as a weight on the life of the mind, it shackles and obscures it. The nature from which our spiritual activity proceeds, does not depend on us either for its being or for its essence. Nevertheless, it unfolds itself in a free and autonomous movement; and by this conscious and free development being knows itself, determines itself, possesses itself.

Its activity is completely immanent and belongs to it in its own right; that is, this selfsame being which acts, belongs to itself truly in its existence as well as in its action. It is a complete and subsistent being.

The distinction between this being and the reality which surrounds it, appears then to be real and fundamental. Subsistent being confers on its activity a meaning and value which are peculiar to it; it assumes the responsibility for this activity, it acts as a person.

What does the world contain which surrounds the person who I am? Things distributed in space, plants and animals of every species, with which I enter into contact by means of my body. It would require a profound study of this world to determine its nature and its relations.

This world contains also certain living beings for whose behavior I have an explanation as soon as I consider them as men, every one of them constituted by a conscious ego, and expressing physically by their attitude and their actions the personal interior life of which they have consciousness. I am, moreover, moved to adopt these views by the social character which my nature possesses. The tendency to social life, which I experience, is in accordance with the data with which my experience of life furnishes me. I am certain that there are men, with whom I can enter into relation and with whom I can come to terms, and with whom I constitute on this spiritual basis a human community.

Here especially this truth that there are many beings, comes clearly home to me. For from the fact that there exist men who resemble myself in as far as I am endowed with conscious life, I must admit that every one of these is the author of free actions, which proceed only from him and of which he alone carries the responsibility. This is tantamount to saying that every man is an autonomous being, sufficiently complete and independent of all others for acting by himself, for subsisting and developing in himself; every man is one being.

To establish this truth we might start with the analysis of human experiences, such as friendship, love, hatred, and sympathy, boredom, remorse, vanity, pride, etc. A number of contemporary philosophers, in particular the phenomenologists and the existentialists, strike out on this path. Their descriptions and their theories here take on a particularly lively character, and their system as a whole presents a strong affective complexion in keeping with the experience whose analysis is found at the very beginning of their researches. But whatever be the experience described and studied in preference to others, it always implies, on the one hand, an affirmation of personal existence and activity, and on the other, an affirmation of limitation, manifesting itself in an attitude of attachment, opposition, dependence or want with regard to other beings. In his whole conscious life man appears as a person, who lives in the presence of other human persons within the framework of the material world.

2. Being, the Basis of Metaphysics

We have good reason to stop at these first data, in order to make them the object of metaphysical considerations. Human experience, such as we have just described, arises and is developed within the heart of existing reality; it is always an apprehension of being. In every act of consciousness the ego is manifested to itself as a real and existing ego. It vouches for its own being as well as its immediate contact with the being of the non-ego. Such an experience implies, in the very first place, an affirmation of being. It guarantees that being is forced upon us by the undeniable fact of its presence; it asserts firmly that being is there.

This affirmation is direct. It is not founded on a reasoning process, or on the testimony of a third party, or on the content of a representation, but entirely on the presence of the being of the ego and the non-ego. It is an incontrovertible affirmation; for there is manifestly an identity between the existing ego and the conscious ego, and this absence of an intermediary and even of distinction excludes all possibility of discordance and error. As regards the presence of the non-ego, it is indissolubly bound up with the consciousness of the limitation of the ego, and it is direct and immediate. Just as no man has ever been able to doubt about his own reality,[10] so neither can he doubt about the reality of the world of things in the midst of which he exists.[11]

This affirmation is categorical and expresses the absolute character of being. From the very moment that we brush up against reality, we affirm it as an incontestable fact, established once and for all. Thus, I feel myself living and existing, and right away it seems quite evident to me that as long as I exist, it is impossible for me not to exist.

---

[10] "No one can assent to the thought that he does not exist. For in the very fact that he is thinking, he perceives himself to exist." St. Thomas, *De veritate*, q. 10, a. 12, ad 7.

[11] This does not mean that we are in a position to define the nature of these things exactly.

Never under any supposition could it be true to say that I do not exist at this moment. I exist, and I must admit it without any qualification. There is question then of a truth which is not hypothetical, but rather unconditional, absolute. Now we affirm this only by reason of the reality which is present to us. It is this reality which possesses an unshakable solidity, an absolutely definitive consistency, an absolute validity. This also holds good for all existence; whatever be its nature and its duration, it etches into reality its indelible traits and it forces itself for ever and ever on the mind. Being exists; and by its own peculiar power, its "virtus essendi," [12] it excludes radically and without condition or any restriction all that would be opposed to it, and would tend to justify a different affirmation. Outside of being there is only nothing, and so there is nothing which could make it conditional. Being rests upon its own unshakable and irresistible force; it is complete in itself, sufficient for itself, absolute.

Some people believe that it is fatuous to wish to find the absolute in the data of experience, seeing that these data are contingent; but this is merely a gratuitous affirmation. First of all, a preliminary remark confronts us. The ontological contingence of things is not at all immediately evident, and it does not form the point of departure of metaphysical reflection. If we are justified in admitting it, this is only at the end of a proof properly drawn up. Furthermore, whether reality is contingent or not, the fact is that its existence is affirmed in a way that is really indisputable and definitively undeniable. It manifests a value of absolute being, forcing itself upon everything and everybody. In the case where this reality would be contingent (and later on we will strive to prove that it is such) the problem would be posed of knowing how contingent being can manifest an absolute consistency. We cannot decide the question in advance; but in any case it would be a vicious procedure to reject immediate data under the pretext that they would give rise to insoluble problems.

For the moment we restrict ourselves to laying emphasis on the absolute character of being in the general sense which has just been indicated. Being is absolute, that is to say, considered as being, it is not relative to anything besides itself; for a relation with non-being could only signify an absence of relation. It means, too, that in no

---

[12] St. Thomas, *In De divinis nominibus,* chap. 5, lect. 1, ed. *Opuscula omnia* by Mandonnet, Paris, 1927, Vol. II, p. 486. *De Malo,* q. 16, a. 9, ad 5. Cf. *Contra Gentes,* Bk. I, chap. 28: "*virtus* essendi . . . essendi potestas . . . posse essendi."

sense, in no order, in no manner, can being have a relation to some term outside itself, and a fortiori that it cannot depend on any extrinsic condition. For what is outside of being is pure nothing.[13] Being is absolute, that is, there is a unique domain of being, which is self-sufficient and which must be explained completely by that which it is in itself, by that which it contains.[14]

"It is" is an expression which borders on the equivocal. It can be used to emphasize the absolute character of being, but it is often used to signify especially certain relative aspects which are encountered in being itself; and it is of the highest importance to distinguish these cases. The present of the verb "to be" is opposed to the past and the future; it indicates the present moment of time, that in which I actually have consciousness of existing, and which is in a definite relation with the moments that precede and with those that are still to come. In this sense, in asserting "it is" of a being we insist on the temporal relativity which characterizes it.

That which exists at the present moment of the course of time, possesses a value of being, which holds good not merely for this mo-

---

[13] The meaning of the term "absolute" is often taken from a very relative point of view. In general, "absolute" signifies non-relative. If we use the term "relative" to designate such a species of relations, all the rest will be called "absolute," but this absolute will contain a number of elements which are not absolute from every point of view, *simpliciter,* but only in a certain sense, *secundum quid,* i.e., as far as they differ from such species of relation. For example, in the Aristotelian system, if one agrees to call "relative" the predicament *ad aliquid,* the predicaments substance, quantity, quality, will be called absolute categories. If one calls every accident relative, because accident has being only in reference to substance, only the predicament of substance will be called absolute; the nine others will be called relative predicaments. In both cases the opposition of relative and absolute is effected within the limits of the particular point of view at which we place ourselves, *secundum quid.* However, if we go beyond every particular point of view to consider things in a general way, *simpliciter,* without any reservation, the word "absolute" will be reserved for what cannot in any sense be reduced to the relative, because it cannot be found in relation with any other term; hence it will be reserved for what transcends all relativity. It is in this sense that being is an absolute value, *absolutum simpliciter,* because it transcends every limit, every relation.

[14] It is quite another problem to consider the intrinsic conditions, the internal multiplicity, the constitutive law of the domain of being. Here precisely is the object of metaphysical inquiries. Is the actual existence of the being necessary, and is it such wholly, or is the being, wholly or in part, content with contingence? The relation of being and knowledge (which must be internal to being under penalty of otherwise identifying knowledge and pure non-being, in other words, under penalty of otherwise denying knowledge): does it require actual knowledge, constitutive of reality? These questions and others will form the subject of a later discussion.

ment but also for all the others. It is absolutely true to say that "that object exists at the present moment"; in other words, that truth holds good not merely for the present but for all times. It will always be true to say that "that object has existed at this particular moment." The validity of this truth does not vanish with the present moment; it does not evolve with the course of time; it transcends the relativity of time It is absolute.

Now this absolute validity which the being of the present moment possesses, is common to being at all moments. It is just as false to state that that which will come to pass in the future, will not be, as to maintain that the past has not existed. And if we must admit that there is purely possible being (this question will be discussed later on) it is absolutely true to say that it is possible. At all times and at all places the same unshakable solidity of being is manifested. Undoubtedly, we must distinguish clearly different times, modes and forms; each one *is* in its own fashion, and this is relative to others, but it is always a value of being absolutely undeniable, which it possesses in its own fashion.

The verb "to be" is conjugated in different moods and tenses, in such a way as to be applied to all particular situations; but there is always question of the same verb, always the absolute value which it signifies, and it is to this value that its different forms are referred.

The form of the present indicative "it is," inasmuch as it is a particular form which is opposed to other moods, other tenses and other persons, expresses the absolute value of being, while connoting a special and relative manner of being. But we can employ it also to indicate the value of being without any qualification, which is common to all. That which was, belongs to being, just as that which is at this moment, that which will be, that which could have been, and that which could be. Of all these we must say "it is," that it is engraved absolutely and forever in being. In this metaphysical sense we say that being is, and that every thing is of being. To being, taken formally in this absolute sense, there is opposed that which in no wise has any relation to the verb "to be"; that which is not, has not been, will not be and could not be in any fashion, in a word, it is absolute non-being, the impossible.

Being embraces everything, since it is opposed only to absolute nothing. It does not do this in the manner of a receptacle, distinct

from the things which it contains. Quite the contrary. It must needs
be the whole of every thing. Hence it is identified with what is most
intimate in all reality,[15] with the fundamental validity of every perfection.[16] It is the constitutive act in which the nature proper to every
subject is inscribed.[17] Its absolute validity, from which nothing could
withdraw without losing all meaning, penetrates everything; it is
omnipresent, and hence it guarantees the fundamental unity of all
things.[18]

At all events, every idea is related to being. "Man" signifies being
human; "God" means being divine; "wise" means being wise; and in
the measure in which the idea would turn aside from being, it no
longer signifies anything and so, it would not be an idea. Every affirmation, too, must be reduced to the unique affirmation of being, under
penalty of otherwise having no meaning and so not being an affirmation. The idea of being, implying the absolute affirmation of being,

---

[15] "*Esse*, however, in anything whatever is more intimate than those things
by which the *esse* is determined." St. Thomas, *In II Sentent.*, Dist. 1, q. 1, a. 4,
solutio.

[16] "But this which I call *esse* is the most perfect of all things . . . This which
I call *esse* is the actuality of all acts, and on this account it is the perfection
of all perfections." St. Thomas, *De potentia*, q. 7, a. 2, ad 9.

[17] "*Esse* itself is the most perfect of all things: for it is compared to all things
as act; for nothing has actuality except so far as it is." *Summa theol.*, Ia, q. 4,
a. 1, ad 3.
"Everything which is in potency and in act, becomes actual by this, that it
participates in a higher act. Through this, however, does something especially
become actual, that it participates in the first and pure act by similarity. But
the first act is the subsistent *esse per se;* hence *esse* is the complement of every
form, because it is completed by this, that it has an *esse,* and it has an *esse*
when it is in act. And thus no form exists, except by means of *esse.*" *Quodlibetum,*
XII, q. 5, a. 5. For the importance which this conception enjoys in the philosophy of St. Thomas, cf. Part II, *infra*, pp. 126–140.

[18] "It cannot be, however, that *ens* should be divided from *ens,* so far as it is
ens; nothing indeed is divided from *ens* except *non-ens.*" St. Thomas, *In Boethii
De Trinitate*, q. 4, a. 1.
Aimé Forest shows that the first idea which metaphysics envisages is the idea
of the absolute, which implies before all else the idea of interiority. The absolute penetrates and envelops all things and therefore requires their radical
explanation. Metaphysics seeks to discover the explanatory principle in which
the very foundation of experience participates. It is toward this that metaphysical
idealism, actualism and the metaphysics of value tend; but this goal is fully
realizable only in a metaphysics of being, because being is the absolute value,
intelligible of itself. It is transcendental, in which therefore all reality participates, and by reason of which everything is comprised in a single order; and
everything ought to be explained by one source of unique and absolute being.
(Cf. *Consentement et création*, Paris, 1944.)

is the foundation and the stuff, as it were, of all intellection. It is transcendental [19] in this sense that it is applicable to everything without exception.[20]

3. The Transcendental Idea of Being; Formal Viewpoint of Metaphysics

If we understand by metaphysics the philosophical discipline which seeks to discover the fundamental explanation of the whole complexity of beings, we find here the formal object which belongs to it. It will be a metaphysics of being, an ontology.

As a matter of fact, as the idea of being is transcendental, it embraces everything under one single aspect. From this point of view one could raise questions concerning the whole complexus of things. On the other hand, being is absolute and cannot be related to anything which would be prior or more fundamental. Hence, the absolutely universal viewpoint of being is likewise an absolutely

---

[19] The word "transcendental" is used here in the sense which the Scholastics give it, especially since Suarez, to designate the absolutely universal extension of certain ideas, such as the idea of being. The Latin verb *transcendere* is used by the Scholastics to indicate that a term goes beyond another because it belongs to a higher order. In this case we have a difference of order and not merely of degree, and we cannot pass from the one to the other by a development in a continuous line. In this sense God transcends the creature, and spirit transcends matter. In the same sense the idea of being transcends the genera and species, because its extension, which includes everything, is not reducible to the limited extension of the species and genera; i.e., we cannot pass progressively from the extension of the categories to the unlimited extension of the idea of being.

The word "transcendent" will be reserved for a reality which transcends another, e.g., God is the transcendent Being. The word "transcendental" will be employed to qualify the ideas whose extension includes everything, e.g., the transcendental ideas of being, the one, the good, the true.

Kant knew this scholastic sense of the term "transcendental." He treats of the transcendentals in the second edition of the *Critique of Pure Reason*, Analytic of Concepts, chap. I, sect. 3, par. 12 (Smith's transl. pp. 118–119). Besides, he attached to the words "transcendent" and "transcendental" new meanings within the framework of his own system. Modern philosophers have generally retained these meanings of Kantian origin or at least their analogous meanings. Cf. A. Lalande, *Vocabulaire technique et critique de la philosophie*, 2nd ed., Paris, 1928.

[20] The difference of extension between the transcendental idea of being and the categories establishes between them a difference of nature and not merely one of degree, for we do not pass gradually from the finite to the infinite. The idea of being "transcends" the categories. The nature of this idea will be examined later on.

first point of departure, just as it offers a point of support that is absolutely irrefragable.

From all this we will conclude that the value of metaphysics does
not rest, in the last analysis, on the formal and subjective structure of
the human mind, no more than it derives from the particular nature
of the empirical data which we can attain to in the narrow limits of
experience. We should rather conclude that the value of metaphysics
stems from the absolute value of being, which is revealed inevitably
to every man who is conscious of his activity.

4. Participation in the Absolute Value of Being.
The Order of Beings, Multiple, Finite, Imperfect.
Being: Metaphysical Problem of the Absolute
and Relative, of the One and the Many

Every thing belongs to being, the ego and the non-ego, their whole
reality and every one of their parts. Everywhere being reveals itself
as an absolute value, neither more nor less, for a thing is or it is not;
there is no middle ground.

Now, the ego acts in an autonomous way; it possesses in itself that
which it needs to exist. In this regard it is not merely a part of a
whole which exists and acts, but it is itself a real and active whole,
a whole being, a complete being. And yet it is not the whole of being;
it does not contain all reality, since there is being outside of it, to wit,
the non-ego. There exist many beings.

In its being the ego is distinct from the others; it is other than they.
It has a kind of being which is proper to it, a mode of particular being.
That is why we say that it participates in being. To participate in or
to have a part in being does not signify, strictly speaking, to form
a part of being, since every one of the participants is a complete and
integral being. Nevertheless, there is a kind of analogy between the
order of the parts and the order of the participants: a part is necessarily contained in the order of particular beings.[21] But whereas the
part has no subsistence, no autonomy (for it is not the part which
acts and exists, but the whole which contains the part) the partici-

---

[21] "To participate, however, is as it were to take a part (*partem capere*)."
St. Thomas, *Comment. in libr. Boethii De hebdomadibus*, lect. 2 (ed. *Opuscula
omnia* by Mandonnet, Paris, 1927, Vol. I, 172). Cf. *Comment. in Epistolam ad
Hebraeos*, chap. VI, lect. 1.

pant is a complete and subsistent being; this it is indeed which exists and acts.

Since particular being is not the whole of reality, it exists only partially,[22] but that signifies that it has a share in being, and not that it is only a part of being, or that it only exists in part. No doubt, some one will say with good reason that a particular being is a finite being; but as it is also a complete being, a subsistent whole, its limitation must be understood otherwise than the limitation proper to a part, which by definition is not a complete whole.

Similarly, we say that particular being, which is limited, is an imperfect being.[23] Actually, it does not contain the other particular beings; it does not possess their perfection, and hence does not contain all perfection. Consequently, it is not completely perfect, it is imperfect. But here again, this cannot possibly mean that it is unfinished in itself, or that the perfections of the other things are wanting to it; this imperfection therefore is not a disorder, an evil. We cannot maintain that particular being is imperfect in the sense of evil, under the pretext that it does not possess the goodness and perfection of the others. Particular being is a subsistent reality; nothing is wanting to it in order to exist. It is therefore ontologically complete and finished, and in this sense it is entirely in order, good, perfect. It possesses its own proper mode of being and the other modes do not belong to it; they could not be added to its own mode in order to perfect it intrinsically. The perfection of every particular being belongs itself wholly to being, and by that token it is to be distinguished in a clear-cut way from every other thing. If we speak of its imperfection, we must be careful not to confound this imperfection with that which characterizes every part of being. The ontological imperfection of a particular being, which is finished and subsistent, can by no means signify the ontological incompletion of this being; but it

---

[22] "And therefore when something receives in a *particular* way that which belongs to another universally, it is said to participate in that." *In lib. Boethii De hebdomadibus*, lect. 2 (ed. Mandonnet, Vol. I, 172). "For to participate is nothing else than to receive from another *partially.*" *Comment. in libros De coelo et mundo*, Bk. II, lect. 18. "For whatever is something totally, does not participate in that thing, but it is essentially identified with it. But whatever is something *not totally*, i.e., having something else joined with it, is properly said to participate." *Comment. In Metaph.* I, lect. 10 (ed. Cathala, p. 54, n.154).

[23] "That belongs to another *participative*, which exceeds its nature, yet participates in some way in it, but *imperfectly*, just as the intellectual element in man, which is suprarational. This is essential to the angels, and yet man participates in some way in this same thing." *Comment. in ad Coloss.*, chap. I, lect. 4.

indicates that the perfection which is proper to that being is necessarily distinct from that of the others. The perfection of the one cannot therefore contain that of the other; and consequently, it is by
reason of its very nature, of its natural law, that it cannot completely
contain the perfection of the ontological order.[24]

The complexus of beings forms the fundamental order, for the
value of being in which all beings participate is absolute, in such wise
that this value of being cannot be referred to a source of participation that is more profound.[25] Participation on the plane of being constitutes the metaphysical problem par excellence, for it has to do
precisely with the formal object of metaphysics. When does a problem present itself? Every time that different data, whose connection
we do not grasp, present themselves together. The problem is solved,
as soon as one discovers the principle of their union. Now being manifests properties which seem to be incompatible in one and the same
subject. It is this which creates the difficulty.

First of all, being possesses an absolute character; it is not opposed
to anything, and consequently it penetrates and envelops everything.
To draw a comparison: just as the acts and the states of the conscious ego are nothing outside the ego itself, so all things, whatever they may be, belong to being, and they are nothing outside of
being.

At the same time, however, being manifests some relativity, since
the real is broken up into multiple unities, all of which participate in
being. Let us resume the comparison just drawn to emphasize the
difference of the cases. The ego carries with it a multiplicity of acts
and states, but it itself is not multiplied; it always remains one and
the selfsame ego, and its acts and manifold states are merely the elements of its internal structure. On the contrary, the value of being
is met with in a variety of beings, and these are by no means founded
in one and the same subject, since each one is autonomous and subsistent. It is true that they belong to one and the same order of participation, and that therefore they go to make up a unity; but this is
precisely a unity of order and the relations which bind the beings together, do not in anyway suppress the subsistence of any one of these

---

[24] The problems concerning the particular modes, their limitation and their
imperfection will be raised and studied in the sequel.
[25] "*Esse* itself is the last act which is participable by all; it itself, however,
does not participate in anything." St. Thomas, *Quaestio de anima*, a.6, ad 2. Cf.
De malo, q.16, a.9, ad 5; *Summa theol.*, Ia, q.2, a.3, *quarta via*, by means of
the degrees of being.

beings. For every element of this order participates individually in the value of being; it possesses it in its own right.

The data of the problem, then, are firmly established: the value of being is absolute, and there are subsistent beings. In other words, participation in being is an undeniable fact. But how are we to understand that the absolute can be allied to the relative, that the unity of being is not lost in the multiplication of beings? Or rather, to look at the problem from the other end, how can we explain the fact that the distinct elements, which are intimately riveted to a real order, preserve nevertheless their autonomy, and form, each one of them, a subsistent being?

The difficulty is to preserve at one and the same time the fundamental unity of the order and the subsistence of its multiple elements. What is required that the order of beings can be conceived without contradiction? The problem of the one and the many, of the absolute and the relative, of participation on the plane of being: this is the fundamental problem of metaphysics.

Reflection on the fundamental structure of human experience furnished us with the point of departure of our inquiries. At the outset we there seized upon being. Being revealed an absolute solidity and thus the whole point of support of a philosophical investigation is indicated. At the same time this absolute is affirmed as a transcendental; it furnishes the formal viewpoint of metaphysics. It is from the angle of being that we will have to treat that which concerns the complexus of things. But how are we to proceed? What question can we formulate? Being never reveals itself without a question mark. The fundamental problem is manifested at the same time as being, and there is no way either to ignore or to escape it. Undoubtedly, being possesses a reliable solidity and it forms the absolute foundation of our certitudes; but surprising as this may seem, this creates a difficulty right away. We always apprehend being at one and the same time in the ego and the non-ego, for the one is never given to us without the other; and we do not see forthwith how this multiplicity and this relativity could be reconciled with the absolute unity of the transcendental. There is question consequently of solving this mystery of participation in being, while discovering the absolute principle of beings and the nature of the bond which unites them to it. In the following chapters we will endeavor to make the data of the problem more precise, as far as this can be done.

CHAPTER III

THE ANALOGY AND THE IDENTITY
OF BEING

1. *The Origin and the Nature of the Idea of*
Being; Universal, Concrete, Collective Idea

THE entire life of the soul, its tendencies, sensations as well as knowledge strictly so called, come into play in the concrete apprehension of being; but it is by means of the knowledge which implies thought, that we succeed in comprehending the meaning and value of the data. Going back then by means of an act of attentive reflection on the idea we have formed for ourselves of reality, we can give an exact account of what we have understood and of the manner in which intellection has occurred.

In the direct apprehension of being always and at one and the same time we get at two characters of the reality of experience, the absolute value of being which this reality discloses, and the finite individuality by reason of which every particular being is distinguished from the others, and by means of which it has relations to them so as to form with them the order of beings. What are the origin, the nature, and the internal structure of such intellectual knowledge?

There are many beings, and of every one of them it must be said that it is, that it is a being. The idea of being is a universal idea. Furthermore, being is absolute; there is no term whatever that can be opposed or related to it. This is the same as saying that every being is, and that every one is such from every point of view; or again, that it is the whole and entire individual reality which, strictly speaking, belongs to being. Hence, the content of being is at once universal and individual.

If the idea of being is universal is it not an abstract idea, as are generic and specific concepts? There is question here of getting clear on the meaning of the term abstraction. In general, in the order of knowledge to abstract means to separate. We might think that sense knowledge is abstractive. Really, every sense reacts only to certain stimuli, to certain forms of energy to the exclusion of a good many others. For example, the eye reacts to vibrations of ether, the ear to vibrations of air. Every sense, then, effects a choice among the physical forces which act on it; it reacts only to those which are adapted to its structure, it discerns and abstracts these from the others. The content of sensations, however, remains always strictly material and individual; it is characterized by its localization in space and time. Sensation gets at this sensible thing here at this precise moment. Ordinarily, we do not employ the word "to abstract" to signify this manner of limiting knowledge.

When we speak of abstraction, there is question usually of concepts or of abstract notions. We designate by it intellectual knowledge which gets at an object only from a certain angle, from a definite point of view. This is the case with every generic or specific notion, for example, animal, man. The individual character of the reality—this thing here and now—is not taken into consideration, so much so that knowledge in getting to the real, remains incomplete; and it is precisely this incompleteness of knowledge which the term abstraction expresses. The content of the concept is an aspect which has been disengaged, separated, abstracted from the individual notes of the real. Here again we must observe that an aspect is not a real part of the object to be known; it is rather the whole object, but grasped imperfectly. Moreover, the abstract concept is known as such; that is to say, we know that it is abstract knowledge and therefore imperfect. By its nature, such a concept is related to the concrete from which it has been drawn, and the consciousness which we have of the imperfection of this means of knowing makes us tend towards perfect knowledge as towards an ideal.

In the development of our abstract knowledge, we are forever turning towards new aspects, which are added to the previous aspects with a view to perfecting these latter. For example, we consider man successively as material, living, animal, rational. These different vocables are not synonyms; the concepts which they express are logically distinct, since their contents are different. Every one of these concepts considers a special point of view of the real; every one takes its place alongside of the others and determines them as from the outside. But all of them make an abstraction from the individual; and we could add indefinitely concepts to concepts, abstract to the abstract, without ever obtaining an exhaustive knowledge of the concrete individual, of the real.

If abstraction is understood in this sense, the idea of being cannot be called abstract; for it is transcendental and it is applied to all that is real, no matter what way we envisage it. The real holds on to being by all that constitutes it, and it is precisely in as far as it is individual that it *is*. As such, the abstract does not exist; in any case it has meaning only as imperfect knowledge which of itself has reference to the concrete. Every concept looks to being; man signifies to be human; animal means to be animal. Divorced from the bond that binds it to being, the concept is devoid of meaning and disappears. Being is the soul of all intellection; it is the formal object of intelligence. Now being is absolute, without any possible opposition; and hence the idea of being is transcendental and expresses all that is, all that is concrete. This is the reason for this scholastic principle: "The differences of being are formally being." This means that it is precisely that reality by which beings differ from one another, namely, the concrete and individual reality, peculiar to every being which *is*, and this is what the idea of being signifies.

If the idea of being cannot be said to be abstract in the precise meaning just indicated, must we see here an intuition? First of all, we must come to some kind of agreement as to the meaning of this word. Intuition is generally understood to be the direct seizure, apprehension of an object perceived in the individuality which distinguishes it from every other object. For example, I perceive this tree here; I have consciousness of discovering myself in this state of soul. Without doubt, the value of being appears to us directly in this or that datum of experience, but we lay hold of it as an absolute and transcendental value, embracing in its extension the whole complexity of objects, whereas in our experience we by no means get at or distinguish the individuality of things. The idea of being concerns everything, without any one of them being represented or defined by it in its individuality. Everything is included in it, but nothing is recognized there in a distinct way. Everything is contained in it, but implicitly and as wrapped up in obscurity; so much so that it is impossible to deduce from it the individual forms of beings. "*Ens* actually contains all things, but indistinctly and confusedly." The idea of being signifies all things only by reason of the confusion of the particular modes of being which it contains.

Now if the idea of being signifies the complexus of individual and concrete beings, must we not consider it as a collective idea? Once again, we must first get clear on the meaning of the terms. A collective word such as forest, army, people, signifies a collection of persons or things; it belongs to this collection taken in its entirety and not to one or other of the elements which make up this collection. Thus a forest is a group of trees arranged in a definite manner, but no tree in particular can be called a forest. Every tree can be taken by itself; besides, we can consider it as forming a part of the forest. The arrangement as a forest is accidental with relation to each particular tree, and it is possible to abstract from it. Similarly, we can have the idea of forest without considering the individual determinations of this or that tree.

It is altogether otherwise with being. The idea of being signifies precisely the concrete and individual reality of each object in particular and of all objects together. In this sense it does not abstract anything, and hence it is in no wise an abstract idea. It is nevertheless universal, because it is transcendental; it applies to all things, and includes all things in one all-embracing complexus, that is, the order of being. But it makes this synthesis by signifying what is proper to each one, its individual reality. Since the order of being holds for what is proper to every being, namely, its incommunicable individuality, it is not possible to think of a particular being without thinking of it in the order of beings. In other words, it is impossible to abstract the universal idea of being from beings in the concrete. Hence, this idea is collective in this sense that it signifies the complexus of particular realities, but at the same time it gets at that which goes to make up completely every one of the realities. Accordingly, by the word *being* we designate the collection of all beings, though all the while we affirm of every member of the collection that it is in the truest sense of the word a being.

The idea of being has something in common with an abstract notion, an intuitive apprehension, and a collective idea. As an abstract notion it is universal: it is formed from contact with a datum, and it is applicable to all other possible data; it is an attribute which belongs to all these subjects. As an intuitive apprehension, it terminates at concrete and individual reality. As a collective idea, it designates a complexus of objects.

The idea of being, however, is not universal in the same way as genus or species. It is not limited to signifying merely one aspect of reality, and in this precise sense it is not abstract. On the contrary, it designates that which is beyond all abstraction, and that from which all abstracts are derived, the concrete individual. Undoubtedly, as an abstract concept, the idea of being is universal and perfectible knowledge, and in this broad sense one could call it abstract; [1] but the imperfection of the idea of being comes from its obscurity, from the confusion of the particular modes which it implies, and not at all from the fact that certain real aspects could be considered as being outside its extension. For by that very fact we would treat these things as belonging to non-being, and we would deny their reality.

The idea of being applies to the concrete but otherwise than does intuition in the usual sense of the word. While being directly applicable to present data the idea of being goes beyond them infinitely, since it is universal and applicable to everything.

It is a collective idea of a special kind, for it is not limited to signifying an order which includes its terms only up to a certain point of view, and which in other respects is outstripped by them. On the contrary, the order which the idea of being indicates is absolutely radical and constitutive of all things, and hence it is inseparable from these from every point of view, logical and real. A reality is conceivable only as an element of the order of being; and this is why the absolute character of being is manifest in everything that is this reality. On the other hand, the order of being cannot be conceived of as outside of the peculiar and individual constituent reality of every one of the elements which it contains.[2]

The idea of being is transcendental; it differs in this from all other knowledge: it is an idea *sui generis*.[3] In scholastic philosophy the

---

[1] It is frequently asserted that the abstraction of the idea of being is an abstraction improperly so called; this is tantamount to saying that, strictly speaking, it is not an abstraction. But in metaphysics it is better to preserve the strict meaning of words. We prefer, therefore, to say that the idea of being can be called an abstract idea, but in the broad sense of the word, i.e., in the sense of a universal and determinable idea.

[2] "Being . . . is everything, i.e. a term whose comprehension and extension are identified." L. Lavelle, *La dialectique du monde sensible*, Strasbourg, 1921, p. XII. Cf. *De l'Être*, Paris, 1928, p. 75.

[3] "We are therefore here face to face with a genuine intuition, a direct immediate perception, not in the technical sense which the ancients gave to the word intuition, but in the sense that we can borrow from modern philosophy. There is question of a very simple vision, superior to all discourse and demonstration, since it is at the origin of demonstrations. There is question of a vision whose richness and virtualities no word pronounced outwardly, no word of language can exhaust or express adequately. It is a vision too, where in one moment of decisive emotion and, as it were, of spiritual fire, the soul is in living, reverberating, illuminating contact with a reality which it touches and which is

thesis of the transcendental character of the idea of being is a classic, and it does not seem to create any great difficulties. There are quite a number of universal ideas, and the idea of being is just one among many. Just how then can it run afoul of our mind? All too often, nevertheless, we lose sight of the fact that the transcendental must signify the concrete formally, and that its universal character cannot be founded on an abstraction. This is why we fail to consider the questions which are bound up with this exceptional situation. Universal ideas have an extension which can be more or less comprehensive; on this point the idea of being goes beyond all the others, since it embraces everything without exception. Are there difficulties here? Undoubtedly, for once it is established that the idea of being is not to be put on the same plane as ordinary collective terms, but that it is also a general idea, which like every general idea applies to many subjects (for being applies to every one of the terms of the complexus of beings and not merely to the complexus as such), there arises an important problem. How can we formally lay hold of in one single idea, at one and the same time, the absolute and the relative, the one and the many, the universal and the concrete? The problem which the transcendental character of the idea of being poses so imperiously, constitutes the fundamental problem of metaphysics.

The idea of being is a mysterious idea whose content and extension mutually imply each other, so much so that from the content, from the absolute value, we pass right away to the transcendental extension, and vice versa. This is the reason that if we could make the content of the idea of being precise, its transcendental character would also be explained in some way.

2. The Content of the Idea of Being; the Order of Being; the Proportionality of Beings

The content of the idea of being, the order of beings, can be expressed in a proportionality. To assert being is really equivalent to asserting at one and the same time the individuality proper to every one of the beings and their complete inclusion in a unique order.

The knowledge which we have of a particular reality is not purely

---

grasped by it. Indeed, what we are now asserting, is that it is being before all else which enjoys such an intuition." Jacques Maritain, "Sept leçons sur l'être et les premiers principes de la raison spéculative," 1932–1933 (*Cours et documents de philosophie,* Paris), p. 54.

and simply convertible with the idea of being. For if it is true that this reality *is* in the fullest sense, it is equally well established that other beings *are*. We will not therefore say that it is *the* being, but rather that it shares in being; it possesses being in a particular fashion, which differs from the manner of being of all other things. It possesses and reveals the value of being precisely by the reality which is peculiar to it, and which is individual to the point of being incommunicable to the others. From this it follows that a particular being could not be conceived in a simple manner; we must always consider at one and the same time that it is, and that its mode of being is peculiar to it. And yet these two elements of thought are necessarily related one to the other, and they remain indissolubly united; for the bond which unites them is not to be added to that which they are in themselves, but on the contrary it is a part of their integral make-up. As a matter of fact, the being of this reality is not found anywhere outside the individuality peculiar to it, and on the other hand its individuality derives all of its meaning from the value of being which it conceals within itself.

Consequently, the knowledge of a particular being implies the proportion or relation of a particular mode and its being. This holds good for all particular beings, and in this respect all are equal; their condition is identically the same. The order of being then makes up a proportionality, a proportion of proportions. Being, number one, is constituted by the relation of its mode and its being, just as being, number two, is constituted by the relation of its mode and its being, just as every one of the other beings is constituted in the same way.

It would be altogether false to apply mathematical processes to this proportionality. This is no solution, nor can it produce results since it is not founded on an abstraction. As we have insisted above the terms of every one of these relations are concerned with the complete and concrete reality of a particular being, and they are not separable one from the other either in their existence or in the thought which we have of them. The relation cannot be abstracted from the terms, nor can the terms be conceived otherwise than united. The proportionality of these relations therefore only helps to bring out the internal structure of the content of the transcendental idea of being. This content is the complexus of beings, the concrete order of beings, and not at all an abstract aspect of reality. The proportionality of being signifies that every being participates in being, that it could not have any consistency outside of the order of participation which binds all beings together without exception.

3. Attribution of the Idea of Being; Analogy or Proportional Univocity

If the idea of being is formed in a different way from generic and specific concepts, it stands to reason that its attribution to the several subjects to which it belongs ought to differ from that of abstract concepts, properly so called. How then can the universal and concrete idea of being perform the function of an attribute? The theory of analogy helps us to answer this question. To get clear on the analogy of being let us recall some notions concerning analogy in general.

It must be observed, first of all, that analogy has reference to universal ideas employed as predicates. Every universal idea can be repeated and affirmed successively of a number of subjects, keeping the while its own proper meaning. Take the concept "man." I thought of him yesterday; I think of him again today; I have formed the same idea twice. Twice, that is to say two different psychological acts are produced in me; for yesterday differs from today, and the act of thought which was produced yesterday cannot be confounded with that which is realized at this moment. Nevertheless, from another point of view these two thoughts are merely one, since they have the same signification, the same content. I have had one and the same idea twice, the idea of man. Hence, intellectual activity subject to time as everything else that is in man, escapes in certain respects from the course of time and transcends it, just as the immanent content of thought bears witness. As the ego preserves its identity through the whole evolution of conscious life, so the ideas which the ego forms for itself remain unchanged and always retain their meaning.

An idea has always only one signification; it is univocal. To speak of one idea with many meanings is to speak of a square circle. There are words and gestures with double meaning; these are equivocal symbols. These symbols are sensible material signs which serve to express a thought, a state of soul or an inclination of internal, conscious life. We can communicate our data of consciousness to another only by means of the body acting as an interpreter. That is why we set up a nexus between psychical facts, strictly personal, and certain physical facts which go to make up the behavior of the body, for example, mimicry, motions, spoken or written language, so as to signify the first facts by means of the second. In bodily behavior there are certain elements which spontaneously translate certain states of the soul, and there are others of these which have a purely conventional meaning. It is evident that different meanings can be attached to one and the same conventional sign. Thus, in an assembly we can stand up to express our respect, and we can also do this by a certain amount of protest. Similarly, there are equivocal words; for example, the French word "mine," which signifies the appearance of the countenance, a subterraneous place from which metals are extracted, and a piece of money among the Greeks.

There cannot, however, be ideas with multiple meanings; for an idea is not a reality to which a meaning is attached by accretion, but it is a spiritual reality whose nature and unity consequently derive entirely from the content of its signification. An idea is defined by its meaning, for it is through this meaning that it is such a definite idea. Ideas of different meaning are by that very fact different ideas, and one and the same idea can be equivalent only to one single meaning of thought.

In the attribution of universal ideas to their subjects we must distinguish several cases. If there is question of concepts strictly abstract, generic or specific, the case is relatively simple. Since these concepts are the fruit of an abstraction, their meaning does not imply the individual notes of the subjects; they are defined without taking these into account, and they can be considered in themselves as absolute, apart from the relations which bind them to concrete subjects. They are logically separate, abstracted from their subjects, and they keep themselves, so to speak, at equal distance from all of their inferiors. Their univocity is therefore absolute, since their meaning is defined independently of the relations which they can have with different subjects. Consequently, these abstract concepts are always predicated of their inferiors in the same way, since they are not affected in themselves by the individual notes of the subjects. Peter is a man, Paul is a man: the attribute "man" is predicated in exactly the same way in both instances, precisely because in the formation of the concept "man" an abstraction has been made from that which is proper to Peter and Paul. As soon as we get away from this absolute univocity, we get relative or proportional univocity, which is called analogy.

In many cases, commonly considered as cases of analogy, this latter is more apparent than real. Take the classic example, borrowed from Aristotle, the predicate "healthy." Health is the state of the organism whose functions are not disturbed by any sickness. Man, for example, can enjoy health; and this disposition of the body depends on a number of external conditions. Now the attribute "health" is predicated likewise of all these external factors: healthy air, healthy food, healthy region, etc. No one is deceived as to the meaning of these expressions; every one knows that neither the air nor the food nor the region can be in good health the same way as man; still no one is unaware that the air, food, and country are not without influence on health, and that on this account the attribute "healthy" is commonly applied to them. If one says: "The air is healthy," he wishes to convey the meaning not that the air itself is healthy, but that it is favorable to man's health. Thus, the attribution of the predicate "health" is extended to a good number of subjects to which, strictly speaking, it does not belong. Nevertheless, there is no equivocation here, since it is not without an evident reason that we thus broaden the field of application of the predicate. This reason is the relation which binds the new subjects to the subject which possesses in its own right the quality expressed by the predicate.[4]

In the present instance which we call the analogy of attribution[5] or the analogy of proportion, the subjects of attribution, contrary to what takes place in strict univocity, are not found on one and the same line. There is one of them, the principal analogue, which is the root of the analogous form expressed by the attribute, and to which this attribute belongs principally. To the other subjects, the second-

---

[4] Aristotle distinguishes two species of equivocal terms: those which are such by chance, "ἀπὸ τύχης ὁμώνυμον," and those which are such by reason of an analogy "ὁμώνυμον κατ' ἀναλογίαν." St. Thomas Aquinas likewise distinguishes "equivocal terms by chance and fortune, and those by relation to one principal thing." Cf. I Sentent., d. 31, q. 2, a. 1, ad 2; In Ethicam, lect. 7.

[5] We call it "analogy of attribution," because the secondary terms are referred or "attributed" to the principal term. As St. Thomas writes in De principiis naturae (1255): "That is said to be predicated analogically, which is predicated about a number of things whose forms (rationes) and definitions are different, but which are attributed to one same thing: just as health is predicated of the body of an animal and . . . of drink. . . . All those forms are attributed to one end, sc. to health."

According to John of St. Thomas, Cursus philosophicus thomisticus, Logica, secunda parte, q. 13, a. 3, edit. B. Reiser, O.S.B., Vol. I, Turin-Rome, 1930, p. 483 b, the name of the analogy of attribution indicates that the term and the concept have been extended from the principal to the secondary terms. The text of St. Thomas permits us to see here, moreover, the reason of this extension, i.e., the relation of the "attribution" which unites these terms to the first.

ary analogues, the attribute can be applied only subordinately by reason of the proportion or the relation which binds them to the principal term. The classification of these secondary terms can be made according to the nature of the relations which unite them with the first term. It is easy to see that it would be impossible to understand the attribution of the analogous form, expressed by the predicate, to the secondary terms without taking the principal attribution into account. In other words, the principal analogue must play a part in the definition of the attribute, as soon as we wish to apply it to the secondary analogues. For it is not possible to define a relative without signifying the terms of the relation.

Strictly speaking in the analogy of attribution the analogous form always retains the same meaning; it is rather the signification of the word which we make elastic, and stretch to the point of applying it to different elements. These latter are extrinsically related one to the other, but nevertheless they belong to the order of the analogous form, in as far as they are connected with the principal analogue.

Another instance generally bound up with analogy is that of metaphor, which at times is called the analogy of proportionality, improperly so called. For instance, the lion is the king of the animals; the meadow is smiling.

Among men the king exercises authority and power over his subjects; on the other hand, the lion makes the effects of his power felt on the animals, and he exercises dominion over them. Nothing prevents us from establishing a comparison between the material power of the man who is king and the physical strength of the lion. We can extend the comparison to the external behavior of the king and to that of the lion, and observe on both sides a haughty and resolute bearing; but the comparison stops at these material aspects, it does not have any bearing at all on the authority or the moral and juridical aspect of royalty. On the contrary, everybody is quite certain that the lion cannot enjoy any moral authority, and that, strictly speaking, it would be nonsense to maintain that an animal is king. If therefore we apply the attribute "king" to a subject which does not possess royalty, we have not modified the meaning of the idea itself; but the word, the expression of the idea, has received a wider field of application by reason of a comparison which has to do only with certain accessory aspects and not at all with the very essence of the signification of this idea. Here again, if we wish to speak of analogy it must be found in the words rather than in the ideas. There is question here of a figure of speech, of a typical expression. As we leave the proper sense to pass over to the figurative meaning we are quite right in saying that the metaphor is only an analogy, improperly so called.

Evidently, the metaphorical or figurative meaning of the attribute cannot be understood without taking into account its literal sense; hence, there is reason to distinguish here also a principal analogue and one or many secondary analogues. The metaphor has to do always with a mode or a quality belonging to subjects. The example used above shows that it can be easily expressed under a form of proportionality. What supreme authority is with regard to the man who exercises it, such are strength and agility with reference to the lion, that is, the principle of dominion over the subjects who are under them. Similarly, the metaphor of the smiling meadow, implies that the flowers are to the meadow as smiling is to man.

There are instances of analogy properly so called, where we get away from the absolute univocity in the use of the idea itself. The analogy of being is the most striking example of this. Absolute univocity is founded on abstraction, properly so called, and the analogy of attribution and the metaphor likewise are based on abstraction. In the former we take our stand at the point of view of certain relations which bind the secondary terms to the principal term; in the latter we consider an accessory aspect under which the terms resemble one another.

In the strict sense, however, the idea of being cannot be abstracted; it is the concrete individuals which it designates, for only the individual can become real. It is nevertheless the most universal of all ideas, since it belongs to all subjects. Hence, the attribution of the predicate "being" cannot be made conformably with the rule of absolute univocity; it implies a certain relativity. We explained above that in certain respects the idea of being at one and the same time has something in common with the abstract idea, the intuitive apprehension, and also the collective idea. It signifies the whole order of beings, the fundamental unity of the whole of reality. Every particular subsistent being clings to the fundamental and transcendental unity by everything which constitutes it, without losing its own subsistent individuality, without being confounded with the other terms. In other words, every being in particular participates in the value of being; it possesses it according to its own proper mode, in the proportion which belongs to it. Hence, the universal attribute of being can only be applied proportionally to every case; that which is peculiar to every subject must be taken into account.

To establish the analogy of the idea of being we are often satisfied in appealing to any real multiplicity whatever without being precise about the nature of this multiplicity. We have good reason at this juncture to wonder whether any multiplicity whatsoever can suffice.

Man thinks, wishes, hears, sees, works, takes a walk, etc.; his life extends through time, and his activity unfolds itself in multiple acts and various subjective states. Thought has to do with being, and so also does willing, hearing, seeing, working, taking a walk; but thought is other than willing, hearing is different from seeing, etc. All these terms have to do with being, but every one is such in its own fashion, and they differ among themselves precisely by the being which goes to make them up; hence, the idea of being is an analogous idea.

This matter must be examined a little more closely. Truthfully, thought and willing do not exist; they are abstractions. What exists is *my* thought, *my* willing etc., that is, I myself exist in the act of thinking and willing. As has been explained in our second chapter, my activity contains exclusively the active ego and nothing else. From this it follows that in the example under consideration we always have to do with one and the same subject: the same ego thinks, wills, hears, sees, works, takes a walk. It is therefore always the same ego which *is*. But then, how can we conclude from this to the analogy of being, if what is peculiar to analogy is the proportional attribution of a universal idea to many subjects?

Undoubtedly, the ego really contains the aforesaid multiplicity: it is not absolutely the same at different moments of its existence, since these moments are different. And just as the thinking ego and the willing ego, the ego of yesterday and the ego of today are not completely identical, I can consider them successively and see there so many subjects to which I attribute always the same predicate "being." The ego of yesterday was, that of today is; they differ from one another as yesterday and today. Consequently, the being which I attribute to one and the other is not absolutely the same, and the idea of being belongs to these different subjects only if their differences be taken into account. The permanent identity of the being of the ego is therefore entirely relative; it is proportional to the differences which affect it, and the repeated attribution of the predicate "being" to the real and active ego can only be made in an analogous way.

Nevertheless, the example of such multiplicity cannot bring out all the profundity of the analogy of the idea of being. As a matter of fact, the ego which develops unceasingly in different ways is a being which is never transformed into another being; it remains the same ego, the same being, it preserves its substantial identity. Hence, the different subjects considered above—the ego thinking, willing, etc. —are all reduced, at bottom, to one and the same subject; and in so far there is no analogy, since this designates the proportionally identical attribution of one and the same predicate to many subjects. In the case of the ego, the differences, while being real, are only accidental, and the analogy which is relative to it could not affect the foundation of the reality.

The idea of being is radically analogical; it is such always. The consciousness which we have of ourselves is indissolubly bound up with the knowledge of the world which surrounds us, and of the men which it contains; and vice versa, the knowledge which we possess of this world is conscious, and is therefore accompanied by the knowledge of ourselves. Thus we always apprehend many beings at once, and it is impossible for us not to observe that the idea of being is applied to every one of them. This idea is therefore characterized first of all by its analogy, and it remains always and necessarily analogical, because, strictly speaking, we cannot abstract it from the real, or dissociate it from the fundamental experience on which the whole edifice of knowledge rests, that is, the experience of the ego-in-the-world, of the ego limited by the non-ego.

We might be tempted to reduce the analogy of being to univocity, in abstracting from the individual and concrete modes which characterize the different realities, the being which is common to them. But this abstraction cannot be made, since the knowledge (undetermined and implicit, but actual) of these modes necessarily affects the proper and essential meaning of the idea of being, to the extent of being inseparable from this idea. Actually, it is impossible to maintain that the modes do not formally belong to being; for that would be tantamount to identifying them formally with non-being. Hence we must admit that the predicate "being" is applicable to them, in as far as they are concrete and individual, and that it embraces them as such in its signification. The plasticity of the idea of being, which permits it to espouse all shapes and forms of reality, and the concrete and infinite riches of its content which give it a transcendental range, distinguish this idea from univocal, abstract, and limited notions.

The Scotists, however, refuse to subscribe to this. According to them the idea of being signifies abstract existence, existence which is perfectly "de-essenced," [6] which abstracts from every quidditative note, specific or generic, and is consequently a univocal idea. And yet its sphere of application extends beyond every genus, since it embraces all reality: "Being is not a genus on account of its excessive commonness." [7] But precisely by reason of its abstraction, this idea of being cannot be held as the equivalent of concrete reality: "The differences of being are being not formally, but only materially." Hence, the transcendence or univocity of being is strictly conceptual, *logical*,[8] and as soon as we apply ourselves to the knowledge and the

---

[6] "Can we not, in fact, strip the concept of the concrete determinations in order to mount up to an extreme datum, supremely abstract, in which the mind, by supposition, would no longer represent to itself anything of the essence of things?" Séraph. Belmond, O.F.M., *Études sur la philosophie de Duns Scot,* I, "Dieu: Existence et cognoscibilité," Paris, 1913, p. 333. "Take the idea of *not-nothing.* It does not evoke of itself a subject of inhesion, either finite or infinite. It is therefore capable of penetrating the definition of the one and the other. It is the transcendence or the logical univocity which Scotus favors." (*ibid.,* p. 331). "Nothing of that which is or can be in any way whatever is excluded from the sphere of extension of the being, de-essenced by an artifice of the intellect." *ibid.,* p. 335.

Cf. article by the same author, "L'univocité scotiste," *Revue de Philosophie,* Vol. XXI, 1912, pp. 33 ff., 113 ff.; Vol. XXII, 1913, p. 137. "Founded exclusively on the fact of existence, this concept signifies exclusively that being is formally something, *quid,* a reality whose how is not yet considered. It is, consequently, absolutely undetermined, without modal content, a pure verification of the objectivity of the beings without defining them in any way." S. Belmond, "Essai de synthèse philosophique du Scotisme," in *La France Franciscaine,* 2nd series, Vol. XVI, 1933, p. 79 (7).

[7] John Duns Scotus, *Opus oxoniense,* I, d. 3 (edit. Wadding, Lyons, 1639, Vol. V, p. 454). In asserting the univocity of being, Duns Scotus wishes to set himself against the ideas of Henry of Ghent, more than those of St. Thomas. Cf. Jean Paulus, Henri de Gand (*Études de philosophie médiévale,* XXV), Paris, 1938, pp. 52–66.

According to Henry of Ghent, the unity of the idea of being is the result of a confusion, due to the obscurity of this idea. In fact, as soon as our knowledge becomes precise, it is either the divine Being, or created being that is signified; and between the two there is nothing in common either in the order of knowledge or in that of reality. Henry of Ghent writes: "Every real concept, therefore, by which something real is conceived by conceiving *esse* simply, is either of the thing which is of God, or the thing which is of a creature, but not of something which is common to both." *Summa,* 24, 14 (J. Paulus, *op. cit.,* p. 57). Understood in this way the idea of being seems to be tainted with equivocity. It is against this conception that Duns Scotus addresses himself, by insisting on the univocity of the idea of being.

[8] "What we must hold on to is that the *ens univocum* is not the equivalent of concrete reality, but an abstraction pushed very far, a stripping of the concrete, carried to its ultimate limits even to the 'de-essencing' of being. This

study of reality, as it is, we must take the modes of being into account and complete the univocity by analogy. "Existence without essence is univocal, but existence with essence is analogous."[9] The metaphysical study of the real therefore demands "ontological analogy as the basis of univocity."[10] Metaphysical being presupposes logical being "which constitutes at the foundation of analogy and transcendence the minimum of univocity that is able to guarantee the internal unity of the transcendental idea."[11] On this point the doctrine of Scotus would complete the Thomistic conception of analogy by providing it with an indispensable logical foundation. In this capital question the opposition between Scotism and Thomism would therefore be less great than it would appear at first blush, and several Scotists like to emphasize this point.[12] What are we to think of this interpretation?

---

operation being achieved in and by the mind, and the 'ens univocum' being in all necessity a pure idea, the univocity is therefore strictly conceptual, logical." S. Belmond, *Études sur la philosophie de Duns Scot*, I, *Dieu*, Paris, 1913, pp. 316–317.

[9] Séraphin Belmond, O.F.M., *op. cit.*, p. 237, note 3.

[10] S. Belmond, "Duns Scot métaphysicien," *Revue de Philosophie*, Vol. XXXVI, 1929, p. 422. The Scotistic thesis can be compared with the doctrine of L. Lavelle on the univocity of being. The latter insists more on the metaphysical value of this univocity. Cf. B. M. I. Delfgaauw, *Het Spiritualistich Existentialisme van Louis Lavelle*, Amsterdam, 1947, pp. 36–53.

[11] *ibid.*, p. 418. The interpretation of the Scotistic univocity which Fr. Belmond proposes, is shared by the majority of the Scotistic authors, e.g. Déodat Marie, Raymond de Courcerauld, Zacharie Van de Woestijne, Ephrem Longpré, Déodat de Basly, etc. See likewise Ét. Gilson, *L'esprit de la philosophie médiévale* (Gifford Lectures, University of Aberdeen), 2nd edit. Paris, 1944, pp. 261–262; "*Avicenne et le point de départ de Duns Scot*," *Archives d'Histoire doctrinale et littéraire du moyen age*, II, Paris, 1927, pp. 89–150; "Les seize premiers Theoremata et la pensée de Duns Scot," *ibid.*, XI, 1937–1938, pp. 5–45. And yet Timothée Barth, O.F.M., maintains that the "ens Scotisticum" is found in the line of the "quiddity," and that far from being purely abstract existence, it is pure essence, abstracting from every mode of determined being. Cf. "Die Stellung der Univocatio im Verlauf der Gotteserkenntnis nach der Lehre des Duns Scotus," *Wissenschaft und Weisheit*, Vol. V, 1938, pp. 235–254. Also, "Zum Problem der Eindeutigkeit, Ein Beitrag zum Verständnis ihrer Entwicklung vom Aristoteles, über Porphyrius, Boethius, Thomas von Aquin nach Scotus," *Philosophisches Jahrbuch*, Vol. LV, 1943, pp. 300–321.

[12] "Thomism and Scotism do not run alongside of each other, but rather cross each other's path from below and above, in such wise that they end up with emphasizing in genuinely scholastic fashion the fact and the infinite extension of the analogy of being." Paul Fleig, "Thomistische und Skotistische Erkenntnislehre," *Franziskanische Studien*, Vol. XXII, 1935, p. 157. From the origin of the renaissance of Scotism at the beginning of this century the studies of

The Scotistic conception tends to bring to light the value of being and to distinguish it from its different modes of realization; but it fails here by excess and at the same time by defect. It is impossible to "de-essence" the idea of being, as Scotism pretends to do. If we were to separate the idea of being from that of its modes, we would end up by relegating these modes to the domain of non-being, denying them, and proclaiming the absolute unicity of existence. This would be precisely the opposite of Scotistic doctrine, since this latter considers the abstract idea of being as a universal idea.

Moreover, the unity of being which Scotism affirms is purely logical and abstract, obtained by an "artifice of the understanding"; [13] but that cannot suffice, for the unity of being is entirely real. An absolute, and therefore a concrete value penetrates individual beings and envelops them in one and the same order. This unity is therefore not reserved for an abstract logical order; it belongs to the concrete, ontological order. Since the idea of being, however, ought to signify all that exists without excluding anything, it must imply in its actual signification every individual being, whatever it be and such as it is; it is at one and the same time universal and concrete. Consequently, the attribution of this idea to its different subjects can never be made on the basis of univocity; it must be founded on analogy.

Neither can we be any more satisfied with the Suarezian theory of analogy. Suarez rejects the univocity of the idea of being and admits its analogy, because he thinks along with the Thomists, that it is the individual reality, differing from one individual to another, which belongs formally to being. The signification of the idea of being is therefore adapted formally to every reality in as far as it is such, in as far as it is individual. In other words, every being, in as far as it is such, is contained in an undetermined manner in the signification of the idea of being. Suarez nevertheless teaches that individual being is contained therein, not inasmuch as it is such, but only inasmuch as it is being.

Parthenius Minges, O.F.M., tended to diminish the distance between Scotus and St. Thomas.

On the contrary, Father Borgman's article, "Gegenstand, Erfahrungsgrundlage und Methode in der Metaphysik," *Franziskanische Studien*, Vol. XXI, 1934, pp. 80–103, 125–150, insists on the opposition between the Thomistic conceptions and those of Scotus, and on the incoherence of the analogy of proportionality.

[13] S. Belmond, *Études sur la philosophie de Duns Scot*, I, *Dieu*, Paris, 1913, p. 335.

This last restriction seems strange, at least in a doctrine which admits in other places that the individual shares formally in being precisely because it is such. Undoubtedly, Suarez took pains, as did the Scotists, to guarantee the idea of being a perfectly constant meaning; for one idea cannot have many meanings. With this in view he thought he was forced to eliminate from the content of meaning of this idea the different "taleities" of being which are opposed as irreducible terms. Scotism, which had taken a similar attitude, had only succeeded in making being a perfectly abstract concept. With Suarez, who does not admit the abstraction of being, properly so called, this thesis of the non-inclusion of the "taleities" in the implicit content of the idea of being is unintelligible.

Certain representatives of the Suarezian school have thrown in their lot with the Scotistic thesis of the abstract and univocal idea of being.[14] Many Suarezians, remaining faithful to Suarezian analogy restrict themselves to taking over the formulae of the *Doctor Eximius* without giving further explanations of the manner in which the "taleities" are contained in the transcendental idea, in as far as they are being.[15]

Father Descoqs offers his own personal solution of this problem: [16] the analogy of the idea of being would be founded in the last analysis on the similarity of objects. This similarity is an immediate and irreducible datum; it implies at one and the same time the distinction of the objects and their resemblance, and it is thereby distinguished from identity just as much as from pure diversity. It would not, however, be necessary to consider it as constituted by a relation between the distinction and the resemblance; and Descoqs refuses absolutely to reduce it to an analogy of proportionality.

If the Suarezian school cannot admit that the fundamental analogy in the order of being is the analogy of proportionality, it is because they do not find there the essential unity of content required by the idea of being. How could the terms of a proportionality, which are distinct one from the other, constitute as such, that is, in so far as they

---

[14] For example, Lorenz Fuetscher, S.J., "Die ersten Seins-und Denkprinzipien," *Philosophie und Grenzwissenschaften*, t. III, Vol. 2/4, Innsbruck, 1930, pp. 103–376.

[15] Among the representatives of Suarezianism we may cite T. Pesch, C. Frick, E. Delmas, J. J. Urraburu, J. Donat, all of the Society of Jesus.

[16] Pedro Descoqs, S.J., *Institutiones metaphysicae generalis; Éléments d'ontologie*, Vol. I, Paris, 1925; *Praelectiones theologiae naturalis; Cours de théodicée*, Vols. I, II, Paris, 1932, 1935.

are distinct, a fundamental unity? The members of this school themselves make use of the analogy of proportionality, but only along the
line of quidditative determinations, essential or accidental, which
can give rise to the formation of abstract notions. For example, in the
order of knowledge it seems correct to them to say that the eye is to
the body as the intellect is to the spirit. This proportionality presupposes many substantial subjects that are perfectly one; it is related to and rests upon it as a basis, since it compares them from a
certain point of view. Still, the Suarezians think that it is impossible
to establish a proportionality on the plane of being, since it could no
longer have a basis, seeing that being cannot be abstracted in the
proper sense of the word.

In truth, the cause of this debate on analogy is the conception of
being. According to Suarez being is the actuality, the reality of things;
it is the concrete quiddity of things, their individual essence in as far
as it is real. There is no other real relation whatever to be established
between being and essence than that of identity; in this sphere a system of proportionality could not even be formulated.

On this all-important point Thomism is opposed to Suarezianism.
Thomism sees in being the fundamental value, the supreme perfect-
tion which every thing possesses in the measure in which it shares in
being. All things participate in being under penalty of otherwise not
being at all, but they all differ among themselves, since they do not
participate in being in the same measure. Consequently, in our knowledge of reality in regard to every particular being, we run up against
a duality of terms, intimately bound up together but irreducible,
namely, the absolute value of being and the quiddity, the "taleity" or
the measure of being. How can we express this if not by the relation
of the measure of being? And since all these beings participate in
the same value, they make up all together a whole, an order; and how
can we express this if not by a proportionality? Therefore, the transcendental idea of being implicitly contains the proportionality of beings, and it is the analogy of proportionality which characterizes the
attribution of this idea to its different subjects.

The Thomistic school has always vigorously defended this opinion,
and in so doing it has remained faithful to the doctrine of the Angelic
Doctor. In the order of being St. Thomas invokes quite often the
analogy of proportion, but he likewise emphasizes the analogy of
proportionality, properly so called.[17] How could he not have done

---

[17] "The different relation to *esse* prevents the univocal predication of *ens*. Now

this, since he develops a metaphysics of *esse*, understood in the sense of the perfection of all perfections, a transcendental value in which every particular being participates?

On this point St. Thomas definitely surpasses Aristotle. The Stagyrite recognizes the analogy of proportionality and often makes use of it,[18] but not for one moment does he dream of applying it to being, since in no wise does he recognize being as a perfection in which things can participate. As soon as the formal object of metaphysics has been defined as "being in as far as it is being," he fundamentally identifies being and substance, and undertakes the study of substance and accidents by posing problems in the order of essence; but he does not suspect that there could be problems along the line of the relation of substance and being. He strives to side-step the equivocity of being by showing that the different meanings of the idea of being do not form an accidental whole whose terms are united only in a purely fortuitous way; rather, they make up a whole that is naturally arranged, an order that is founded on the bond of their relations. Actually, substance is being par excellence, whereas accidents can be called being only by reason of their relations to substance.[19] We can admit that these views of Aristotle hold good in the case of a series of predicates which are related to one and the same substantial subject; for example, Peter is a man, he is intelligent, in good health, a musician, etc.; but if the substances themselves are multiplied, would we not have to conclude from this that the idea of being, taken

God has a different relation to *esse*, from that of any creature whatsoever; for He is His own *esse*, a thing which does not belong to any creature." *De Potentia*, q.7, a.7, corp. Cf. *De Veritate*, q.2, a.11.

Avicenna expresses himself practically in the same way. Cf. M. Goichon, *La distinction de l'essence et de l'existence d'après Ibn Sina (Avicenne)*, Paris, 1937, pp. 176–178. "Just as substance is to the *esse* due to it, so also is quality to the *esse* that belongs to its genus." St. Thomas, III *Sentent.*, d.1, q.1, a.1. For the classification of the different species of analogy according to St. Thomas, Cf. L. Penido, "Le rôle de l'analogie en théologie dogmatique" (*Bibliothèque thomiste*, XV), Paris, 1931, pp. 27–52; L. B. Geiger, in *Bulletin Thomiste*, Vol. VI, n.1–12, Jan. 1940–Oct. 1942; Paris, 1946, pp. 256 ff.

[18] "Intelligence is in the soul as the sense of sight is in the body," *Nicomachean Ethics*, I, 1096 b25; Cf. *Topics*, I, 17, 108 a7; *Prior Analytics*, I, 46, 51 b22; *Physics*, I, 7, 191 a7; *On the Parts of Animals*, I, 5, 645 b6, 9; *Metaphysics*, V, 6, 1016 b31; IX, 6, 1048 b5; XII, 4, 1070 a31, b16, b26; 5, 1071 a30; XIV 6, 1093 b18 etc. Cf. G. L. Muskens, *De vocis ἀναλογίας significatione ac usu apud Aristotelem*, Groningue, 1943.

[19] *Metaphysics* IV, 2, 1003 a33–b18; VII, 1, 1028a 10–31; XI, 3, 1060 b30–1061 a17. Today they call this the analogy of proportion or of attribution. Aristotle uses in this case the expression "πρὸς ἕν" or "πρὸς μίαν ἀρχήν." He reserves the term "ἀναλογία" to designate proportionality.

in the primordial sense of substance, can only be equivocal? Aristotle does not examine this question explicitly, but merely touches upon it in passing in the study which he devotes to the nature of first philosophy. He asks whether this fundamental philosophy ought not to be called a particular science, seeing that it studies immaterial reality; or whether it ought not to be considered a universal science whose object would embrace material as well as immaterial things. He finally accepts this second alternative, and the reason for his decision is that in the last analysis material things belong to the same order as immaterial reality, since they are bound to the latter by relations of dependence. Once again he side-steps equivocity, thanks to the analogy of proportion [20] whose principal term in the present case is the Supreme Being.

This solution, nevertheless, is obviously inadequate. For according to Aristotle the dependence of material things on the Supreme Immaterial Being has to do only with movement which on his own admission is an accidental reality, and in no wise forms the substance of things. Consequently, the dependence on the Supreme Being also has to do with the accidental order and not with substance; the Supreme Being is only the first mover, but in no wise the creator of things. Must we not conclude from this then that substance itself does not belong to this analogy of proportion of which there was question above? It is only too evident that the Stagyrite does not succeed in explaining in what the unity of the meanings of the idea of being consists. Just as he does not think of being as a perfection, so he cannot speak of the relations which unite being and its different modes or essences; by the same token it is impossible for him to reduce the many meanings of the idea of being to a relative unity, to the unity of an analogy of proportionality.

Cajetan in his *De nominum analogia* (1498), supporting himself on St. Thomas, makes a systematic study of the nature and the divisions of analogy,[21] and it is particularly from him that present-day Thomists draw their inspiration.[22] And yet Cajetan fails to throw light

[20] Metaphysics VI, 1, 1026 a7–32, and XI, 7, 1064 a34–35. Cf. Aug. Mansion, "La genèse de l'oeuvre d'Aristote d'après les travaux récents," *Revue néoscolastique de philosophie*, 1927, pp. 327–328.

[21] Cf. Cajetan, *De conceptu entis ad Ferrariensem*, 1509; *In Iam Summae theologicae*, q. 13, a. 5. Cf. also Franciscus de Sylvestris Ferrariensis, O.P. *In Iam Summae contra Gentiles*, 1516, c. 34; Joannes a St. Thoma, O.P., "Cursus philosophicus thomisticus, Ars logica," p. II, q. 13, a. 5.

[22] It was the modernistic crisis that first of all provoked special studies on analogy. Up to then scholastic authors treated of analogy only in logic or

on what characterizes the analogy of being and what distinguishes it from every other instance. Following his lead, philosophers generally restrict themselves to seeing here merely an application of the general theory of analogy. The case of being, however, is unique and the analogy of the idea of being differs profoundly from that of other concepts, for the idea of being is transcendental, and quidditative concepts are not such. The difference between a transcendental idea and a concept of limited extension is not merely a difference of degree; the first transcends the second, it is of a different nature; both as regards its comprehension and its extension, in its origin as well as in its mode of attribution, it belongs to a different order.

In the realm of essences the analogy of proportionality is illuminating in this sense that it advances the knowledge we have of an object by solving questions concerning this object. It is thus that we determine ever more and more the divine nature by establishing the fact that the ideas of life, knowledge, will, liberty, justice etc., are applied proportionally to God and to man; but in the order of being it is not thus. The analogy of proportionality does not solve a difficulty, but rather poses one, and it is illuminating only because it makes the data of the fundamental metaphysical problem stand out clearly. In the idea of being the relative and the absolute, the one and the many, the essential modes and the source of all participation, collide with one another and are grounded in the indistinction of an implicit proportionality It is quite understandable why some declare that they do not see right away how such an idea could possess an essential unity and how it could be an idea, but this is because they do not see at once how to solve the metaphysical problem. And yet, it is not astonishing that the end of metaphysics is not found at its beginning, and that we cannot offer the solution of problems before having placed them. What creates the difficulty in the case of being is that the proportionality has to do entirely with the concrete, that the terms brought together are subsistent and hence radically dis-

---

theodicy, and they did not speak of it in metaphysics. About 1907 they took up the study of analogy by itself, in the Thomistic, Cajetan, Suarezian, and Scotistic interpretations. Later the study of analogy was taken up from a wider and more critical point of view, e.g., by J. Maréchal, S.J., E. Przywara, S.J., P. Fackler, P. Fleig.

Among the followers of Cajetan we may cite: R. Garrigou-Lagrange, Gardair, A. Gardeil, Ed. Hugon, Nic. Balthasar, Jos. Gredt, Jos. Bittremieux, G. M. Manser, Del Prado, Jos. Habbel, K. Feckes, F. A. Blanche, J. M. Ramirez, J. Le Rohellec, St. De Backer, A. Forest, A. Marc. For the Scotistic school, cf. pp. 47, 48; for the Suarezian, cf. pp. 49–51.

tinct, and that without making an abstraction of anything, we reduce them nevertheless to a unity of a single content of meaning on the basis of the absolute value of being. We cannot escape either this principle of absolute unity, or the multiplicity of subsistent terms; for the one and the other are thrust on us with equal force in every act of knowledge. These two data are firmly established and assert themselves at one and the same time; the idea of being embraces both of them, and by that same token it strikes us, makes us wonder, confronts us with a problem. It belongs to metaphysics to solve this problem by discovering what is the unique and absolute principle which has to do with, penetrates, and unifies the ensemble of the subsistent terms of the proportionality of being. The idea of being implies the existence of this fundamental principle of unity of the subsistent terms; and it is precisely here that we find the reason for the unity which it itself possesses as an idea, but it does not determine in any way the nature of this principle.

From this point of view it is easy to pass judgment on a controversy which has developed in the Thomistic school on the subject of the analogy of being. Some have asked the question whether this analogy of proportionality implies a principal term and secondary terms, as is the case with the analogy of attribution and the metaphor.[23] The answer depends on the meaning we give these terms.

---

[23] Cajetan and John of St. Thomas answer in the negative, Franciscus de Sylvestris Ferrariensis in the affirmative. Cf. (for the view of Cajetan) Jos. Habbel, "Die Analogie zwischen Gott und Welt nach Thomas von Aquin," Regensburg, 1928. "Die Lehre des Thomas v. Aquin von der nur analogen Bedeutung unserer Aussagen über Gott als Zeugnis seiner Anschauung über das Verhältnis der Welt zu Gott," Regensburg, 1928.

Karl Feckes, "Die Analogie in unserem Gotteskennen, ihre metaphysische und religiöse Bedeutung," *Probleme der Gotteserkenntnis* (Veröffentlichungen des Albertus-Magnus-Akademie zu Köln, t. II, vol. 3), Münster, 1928, pp. 132–184.

L. Penido, *Le rôle de l'analogie en théologie dogmatique* (Bibl. Thomiste, Vol. XV, sect. théol. t. II), Paris, 1931, pp. 46–53. "Cajetan et notre connaissance analogique de Dieu," *Revue Thomiste,* new series. Vol. XVII, 1934, pp. 149–198. G. Manser, O.P. *Das Wesen des Thomismus,* Fribourg in Switz., 1932.

For the meaning of Ferrara, cf. F. A. Blanche, "Sur le sens de quelques locutions concernant l'analogie dans le langage de saint Thomas d'Aquin," *Revue des sciences philosophiques et théologiques,* Vol. X, 1921, pp. 52–59. "La notion d'analogie dans la philosophie de St. Thomas," *ibid.,* 1921, pp. 169–193 "L'analogie," *Revue de philosophie,* Vol. XXX, 1923, pp. 248–270. "Une théorie de l'analogie. Éclaircissements et développements," *ibid.,* new series. Vol. III, 1932, pp. 37–78. Jac. M. Ramirez, O.P. "De Analogia secundum doctrinam aristotelico-thomisticam," *La ciencia tomista,* Vol. XIII, 1921, pp. 19–40, 195–214, 337–357; Vol. XIV, 1922, pp. 17–38.

Jos. Le Rohellec, C.S.Sp., "De fundamento metaphysico analogiae," *Divus*

The idea of being is transcendental, it includes in its signification all particular beings; and these latter enter completely into a unique order, and the relation which binds them to it constitutes their own distinctive reality. On the ontological plane we cannot then designate them without signifying also the fundamental principle to which they are related by all their reality; for we cannot make a relation known without making mention of its term. In this sense the analogy of being implies a principal analogue and secondary ones; but it is this very fact which constitutes the metaphysical problem: what can be the nature of the relations which bind the secondary terms, which are subsistent beings, to the principal term? If the first term is a being entirely independent of particular beings, it is a principal analogue in the full sense of the word; but if on the contrary it must be identified in any way with the reality of every particular being, it is only in an entirely different sense, and one which hardly preserves the proper meaning of the word, that we will be able to speak of a principal term.

4. The Absolute and the Relative in Affirmation and Negation

To formulate the ontological problem the better it will help us to consider it in the light of the negation of being; for the contrast emphasizes the meaning of the terms under discussion. It has been remarked, and not without reason, that from the psychological point of view, knowledge of the negative is more difficult than that of the positive.[24] As a matter of fact, whoever wishes to think of a negation must first of all posit the affirmation so as to be able later to exclude it. For example, I find myself in a furnished apartment which I can represent to myself now as empty. The articles of furniture were there, but they are there no longer. The negation falls upon a positive

---

Thomas (Plaisance) 3rd series, 3rd year, pp. 77–101, 664–691. "Cognitio nostra analogica de Deo," *ibid.*, 1927, pp. 298–319 (Article reprinted in *Problèmes philosophiques*." Articles and notes collected and published by C. Larnicol and A. Drellemmes, Paris, 1933).

Nicolas Balthasar, "L'abstraction et l'analogie de l'être," in *Miscellanea Tomista* (*Extraordinari d'Estudis Francescans*, Vol. XXXIV), Barcelona, 1924. *L'abstraction métaphysique et l'analogie des êtres dans l'être*, Louvain, 1935.

[24] Cf. H. Bergson, *L'Évolution créatrice*, 20th ed., Paris, 1917, pp. 298 ff. (English transl. by Arthur Mitchell, Henry Holt & Co., New York, 1931, pp. 285 ff.)

content which has been removed, denied. This is a relative negation; it has relation to a positive content of thought.

In the example just mentioned, the articles of furniture have been effectively replaced by some other thing; all the space which they occupied has been invaded by the air which fills the apartment. Two positive contents of representation form the object of comparison: the furnished apartment and the same apartment devoid of furniture and filled only with air. The first content is distinct from the second, the second is not the first; and in this sense we speak of the apartment *not* furnished. When one follows the other and replaces it, the second, so to speak, serves to blot out or suppress the first. In this case the negation rests on two affirmations: it is relative [25] in this sense that it requires a positive foundation; negation presupposes affirmation.

By imagination and thought we can successively deny all things, we can replace them by other things, but it is evidently impossible to deny the whole complexus of things; for if we take all things at one and the same time, we cannot replace them with anything. Total transcendental negation would be equivalent to a thought without any content of knowledge, and this would be reduced to no thought at all. Transcendental negation is simply a word devoid of all meaning.

The transcendental idea of being does not merely signify a multiplicity of isolated beings, it envisages at the same time the absolute in which all these beings find their fundamental unity, and by reason of which each possesses its own proper consistency. To deny this absolute value in a being is to deny the principle on which this being, and likewise the whole order of beings, are founded; such negation is nonsense. It is impossible to deny the absolute, which is always present to consciousness. Consequently, negation cannot be brought to bear either on all things at once, or on the value of being which manifests itself in everything. In a word, it cannot be brought to bear on transcendental and absolute being; transcendental and absolute negation is impossible. The following problem therefore suggests itself: if absolute negation must be ruled out, how far can we extend relative negation? Can we conceive that certain realities

---

[25] Likewise according to Plato, non-being can constitute an "idea" and form an intelligible content only in the sense of otherness, i.e. of relative non-being. Parmenides according to Plato was wrong in not distinguishing this relative and intelligible non-being from absolute, and by that same token, absurd non-being. Cf. *Sophist*, 255c–e.

which exist could not have been? This question has to do with the pure possibility and contingency of beings, and it will be shown later on that it is quite closely connected with the fundamental problem of metaphysics.[26]

5. *The Absolute and the Relative in Identity*

The opposition of affirmation and negation permits us to make more precise the content of the idea of being. Every experience of being implies an affirmation of being; here we firmly apprehend the absolute. The absolute is complete, it has reference to itself, without relation to any other thing; it is itself and nothing more. The fundamental law of being is its full and complete identity.

Contrary to what the subjective criticism of Kant maintains, unity is not reducible to an a priori form of thought. The law of identity governs the content as well as the form of knowledge; it dominates

---

[26] According to Jean-Paul Sartre, consciousness, the "being for itself" belongs to relative non-being, the "other" (of which Plato speaks in the *Sophist*), and it is a perpetual source of the "annihilation" of the "being in itself." Cf. *L'être et le néant*, Paris, 1943, pp. 59–84, 711–713. It is therefore fundamentally negative.

Existence is the "very batter of things." (Cf. *La Nausée*, Paris, 1938, p. 162). When consciousness arises here, it recoils, it settles down at a distance, face to face with being, all the while being essentially related to being. And whereas in stretching itself out in the successive moments of time it strips itself of the perfect identity, which is the characteristic of being in itself, it lays hold of knowledge of existing reality by introducing everywhere distinctions between this and that (and therefore negations, since it opposes distinct terms), and by seeking to form a foundation for the different terms which it has thus recognized. In a word, consciousness raises problems unceasingly; it calls everything in question; under the pretext of wishing to found everything, it annihilates being.

As a matter of fact, in the perspective of such philosophy being is volatilized in a universal relativism. "The essential, this is contingency; . . . contingency, this is the absolute, and consequently, perfect gratuity. Everything is gratuitous, this garden, this city and myself." *La Nausée*, p. 167.

Such a philosophical attitude cannot be defended. It is impossible for us to call everything in question, for it is not negation which is first, but affirmation. Consciousness is anchored in being; before all else it lays hold of itself, by identity, as belonging to conscious being. In so far, it does not keep at a distance from being, but it lays hold of it as it is, in its real value, which is absolute. At the same time it recognizes there multiplicity, real oppositions, relativity. And so the problem is not to know if the absolute and the relative are reconciled, but how this reconciliation is to be conceived. We cannot assert offhand that everything is contingent, or that everything is necessary; no more than we can at first maintain that there are necessary beings and others which are not necessary. The problem precisely is to know what is implied by the fact that all reality of experience manifests at once the absolute and the relative, and in particular what this implies on the plane of the necessary and the contingent.

everything without exception, since it is reduced to the fundamental character of being which is of itself altogether sufficient, just as it is absolute and transcendental.

As all truth, so this identity of being is expressed under the form of a judgment: Being is being. Some have erroneously pretended to see here a mere tautology.[27] Undoubtedly, the subject and the predicate of this proposition are expressed by the same word "being," but they do not exercise the same logical function, and in so far they differ, one from the other. Logically, being-as-subject cannot be confounded with being-as-predicate. The predicate can be attributed to the subject when it says something of the latter, that is, what we have understood of the subject. Now when we find ourselves in the presence of being we lay hold of its most fundamental, its absolute character; we comprehend first of all that being is itself absolutely, that it is being without supporting itself on the relations which bind it to some other thing. By this very fact we understand that there is nothing to add to the affirmation of this identity; it is unconditional, self-sufficient, complete.

The negation of being is unthinkable. When I write: "Being is not non-being," the term "non-being" which should function as the predicate, does not express an idea. It is merely a word, devoid of meaning, and as such it cannot fill the role of an attribute. If it is altogether impossible to oppose a second term to that of being, we could not a fortiori find a third term which would be situated between these first two. Consequently, the principle of excluded middle, expressed in terms of absolute being, contains likewise a so-called attribute which is only a sound stripped of all signification. The identity of being is absolute; it is impossible to oppose no thing, non-being, to transcendental being.

The identity of being is found necessarily in everything which contains the value of being, and hence in the order of beings; since being is being, this being here is this being here, and that being there is that being there. The order of beings is adequately the order of identity,[28] and this order contains correlative terms. The identity of being

---

[27] J. Laminne maintained that the principle of identity is tautology. Cf. *Revue néoscolastique de Philosophie*, Vol. XXI, 1914, p. 358.

[28] If we posit as a principle that A is A, we cannot deduce from this that B is B. But if being is being, it follows from this that A is A, and B is B, since being is transcendental. The metaphysical principle of identity must be formulated in terms of being, since it is being which is the formal object of metaphysics, and since, moreover, by that same token the principle is of absolutely universal application.

implies therefore the identity of terms which are characterized by their relativity. Now the nature of a relative term depends fundamentally on the corresponding term, and the identity of the first is therefore bound up with that of the second. A is A, B is B, A is related to B. Furthermore, we have shown above that the order of being does not consist in a network of relations superadded to the beings already in being; on the contrary, it is the mark that is characteristic of the whole reality of these beings. Hence we must conclude that in the order of being all things are concatenated, and negation of the identity of one thing destroys the order and the reality of all things. The identity of every particular being depends on that of all the others: A is A, if B is B; or again, A is A, since B is B, and conversely. Absolute identity is manifested at the same time as relative identity and through this latter just as the absolute value of being is revealed in particular beings united in one all-embracing order.

When there is question of particular beings, therefore, the identity of the one implies intelligible negation, that is, the relative negation of the other; A is A, and it is not B. Identity keeps step with non-identity or opposition. In this case the principle of non-contradiction can be formulated in intelligible terms: A is not B. The predicate B is not a word, devoid of meaning, but a positive term. This principle of non-contradiction rests, by reason of the negation which it implies, on the principle of identity: A is not B presupposes that A is A, and that B is B.

Every being gives rise to the enunciation of two judgments of identity: it *is*, it is *this* and not that. The first has reference to the absolute character of being, and the second to the limited and relative character of particular being. Metaphysics inquires how these two identities, the one absolute and the other relative, are reconcilable. How can being exist under the form of an order of beings?

CHAPTER IV

THE UNITY AND THE INFINITY OF BEING

1. Unity and Identity: Unicity and Plurality

THE problem of being is that of the one and the many; to make this precise we must determine the meaning of these terms. Unity is defined by identity: that is one which is one and the same, that which is identical with itself. The classical formula enunciates this negatively: "The one is undivided in itself and divided from another." It is undivided in itself, it is that which is entirely itself, and not partly another; for it is a contradiction to be at one and the same time another and itself. It is distinct from any other thing, it is only itself and not at the same time another; for otherwise, there would once again be a contradiction. And since being is characterized by identity, the idea of being and the idea of the one are convertible: *Ens et unum convertuntur.*

Being, as being, is absolute; it is absolutely one. It excludes the other, it is unique, but there are many beings; every one of them is a being. As beings, they all belong to one and the same order; these unities are correlatives, necessarily united on the basis of their unique value of absolute being.

The unity of a whole is relative, since it implies multiplicity; but in its turn all multiplicity is relative, since it forms necessarily one whole. All multiplicity, therefore, presupposes a principle of unity, an element which unites the different terms and renders them in this regard similar; one and the same unity of measure is adapted to all the terms. The wholes differ among themselves according to the modes of unity which they possess, and therefore according to the measure which we can apply to them.

The analogous idea of being indicates the principle of fundamental unity, since it permits us to reduce all things to one unique synthesis. Besides, limited groups can be formed on the basis of a

61

specific determination common to all the members of one and the same group; the universal idea which corresponds to it is univocal, for example, the notion of man. In other cases the principle of unity is purely accidental and the complexus thus produced is fortuitous or accessory, for example, a heap of stones, or a dream.

Unity is encountered not merely in the real order but also in that of knowledge, considered as such. As a matter of fact, knowledge takes place in time and it embraces a concatenation of distinct contents. Logical unities are found here, for example, the ideas of man, animal, mortal, which retain the same meaning, that is, a logical unity throughout the successive psychological acts by which they are evoked. These ideas are combined in judgments and reasonings, in such a manner as to form one logical order.

2. Unity and Distinction; the List of Distinctions; the Problems of Distinction in the Order of Being

Since philosophy seeks above all for a solution to the problem of the one and the many, which is presented moreover under various forms, it ought to determine accurately the nature of the unities which it studies. And just as there are unities of very different species, it must avoid confounding them, and it must endeavor to distinguish them. The question of distinction which is merely the opposite of that of unity presents, therefore, a thing of capital importance. History bears witness to the fact that the progress of philosophy always reveals itself by a finer and more delicate understanding of the modes of distinction.

Aristotle took a decisive step in this matter, when in the light of his theory of abstraction he distinguished the order of knowledge and that of reality. From then on he was able to avoid Platonic idealism and to show that the course of knowledge is not the literal replica of the development of things, and that the articulations of thought do not correspond entirely to real distinctions. But more than this, on both sides, that is, in reality and in knowledge, degrees of distinction are presented which it is important not to confound. Let us single out a few.

First of all, in the logical order. When we find ourselves in the presence of reality, we consider successively different aspects of it in such a way as to form several ideas which have different contents, distinct significations. Thus we say that man is a being, corporeal, living, an animal, rational. These attributes are not synonyms; they express, every one of them, an idea, a logical unity. All these ideas are formally distinct one from the other since their contents of signification envisage different formalities, points of view, aspects of one and the same reality. Such distinction is founded in reality since the different aspects considered are prescribed by reality; they are real aspects, even though they are not really distinct. Man is really corporeal, living, animal, rational; but corporeity, life, animality, and rationality are not so many really distinct parts in him.

This formal distinction is called virtual, since it is founded on an analysis of the activity manifested by the real subject. The activity of man is really developed in different ways; it comprehends different virtualities. Man reacts as a body; he develops as a plant; he moves as an animal, and more than that, he possesses a personal activity. We can then distinguish here forms of activity which make him similar to beings of different perfections; man acts as a body, as a plant, as an animal, as a person. He is one single being, and yet by his activity, *virtute,* he is equivalent to many; he is virtually many beings.

Formal or virtual distinction between two ideas is called complete when the content of the one is entirely outside the content of the other; for example, the concepts of corporeity and rationality are completely different. It is said to be incomplete when the content of the one partially overlaps that of the other; thus the idea of man, defined as rational animal, and the idea of rational are formally identified in part and distinct from each other only in part.

As regards this last point, we have to distinguish several cases, for we must take into account not merely univocal concepts but also analogical notions, and especially transcendental ideas. The univocal concept of animal lies entirely outside the concept of rational; put together they are adapted one to the other, and they complete each other. It is altogether different with transcendental ideas, as that of being, since they cannot receive any extrinsic complement and their development must be effected from within, by additions improperly so-called, that is, by being made more explicit. Consequently, the idea of being is not completely distinct from any other; it implicitly contains the content of all ideas: man signifies being human; God is the divine being; rational means being rational. Again, we must not confound different cases; there are ideas which go to determine that of being and which have a limited extension, for example, that of man; others determine the idea of being while possessing a transcendental extension: one is a transcendental just as is being; both have the same extension, and that is why they are convertible. Thus, in starting from a virtual, complete distinction we gradually get nearer and nearer to logical identity.

We call a distinction of pure reason, or a purely logical distinction, that which obtains between two concepts which have to do, both of them, with the same aspect of the same object. They are not therefore formally distinct, and the words which express them are synonyms. There is only a difference of clarity between them, in such wise that the reason of the distinction is found on the part of the knowing subject and so has no foundation on the part of the object known.[1] For example, there is a distinction of pure reason between man and rational animal, if I begin by not clearly distinguishing what man is, so as to arrive later at a clear apprehension of his definition.

The order of knowledge is bound up with the real order since it comprehends the idea of being, which establishes the contact of the mind with all reality. However, the first differs from the second, and for every distinction between ideas there arises the question of knowing, if a real distinction corresponds to the logical distinction, and further, what the nature of this real distinction is. In reality as well as in knowledge, there are many degrees of distinction. We will admit without hesitation that there is a real distinction between a man and a horse, between a star and an apple; similarly, that there is such a distinction between a man and his head, but all will likewise agree that all these cases are not the same. How are we to classify the distinction between a man and his soul? Is it the same as that which exists between the entire body and the head? Or the distinction between soul and body? Is it the same as the distinction between the head and the other parts of the human organism? Are thinking and willing as different as the sense of sight and that of hearing? In what way is God distinct from finite beings? Is this distinction reducible to that which obtains between two men, or between an animal and a plant, or between a part and its whole, or being a substance and its active evolution?

In determining the nature of distinction, we define at least im-

---

[1] This is the reason why the Scholastics oppose the "distinctio rationis *ratiocinantis,*" which is founded entirely on the *knowing* subject, to the "distinctio rationis *ratiocinatae*" (the virtual distinction), which is founded also on the object *thought about.*

plicitly the nature of the terms which we distinguish; the two involve each other. Suppose that there is no agreement on the nature of the world and the things it contains; there could then no longer be any agreement on the way in which beings are distinct one from the other.

Hence, it is just as completely impossible to draw up a priori a complete and exact list of distinctions, as to offer a priori the solution of philosophical problems. We are at times tempted to wish that philosophers would agree on a precise terminology of distinctions; but how could they do this if they do not come to some understanding on the fundamental theses of philosophy? [2] Undoubtedly, we could in advance define in some very general fashion the meaning of certain expressions; it is possible to indicate in this way the difference to be drawn between a real distinction and a logical one, but the exact meaning which we give to the different real distinctions depends inevitably on the philosophical opinions which we profess. In a monistic system these distinctions will not have the same importance as in a dualistic or pluralistic system. Moreover, the question arises how are we to know if we are in a position to discover non-logical distinctions outside of those which obtain among realities which are separable, and how must we conceive these distinctions, if such should be the case? On this point opinions are quite divergent, but let us single out those of St. Thomas and John Duns Scotus.

The Angelic Doctor admits certain distinctions which have to do with reality (and not merely the knowledge which we have of this reality), and whose terms cannot be separated in any case. For example, the distinction between essence and existence in every creature. There is question in this case of a real structure of every finite being. How must we conceive the elements of this structure and what is the nature of their distinction? This question will be discussed later on; but we must always remember that this is not a distinction between two beings, or between two separable parts of one and the same being. This is why it could not be called a real distinction in the sense which this expression always has in some non-Thomistic

---

[2] It is the same with all philosophical terms. An agreement could be made on the general sense which must be attributed to them, but not on the precise sense. From the fact that St. Bonaventure, St. Albert the Great, St. Thomas and Duns Scotus use the same terms, *esse, essentia, actus, potentia, substantia, accidens*, etc., we would be wrong in concluding that they attribute to these terms the same meaning, and that they are in agreement on the broad lines of a philosophical system. Every one of these understands these words in a particular sense, which can be understood only in the light of his fundamental theories.

schools, that is, a distinction between one thing and another, a "distinctio inter rem et rem"; [3] but if we call every non-logical distinction a real distinction, the distinction between essence and existence is real. Let us rather call it a real, metaphysical distinction. According to this same pattern of real structure of finite being St. Thomas conceives the union of prime matter and substantial form, and that of substance and accidents; but in every case it will be necessary to determine with precision the meaning of the structure.[4]

Duns Scotus likewise makes an effort to define a kind of distinction which is not of the logical order and which nevertheless is not reduced to a real distinction between elements which are separable. The "distinctio formalis *ex natura rei*" is a distinction "from the nature of a thing." Without being a distinction between entities which are separable [5] it has to do with reality in that which it is in itself,

---

[3] "On the part of the Scotists as on that of the Suarezians, a real distinction obtains only where you have the possibility of separation (if not mutual necessarily, at least non-mutual) and composition in the manner of oxygen and hydrogen resulting in water. The real distinction is a distinction of the physical order in the strict sense, (I almost said "gross" sense) of the word; a man and a dog, sodium and chloride. The distinction of matter and form is real for them only because they suppose the two terms are capable of subsisting by themselves, if not naturally at least as an effect of the divine omnipotence." P. Descoqs, S.J., "Archives de Philosophie," vol. IV, cahier 4, "Bibliographie critique," (Paris, 1927), pp. 141–142; cf. *ibid.*, p. 109.

Descartes on his side writes that "there are distinctions of three sorts, real, modal and of reason, or that which is made by thought. The real is found properly between two or more substances. . . . There are two kinds of modal distinctions, the one between the mode, which we have called *façon*, and the substance on which it depends and which it diversifies; and the other between two different *façons* of one and the same substance. (For example, between the form and the movement of a material thing. Author's insertion) Finally, the distinction which is made by thought, consists in this that at times we distinguish a substance from some one of its attributes, without which, however, it is not possible for us to have a distinct knowledge of it; or it consists in this that we strive to separate from one and the same substance two such attributes by thinking of one without thinking of the other, e.g., substance and its duration." "Les Principes de la Philosophie" I^e partie, ch. 60–62 (édit. Ada n–Tannery, t. 9, Paris, 1904, pp. 51–53).

[4] The controversies about the distinction between *esse* and *essentia*, immediately after the death of St. Thomas in 1274, provoked a number of studies on distinctions, and attempts to find the kinds of distinction, differing from the purely logical and the real distinction "inter rem et rem." Thus it was that Henry of Ghent, in his *Quodlibet* I, in 1276, proposed a *distinctio secundum intentiones;* others speak of a logical distinction *secundum diversas rationes.* Cf. Jean Paulus, "Henri de Gand. Essais sur les tendances de sa métaphysique." (*Études de philosophie médiévale*, Vol. XXV) Paris, 1938, pp. 199–257.

[5] "It is not properly real and actual, understanding (as is commonly said)

independently of our knowledge.[6] Hence, it is not a mere distinction of reason, or a logical, virtual distinction.[7] We must admit such a distinction every time that we find ourselves before concepts that are formally irreducible [8] since all agree that knowledge has bearing on reality.[9]

Scotus thinks that there is such a distinction between being and its transcendental properties, one, true and good; similarly, between the substance of the soul and its faculties, between the different aspects of one and the same form, for example, between the formalities living, animal, rational, of the human substance. Likewise, he finds it in God, between the essential divine attributes, such as the divine intelligence, will, justice, wisdom; as also between one divine person and his personal properties, as between the act of generation and the act of spiration of the Father. Nevertheless, in God there obtains

real and actual as that which is the difference of things and in act." Johannes Duns Scotus, *Opus oxoniense, Sentent.* I, dist. 2, q. 7 (edit. Wadding, t. 5, p. 335).

[6] "(It is) a difference which is posited as preceding every act of the intellect." *Ibid.*

[7] "It can be called a difference of reason, as a certain doctor (Bonaventure) says, not because *ratio* is taken for the difference formed by the intellect but as *ratio* is taken for the quiddity of the thing, inasmuch as the quiddity is the object of the intellect."
"Or in another way it can be called a virtual difference, because that which has such a distinction in itself, does not have one thing and another, but it is one thing, having virtually or eminently as it were two realities; for to each reality, as it is in that thing, there belongs that property, which is in that reality, as if it itself were distinct. For thus this reality distinguishes, and that does not distinguish, just as if these were one thing, and those were another." *Ibid.*

[8] "From the difference of the formal objects, of which neither is contained in the other eminently, and this in the intellect, considering intuitively, we conclude to some difference (before the act of the intellect) of those things which are known intuitively." *Ibid.* "One is not of the formal definition of the other." *Reportata parisientia,* I, 45, q. 2 (t. II, p. 233). "I understand by the formal non-identity of some things, when one is not of the formal definition of the other, so that if it were defined, it would not belong to its definition. Therefore by formal non-identity I understand quidditative non-identity, i.e. not belonging to the definition of the other, if it were defined." *Ibid.* (t. II, p. 234).

[9] "Definition indicates not merely the form caused by the intellect, but the quiddity of the thing." *Opus Oxoniense, Sentent.,* I, d. 8, q. 4 (t. 5, p. 766). "Thus in the divine attributes there is a formal non-identity of wisdom and goodness, in as far as there would be distinct definitions of them, if they were definable. . . . I understand this thus, that the intellect judging 'wisdom is not formally goodness,' does not by its act of comparison cause the truth of this composition, but in the object it discovers the extremes, from whose composition the act becomes true. . . . Thus I grant that truth is identified with goodness in reality, but still truth is not goodness formally." *Ibid.*

a minor distinction, for there is neither formal nor real composition
in the divine Being.[10]

Scotus applies his theory of formal distinction in the essential order
and not in the order of the absolute value of being; St. Thomas admits
a real metaphysical distinction between essence and existence. Scotus
places a real distinction, "inter rem et rem," between prime matter
and the substantial form as well as between substance and accidents;
St. Thomas places here only a real metaphysical distinction, and not
a "distinctio inter rem et rem." In certain cases where Scotus admits
a formal distinction, St. Thomas insists on a real metaphysical distinction, as between the soul and its faculties; in others, St. Thomas
admits at most a logical virtual distinction, for example, between the
transcendental ideas, between the abstract aspects of one and the
same reality, the degrees of the Porphyrian tree, as well as between
the essential attributes of God. In general, the formalism of Scotus [11]
is in comparison with the philosophy of St. Thomas an exaggerated
realism which tends to project into reality the whole formal structure
of the order of ideas.

A lively reaction set in against the formalism of the Scotistic school,
and it also assailed the Thomistic theories on metaphysical composition, which were moreover all too often presented without their
shades of difference, and were understood in the sense of a composition of things or of parts, as "inter rem et rem." In modern philosophy,
Cartesian rationalism, quite as much as English empiricism, refused

---

[10] The plurality of formalities does not imply any composition in God, either
real or formal, for God is infinite. "Every perfection in God is infinite and therefore it cannot properly be said to be a part of one total perfection." *Quaestiones
in Metaphys. Aristotelis,* lib. IV, q.2 (t. 4, p. 587, col. 1). "Some composition is
in whiteness, although not of one thing and another, still such as is not conceded
to be in God on account of formal non-identity." *Opus oxoniense, Sentent.* I,
d.2, q.7 (t. 5, p. 356).

[11] Duns Scotus (1266/74–1308) is the most famous representative of this
formalism; he is not the inventor of the formal distinction. It was St. Bonaventure
who was the first to speak in his studies on the Trinity, of a "difference of attribution," of a "different mode of being." Peter of John Olivi, O.F.M. (1248/9–
1298) and especially Alexander of Alexandria, O.F.M. (+1314) studied ex
professo the possibility and the foundation of such distinction. Matthew of
Aquasparta, O.F.M. (1235/40–1302) was the first to use the word "formaliter"
to designate this formal distinction. Among the authors of the 13th century who
admit the formal distinction "ex natura rei" we may also cite: Peter of Trèves,
O.F.M. (end of 13th century) and Peter de Falco, O.F.M., both at Paris; at
Oxford: John Berwick, O.F.M. (circ. 1290), Adam of Lincoln, O.F.M. (circ.
1292), William of Nottingham, O.F.M. (1336), William Macklesfield, O.P.
(1304). Cf. Bernard Jansen, S.J., "Beiträge zur geschichtlichen Entwicklung der
distinctio formalis," in *Zeitschrift für katholische Theologie,* Vol. LIII, pp. 332 ff.

to admit a metaphysical explanation of reality by means of the internal composition of finite beings. This reaction was exaggerated, and was bound to render insoluble some fundamental problems, such as that of the unity of human nature. Contemporaneous thought, by introducing everywhere but especially in psychology and physics, the idea of structure, opposed to that of an association of pre-existing elements, once more seems inclined to admit also in metaphysics this scholastic conception of the non-simplicity or internal composition of beings that are substantially one. In other words, these moderns admit the metaphysical structure of finite beings.

Besides the question of the real distinction between the constitutive principles of one and the same finite being, there is also that of the distinction of beings and their fundamental principle of unity. This latter, if we admit its reality, ought to differ fundamentally from the distinction which obtains between particular beings; but once again, we cannot define it a priori, and every author will conceive it as functioning in his whole system of philosophy. Besides, this question is bound up with that of the finite and the infinite, whose terms we must make precise.

3. Unity, the Absolute and the Infinite. Finite Number and Unlimited Multitude. The Problem of the Unlimited Order of Particular Beings, and the Infinity of Being

There is a very close relation, on the one hand, between the many and the finite, and on the other, between the one and the infinite. The units constitutive of a multitude are distinct one from the other; that which is proper to one is not found in the other; in other words, every one is finite. Inversely, that which is finite is limited by that from which it is distinct; it is opposed but related to that which is found outside of it; it belongs to a multiplicity, to a whole, to an order. The notions of finite, relative, multiple, mutually imply each other.

The infinite is the negation of the finite, and hence it is also the negation of the relative and the multiple; it is absolute and unique; and just as every order is made up of finite elements, the infinite can be conceived by relation to every order. For example, space: the different places which it includes, limit one another; but the ensemble of all possible places cannot be limited by other places, it is unlimited. So also time: every moment is limited by that which precedes it and by that which follows it, but the ensemble of all the moments is not preceded or followed by any other; it is not further limited by anything, it is unlimited. It is not otherwise with the species, such as human nature. No one man is identified with the whole human species, for there are other men who possess human perfections which this man has not; and by this very fact every individual is limited in the species, but the ensemble of all possible men embraces all, unlimited, unbounded human perfection.[12] We might say in the same sense that every person possesses his own individual perfection in an unlimited way, since his personality is unique and incommunicable. The ego cannot be duplicated; it completely exhausts the possibility of its personal nature.[13]

All these totalities are unlimited only in a relative way, that is, in their order; for they are distinct one from the other, and therefore they limit one another mutually. If, however, we were to take the ensemble of finite beings, real and possible, there would be no other finite being to limit it, since by definition this ensemble would include all of them. This would be the unlimited order of beings.

From the moment that a complete and finished whole, unlimited or infinite in the sense just indicated, gives rise to intrinsic distinctions, questions are raised as to the subject of this multiplicity of terms which it contains. Among others there is the following question: do these terms form a multitude which it is possible to number? We are tempted to deny this; in fact, every number can be increased by another unit, and therefore it is finite and has relation to the unit which could be added to it, in such wise that it does not include the ensemble of the actual or possible terms in the order under discussion. Consequently, an ensemble of terms which we can number does not seem to be able to form a whole entirely complete, unlimited,

---

[12] In this sense St. Thomas writes that every angel, considered in its species, is infinite because according to the Angelic Doctor every angel is unique in its species; it is identified with its species, and it possesses the perfection of its species in an unlimited manner, since it does not share it with any other. Cf. *Summa theol.*, Ia, q.7, a.2; q.50, a.2, ad 4; *De ente et essentia*, c.6 (edit. Laurent, n.115, pp. 184–185).

[13] The reality of the ego is not simple; we can distinguish in it the principles of a structure, which are distinct one from the other, are correlative, and limit one another in the interior of the structure. Similarly, human existence extends into time, and we can here distinguish successive periods, mutually limited by one another. But if we take the existence of the ego, in its complexus, in its eternal duration, it includes the unique and incommunicable plenitude of the ego, its complete and in this sense, infinite value.

absolute, that is to say, a whole which in its order is exclusive of every relation with something outside of it. This would amount to maintaining that the multiplicity of terms, constitutive of a complete whole, is necessarily innumerable; in which case the infinite, in the sense indicated until now, would imply an infinite, understood in another sense, namely, that of an inexhaustible multitude. But can such a multitude be conceived and can it be such in every order? The history of philosophy bears witness to the fact that these questions have given rise to divergent solutions, which formed the object of numerous controversies.

Spinoza maintains that we know two properties of the fundamental substance, thought and extension; but he thinks that this substance, being infinite, must be affected by an infinite multitude of properties. According to him it is impossible for a finite number of properties or modes to express adequately all the riches of reality. Hence we must admit an infinite multitude of possibles, all of which come to be realized. Leibnitz is of the opinion that all the possibles could never come into existence, because there are some which exclude one another; if one is realized, by this very fact a series of other possibles cannot be produced. Only those things are actually realized which are capable of existing together, which are compatible, compossible.

The Scholastics, too, are generally in agreement in admitting an infinite multitude of possibles, and in declaring that they are, all together, known by God and our divine Lord; they think, moreover, that these possibles cannot be realized all at once. Even in this case, however, the question arises whether the multitude of things which are realized, is infinite. For if it is true that it is not enough to add one unit to a finite number to obtain an infinite multitude, it seems equally true that it is not enough to take away some units from an infinite multitude to render it finite. The Scholastics distinguish two cases, that of the simultaneous existence of the multitude of units, and that of their successive existence in time. For the first case, they pronounce generally in favor of the opinion which declares the realization of a simultaneous infinite multitude to be impossible; as for the second case, the majority is likewise in favor of the negative opinion.

St. Thomas, however, adopts an attitude that is more prudent. As regards a successive multitude, he states that he does not see any way of solving the question merely by reason; arguments have been brought forward in favor of the possibility of the eternity of the world, and others in favor of its impossibility, but none of these arguments is apodictic; "up to now it has not been demonstrated."[14] As regards an infinite multitude of things which would exist simultaneously, the Angelic Doctor hesitates a long time before declaring it impossible in all cases.[15]

Kant, on the contrary, takes great pains to prove two contradictory theses, that of the possibility and that of the impossibility of the eternity of time *a parte ante* and of the infinite extension of space.[16] In this antinomy he sees evident proof of the fact that the problem is poorly enunciated.[17] It is a mistake, he says, for speculative reason to be occupied with such problems; a critique of pure reason makes us discover the root of the evil, and his subjectivistic formalism furnishes the key to the enigma.

This is not the time to examine the foundation of the question whether an infinite multitude of terms is necessary to constitute a complete order, and in this sense an unlimited order (for example,

---

[14] Cf. *Summa theol.*, Ia, q.46, a.2; II *Sentent.*, d.1, q.1, a.5; *Quodl.* III, q.14, a.31; II *Gent.*, c.38; *De Potentia*, q.3, a.17; *De aeternitate mundi.*

[15] In *II Sentent.*, d.1, q.1, a.5, ad 17 (1254–55), and *De Veritate*, q.2, a.10 (1256), St. Thomas does not commit himself on this question. While rejecting the possibility of an infinite multitude in act *per se*, he calls attention to the opinion of Algazel, according to whom an infinite in act *per accidens* would be possible.

In the *Summa theol.*, Ia, q.7, a.4 (1266) he rejects this opinion of Algazel: "But this is impossible, because every multitude must be in some species of multitude. . . . Everything created is comprised under a certain intention of the one creating; hence it is necessary that all things created should be comprised under a certain number." Besides, "it is possible that there should be an infinite multitude *in potentia.*"

And yet a certain hesitation lingers in Thomas' *De aeternitate mundi* (1270): "Still it is not determined that God cannot bring it about that there should be infinite things *actu.*" The same thing occurs in III *Phys.*, lect. 86, and XI *Metaph.*, lect. 10, which are dated from this same period.

On the other hand, *Quodlib.* XII, q.2 (December 1270) is categorical: "When therefore it is asked whether it is possible for God to make something infinite in act, we must answer: No." The motive invoked is the following: "All things which (God) does must be formed; but the infinite is taken to be as matter without form, for the infinite is classed on the side of matter." *Quodl.* IX, which dates from before 1258 (since it was used that year by a disciple of St. Thomas, Hannibald de Hannibaldis, in the second book of his commentary on the Sentences) is also completely categorical in its question I. In this it is opposed to the other writings of St. Thomas of this period. This is one of the reasons which has weight with Glorieux to make him doubt the Thomistic authenticity of this *Quodlibet. Cf.* P. *Glorieux*, "Le plus beau Quodlibet de S. Thomas est-il de lui?" *Mélanges de Science religieuse*, t. III, Lille, 1946, p. 241.

[16] *Prolegomena to Any Future Metaphysic*, paragraph 52 and Appendix (transl. by Mahaffy and Bernard, London, 1889).

[17] *Critique of Pure Reason, Transcendental Dialectic*, Book II, Chapter II, Section 2 (Norman K. Smith's transl., pp. 393 ff.).

that of time, of space, of species or of personal activity), or if on the contrary such a multitude can be infinite only in certain cases or even whether it is possible in any case. It suffices for the time being to remark that to solve this problem we cannot limit ourselves to considering the point of view of unity, of number and of multitude in general, but that it is imperative to take into account the nature of every order considered. Furthermore, it is not at all certain that it is in man's power to answer this problem. Perhaps it would be more discreet to take the modest attitude of St. Thomas and to recognize that in this connection apodictic arguments in favor of either alternative are not at our disposal. As regards Kant's point of view, we cannot forget that he has failed to notice the absolute value and the transcendental character of the idea of being, and that therefore he did not see his way clear to justify the possibility for man to busy himself with metaphysics.

If we come back to the first sense of the word infinite, that is, complete in its order, the following problem inevitably arises in metaphysics: Does the unlimited ensemble of finite beings (real and possible) constitute the complete and unlimited order of being, the absolute infinite? This problem is the same as that of the one and the many.

As a matter of fact, if the unlimited ensemble of finite beings forms the absolute infinite, every finite being is a constitutive element of this infinite. In this case the fundamental principle of unity of all things is completely immanent in these things: it consists in their own cohesion and in their structure. Does this not, however, imply a contradiction? Every being is a subsistent whole which participates in the absolute value of being, it has part in it; but this is not the same thing as to be a part of being.[18] Must we not conclude from this that the fundamental principle of beings is transcendent to the order of these beings? An affirmative answer to this question would imply that the fundamental principle of unity is distinct from the complete order of finite beings, and that this order is not absolutely infinite, since it would not embrace all reality. On the other hand, however, the fundamental principle of unity would not limit this order in the sense attributed up to now to the word "limit," for it would not constitute a realm adjacent to it. In other words, such a principle could not limit the ensemble of finite beings in the way in which one finite being limits another finite being; otherwise, it would also be a limited

[18] Cf. *supra*, pp. 29–30.

being itself, and it would be in its place only in the interior of the order of beings. All this would in fine be tantamount to distinguishing two infinites: first of all, the ensemble of limited beings, whose infinity (while being perfectly unlimited, not bounded by an adjacent domain) is declared relative, since it is related to a real principle distinct from this ensemble; and in the second place, this last principle itself, in no limited or finite sense, whose infinity, without relation to anything, is consequently perfectly absolute.

How are we to solve the problem of the unity of the diverse, of the infinity of the finite? What explanation should we prefer, that of immanence or that of transcendence? This is the principal problem which metaphysics has to solve.

CHAPTER V

THE INTELLIGIBILITY OF BEING.
POSSIBILITY.

1. The Intelligibility of Transcendental Being; That Which Is, Has a Sufficient Reason. The Intelligibility of Particular Being Implies Both Intrinsic and Extrinsic Reasons

ON THE plane of being, unity and identity are absolute. The proposition which expresses this identity is enunciated thus: Being is being. In this judgment being itself performs the function of an attribute; it indicates what the intellect has grasped of the subject. This is tantamount to saying that being is formally intelligible. Since being is transcendental, nothing escapes its intelligibility; everything is adapted to the intellect; everything speaks to the mind; everything has a meaning.

Being is absolute, sufficient unto itself. It contains in itself what is necessary for being; it is explained by itself. It possesses therefore in itself what is required to enlighten and satisfy the mind in its quest for intelligibility. Now we call that a reason which speaks to the mind, that which can be comprehended. From this we must conclude that everything ought to find a sufficient reason in being: *Quidquid est, habet rationem sufficientem.* If once we admit that it is to being that the intellect is formally adapted, it seems that what is opposed to intellect is just as much opposed to being. A contradiction corresponds to the impossible, to the unrealizable. Now if the transcendental is intelligible, the absurd does not correspond to anything, it has no value of being at all. On this foundation the argument *per absurdum* rests. If we suppose that we do not have any direct comprehension of this or that reality, we have grounds for rejecting every explanation which would appear self-contradictory since it must be admitted once and for all that the absurd cannot express the real.

Being includes the relative, for there exists an order of beings. Every particular being, by its whole reality, is necessarily in relation with others since it cannot exist outside of the order of beings. Hence, its intelligibility, just as its being, its unity, its identity, is relative to the intelligibility of the others. It would therefore be a mistake to wish to find in a particular being, taken separately, the sufficient explanation of its being. The foundation of its explanation extends much farther; it must comprise the others. The intrinsic reason of a particular being cannot then suffice to explain it; it must be completed by an extrinsic reason.[1] What is the nature of this extrinsic reason? Is it productive causality? This question must be solved later on, but meanwhile it seems certain that the adequate reason of every particular being must imply both an intrinsic principle and another which is extrinsic. Still, it is no less certain that every particular being bears witness to its value of absolute, non-relative being. How are we to reconcile this absolute and relative intelligibility in one and the same reality? The metaphysical problem of the one and the many, of the absolute and the relative, crops up once again.

2. The Intelligibility and the Truth of Being; Being and the True Are Convertible

The intelligibility of being is called its truth. Truth is defined traditionally as the conformity of thing and intellect.[2] Hence, it consists

---

[1] Hegel insisted emphatically on this fundamental relativity of all things. Every finite being "looks to something outside of itself," is relative to the rest. "By all means must their due be allotted to finite things as such, in that we consider them as something not-ultimate, and as pointing to something over and above itself." Hegel, *Encyclopedia*, First Part, *Logic*, Sect. III, paragraph 205, edit. H. Glockner, t. VIII; *System der Philosophie*, Stuttgart, 1940, p. 417.

Far from being added to this being, this relation is constitutive of all of its reality. Things, therefore, are by no means absolute, closed realities; they are entirely relative one to the other, and they mutually call up one another. This is the reason that it is possible to pass from the one to the other by knowledge. Cf. Fr. Grégoire, "Hegel et l'universelle contradiction," *Revue néoscolastique de Philosophie*, t. 44, 1946, pp. 36–73.

Hegel, however, sees in things only "parts" of one, unique being; his system is an ontological monism. We oppose pluralism to it: there are subsistent beings, and yet these beings "participate," all of them, in one and the same absolute value. Hence, while being subsistent unities, they are radically relative, one to the other, and they can in no way withdraw themselves from the order of being. This means thorough-going relativity of "participants" and not of "parts." Cf. *supra*, pp. 29–30.

[2] This definition of truth, *adaequatio rei et intellectus*, is attributed by St. Thomas to Izaak Israeli, a Jewish doctor and philosopher, who lived in Egypt

in a relation, one of whose terms is the intellect. As the second term of this relation of conformity we often take one or other symbol (for example, a word or a gesture) designed to translate and communicate a thought. If there is an adequation, there is truth; if not, there is a lie. At other times, the second term of the relation is the reality to be known. If there is agreement between the intellect and this reality, there is truth; if not, there is error.

A relation can be considered in two ways, either starting with the first term or with the second. If we consider the conformity of the intellect and reality from the side of the intellect, that is, if we insist that the intellect is conformed to the real, we observe that the intellect is in possession of truth; it is true. This is logical truth, a property of our cognitive faculty. If we place ourselves on the side of the real so as to bring out its conformity with the intellect, it is reality which we recognize as true. This is ontological or metaphysical truth, a property of the real.

When we enter into communication with other men, we must adapt our expressions to our acts of knowledge; it is the content of these latter which is the rule and which imposes its law on the expression. When there is question of our acts of knowledge and their truth, our intellect must conform itself to the real and submit to its law. In two cases truth can be defective; on the one hand, if the expression is inadequate or deceptive; on the other, if the intellect is not adapted to its object, and by that very fact falls into error.

Generally, we speak of truth by placing ourselves at the point of view of the term which must submit to truth, that is, by conforming to the rule which is the other term for it. For we hold truth in high esteem, and psychologically speaking, it is natural that attention be brought to bear first of all on the terms where it could possibly fail, namely, on the expression of thought and thought itself. We must not, however, lose sight of the fact that the ontologically true is always necessarily present; for it is being itself, considered in its relation with the intellect, being inasmuch as it is intelligible. Hence, the ontologically true is the foundation of every other truth. It is absolute, transcendental, analogical just as being is. Being and the true are convertible.[3]

---

between 845 and 940, and was the author of a work, entitled *De definitionibus*. Various passages of Aristotle could have inspired this formula, notably, *Categories*, c. V, 4 b 8; *Metaphys.*, IV, c. 7, 1011 b 26; VI, c. 4, 1027 b 20; IX, c. 10, 1051 b 3, 6–9, 17, 24.

[3] In the analogy of truth, logical truth, psychologically speaking, is the prin-

3. The Unlimited Value of Our Intellect, Founded on the Unimpeachable Idea of Being. The Limited Value of Our Intellect, the Indefinite Tendency Towards an Understanding Always More Precise of the Modes of Being. The Irrational Strata of the Intelligible

Of its own nature our thought is oriented towards being. Its intelligible content bears the mark of the absolute and the transcendental. Hence, it is a mistake to believe that the truth of our knowledge is measured by the form of our human mind; its measure is neither subjective nor objective; it is absolute. Nevertheless, it is undeniable that we feel ourselves quite small in the world, limited in our existence as much as in our activity. But how are we to understand the fact that the content of a finite act of thought could have a transcendental extension, and that our intellect borders on the infinite? And yet nothing is more certain, and this is the very foundation of all certitude since it is by this that our intellect is defined. It is impossible to doubt the fundamental value of thought. As has been shown above doubt is never first; it can come into being only by resting on the truth of consciousness, and this is nothing other than consciousness laying hold of reality in which being asserts itself in an absolute manner. Even negation implies the affirmation of being; for, just as doubt, it rests on being.[4]

---

cipal analogue, and the ontologically true is the secondary analogue. On the contrary, from the metaphysical point of view the ontologically true is the first term and logical truth the second.

[4] St. Thomas makes the same remark on the subject of the true (but being and the true are convertible): "It is *per se notum*, that truth exists, because he who denies that there is truth, concedes that it is; for if some thing is true, truth must exist." *Summa theol.*, Ia, q.2, a.1, ad 3um. Cf. Aristotle, *Metaphysics* IV, 4, 1006, a26; St. Thomas *In IV Metaph.*, c.4, lect. 7, 9 (edit. Cathala, n.611, p. 206 b).

We would be mistaken if we saw merely a *petitio principii* in this reasoning. "Let us emphasize the general sense of this subtle sorites, which under the appearance of a reduction to absurdity is, at bottom, merely the verification of a transcendental necessity; the relation of truth is inherent in objective thought, for, if denied, it is reborn from the very negation. The moment you say 'There is no truth,' you affirm implicitly the agreement of your negating thought here and now with a certain objective lack of harmony, which you suppose to exist between thought in general and things. In other words, you affirm the existence of a relation of truth in the very act by which you pretend to deny this relation universally." (J. Maréchal, "Le point de départ de la métaphysique," Cahier

Difficulties force themselves on us when we compare thought to the sensible aspect of knowledge, and when we happen to lose sight of the insuperable chasm which separates them. On the side of our faculty of sensible knowledge we distinguish the different realms of the senses. No one of them includes all reality; each one of them (sight, hearing, taste, etc.) only contains a part. Must we not say the same of the sphere of the intellect? Why should we be justified in declaring it unlimited?

First of all a remark must be made which suffices to show that we cannot without further ado arrange the senses and the intellect on one and the same plane. The proper object of each sense is outside the object which is proper to the others; as such, a color is not a sound; we can see but not hear it. As such, a sound is not a light; we can hear but not see it. It is quite otherwise with the intellect. In point of fact, the intellect lays hold of colors, sounds and all the other objects of the senses; for of all of them it must be said that they *are* in some way or other, and that the intellect discovers there its formal object, namely, being. The sphere of the intellect is not alongside or outside of the sphere of sensible knowledge, as that of one sense is next to that of another sense; but the objects of the senses are, all of them, included in the extension of the object of the intellect. This last is not a sense; it transcends the senses and lays hold of their objects in the synthesis of being. And not merely does the range of the intellect extend beyond that of each sense in particular, but it is unlimited, since it extends just as far as absolute and transcendental being.

Thanks to this, man is in a position to know his own self, just as he can know the external world. He is endowed with reflection, and it is here that we put our finger on the vast distance that separates the senses and the intellect. By my eyes I do not see myself seeing; by my intellect I know myself knowing. Thought tends towards reflection; man recollects himself, he goes back over his actions, he follows their course, he takes account of the difficulties which he encounters, he notes the limits which he runs up against. He succeeds in formulating the "critical problem" on the subject of the validity of his cognitive faculty. Now, the sovereign worth of his intellect evidently

V, *Le Thomisme devant la philosophie critique*, Louvain, 1926, p. 42. "One who tries to destroy reason, sustains reason." (*In IV Metaph.*, lect. 7). In other words: "The sophist, who denies every objective signification (of the words he uses), restores an objective signification by his very negation." *Ibid.*, note.

derives from this simple fact that it is capable of raising this problem; for it could not do this if it were not already in possession of the solution.

To be able to inquire about the validity of knowledge and about its ultimate limits, we must have already gone beyond all limits. For conscious limits can only serve to set up relative limits. He who is imprisoned and knows it, has no longer the freedom of his bodily movements, but he has preserved the liberty of his mind. This imprisonment, therefore, is relative, relative to the body. To be aware of a limit we must know in some way the adjacent terrain, and so have gone beyond the limit.[5] He who apprehends limit as such, inasmuch as this constitutes an impediment, tells himself that there is a beyond, whose precise nature perhaps he does not know; but at least he knows that it is there. This beyond is no longer for him something absolutely unknown, since he is concerned with it; and the limit in question has only a relative value, since he had to have gone beyond it in order to take cognizance of its presence and its meaning. Consciousness of self implies undoubtedly a consciousness of limits, for the ego is limited; but this consciousness of limits can be effected only by supporting oneself on a consciousness of being thanks to which the ego and the non-ego are united in the unlimited synthesis of absolute and transcendental being. Thought, whose formal object is being, rests on an absolutely unshakable foundation, and on this point it attains to, right from the start and ever after, an unconditional certitude. The denial of this is unthinkable, and we can only formulate such a denial in terms devoid of all meaning.

We should not conclude from this that human knowledge is thus declared perfect in every point. It is finite and its content necessarily has limits; but these are relative, they have to do with the clear and precise understanding of reality. As has been said above, our intellectual activity is intimately bound up with experience, with the conscious apprehension of reality actually present. This reality is nothing other than that of our own person and that which surrounds it: we ourselves and a paltry part of the universe. This is what the Scholastics call the "proper and proportionate object" of this cognitive faculty. Here we enter into contact with existing things, and

---

[5] "The knowledge which we have of a limit shows that we have already cleared the limit; it shows our infinity." Hegel, *Philosophy of the Spirit*, transl. by A. Vera, Paris, 1867, t. I, p. 68.

Cf. *Encyclopedia*, III., edit. H. Glockner, t. X, Stuttgart, 1929, pp. 43–45.

we strive to distinguish one thing from the other, to recognize their modes of being. And yet this labor of recognition ends with only meagre results, for we succeed in defining these modes of being only by means of abstract notions, which do not contain the individual, as such, and which therefore can only provide us with a deficient knowledge of the data. Undoubtedly, we are not unaware of the fact that all reality is concrete and individual (otherwise, we could not even suspect that our concepts are abstract), but we never succeed in grasping the concrete modes of being by means of adequate concepts.[6] Generic and specific notions do not penetrate very deeply into reality; they are the fruit of an inductive generalization and they merely give us a superficial view. For example, the definitions of the species of plants and animals, while grounding themselves on the data of experience, merely take notice of the typical and regular groupings of certain phenomena. Certain groups of plants and animals possess such an external form and such an anatomical structure; they follow such a line of development, etc.

The ideal would be to get to the essence of things, the kernel of reality, the source from which the properties of things flow and from which the phenomena result. For if we could deduce from the essence of things the facts of experience, we would by this very fact have comprehended and explained them. But our knowledge follows exactly the opposite path; it starts with facts of experience, it uses the inductive method to establish their different groupings, and far from finishing with a direct knowledge of the profound nature which is at the source of the immediate data, it has to resign itself to affirming merely the necessary presence of such an essential principle of unity.

We are constrained to follow this inductive path, even in the study of our own person; at the same time, however, we penetrate profoundly into ourselves, for internal experience reveals to us the reality of the ego, the source and root of our vital development. This perception of the fundamental nature of our conscious life becomes more

---

[6] The following text shows that St. Thomas was under no illusion as to the weakness of our knowledge: "Our knowledge is so feeble that no philosopher has ever been able to investigate perfectly the nature of one fly: hence we read that one philosopher spent thirty years in solitude in order to know the nature of a bee." *In Symbolum apostolicum expositio* (edit. P. Mandonnet, *S. Thomae opuscula omnia*, t.4, op. 33, p. 350). St. Thomas delights in insisting on the difficulty of defining material things exactly. See the references indicated by M. D. Roland-Gosselin, O.P., *Le "De ente et essentia" de S. Thomas d'Aquin* (Bibliothèque thomiste, VII), Le Saulchoir, Kain (Belgium), 1926, p. 40, note 2.

accurate and more penetrating in the measure that consciousness becomes more detailed, and in the measure that we acquire a mastery over ourselves sufficiently complete to adopt a personal attitude and to act in fullest freedom. Substantial unity which sustains and inspires our acts, strongly asserts itself then; nevertheless, so many things remain in the penumbra or in complete obscurity, that our own nature is a big mystery for us, and we must adopt the humble inductive method to put at least a superficial order in the data of experience.

However, it is still true that the existence of the principle of central unity of our life can no longer give rise to doubt, once it is revealed to consciousness. According to this model of profound essence we form an idea of the realities of the external world; we consider the regular groupings of verified facts as the active expression of a non-perceptible nature, which ought to have some resemblance to the nature of the conscious ego.

These conditions of our experience provoke an internal tension, which betrays itself by a perpetual movement of research. In the content of knowledge there is manifested the opposition of being, a unique and absolute value, and its multiple and correlative modes. The opposition appears in the very interior of the idea of being; for, strictly speaking, this idea is not abstracted from the different modes of being, and it contains all of them. The idea of being is analogical and transcendental.

The idea of being gives us an indeterminate knowledge of the whole order of reality. We are conscious of the imperfection of this knowledge, and we have naturally a tendency to remedy it. The experience of our own nature and of what surrounds it, illumines the idea of being in making certain modes of being a little more precise, notably that of the ego and those modes of the divers things with which I find myself in relation. Nevertheless, it cannot escape us that the actual limits of our experience are extremely narrow, and hence, we endeavor to enlarge them. If this experience had the dimensions of being, all would be present to us; all would appear to us clearly; but this is not possible, since we are limited beings, incapable of being in immediate and adequate contact with infinite reality wholly and entirely. It will never be possible for us to suppress the tension which exists between our grasp of the transcendental and that of the finite, between being and its modes; and as we have consciousness of this, we can no more keep ourselves from applying a remedy here as much as possible, by pursuing our intellectual development indefinitely. We will never rest satisfied with the acquired result; every end attained furnishes the occasion for new researches. This insatiable desire of perfection, which is observed in our cognitive activity, betrays itself just as evidently in the other spheres of our conscious life, in those of the will and sensation. The philosophy of the romantic period, notably that of Fichte, Schelling and Hegel, emphasized very vigorously this thirst for the infinite, this perpetual tendency to have new experiences and to acquire new values.

Irrationalism, a theme of contemporaneous philosophy, can likewise be understood in the light of the tension of being and its modes. According to these moderns, discursive reason in its search for the nature of things, obtains only meagre results; practically everything escapes it. Only with difficulty does it succeed in defining in some fashion, hardly precise, the specific perfection of man. At bottom, being is irrational.

On the other hand we should be wrong in forgetting that being is nevertheless intelligible, that it is such completely, and we know that it is such. For, once again, by our intellect we formally get to being, since we use it as a predicate of the principle of identity. We declare with full right that the absurd is unrealizable, and we refuse to admit that a contradictory explanation can, inasmuch as it is contradictory, teach us anything about reality.

If we call the mind, inasmuch as it is intellect, the faculty of being, and if we attribute to it, in as far as it is discursive reason, the search for essences or modes of being, we will say that reality, as being, is intelligible, and that it is governed unconditionally by the principle of identity; but that, beyond this, the modes of being, the "taleity" of the real, the particular nature of things, generally escape us. They are accessible to us merely on the surface (with exception in some way for the apprehension of the ego), and we can in so far call them irrational.

The determination of the nature of things is achieved by availing oneself of experimental observation. On this point, we notice that between ancient philosophy and that of the moderns an opposition still obtains. The ancient philosophers freely turned their attention to the data of the external world, animals and plants, the heavens and the stars; they made them the object of their reflections. The moderns turn by preference to internal experience; they have a predilection for what is most intimate and the least communicable, namely, for our inclinations and sensations, very little of which the abstract concept succeeds in grasping. We cannot deny the importance of this irrational segment of human life, and it is fortunate that philosophical research is striving to explore it; but we have to be on our guard against all exclusiveness. The ego never grasps itself without perceiving at the same time the non-ego, just as it is impossible to know the non-ego without having consciousness of it, without experiencing the ego itself. Internal and external experience are united indissolubly. Without doubt, we can focus our attention on one side rather than on the other; and we will freely grant that internal experience possesses a richness, a warmth, and an intimacy at the same time, which cannot be found in external data; but we can never forget that the two fields of observation, altogether distinct as they are, remain inseparably united, and that together they form the object of only one human experience.

4. Two Extreme Theories: Exaggerated Idealism, and Agnosticism. The Absolute and the Relative in Human Cognition, Founded on Experience

In our appreciation of the validity of human knowledge we must be on our guard against extreme solutions; idealism, properly so called, is one of these. It would wish to immure itself in the mind as in an ivory tower, there to construct by its own powers the system that is to explain the real. This is an unrealizable goal, at least if we do not admit that in apprehending the ego in consciousness, the mind recognizes itself as real, as being. Furthermore, this apprehension on the part of consciousness can be effected only in the act by which we lay hold of ourselves just as we are, that is, in the world; consciousness awakens only on contact with the world, under the shock of what is external. The value of being which we discover in ourselves by our mind, we see realized and extended outside of ourselves, in the non-ego. Idealism will never discover being, if it has begun by eliminating it and thereby isolating itself in a function of the mind; and it will not be able to discover the true value of being, if it admits that we can lay hold of it in the reality of the ego, while altogether excluding the perception of the reality of the non-ego. It will be impossible for it to deduce from the human mind (the only being which man can get at directly) the law of existence and of the nature of all reality. For the mind of man is finite; it is not the absolute, and so the very basis of the idealistic construction becomes hypothetical, that is to say, the whole edifice collapses.[7]

The exaggerations of certain idealistic philosophers, starting with the German romantic epoch at the beginning of the nineteenth century, have unleashed various reactions against all speculative philosophy. Puffed up by the success of the natural sciences, some have believed that philosophy should itself be held to the strictly empirical method, and consequently should banish every metaphysical explanation. This philosophical empiricism is equivalent, in fine, to condemning all philosophy.

A fact which is not without interest is this, that never in any period have philosophers of ability resigned themselves to being shut up among empirical data. Acting in this way they conform themselves to the law of being, which is the law of the mind. Assuredly we are not the creators of the contents of our knowledge, and we cannot deduce them from a principle, conceived by our mind; neither do we hold ourselves merely receptive in regard to facts. For we actively elaborate these facts in the light and under the direction of being, whose value and properties are revealed to us, as soon as a reality appears to us in our complete experience, external as well as internal.

In this experience being is affirmed everywhere as absolute, and the idea which we form for ourselves of it is necessarily transcendental. Its unconditional value goes beyond the limits of all human experience, and transcends all the results which we can get at by the empirical method. There is no question here of denying the limits of our knowledge, but we must give an exact account of their nature and their role. As we have shown above, they are relative, since we have consciousness of them, and consequently they are not the ultimate limit with which we collide definitively. They demand a further foundation, the absolute, which transcends these limits. The categorical affirmation of being is first; this forms the foundation of all knowledge and all certitude.

We must, therefore, reject every system which would place on our knowledge limits that are altogether insuperable by taking from it any sphere whatsoever, and by subjecting it by the same token to conditions which would always remain unknown to it, since they would be absolutely outside of that to which our knowledge can at-

---

[7] Cf. Alb. Dondeyne, "Idealisme of realisme," in *Tydschrift voor Philosophie,* III, 1941, pp. 607–648. *Aimé Forest, Du consentement à l'être,* Paris, 1936, pp. 38–41.

tain. Skepticism, sensualism, empiricism, positivism are merely different forms of relativism; but philosophical relativism is unthinkable. If everything is relative, nothing holds good, and it becomes impossible to formulate either an affirmation or a negation, or even to put forth a doubt.

Relativism denies the absolute, which is the foundation of all knowledge. Idealism affirms the absolute, but it loses sight of the fact that the human mind is not purely and simply identified with this absolute which it apprehends, and that the finite mind of man is bound to conditions which it would be vain for him to wish to ignore. Man is not a pure spirit nor is he merely a material organism; he is a conscious, subsistent being in the world. His knowledge rests on the only conscious contact which he could have with reality, on the sensitivo-intellectual experience which he has of his own reality in the place where it is inserted in the material world. The apprehension of the absolute value of being in this experience, which is at the same time internal and external, and whose soul is the consciousness of the ego: this is the ineluctable principle of the life of the mind.[8]

5. The Metaphysical Problem of the True

The metaphysically true poses a problem which is at bottom merely that of being. Being is true, intelligible; it is such in its whole tran-

---

[8] According to St. Thomas, God knows all things in the same act by which He creates them, which, moreover, is identified with the divine Being, absolutely simple and infinitely perfect. (Cf. *Summa theol.*, Ia, q.14). The angels know things by means of infused universal ideas, which are participations in the creative Idea of God. By this they get down to the individual determination of reality. (*Ibid.*, Ia, q.55, a.3). Man, on the contrary, forms for himself universal ideas, starting with a human experience: transcendental ideas (as those of being, the one, the true, the good) on the one hand, and on the other, abstract ideas, representative of the different modes of being of things. Without doubt, the universal character of these last ideas permits us to extend the domain of knowledge beyond the data of actual experience, but it is only at the expense of understanding the individuality of things that this extension can be effected. For it is not possible formally to get to the individual, which is concrete, by an abstract idea. (Cf. *ibid.*, Ia, qq.84–85). Nevertheless, all abstract notions are founded on the transcendental (universal, but concrete) idea of being.

The conception which St. Thomas forms of the divine and angelic knowledge implies a remarkable critique of human knowledge; for it is only in the light of the critical study of the imperfect manner of knowing, peculiar to man, that the Angelic Doctor succeeds in conceiving more perfect forms of knowledge. His theory of angelic knowledge is pretty close to certain forms of contemporaneous idealism, and by that same token it constitutes a refutation of exaggerated idealism.

scendental extension and it is such for the human intellect, whose formal object it constitutes. This relation with our intellect, therefore, enters into the very constitution of being, of all being. Every relation depends on its terms, and so the intelligibility of being is bound up with the human intellect. To be able to affirm that being, whose value is absolute, is of itself intelligible for us, the possibility of our intellect must not in any case be called into question. Hence, the order of being requires this possibility as an absolutely essential element. This fundamental and absolute character of the human intellect idealism has helped to bring out into clear light. However, it would be a mistake to wish to discover the absolute source of all ontological truth in the human intellect; for this latter is marked with the evident indication of its finitude and dependence, that is, with relativity. It is the intellect of an ego which is in relation with the non-ego, against which it collides as against an irreducible fact; the non-ego is the other, and it will never be able to be reduced to the ego perfectly. Hence, every human intellect will seize upon reality in its own individual manner; its activity will invariably bear the "color" of the particular finite ego, which is distinct from the other subjects of knowledge just as much as the objective data.

The problem arises, then, of reconciling the absolute and the relative in the order of knowledge. By the intellect, the faculty of absolute being, I hold fast to a transcendental point of view, over and above every particular angle, subjective or objective; and on this plane all the subjects of knowledge meet and are comprised, since the point of view is identically the same for all. On the other hand, by this same intellect, an activity of the ego, I know things in a limited and particular manner, since I am myself a particular, finite person, and my way of knowing is not reducible to that of the other subjects, just as the ego is not communicable to any other person. Truth, then, is analogical; it is absolute, since it is a property of being, that is, its intelligibility; and at the same time it is affected with relativity, for intelligibility being a relation it must vary with the terms of this relation, on the one hand with the different subjects of knowledge, and on the other with the different realities to be known. How are we to conceive the synthesis of the metaphysically true? How reconcile the particular modes of the true with its absolute value? Thus, the problem of the one and the many, of the absolute and the relative, comes up in regard to the metaphysically true, just as in regard to being.

6. *The Possible*

The observations made on being and the true allow us to formulate
the metaphysical problem from the point of view of possibility. The
possible in the strict sense of the word is that which does not actually
exist but which can exist. In this sense, that which can be differs from
that which is. That which is is opposed to that which is not. In the
strictest sense of the phrase "that which is" indicates "that which is
realized at this moment"; and opposed to it are: "that which was,"
"that which will be," and besides, "that which is not," "that which
was not," "that which will not be," "that which cannot be."

In a less strict sense, the phrase "that which is" can be used to
designate all existing reality, abstracting from the moment of its
realization. Understood thus, it signifies that which belongs to the
past and the future just as well as that which exists here and now;
these are all real facts, they exist. Taken in this sense, "that which is"
is opposed to that which is not realized in any way, to that which was
not, is not and will never be.

When the term possible is used to express "that which is not realized actually, but could be," it is opposed on the one hand to that
which is realized at any moment whatsoever (that which occurs in
the past or in the present or in the future), and on the other hand, it
is opposed to that which could not be in any way, that is, the impossible.

The real is of real being, and the possible is of possible being; the
one and the other belong to the order of being, both bear witness
to the same absolute value of being. "That which can be" is absolutely
possible; "that which is realized" is absolutely real.[9] If the clause "that
which is" serves to express being inasmuch as it implies an absolute
value, the possible belongs to the order of being just as much as that
which is realized. The possible belongs to possible being; it shares in
the value of being; the possible *is*. At times also we give this last
meaning to the expression "that is possible"; and this is especially the
case in the aphorism *ab esse ad posse valet illatio;* that thing is, therefore it is possible. In fact, in this clause "that thing is" is taken in the
second sense indicated above, namely, that which must be admitted
as a real fact, either of the past or of the present, or of the future. In
the same phrase "that is possible" it is not used to mean "really that
is not, but it could be," since we apply this precisely to a real fact;
but it is used to express that that is not impossible, in other words,

---

[9] For the meaning of the term "absolute," cf. *supra,* pp. 24–25.

that that thing shares in the value of being; or simply that that thing
is.

Used in the strict sense "that thing is" and "that is possible" are opposed as different states of being: the first of reality actually existing,
and the second of the possibility. This is a relative sense. On the contrary, taken in transcendental sense, "that is" and "that is possible"
are no longer opposed; they take on the same meaning: they designate, both of them, the absolute value of being.

The word "impossible" is used only in connection with this last
meaning. It means: that which cannot exist under any condition, that
which is not merely unreal, but unrealizable; that, namely, which is
opposed to the value of being and is therefore absolutely impossible.[10]

7. The Problem of the Foundation of Intrinsic Possibility

Possibility implies intelligibility, for being and the true are convertible. That therefore is possible which is not contradictory. We
call intrinsic possibility the compatibility of the different elements
united in thought; for example, animal and rational do not exclude
each other, they can be thought of together: rational animal is possible.

The absolute value of intrinsic possibility was brought to light even
in ancient times.[11] St. Augustine found here a foundation for proving

---

[10] Possible, therefore, is used in a wide and a narrow sense. Impossible is
never used as a negation of the possible in the restricted sense of the word; otherwise, that which is realized (and therefore is no longer simply possible) would
have to be called impossible! Impossible is used only as the negation of the
possible in the transcendental sense; it expresses that which is impossible in an
absolute way.

[11] The words "to be able," "possible" are often used to indicate a relative
intelligibility, which is bound up with a certain hesitation of the one speaking.
For example, we ask some one whether it will rain tomorrow; he examines the
heavens, and answers: "It could well be." We tell him that a friend has made
such or such a decision; he reflects a moment and observes that at bottom that
is not "impossible." There is question always in these cases of some one who
does not possess the elements necessary to form for himself a conviction, which
is solidly grounded. He is content, therefore, to examine the data at his disposal,
and he ends with a conclusion of relative value: In as far as I have been able
to examine the question, and under the reservation of unknown factors which
could weaken my conclusion, I think that this will happen or will be able to
happen. In other words, (in my system) "this seems intelligible to me."
There is question, therefore, of a relative, limited intelligibility. To affirm in
cases of this kind that intelligibility is absolute, that possibility is unconditional—
(hence, if there is question of events, governed by the determinism of the
physical laws, in order to say that this fact will certainly come about)—the in-
formation would have to be complete.

the existence of God, and many have followed him on this point. The analysis of the absolute properties of this possibility was made always under the influence of Plato's philosophy. Plato had realized that general ideas, such as man, good, virtue, etc., possess an eternal, immutable and necessary content. In the sequel those who raised the problem of possibility held their eyes fixed on these general ideas, called essences or possibles. A good number of philosophers have remained skeptical with regard to the Augustinian argument, because the general ideas which are put in relief there are abstract concepts, and it seems rash to conclude from the properties of abstract ideas to the existence of a real being. In point of fact, some might think that the properties of these ideas ought to find their explanation in the human intellect, since these ideas are the fruit of man's faculty of abstraction.

Cardinal Mercier adopted this last way.[12] According to him, the abstract is explained by the activity of our mind and by the concrete reality on which this activity is exercised. Hence, the abstract is founded on the concrete; its properties are hypothetical, since they depend on man's intelligence and on things. And yet this solution is not adequate, for it rests on a misunderstanding. Even the Scholastics of the Middle Ages had remarked that in the study of knowledge, we must avoid confusing the psychological and the metaphysical aspects of the problem.[13] I could not have any content of knowledge if I never succeeded in knowing, if there were no real objects to know, or if my activity were never exercised on them; but from this we may not conclude that the value of the content of knowledge depends entirely on my activity. For example, two plus two equals four; the reason for this truth is not found in myself; on the contrary, I have to take it as a rule of thought, I have to conform myself to it, and I know it. I get to truth only if I recognize its absolute value; I understand precisely that truth is not relative, that it possesses an absolute and eternal value. It is the foundation of this value which formed the object of St. Augustine's reflections. The Scholastics, besides, maintained that the absolute value of ideas or essences did not depend on the fact of the existence of things. Even

---

[12] Cf. *Métaphysique générale ou Ontologie* (Cours de Philosophie, vol. II), 5e édit., Louvain, 1910, p. 31 ff.

[13] St. Thomas Aquinas, *Quodlibetum* VIII, a. 1. The threefold division, which is there indicated, *scil., natura in re, in intellectu, et absolute considerata,* is taken from Avicenna. In regard to Avicenna's ideas, cf. A. M. Goichon, *La distinction de l'essence et de l'existence d'après Ibn-Sina (Avicenne),* Paris, 1937, pp. 71 ff.

if Socrates and Plato, human persons, would not have existed, man would none the less remain possible and thinkable.

It is striking to discover that in the exposition of the theory of the possible, appeal is always made to abstract examples. This is a regrettable effect of the influence of Plato. Nevertheless, it is evident that the abstract must find its explanation in the concrete, and this, from the point of view of metaphysics no less than from that of psychology. The ontological value of the abstract content of knowledge must have its roots in the value of the concrete. The absolute, the eternal and the immutable of the abstract and universal object are derived characteristics, whose source must reside in the individual reality. To revert to the example cited above: if no individual human being were possible, the essence "man" would not be possible either. It is not the abstract, as such, which can exist, but the concrete individual; it is not the abstract essence "man" which is possible, it is this or that man, Socrates or Plato.

This indicates the path which our discussion must take. Do we have a knowledge whose content is at once concrete and universal, and to which we could reduce the abstract universal? Undoubtedly, since we form the idea of being, which is transcendental; [14] by it we get to concrete reality in its totality, and in it we discover the fundamental value to which every other value must be reduced, under penalty of otherwise being nothing. At the very beginning is being, an absolute value: "*Esse* (existence) is the perfection of perfections." [15] The problem of the foundation of the possibles, as tradition raises it, must then be reduced to that of the foundation of the order of beings.

8. The Problem of the Relation of Extrinsic and Intrinsic Possibility

Intrinsic possibility is distinct from extrinsic possibility. That is intrinsically possible which is intelligible; that is extrinsically pos-

---

[14] *Scientia est de universali:* there is science only of the universal, not of the individual. This is an axiom since the time of Plato. Aristotle admits this principle. As a matter of fact, science seeks the law, necessity, *scientia est de necessario;* and in the individual we see only a contingent fact. And undoubtedly, there is no science of the individual, in as far as it seeks to define the modes of being, natures and the law of their activity; but besides, science must be occupied with being, as such. Now this study is developed on the fundamental plane of absolute being, whose idea is at once concrete and universal, since it is transcendental.

[15] St. Thomas Aquinas, *De potentia*, q.7, a.2, ad 9.

sible which can be, inasmuch as the cause (an extrinsic principle) on which its existence depends is in position to act. The
foundation of extrinsic possibility is therefore the existence of this
cause.

What is the relation between these two possibilities? That which
is contradictory cannot in any case be realized, no cause can produce it; extrinsic possibility must be regulated by intrinsic possibility. But must we likewise think that no intrinsic possibility is
conceivable, if there is no cause to realize this possible? The answer is "yes"; it is contradictory to declare possible, that is, able to
be, that which can not be, because there is absolutely no cause to
realize it.

This last question, at bottom, comes to this: Is the internal reason, the real identity of a being (corresponding to the compatibility
of the notes of its idea), closed or absolute, to the point of not being
able to lead us to recognize an external reason, an extrinsic cause?
On the plane of causality we can put the question as follows: What
relation is there between the principle of identity and the principle
of causality? Does the denial of the second carry in its train the
denial of the first?

We have shown above that the principle of sufficient reason applied to a particular being, always looks to an intrinsic and an extrinsic reason at one and the same time; the two are indissolubly
united, because finite being is necessarily contained in an order of
beings, and consequently all its reality bears the mark of relativity.
The identity of a finite being is "open"; it implies a reference to the
exterior, it must be bound to that of the other terms of the same
order. What is the nature of this bond? Is it a causal nexus? This is
a problem to be studied later on.

We will have to ask, moreover, if this reference to other members
of the order constitutes the whole relativity of the finite. Perhaps the
whole order, considered in all of its terms, is based on a reference to
a source of transcendent being. In this case the intrinsic reason of
identity would be relative in a twofold sense to another thing: it
would have to be related to the finite terms, and with them to the
Infinite. But once again, this question is bound up with the fundamental problem of being. In whatever way we consider the question of possibility, either intrinsic or extrinsic, we end up with the
metaphysical problem of being.

9. The Problem of Purely Possible or Contingent Beings

This same problem can be illustrated also by the examination of possibility, understood in the restricted sense of the word; we mean by this possibility a state of being, which is opposed to the state of actualized reality. In the light of the data of experience, we distinguish that which is, which was, which will be; in these three cases there is question always of existing reality. We oppose to it the purely possible which is not, was not and will never be, which therefore does not belong to reality actually existing; but of which, none the less, we declare that it is possible, that it could exist or could have existed. This purely possible, whose realization is in fact forever excluded, is held to be non-contradictory, thinkable; it is, we say, an essence or an idea, purely possible. But the question arises whether such a possible is truly intelligible.

Nicolai Hartmann considers that as really possible or as possibly real all of whose conditions of realization are presently given. If one of these conditions happens to be wanting, there would no longer be real possibility; if any one is not lacking, the possible is realized infallibly. Possibility and necessity lie concealed in reality; [16] nothing here is possible which is not necessarily realized, nothing is realized necessarily without being possible. The real is the synthesis of the possible and of the necessary.[17] Every distinction between the real and the possible is suppressed by very definition. That which can be, must be realized; we cannot think of anything, which is really possible, as outside the existing real (in the past, the present or the future). But are these ideas of Hartmann accurate?

The problem of the purely possible which arises here, is none other than that of contingence. Contingent facts occur in our personal life: we feel ourselves free, at least in a certain measure. That means that if we perform this definite action, we could have pre-

---

[16] He opposes to it *Seinsollen*, i.e. the ought-to-be of value, which is the measure of everything which is realized, but which cannot be realized itself; this ought-to-be, therefore, is "really impossible." It is a being, *Sein*, but of the irrational order.

[17] "And precisely this at-the-same-time-possible-and-necessary-being is its actuality." Nicolai Hartmann, *Ethik*, 2nd edit., Berlin, 1935, p. 197. Hartmann takes up again the thesis of the Megarians of ancient Greece, as he himself admits. Cf. *Möglichkeit und Wirklichkeit,* Berlin, 1938, pp. 12 ff., pp. 174 ff.

ferred another to it. We were not forced to place such an action; another, which will never be realized, was possible and it was such, just as much as the action which de facto was realized. The action which has been placed, could have not been chosen: it would then have remained purely possible; the action which did not have the preference, could have had it: it would then have ceased to be purely possible. Such actions are therefore contingent; they are events which occur, but which could just as well not happen. The contingent does not carry within itself the reason of its existence or that of its non-realization; it rests on a free power, which is not shackled by determinism. If this power were not free it would be determined to act in this way and not in that other; and the act which it produces would itself be a necessary fact and not a contingent event. Contingence presupposes the choice between pure possibility and realization; it implies liberty. If there is no liberty, there is no contingence, and neither is there any pure possibility.

Our freedom concerns only our acts, and not our existence. We do not bear the responsibility for our existence; we have to answer only for our actions. Our free decisions are themselves attached to the natural and necessary tendency of our being; but would not these beings also be the product of some fundamental freedom? Would not that which is finite and relative proceed from a source of being, which is infinite and absolutely independent? All would be the result of a creative act. Ultimately, the question is whether beings can be conceived as purely possible, or whether we must admit that they exist necessarily.

From these considerations it emerges that the problem of possibility cannot be solved on the threshold of metaphysics. In order to know whether beings purely possible are conceivable, we must have proven their contingency, and so have shown that they depend on a free, creative cause. Hence, there is question of the fundamental problem of being, and its solution is found not at the beginning but at the end of metaphysics.[18]

---

[18] When some writers treat of the possibles, they often make the problem too easy, since they fail to define the terms of the problem. "Before existing," they say, "I was not, I was possible then; I do not exist, therefore, necessarily: I am contingent." Exactly what do they wish to say? The year 1944 did not yet exist in 1940; could they conclude from that, that it was then possible, and that it could have occurred at that period, i.e. immediately after 1939? Or again, could they conclude from this that the course of time does not follow a natural and necessary order, and that the order of the years could be turned around? For example, the year 1950 would be placed before 1944, and this latter would

take the place of the year 2000! Or rather, do they wish to say (and this is an altogether different question which belongs to metaphysics) that the temporal order, whose course is subject to necessity, is contingent in its entirety, and that it could just as well not have been realized? We grasp the significance of this problem, and we will admit without much hesitation that its solution demands a profound study of reality.

PART II

THE INTERNAL STRUCTURE
OF
PARTICULAR BEING

CHAPTER VI

THE STATIC ORDER ON THE PLANE
OF BEING

PARTICULAR beings participate, all of them, in the same value of absolute being; they constitute a unique order which contains them all. How can this order be explained? On what principle is it founded? And first of all, what is required in every particular being that it be comprised in the universal order? How must it be constituted in itself in order to participate in the value of being?

Beings exist and they are active. Is it necessary for them to act in order to be able to exist? This is a question to be examined later. It is always true that their being is a condition of their activity, for being is transcendental. Let us then first of all consider particular being from the static point of view, without for the present raising, *ex professo,* questions which concern action. This procedure does not imply in any way that a being could ever fail to have some activity, but merely that we cannot treat all problems at one and the same time.

I. STRUCTURE ALONG THE LINE OF THE
VALUE OF BEING

THE REAL PRINCIPLE OF BEING AND THAT OF THE MODE
OF BEING

1. The Proof of the Non-Simplicity of Particular Being
Along the Line of the Value of Being

The study of participation and of the analogy of being showed us that the adequate knowledge of a particular being carries with it always a double affirmation: "It is," and "It is this." The first of these propositions states that particular being manifests a value of

being which is absolute: it is. In this respect there is nothing to oppose it; for nothing is found outside the field of the value of being;
in a word, the attribute of the proposition enunciated possesses a
transcendental extension. Hence, this attribute could not serve to
distinguish different beings since it belongs equally to all; in the
transcendental idea of being the opposition of the terms disappears.

The second proposition states that particular being carries with
it a mode of being which is relative: it is *this*. In this respect another
being is opposed to it inevitably: this is distinct from that. In a
word, *this* is not a transcendental attribute; it has a limited extension;
this does not signify the absolute but the relative. By this attribute
we emphasize that which distinguishes this being here from every
other reality.[1]

The two affirmations formally enunciate being, wholly and entirely concrete. For example, the particular being of which I have
consciousness: I am wholly and entirely; nothing is in me which
could be withdrawn from the domain of being. Also, I am wholly
and entirely this being here, and no other thing is found here save
myself. Nothing is more concrete than being, and nothing is more
concrete than that I myself am being; and though the two affirmations
are, both of them, predicated of every particular being, they do not
predicate the same thing; the two attributes, being and the ego, are
not synonyms, they do not have the same signification. Consequently,
the adequate knowledge of a particular being reveals that this being
is not simple, that it conceals a real composition.

The foregoing argumentation only serves to resume the considerations on which is founded the doctrine of the participation and
the analogy of being. That which participates in being "is" truly,
but in its own particular mode; [2] the idea of being applies in the
proper sense to every particular being, but under a certain relation.[3]
We are satisfied in this present question to emphasize that all these
considerations formally envisage only concrete reality, and that in
consequence the distinctions made are not the products of our
mind, articulations of the logical order, but distinctions which con-

---

[1] "It cannot be that that being is divided from being, in as much as it is being.
Nothing is divided from being except non-being. Similarly, another being is
not divided from this being, but by this that in this being there is included a
negation of that being." St. Thomas Aquinas, *In Boethii De Trinitate*, q.4, a.1.
[2] Cf. *supra*, pp. 29–30.
[3] Cf. *supra*, pp. 44–46.

cern every particular being in itself, independently of the knowledge which we have of it.

It is not altogether useless to insist on the legitimacy of this conclusion. If there were question of intellectual operations, fundamentally abstractive, such a conclusion would not be well founded.
For example, there is a distinction between genus and specific difference, between animal and rational. These two concepts furnish us
with imperfect notions of the essence or the particular mode of being to which they are applied. They complete each other mutually,
and they fuse together to constitute the concept of species; they are
therefore not irreducible. In passing from the one to the other, our
knowledge of the mode of being in question is developed (in this
sense we say that these concepts are on one and the same line of
intellectual development), and it gets to a progressively more perfect understanding of this mode of being. But this understanding
will never be complete because it is abstractive, while the real is
concrete; we could keep on adding the abstract to the abstract and
never get to the concrete. The distinction between two abstract notions is therefore logical. It marks a step in the movement of discursive reason; but the course of the logical development of our
knowledge is not a faithful replica of a corresponding evolution of
reality. The articulations of the one are not the simple reproduction
of one and the same number of ramifications of the other; for by
definition the process of abstraction sets up a cleavage between the
intellect and the reality to be known.

On the contrary, in the two affirmations of which there was question above—this being is; it is this thing here—we constantly keep
in contact with reality, and we express it as it is, as a concrete reality. It is therefore impossible to reduce the one to the other, or
both of them to a third, since each one of them ends formally at
the concrete, and once arrived there, it is at the end of its course and
cannot go farther. Once the real is attained, we cannot get any
nearer to it. Hence, there is question of two affirmations, equally
apodictic and irreducible, because they are concrete. They remain
two distinct affirmations, being applied all the while strictly to the
same real thing. That which the first signifies concretely is not that
which the second signifies concretely; hence, the concrete reality of
particular being itself is not simple but composite, and in this our
intellect discovers the duality which it expresses. If we do not wish
to maintain that being is not the formal object of the intellect and

that there is an hiatus between being and knowing, we must admit that if particular being is known to us as being concretely not-simple, it really contains a composition.

To prove this thesis two other arguments are often presented, and it is well to subject them to examination before making more precise the meaning of the conclusion we have just reached. First of all, we reason like this: Being is of itself unlimited; now there exist limited beings; therefore, there must be in these beings not merely a real principle of being, but also a real principle of limitation, not reducible to the principle of being.

What is meant by the non-limitation of being of which there is question in the major? It can only be that which is expressed by the transcendental idea of being; the value of being is absolute, undeniable, without possible opposition. It holds good without conditions and without limits; that is why it is present everywhere. But it is possible for us to encounter this value only in particular beings, in the ego and the non-ego, which possess it by participation; and it penetrates all of them completely, to the point that it cannot be abstracted from them by the intellect. Also, the transcendental idea of being is analogous and contains implicitly all the particular modes according to which the value of being can be realized. In other words, it is not possible for us to have a knowledge of the value of being without knowing that it is found in limited beings. Really, we cannot ever form for ourselves an idea of being which is not analogous, since the perfection of being, far from being abstractable from its different modes, on the contrary always implies these modes.

Consequently, the major of the argument we are now examining, does not enunciate an abstract principle but a truth, which is transcendentally concrete; and it already contains the knowledge of that which the minor enunciates, that is, the actual existence of limited beings. Therefore, there is no reason to distinguish this major and minor; it is only necessary to consider the fact of participation, which provokes the formation of the analogous idea of being, since it makes us know at once and indissolubly the value of being, which is absolute, transcendental, unlimited, and the multiple particular modes, opposed one to the other, and therefore finite. In this way, however, we come back to the considerations which are found at the basis of the argumentation which we ourselves presented above.

The following argument is often met with: À propos of every being two questions are raised: "Is it?" and "What is it?" These ques-

tions are as irreducible as their answers. To one who asks what is
man we do not answer by saying that men actually exist; and to one
who asks if men exist it is not at all opportune to answer that man
is a rational animal. This adequate opposition ought to make us
conclude to a real distinction. To examine the significance of this
reasoning, we must carefully fix the meaning of the two questions
just raised; otherwise confusions can easily result.

We examined above [4] the different significations which the affirmation "it is" can have. At times we express by this a relativity, either
the state of actual existence at this moment of time (opposed to the
past and the future), or the state of actual existence at any moment
whatsoever (opposed to the state of possibility). At times also, "it
is" expresses being, considered in its absolute value which transcends the opposition of particular beings and that of the states in
which these beings can be found. To one of these first two meanings
we refer when we place the question: "*Is* that thing?" "Does that
thing *exist?*" But there is a third meaning, which furnishes the formal
object of metaphysics, which we must choose in this present study.
"Is it?" then means: Has it a value of being? Does it participate in
being? Or again, since being and the true are convertible, is it intelligible? Is it not contradictory and therefore impossible?

To the second question, "*What* is it?" we are tempted to answer
with an abstract definition, that of species; for example, it is a man.
And yet the problem here raised demands that reference be made
to the mode of concrete and individual being, such as, this man here.
Now it is possible for us to encounter the value of being only in particular beings. For us, the question "is it?" comes practically to the
following: "Does it participate in being?" But this implies a mode of
being to be defined in answer to the question: "What is it?" In other
words, on the metaphysical plane, that of the transcendental, the
two questions: "Is it?" and "What is it?" are presented at once and
as indissolubly united, since they have relation to an order of participation. By this means we are brought once again to the considerations which governed the argument developed in the first
place.

The conclusion of this argument is that particular being cannot be
simple, since it gives rise to the simultaneous affirmation of two
judgments: "It is" and "It is this," which are irreducible, although
each one of them has to do with the concrete and complete unity of

---

[4] Cf. *supra*, pp. 25–26; 88–89.

the being considered. It is only when taken together that these judgments express reality adequately; they are correlatives and lean upon each other as the groin of an arch; together they express the fundamental relation, the interior tension which constitutes particular being. Each of the correlative terms of a relation is distinct from the term which corresponds to it, but in being referred to it marks it with its seal, so that the second shares in that which is peculiar to the first. As the two fundamental affirmations which express particular being are correlatives, they must communicate to each other mutually what is peculiar to each one; in each one will be found a character which it possesses only by reason of the bond which unites it to the other. The first affirmation—this being *is*— expresses the absolute value; on its part the second affirmation—this being is *this*—which has reference to the mode of individual and relative being, communicates its relativity to the first. It is therefore the particular being wholly and entirely which reveals the absolute value, and it is the same being wholly and entirely which manifests relativity. It is absolutely true that it is, and it is also true that it is relative; on the other hand it is by reason of its mode of being that it is relative, and it is such in all its reality, in its being as well as in its mode. For it is precisely in being that it participates, and hence its value of being itself is affected by relativity since it possesses this value as its own only in the measure of its own particular, finite and relative mode.

2. *Internal Composition, Conceived as a Correlation, a Structure of Transcendental Relations*

The terms of the fundamental relation which the intellect discovers in particular being are not subsistent beings: one being is not composed of many beings. Neither are they, strictly speaking, quantitative parts of this being; no one would maintain that one half of a being "is" (without being *this*), while the other half is "this" (without *being*). And yet there are two terms, which in reality are not identified; and hence, we desire to know how they ought to be conceived.

At first glance it appears that they are correlative, and to this we must hold fast. It is in their correlation that the whole reality of the particular being which contains them, exists; and since they are identified with this being, it is in their correlation that all their reality consists. It is impossible to conceive them outside of the mutual relation which binds them together. Undoubtedly, we must distinguish them, but without ever separating them, isolating them, even logically.

Hence, it is an error to believe that each of these principles can be considered as being real in itself, abstracting from its relation with a corresponding principle. For it would then be necessary to maintain that this relation comes to be added to the reality of these principles; and yet they have no reality outside of their correlation. Each principle is a constitutive principle and it is only that; its function is to be referred to a corresponding principle to form with it particular being; it has no other function. It is identified entirely with the relation which binds it to its co-principle, and it does not contain anything which is not referred to this other principle. Consequently, a constitutive principle of particular being cannot be defined without making mention of its co-principle; a relation cannot be defined without its term being indicated. It is impossible to separate logically a principle from its co-principle, to think of one without thinking of the other, even though it is always necessary to distinguish them, just as it is impossible for us to think of a relation without thinking of its term, even though we distinguish the relation from the term.

That which exists is the structure which forms the correlation of the principles, the particular being. A principle taken apart from the other principles, is nonsense and, as such, does not exist. It is conceived and it is real only in the structure which contains it; it is not "id quod est," that is, that which is in itself, but "id quo est" (tale ens quod est), that is, the real, intrinsic principle by reason of which such a being, which is a subsistent subject, presents such or such character. Let us call these correlative principles which form the internal structure of particular being transcendental relations, to distinguish them from predicamental relations, which bind subsistent beings together.[5]

---

[5] By transcendental relation we understand a reality which is related to another by everything which constitutes it in itself. Such a reality is, therefore, completely penetrated with relativity. It is in this manner that we conceive the constituent principles which form the structure of particular being, such as essence and existence, matter and form, substance and accidents, faculties and their actions. The relation of every particular being to the other finite beings, its belonging to the order of beings, must likewise be conceived in this way; so also the relation of dependence of all particular beings in regard to God, their Creator.

As the reality of the constitutive principles is wholly reduced to that of these transcendental relations, and since a relation always carries in itself the imprint of the term to which it is referred, transcendental relations communicate, one to the other, the character which is proper to each, in such wise that particular being is altogether impregnated with it. Each principle is the real reason of a character which affects the whole particular being. This being must contain as many principles or transcendental relations as the irreducible characters it presents. Consequently, particular being is not simple; it consists in a structure whose principles are adequately defined by their correlation, so as to borrow all their value from their synthesis and all their meaning from the place which they there occupy.

3. The Structure of Existence, or the Principle of Being, and That of Essence, the Principle of the Particular Mode or of the "Taleity" of Being

On the plane of the absolute perfection of being, particular being is composed of a real principle of being and of a real principle of the mode of being. The first is the reason of the value of being of the whole subject, and the second is the reason of the individuality (and therefore of the limitation and the relativity) of the whole

---

In this present work we have used this expression of transcendental relation only to designate the constituent principles of particular being.

The transcendental relation is called such because it is not contained in one single category, but transcends every category since it applies to all, that of substance as well as those of the accidents, and even to the whole particular being. It differs, therefore, from the predicamental relation which, as such, presupposes a subject from which it is formally distinct. The real predicamental relation considered as a metaphysical accident, is itself a transcendental relation, under the same title as the other constituent principles of particular being.

We can reconcile what we have just said with this text of Cajetan: "The relation belonging to the predicament of relation differs from other relations belonging to the other genera, which by some are called transcendental, in this that the relation, belonging to the genus *ad aliquid*, is essentially referred to another, not as to something receptive or to an efficient, final or formal cause, but precisely as to its *terminus*. For one of the relative terms is neither the formal nor the final nor the efficient cause of the other relative, but it is its *terminus*. For this reason Albertus Magnus says that one of the relative terms is not to be defined through the others, but as referring to the others, because 'through' denotes causality. The relation of the other genera, which on account of the poverty of language is called relation, looks essentially to another, but as to its subject or to matter or to form or the like; for thus matter essentially looks to form, and vice versa." Cajetan, *De ente et essentia*, c.7, q.16, (ed. H. Laurent, p. 222, n.136).

subject.[6] Strictly speaking, it is not the principle of being which is; it is not in itself, it is not a being, a subsistent reality,[7] just as it is not the principle of "taleity" which is "this" or "limited"; it is not a finite being. But it is the whole particular being which "is" (by reason of its principle of being); and just as it is real through and through, it is such in all of its principles taken together. This is why we say of each principle that it is, but then we speak loosely. Similarly, it is the whole particular being which is "such," finite and relative (by reason of its principle of the mode of being); and this is why its "taleity" affects all the principles taken together. This is why we say, but not strictly, that the principle of the mode is itself "such," finite.

The real principle of the value of being is commonly called *esse*, to be, existence; and the real principle of the mode of being, the principle of individuality or of limitation is called essence [8] or again

---

[6] "Essence and existence, in the finite being, are principles of being, incomplete beings, really distinct. They do not constitute a third thing, since existence does not add to the essence a determination in the order of definition. Their union constitutes a composite with these two; existence places in the last actuality the content of the essence, either simple, or itself composed of matter and form and on this score a third thing already. (The composite of matter and form is called a *compositum ex his:* Author's observation.) Matter and form constitute the essence of the finite sensible thing; the existence actuates the complete essence, as essence, and it is its proper substantial act, its *actus ultimus.* Matter and form are one single receptive principle." Nic. Balthasar, *L'abstraction métaphysique et l'analogie des êtres dans l'être,* Louvain, 1935, pp. 56–57.

[7] "Just as we cannot say that the running itself runs, so we cannot say that the *esse* itself exists." St. Thomas Aquinas, *Libr. de Hebdomadibus,* lect. 2, *explanatio.*—"Existence itself is that by which the substance is, just as running is that by which the runner runs." *Summa theol.,* Ia, q. 50, a. 2, ad 3; q. 75, a. 5, ad 4.

[8] It was Plautus, a philosopher of the Augustan age, who first used the Latin word *essentia* to translate the Greek *ousia.* Quintilian (first century) found the term very inelegant: "and this interpretation (namely, *oratoria* or *oratrix,* corresponding to the Greek word ῥητορική, is not less harsh than those words of Plautus *essentia* or *entia*" according to another reading "*et queentia*"). Seneca 2–66) did not like the word, but he did not find a better one. Apulius, in the second century, uses it without hesitation.

Tertullian (160–240) is the first Christian writer who uses the term *essentia,* but less often than the word *substantia.* Marius Victorinus (fourth century) prefers *substantia* to *essentia* or *essensitas.* Macrobius (fifth century) accepts the word *essentia.* Boethius (circ. 470–525) definitely introduces this word into philosophical and theological language. However, he uses it only ten times in his theological writings.

On the meaning of the words *esse, essentia, existentia* etc., in the first days of Scholasticism, cf. Ferd. Sassen, *De vraag naar het zijn in de eerste eeuwen der Scholastiek, in Mededeelingen der Koninkl. Academie van Wetenschappen* (Amsterdam), afd. Letterkunde, Deel 83, serie A, num. 5, 1937, pp. 1–46.

In the thirteenth century, a juridical meaning was also attached to the term

quiddity and nature.[9] The use of these terms is not without danger, because they do not at all draw attention to the completely relative character of the constitutive principles of being, and they make us run the risk of forgetting that these principles are transcendental relations which have meaning and reality only in the structure which they constitute. Another reason is that the words essence and quiddity, existence and being border on the equivocal. As the first two are employed very often in an abstract sense, we are tempted to lose sight of the fact that in metaphysics we look to the individual and concrete essence. As regards the terms "to be" and "to exist," we have already had occasion to say [10] that they can be understood in more than one sense; in metaphysics they ought to signify the value of being, which is transcendental and, as such, goes beyond all relativity.

We have already emphasized the close relation which unites participation in being, the analogy of the idea of being and the correlation of essence and existence which goes to make up every finite being.[11] Strictly speaking, participation in being and the profound analogy of the idea of being [12] imply on the one hand the absoluteness of the value of being and consequently the transcendentality of the idea of being, and on the other hand the existence of many subsistent beings. It has been shown above that these subsistent beings are found de facto in reality, since they give evidence of free and autonomous activity, and since by this same token

essentia: property, possessions, usufruct. Cf. J. De Ghellinck, S.J., "L'entrée d'essentia, substantia et d'autres mots apparentés, dans le latin médiéval," in Archivum Latinitatis Medi Aevi (Bulletin du Cange), t. XVI, 1941, pp. 77–112: Essentia et substantia. Note complémentaire, ibid., t. XVII, 1942, pp. 129–133.

The Greek ousia, which signifies essence, substance, and at times existence and life, had generally in the current language the meaning of goods, fortune, money, as the Latin word substantia.

[9] To indicate the essence, the Scholastics also used the words "quod quid erat esse," a literal translation of the Aristotelian expression "τὸ τί ἦν εἶναι." This expression includes the words "τὸ . . . εἶναι," which the Scholastics translate by "quod . . . esse," and the question "τί ἦν," "quid erat?" We do not see clearly the reason of the use of the imperfect "ἦν," in place of the present "ἐστί." In Greek the words "τὸ εἶναι" accompanied by a substantive in the dative, e.g. "ἀνθρώπῳ," signify the being proper to such thing, e.g. to man, therefore the human being, the essence of man. "τὸ ἀνθρώπῳ εἶναι" signifies the being which is proper to that which answers the question "quid erat," i.e. what was it?, hence, the quidditative being, the quiddity or the essence. "Quod quid erat esse hominis" means "the essence of man."

[10] Cf. supra, pp. 25–26.
[11] Cf. supra, pp. 100–101.
[12] Cf. supra, pp. 44–45.

they manifest, at least within the limits of these actions, that they are perfectly independent, the one of the other.[13]

The proof of the real correlation of the principle of being or existence, and of the principle of the mode of being or essence in the finite being is grounded on the same data: the absolute value of being, and the relativity of subsistent and multiple beings. In point of fact the problem is to discover whether each of these beings includes, besides the real reason of its "taleity," its own peculiar principle of existence or of value of being. It would not suffice to begin with a real but superficial multiplicity in order to end with this conclusion. For example, an act of the will and a thought, sensations of sight and hearing, the head and the heart, the hand and the foot, the spiritual soul and matter, are so many realities, distinct one from the other; and yet we could not conclude, for all that, that each one of them possesses, in addition to its essence, its own peculiar principle of existence. It is not the part which exists but the whole; for it is not the part but the whole which acts. Hence, as long as it has not been established that there are subsistent beings, whole beings, "supposita," we cannot raise in regard to the given reality the problem of the internal correlation of the principles of being and the mode of being, since we do not know if this reality is a part or a whole. It is only in regard to the whole which subsists in itself, and which possesses therefore in itself the intrinsic reason of its existence,[14] that we can ask if this *esse proprium* (its own *to be*) is identified with its essence, or if it is really distinct from it. The thesis of the distinction of essence and existence implies, of itself, the multiplicity of beings.

4. Objections Against This Thesis of the Real Distinction of Essence and Existence

The objections which our adversaries commonly bring against the thesis of the real composition of the principle of being and the

---

[13] Cf. *supra*, pp. 17–22.

[14] It is generally admitted in the Thomistic school that the *esse proprium* is itself *the* "formal" constitutive principle of "suppositality," i.e. of the subsistence proper to a complete being. A "part" of a being does not possess this complete character, this incommunicability; it does not have subsistence, it does not include in itself an *esse proprium*. It is real by reason of the principle of existence of the whole (which is the subsistent being) of which it forms a part. Cf. *infra*, Part II, chapt. VIII, § 2, pp. 240–43.

mode, are derived from an erroneous conception of this composition. First of all, it goes without saying that the terms to be or existence and essence ought to be taken in the metaphysical sense, indicated above. In taking the word essence in an abstract signification or the word to be in a relative sense (for example, that of the state of realization opposed to that of possibility), we could without doubt spin out philosophical considerations which would not be wanting in interest, but which would not come to grips directly with the thesis of the real distinction between essence and the principle of existence, since these words have here a different signification.[15] Before all else our discussion ought to be concerned with the legitimacy and the importance of this signification.

The principal objection which has been made to the thesis of the real distinction is that of being unintelligible, of implying contradictions. It is impossible, our adversaries object, to give an acceptable meaning either to essence or to existence as long as we suppose that they are really distinct one from the other. This objection proceeds as follows: Essence is a principle of limitation of the existent being; it must be real in order to exercise this function. For we cannot understand how a non-real essence could still produce a real limitation in the being. Hence, we must give to the reality of the principle of limitation at least a logical priority over the principle of existence. In other words, the reality of the essence is a condition for the exercise of its function, and we must think of it as logically antecedent to this function. But from the moment that we see ourselves forced to consider the essence as real, abstracting from the function which it exercises in regard to the principle of existence, we admit that it possesses its own reality outside of this relation with the principle of existence. This is the same as declaring that the principle of existence is perfectly superfluous, since it does not enter in to explain the existence of the essence.[16]

---

[15] A current example of this class of objections: "All entities, which are found in some really existing thing, must be thought of as also pre-existing in the possible state. If, therefore, existence adds some entity to the essence, this is to be thought of also in the possible state. But existence in the possible state is nothing other than the very possibility of the thing, and this possibility does not bespeak any other entity than the possible entity itself. Therefore, neither does real existence bespeak any entity other than the real entity, which is." Nic. Monaco, S.J., *Praelectiones metaphysicae generalis*, 3rd ed., Rome, 1928, p. 175.

[16] "And surely real objective potency of this kind cannot limit the act of being unless it is supposed to be real already, even before it receives the act of existence, at least prior with the priority of nature. But this is repugnant. Therefore . . .

Some philosophers make analogous reflections à propos of the real principle of existence.[17] When we admit, they say, that the existence is limited by the essence, we suppose that before existence has been united to the essence (to exercise its function of the principle of being) this existence was unlimited. How should we conceive this infinite existence? There cannot be any question of a purely logical infinity, of the universality proper to abstract concepts, that is, of the property which the concepts have of being attributable to an indefinite multitude of subjects. As a matter of fact, the problem concerns reality and not the logical order; but neither can there be question of an infinite reality, which could only be the divine reality; for we do not see how that could allow itself to be limited or divided by the essences. Hence, the principle of existence must itself be finite in order to be able to exercise its function of a principle of being in regard to essence; and this is to say that the limitation of the principle of existence is the condition of the exercise of its function, and that we must think of the one in order to be able to think of the other. But as soon as we admit that the principle of existence is limited, independently of the function which it must exercise in regard to the essence, we concede that it is limited, even abstracting from its relation with the principle of limitation. This implies that it becomes superfluous to appeal to an essence, distinct from existence, to explain the limitation.

This whole argumentation rests on this presupposition, that every constitutive principle can be considered in two ways: first of all,

The major is evident; for although both this subjective potency and the act of being are produced simultaneously, still in order that this act may be understood to be limited by that potency in which it must be received, it is necessary first to suppose that potency as real and as capable of receiving and limiting the act of existence. For what is not real, cannot receive anything real into itself and limit it. Therefore . . .

Proof of the minor: Subjective potency can be understood to be real in as far as it has the act of existence, whose function it is to render real the subject which it affects. Therefore, considered in itself, even before it is understood to receive the act of existence it cannot be or be understood to be real, just as a body is understood to be alive through the soul, and therefore considered in itself alone it cannot be or be understood to be alive. But if a real subjective potency must limit the act of existence it would have to be real before it would have this act, at least with a priority of nature. Therefore it would be real, before it would become real, which is a manifest contradiction." N. Monaco, *op. cit.*, p. 198.

[17] Cf. N. Monaco, *op. cit.*, p. 159, 162. Cf. the exposition of this difficulty by Father Pedro Descoqs, S.J., "Essai critique sur l'Hylémorphisme," Paris, 1924, pp. 144–148; *Archives de philosophie*, Vol. IV, cah. 4, *Bibliographie critique*, Paris, 1927, p. 135 (487); Vol. V, cah. 1, *Thomisme et Scolastique*, Paris, 1927, pp. 114–137.

in itself, and then in its relation with the other principle. Our adversaries strive to show that in order that it may be considered in itself, this principle must already possess all that ought to come to it from the other, so that this latter appears to be altogether superfluous. Whether you start from the one or the other of the two correlative principles you always end up with the same result. And so, we must conclude from this that there are not two real principles but one single reality in which, it is true, we can distinguish different aspects but not really distinct elements.

The flaw in this reasoning is its "suppositum," its presupposition. The principles of which there is question are not beings which we could in any way consider in themselves, absolutely. They are transcendental relations and nothing else; [18] all that we can say of them formally concerns their correlation. That which is a principle in itself is therefore not a condition, antecedently to the exercise of its function; to say what it is in itself is to declare what it is in relation to its co-principle. It is not possible to make the distinction, even logically, between the two moments which the objection presupposes. A principle is not conceived outside of its connection with another corresponding principle; we cannot from any point of view abstract it, separate it mentally from this other. For this would be as much nonsense as to wish to speak of a relation without taking into account the reference which binds it to its term, and therefore without taking this term into account. The constitutive principles of particular being have no other reality than that of their correlation: they form a structure; they have meaning and existence only in this structure. But such a distinction, is it still real?

Many philosophers, scholastic and others, call only that distinction real which exists "inter rem et rem," that is, between being and being, or between parts of beings, between terms which are separable at least de jure.[19] In this case the elements to be distinguished must

---

[18] Cf. N. J. J. Balthasar, *Mon moi dans l'être*, Louvain, 1946, pp. 104–114, answer to the objections of Fr. Descoqs, S.J.

[19] Starting with this presupposition certain authors attack the real distinction between essence and existence: "If existence is a thing distinct from the real essence, it can be separated by the power of God. Suppose that this separation has been made; then we will have an essence existing even after rejecting that existence; and on the other hand we will have an existence which has been received into nothing." Tilmann Pesch, S.J., *Institutiones logicales* (Philosophia lacensis), p. II, "Logica Major," vol. 2, "Logica realis," Freiburg in Breisgau, 1890, p. 81, *Ratio quarta*. (In the following edition prepared by Charles Frick, S.J., Freiburg, 1919, this objection has been suppressed.)

be considered, on the one hand in themselves, abstracting from their union, and on the other hand in their mutual relations; but the philosophical study of reality forces us to press on farther. It makes us discover distinctions which are not distinctions between separable realities, and which are not logical distinctions either, that is, the fruit of abstractive and discursive reason. Since they have to do with the internal structure of real being they can on this title also be called real distinctions.

To overthrow the thesis of the real distinction of the principle of existence and that of the essence, and to raise difficulties against it, our adversaries would have to try to show that the two fundamental characters—this being *is*, it is *this*—both of which affect the totality of the particular concrete being, are not irreducible. More accurately, it would have to be shown either that one of them is abstract and can be reduced to the other; or that both of them are abstract and are reduced to an affirmation still more fundamental.[20] At bottom, the

---

The same reasoning had already been proposed by Soto: "The *esse* of existence is not another second thing distinct from the essence, as many disciples of St. Thomas (I don't know about St. Thomas himself) hold for certain. For surely if existence were really distinct from me, God could destroy it, while I would remain safe; hence I would exist without that thing, and therefore it is useless to posit something other than myself and my parts by which I exist. But existence is said to be distinct from essence just as to sit down is distinct from man, because it is not of the essence of man that he should be, since even before the creation of the world man was a rational animal." Dominicus Soto Segobiensis, O.P., *Super libros Physicorum Aristotelis Quaestiones,* II, q.2, Venice, 1582, p. 123 E.

Suarez develops the same objection but in more technical terms: "At least by the power of God the actual entity of the essence could be preserved without that other further formal act, because although God cannot supply a formal cause that is intrinsically component, He can nevertheless supply the dependence of one component part on the other, even though this is a formal act. . . . If, however, God were to conserve an actual essence without that further act of distinct existence, that entity thus conserved is truly existing, and consequently whatever is imagined to be added to it cannot verify the true definition of existence, and without cause it is said to be naturally necessary for the formal effect of existence." *Disputationes metaphysicae,* d.31, s.6, n.8.

[20] Father Pedro Descoqs reasons in the following manner: "The individual essence of the finite being, considered absolutely in as far as it prescinds from existence, is by no means irreducible to the existence as such. On the contrary, it bespeaks an essential relation to the existence, itself considered absolutely, i.e. to existence either possible or actual. . . . Father Garrigou-Lagrange adds that one cannot find a third concept in which to unify the essence and the existence. But what does he do then with the subsistent individual? And because we do not have an exhaustive concept of it, does that prevent us from getting at and knowing by ways complementary of the concept this one reality, which is reality "κατ' ἐξοχήν" (par excellence) infinitely superior to the quidditative

discussion would have to do with the analogy of the idea of being, with participation in being, and ultimately with the meaning which must be attributed to the idea of being in metaphysics. Being: does it designate a relative state or an absolute and transcendental value? It is the conception of metaphysics itself, of its formal object, which is in question.

5. The Structure of the Principles of Essence and Existence and the Metaphysical Problem

The thesis of the real distinction between the real principle of existence and that of essence in every particular being allows us to pose the metaphysical problem with considerable clarity; and in this sense it marks a step towards the solution of this problem. The proportionality which characterizes the content of the analogous idea

---

reality? Once again, the concept does not exhaust the reality." P. Descoqs, *Essai critique sur l'Hylémorphisme* (Paris, 1924), pp. 152, 153, 154.

"Essence and *esse* belong to different orders; they are realities which are dependent on disparate modes of knowing, *scil.*, abstraction and intuition. If one posits a priori that where you have different orders and disparate modes of knowing, there must necessarily and by conventional definition be a real distinction between the terms of these opposite pieces of knowledge, we do not see any inconvenience in admitting a real distinction between essence and *esse*. The quarrel then is reduced simply to a manner of speaking." *op. cit.*, p. 160.

"Let us distinguish: The metaphysical or real concept is that which represents reality without having need of being corrected or complemented in its formal line; it is that which expresses simply objective reality, being. The logical concept is the product of an imperfect abstraction which demands a complement or a correction because, as such, it does not express the reality which is; v.g., genus is a logical concept because 'the form of genus does not exist'. . . . This is why we shall say that the real and adequate metaphysical essence of contingent being, the possible as well as the actual, includes by identity, undoubtedly not formal identity (the quiddity does not answer the question *an est*) but real and truly necessary identity, the *esse* either possible or actual, and so (this metaphysical essence) is thought of only through it. . . . Actuality, as such, falls under the concept only indirectly in the apprehension of the individual essence; it falls under our knowledge on the score of actuality, as such, only by means of intuition." P. Descoqs, S.J., *Archives de Philosophie*, vol. V, cah. I, "Thomisme et Scholastique" (Paris, 1927), p. 109, note 2, pp. 111–112.

In the last paragraph Father Descoqs correctly distinguishes the logical, abstract concept and the metaphysical idea which lays hold of being in its concrete quiddity. He observes that this last idea is inseparable from the idea of *esse*, even though it is not formally identified with it. But how is this possible, if there is no real structure? It is in this "formal" distinction (i.e. dealing with the content of the ideas) which has to do with the "concrete" and which consequently indicates a concrete irreducibility, that we see the reason for admitting a real irreducibility, since the concrete is precisely the real.

of being corresponds to that which constitutes the foundation of the reality of beings. Consequently, relativity is not a superficial but a fundamental character of finite reality, and the absolute, ontological value of every being is inseparable from it; the intrinsic reason of the absolute value of being, the principle of existence, consists in a transcendental relation. It is conceived only in relation with another transcendental relation, the essence, which is the reason of a mode of individual being, by which particular being is opposed to others, and is necessarily contained in an order. In particular being the internal reason of the value of being is not identified with subsistent reality, but with only one of the principles, constitutive of the whole, therefore, with the relative. In technical language, this internal reason is not *id quod est,* that which is, but merely *id quo est,* that by which it is. It is indeed being itself considered in its absolute value, which is affected with relativity; and so there arises the problem of discovering what reality requires in itself so that such a situation may be intelligible. How are we to explain the fact that being, an absolute and unique value, can really be found in each of the multiple, distinct, and subsistent beings, which form the universal order?

6. *Historical Notes*

It will not be altogether devoid of interest to run through the history of ideas rapidly, and to take cognizance of the various solutions which philosophers have given to the problem of the composition of essence and existence. In comparing the various opinions which have been brought to light on this question, we give a better account of the exact meaning and of the importance of the doctrine we have expounded in this chapter.

Some have erroneously believed that they find the real distinction between essence and existence in the writings of Aristotle. Undoubtedly, the Stagyrite teaches that every definition to be real and not merely nominal, must imply a reference to existence; and he adds that this latter does not form part of the quiddity to be defined.[21] According to him it is not by starting with the definition of a thing that we are in a position to conclude to its existence; this latter can

---

21 "τὸ δὲ τι ἐστι ἄνθρωπος καὶ τὸ εἶναι ἄνθρωπον ἄλλο" i.e., the quiddity of man is one thing, the fact of his existence is another. *Posterior Analytics,* Book II, c. 6, 92 b 10.

be established only by an appeal to experience.[22] But "it is all too evident that Aristotle never dreamed of (even to reject it) a composition of two real co-principles, namely, essence and existence, in the heart of existing substance; and that in the two questions, "τί ἐστιν," "What is it?," and "εἰ ἔστιν," "Does it exist?," whose difference and independence he does indeed emphasize, he saw first of all only a logical problem. He did not dream at all of the consequences in the ontological order which it implies, when it is transferred to the field of metaphysics and the real constitution of beings in themselves." [23]

It is quite true that Aristotle insists on the transcendental character of the idea of being which he makes the formal object of first philosophy; [24] he clearly perceived that it is not a generic idea, that it signifies what is common to all the categories,[25] and that it is not capable of being determined *ab extrinseco*.[26] However, he fails to tell us how the intrinsic determination of the idea is effected; he is content to emphasize vigorously the analogy of this idea. Unfortunately, he stops at the analogy of proportion, which can serve, up to a point, to characterize relations which exist between the category of substance and those of the accidents; but it can by no means serve to mark the relations which bind the different subsistent beings together in the absolute unity of being.[27] As a result of his criticism of Plato's system the Stagyrite turns away from every theory of participation,[28] and not for an instant does it enter his mind to consider existence as a perfection in which different beings would participate according to different modes, in the measure of their quiddity or essence. Between being and the quiddities, distributed

---

[22] Cf. Suzanne Mansion, *Le rôle de la connaissance de l'existence dans la science aristotélicienne,* Louvain, 1941, pp. 8–23.

[23] Augustin Mansion, *Bulletin Thomiste,* 4ᵉ année, 1927, p. (23).
The fact of existence, says Aristotle, would result from the definition, only if the existence itself made up a substance. Cf. *Posterior Analytics,* Book II, c. 6, 92 b 14. According to the Scholastics this is precisely the case with the divine existence, but the Stagyrite does not even suspect this.

[24] *Metaphysics,* Book IV, c. 1, 1003 a 20 sqq.; c. 3, 1005 a 19 sqq.; Book VI, c. 1, 1025 b 15–20; Book XI, c. 7, 1064 b 6–14.

[25] *Metaphysics,* Book IV, c. 3, 1005 a 27.

[26] *Metaphysics,* Book III, c. 3, 998 b 15–30; Book VIII, c. 6, 1045 a 36; Book XI, c. 1, 1059 b 30.

[27] Cf. *supra,* pp. 52–53.

[28] *Metaphysics,* Book I, c. 5, 987 b 11–14. Cf. L. B. Geiger, O.P., *La participation dans la philosophie de St. Thomas d'Aquin* (Bibiliothèque thomiste, XXIII) Paris, 1942, pp. 9–11. Cornelio Fabro, C.P.S., *La nozione metafisica di partecipazione secondo S. Tomaso d'Aquino,* Milan, 1939, pp. 144–147.

into ten categories, and especially between being and the first category, that of substance, he admits an identity, pure and simple.
Hence, substances, or subsistent beings, are placed side by side as
absolute terms which can be bound together at best by superficial
ties; and thus moving things depend, all of them, on the Prime Mover,
and in so far they belong to one and the same order; but this dependence does not at all penetrate to their substance, to being: it
does not get out of the zone of motion.

Before Aristotle, Plato strove in the *Sophist* to solve the problem
of being by a circuitous study of non-being. While declaring himself
in agreement with Parmenides in admitting that absolute non-being,
the pure negation of being, is nonsense,[29] Plato believed he had to
attribute a certain meaning to non-being. In this connection he
could only envisage relative non-being. In his previous works he had
already opposed the reality of the "idea" which is bona fide being,
to that of matter which is in constant becoming, and which (since
it is never completed and has no consistency) in this sense is not.[30]
There are, however, many ideas: one idea is distinct from the
other; the first is not the second; it is other than the latter. In this
case non-being is reduced to "otherness"; this relative non-being
is therefore intelligible, and so it is itself likewise an idea.[31]

Aristotle remarks with good reason that this detour through non-
being is useless. Every negation rests on an affirmation; relative non-
being therefore presupposes relative being.[32] In fact, if this thing
here is not that, it is because this thing is, and that thing is. The
Stagyrite concludes from this that being is analogous, that it implies
an order, and therefore belongs to the relative: it is now this, now
that, and it is really and truly this as well as that.

Plato always distinguished the ideas of being and non-being, to
which he also added that of identity; all three are said of everything, they are participated in by all subjects.[33] They are also predicated of one another, they participate in one another, and from this
point of view no one of them possesses a priority; being participates

---

[29] *Sophist,* 258 c.

[30] *Timaeus,* 27 d–28 a; *Republic,* Book VI, 507 b, 509 d.

[31] *Sophist,* 257 b–259 b.

[32] Aristotle, *Metaphysics,* Book XIV, c.2, 1098 a 16–18, 27–29.

[33] Plato here adds two other supreme genera, the ideas of motion and of rest,
but these do not enjoy the complete universality of the first three, as he himself
observes. For motion cannot be predicated of rest as such, nor can rest be
predicated of motion, as such.

in identity and in non-being (since it is identical with itself, and is distinct from identity and from non-being); just as non-being in the sense of otherness, participates in being and identity (it is, and it is itself); and also just as identity participates in being and non-being (in as far as it is and is distinguished from the other ideas).[34]

In fact, without being clearly conscious of it, Plato had in this way disengaged the idea of being (which does not admit any absolute opposition, as Parmenides had quite well seen) from the idea of essence, this latter being considered entirely under its negative aspect,[35] as the reason of otherness and of relative non-being. Essence from this viewpoint is not at all the reason of that which is not absolutely (this would be unthinkable), but it is the reason of this which is not that (therefore this which is this).

Meanwhile, Plato lost sight of the fact that being is the reason of the absolute, although he had previously affirmed this, at least implicitly, in admitting as self-evident that the negation of being is unthinkable.[36] He declares, in point of fact, that being participates in otherness, in non-being, as this latter participates in being,[37] and in saying this he does not seem to observe that it is precisely here that we have the fundamental problem of philosophy, raised by Parmenides.[38] This problem is: How are we to understand that there is participation (and therefore otherness, multiplicity and relativity) on the plane of being, which is of itself the absolute?

Plotinus takes up and develops these conceptions of Plato. In regard to bona fide reality, that of the intelligible world, constituted by the second hypostasis, Intellect ($\nu o\hat{v}s$), matter can only be called

---

[34] *Sophist,* 258 e–259 a. Cf. 255 e.

[35] A point on which Aristotle justly reproaches him, as we have observed.

[36] "Let not any one say, then, that while affirming the opposition of not-being to being, we still assert the being of not-being; for as to whether there is an opposite of being ($\dot{\epsilon}\nu\alpha\nu\tau\dot{\iota}o\nu$ $\tau\iota$ $\tauo\hat{v}$ $\ddot{o}\nu\tauo s$), to that inquiry we have long said good-bye—it may or may not be, and may or may not be capable of definition ($\pi\alpha\nu\tau\dot{\alpha}\pi\alpha\sigma\iota\nu$ $\ddot{\alpha}\lambda o\gamma o\nu$)." *Sophist* 258 e.

[37] As we have said, to the two absolutely universal attributes, being and otherness, Plato adds a third, identity. He does not see that identity is only a precision of being whose unity he emphasizes. Being is of itself, one and the same. There remains, therefore, only the opposition being—other, i.e., absolute being and relative being (or non-being).

[38] In reality Parmenides pretended to solve this problem by denying it, since he safeguards only one of the terms of the problem, the absolute of being, and denies the other without further ado, *scil.,* multiplicity, i.e., the modes of being or essences. But this negation is futile, for this multiplicity continues in spite of everything to assert itself, even though under the form of "opinion" or illusion.

unfinished, imperfect being, belonging to non-being (μὴ ὄν).³⁹ Nevertheless, if we consider the multitude of ideas which the Intellect understands, we must indeed admit that this Intellect also includes the idea of "otherness," that of a certain non-being (μὴ ὄν), which just as the ideas of being and identity belongs to all subjects.⁴⁰ Otherness is, therefore, predicated even of being, and this reciprocally, so that being participates in non-being just as non-being participates in being.⁴¹ Hence, the idea of being is intrinsically affected with relativity. Being, too, is analogous in the sense in which Aristotle understood it, and it is common to all the categories without exception, although it is predicated in the first place of substance (οὐσία).⁴²

Besides this, however, Plotinus does justice to all the exigencies of the absolute, as Parmenides wished. The absolute is the One, which is outside of all multiplicity and all composition. It is therefore outside of being (ἐπέκεινα ἄρα ὄντος),⁴³ for being is not the One, contrary to what Aristotle contends,⁴⁴ since being and thought are essentially in correlation in the Intellect, and since they necessarily constitute a duality.⁴⁵ The One is therefore also of non-being (μὴ ὄν), not indeed by defect but by excess; ⁴⁶ it is that which transcends all things (τὸ ἄνω ὑπὲρ πάντα),⁴⁷ and that in which all things participate and

³⁹ *Enneads*, I, c.8, 5; II, c.5, 5. πλειόνως μὴ ὄν, II, 5, 4. The sensible has reality only by participation (κατὰ μετάληψιν) in bona fide being (τὸ ὄντως ὄν) which is the intelligible. *Enneads*, VI, c.3, 6. Cf. V, c.6, 6.

⁴⁰ *Enneads*, V, c.1, 4. This whole passage refers to Plato, *Sophist*, 145e–147c. Cf. *Enneads*, VI, c.2, 8; c.4, 11.

⁴¹ *Enneads*, VI, c.2, 8.

⁴² *Enneads*, VI, c.3, 6. Besides, we must distinguish the categories of the intelligible world and those of the sensible world. *Ibid.*, c.3, 3.

⁴³ *Enneads*, V, c.5, 6. Confer VI, c.8, 8.

⁴⁴ "The one is being in a sense, and being is one." Aristotle, *Metaphysics*, Book XI, c.3, 1061 a 18. Cf. *Enneads*, V, c.1, 9; VI, c.2, 1; c.4, n.5, 6, 9. In *Enneads*, V, c.1, 8 Plotinus appeals to Plato, i.e., *Republic*, 509 b.

⁴⁵ CF. *Enneads*, V, c.3, 13; VI, c.2, 8. Plotinus cannot make Being and the One coincide, because "by identifying correctly the intelligible and Being, but confounding our concept with the intelligible, he regards as an essential property of Being, as such, that which is only an inferior condition of our concepts, which are doomed to seek their object outside in the sensible world, and consequently are themselves doomed to be, necessarily, only a synthesis of the One and the many." René Arnou, *Le désir de Dieu dans la philosophie de Plotin* (Collection historique des grands philosophes), Paris, n.d. (1922), pp. 137–138. Contemporaneous idealism itself likewise considers that the opposition of the subject and the object, the constituent element of human consciousness, forms the essence of all cognitive activity; and from this it deduces that knowledge must be denied in a God conceived as a simple and perfect Being.

⁴⁶ *Enneads*, VI, c.9, 5.

⁴⁷ *Ibid.*, c.8, 1.

from which they borrow their perfection completely. It is the absolute One, which is opposed of itself and unconditionally to pure multiplicity, to that which is unthinkable and impossible, to absolute non-being (παντελῶς μὴ ὄν).[48]

Neo-Platonism will always place emphasis on the simplicity of the One, the supreme good, the absolute perfection. All other reality, which participates in the One, can only be a degree of perfection, distinct from other degrees; it is such a particular reality, this thing here, which is not that other thing, that over there. Further, this philosophy will insist on the internal composition of things. That which exists by participation, says Proclus, presents a double character, since it must at one and the same time resemble this thing (in which it participates), and also differ from it.[49] Hence, that which participates in the One, that is, any particular reality whatever, cannot be simple; every being is composed, at least of the finite and the infinite (ὡς εκ πέρατος ὄν καὶ ἀπείρου).[50] Let us observe, finally, that Neo-Platonism will strive to bring to light the hierarchy of the terms which compose the universal order. The *Institutiones theologicae* of Proclus, and dependently on this work, the writings of the Pseudo-Dionysius, the Areopagite, and the *De Causis* present among other things a scale of the degrees of perfection which are reduced essentially to the following terms: being, life, intelligence.[51]

---

[48] *Enneads*, I, c.8, 3.

[49] "It is necessary that that which participates in anything (τὸ μετέχον) should be partly similar (ὅμοιον) to that which is participated in, and partly diverse and dissimilar (ἕτερον καὶ ἀνόμοιον). Since therefore that which participates in any thing is something from the number of Beings, Unity itself is superessential, and on this account these things are dissimilar among themselves. That which participates in something, therefore, must be one, in order that on this account it may be similar to the One itself, which is participated in, although the one indeed, which is One in such a way, is Unity, and the other is as that which has suffered the One itself and the United, on account of communication in (μέτεξιν) that Unity." Proclus, *Institutio theologica*, c.135 (edit. Didot, Paris, 1896), p. XCV.

[50] *Ibid.*, c.138, p. XCV; cf. c.102, p. LXXXIV. For the meaning of this opposition of the finite and the infinite, cf. c.90 (p. LXXX), and c.92 (p. LXXXI). Similarly in the *Liber de Causis*, propos. IV: "And the (caused existence) itself is not made many things, unless because existence itself, although it is simple, and there is not in things caused something more simple than it, is nevertheless composed of the finite and the infinite."

[51] Cf. Proclus, *Institutio theologica*, cap. 101, pp. LXXXIII–LXXXIV; also Pseudo-Dionysius, the Areopagite, *De divinis nominibus*, c.5, paragraph 3, 5. Cf. also *Liber de causis, initio.*—With this we can reconcile the following text: "Stones, therefore, exist but they do not live. Shrubs, however, exist and live, but they do not sense; brute animals exist, live, and sense, but they do not dis-

Being is considered as a degree of perfection on the same title as life and intelligence. It is inferior to the two other degrees, for living things surpass in perfection non-living which possess only being, just as persons endowed with intelligence, are more perfect than living things which are deprived of reason. On the contrary, being is a perfection more widely extended than life and intelligence, and it is more resistant than these latter, since it remains even where life and intelligence are completely defective or even where they have disappeared. Being is a "(formal) cause more powerful than the others." [52] Moreover, life and intelligence are never found without being; the perfection of being is the very first of the participations; it is the fundamental degree of perfection. The other degrees, life and intelligence, necessarily participate in being,[53] and hence they are at once degrees of perfection (in the sense of degrees of the good) and degrees of being, participations in the fundamental degree of the good, in the perfection of being.

If we take into account Proclus' doctrine of participation, we must conclude from it that all reality, stamped with any degree of perfection whatever, presents the twofold character of similarity and otherness by reason of its relation to the perfection of being. In other words, this reality contains being and relative non-being or otherness; it is, but according to a mode which differs from every other mode. We will say later that it is composed of existence and essence; but this conclusion was not yet accurately formulated by the Neo-Platonic philosophers of antiquity.

---

cern. Angels indeed exist, live, sense (*sic*) and discern. But man has something of every creature; for he has existence in common with stones, life with trees, sensation with animals, understanding with the angels." St. Gregory, the Great, *Homily 29 on the Gospels* (P.L. LXXVI, col. 1214). The list of these degrees of perfection often crops up in the writings of the medieval Scholastics.

In the *Sophist*, 249 a, Plato asserts that life and thought "have place really in the bosom of universal *being* ($\tau \hat{\varphi} \ \pi \alpha \nu \tau \epsilon \lambda \hat{\omega} s \ \ddot{o} \nu \tau \iota$)." Plotinus on his part writes in *Enneads*, V, c. 6, 6: "in that which is, there is at once thought, life, and being." But in these places they do not set up any hierarchy among these three perfections.

[52] *De causis, loc. cit.* Confer Pseudo-Dionysius, *De divinis nominibus*, c. V, § 3.

[53] "Being precedes all things. . . . The first of all participations is existence; beings possess existence in themselves before possessing life in themselves, wisdom in themselves . . . ; before participating in every other mode of this kind, they have part first of all and before all else in existence." Pseudo-Dionysius, *De divinis nominibus*, c. V, § 5 (translation of Maurice De Gandillac, Bibliothèque philosophique, Paris, 1943, p. 131).—"The first of things created is *esse*, and there is nothing else created before it." *De causis*, propositio IV.

Christian authors were induced to attribute formally to God Himself the perfection of being, relying on the text of the Book of *Exodus,* chapter 3, v. 14: "I am who am. . . . He who is sent me to you." [54] The Christian Neo-Platonists, as the Pseudo-Dionysius, insist on the transcendent character of this divine perfection. "God is being not according to such or such a mode, but in an absolute and undefinable way; for He contains in Himself synthetically and antecedently the plenitude of being." [55] Besides, only in the second place do they attribute to God the perfection of being; the fundamental perfection is called the good.

Nevertheless, in the Christian tradition, authors are inclined more and more to accord the primacy to being, and to consider it as the name of God. Hence, they are oriented towards a system of philosophy which no longer considers being as the first participation, in which moreover all other things participate, but rather as the fundamental perfection, which does not itself participate in anything and in which everything else does participate. Hence, being is conceived as the source of all perfection. This point of view can easily be reconciled with that of Aristotle, when he says that the idea of being is a transcendental idea. This is ultimately the synthesis which St. Thomas proposed.

Boethius throws in his lot with the Neo-Platonists, when he declares with insistence that God alone is simple perfection and everything else is composed, since it is finite. He expresses this in terms of being. "To be and that which is, are different. . . . That which is, can participate in something; but to be itself in no way participates in anything. . . . Everything simple is its to be, . . . but in a composite thing the to be is one thing, and the being is another thing." [56]

---

[54] Cf. St. Gregory of Nyssa, *Catechetical Discourse,* c. XXV.—Pseudo-Dionysius, *De divinis nominibus,* c.V; St. Augustine, *De Trinitate,* Book V, c.2 n. 3 (P.L. 42, col. 912); Étienne Gilson, "L'esprit de la philosophie médiévale," *Gifford Lectures* (University of Aberdeen), 2e édit. (Études de phil. médiév. XXXIII), Paris, 1944, p. 66, note 1.

[55] Pseudo-Dionysius, *loc. cit.* § 4 (Transl. of De Gandillac, p. 130).

[56] "*Esse* and that which is are different; for *esse* itself does not yet exist. But that which is, having received the form of existence, is and persists in being. That which is, can participate in something; but *esse* itself by no means participates in anything. For participation takes place when something already exists. Now something exists when it has received an *esse.* That which exists can have something besides the *esse* itself; but the *esse* itself does not have anything besides itself mixed with it. Merely to be something in that which is, is different from being something; the former signifies an accident, the latter a substance. Everything that is participates in that which is *esse,* in order that it may be; but

In reality, he does not formally envisage the perfection of being, in as far as it would be distinct from every other perfection, and hence he does not treat of a composition of essence and existence.[57] He follows the way of thinking and speaking of Aristotle, who reduces being to the categories by identifying being and its modes. The participation and composition which Boethius treats of, are then found along the line of quiddities; in every created being we must distinguish the nature or quidditative reality (esse), for example, humanity, and the individual subject (that which is) which possesses this reality. A goodly number of Scholastics in the Middle Ages use these expressions in the same sense.

On the contrary, in the Arabian philosophy, which likewise depends on Aristotle as well as on Neo-Platonism, the thesis of the real distinction between essence and existence is found neatly set forth; and it is there considered as a fundamental truth. It is met with already in Al-Farabi (+949/950). Avicenna (980–1037) actually made it the masterpiece of his own system.

It is difficult to indicate with precision what is the origin of this doctrine. It depends, among others, on the well-known passage of the *Posterior Analytics*,[58] where Aristotle makes the remark that it is one thing to say what a being is, and another to state that this being exists. Really, to establish the distinction between the quiddity and its existence, Avicenna rests on this consideration, that existence is not an element entering into the constitution of the quiddity, and that it is always possible to form for oneself an idea of this quiddity without being concerned about its existence. That is why existence ought to be considered as an extrinsic, adventitious,

---

it participates in something else in order that it may be something; and through this, that which is participates in that which is *esse* in order that it may be, but it is in order that it may participate in something else. Everything simple has its *esse* and that which is one has its *esse*. In every composite thing the *esse* is one thing, and that which is, is another." *De hebdomadibus*, c. II (P.L. 64, 1311 BC).

[57] Cf. M. D. Roland-Gosselin, *De ente et essentia de St. Thomas d'Aquin* (Paris, 1926), pp. 124–145. Aimé Forest, "La structure métaphysique du concret selon saint Thomas d'Aquin" (*Études de philosophie médiévale*, XIV) Paris, 1931, pp. 134 sqq.—H. J. Brosch, "Der Seinsbegriff bei Boethius" (*Philosophie und Grenzwissenschaften*, t. IV, 1), Innsbruck, 1931.—Ferd. Sassen, "De vraag naar het zijn in de eerste eeuwen der Scholastiek, Mededeelingen der "Koninklijke Akademie van Wetenschappen," Afdeeling Letterkunde, Deel 83, Serie A, n. 5.—Cornelio Fabro, C.P.S., *La nozione metafisica di partecipazione secondo S. Tomaso d'Aquino* Milan, 1939, pp. 96–99.

[58] Book II, chap. VI, 92 b 10; cf. *supra*, p. 115, note.

"accidental" element which comes from the outside to be added to the quiddity.[59] Avicenna does not mean to say that existence is a predicamental accident, as quality and quantity; he contents himself with emphasizing that finite being is never defined by its existence, and that consequently this latter is distinct from that by which finite being is defined. Now if this existence is not implied in any way in the quiddity, it is not possible that it should proceed from it or that it should be produced in virtue of the quiddity itself. Existence, then, will be able to come on the scene only through the intervention of an extrinsic cause; considered in its existence every finite being is a creature of God.[60] On the contrary, God has no external cause, for His essence is to exist: God is defined by His existence.[61]

At the bottom of this doctrine there lies a certain conception of quiddity or nature. According to Avicenna nature can be considered in three ways: first of all, in an absolute way, nature taken in itself ("in se"), for example, human nature, man, in as far as he is a rational animal; in the second place, nature, considered as realized ("in re"), and in this state it is always individual, for example, Peter or John. Lastly, nature can be taken as a content of knowledge ("in intellectu"), and it is characterized in this case by its universality, the attribute man as applicable to all human beings. Taken in an absolute way nature is neither individual nor universal. The two relative states, "in re" and "in intellectu" bring with them two kinds of existence; and just as these states of real individuality and intelligible universality are distinct from the nature considered in itself, so also the existence really differs from the quiddity to which it corresponds.

It happens at times that to the quiddity elements are added which are already implied in it, and which are derived from it; for example, oddness is a necessary property of the number three. In other

---

[59] To express the adventitious character of the existence of finite being, Avicenna makes use of the Arabic term "lazim" (concomitant, accident). For the meaning of this term, cf. A. M. Goichon, *La distinction de l'essence et de l'existence d'après Ibn Sina (Avicenne)*, Paris, 1937, pp. 112–123.

[60] *Op. cit.*, pp. 130–151.

[61] Avicenna distinguishes the two terms essence and quiddity. God has an essence but not a quiddity; the creature has an essence which is a quiddity. Avicenna establishes the following proportionality: necessary existence belongs to the divine Being, as quiddity belongs to the other beings. Or again: existence is the essence of God, as quiddity is that of creatures; the existence of God is essential, *per se*, whereas that of creatures can only come from God; it is *per aliud*. Cf. *op. cit.*, pp. 176–177.

cases these elements come to the quiddity only through the intervention of an external cause; it is thus, that thanks to the activity of
God, existence comes to be added from the outside to the quiddity
of finite beings. In this chiefly logical conception, the doctrine of
participation cannot play an important role. Quiddity and existence
are presented as absolutes, each having meaning by itself; and it
would only be *ex post facto* and from the outside, that the relation
with the existence would be added to the quiddity; so much so, that
from this quiddity considered in itself, in an absolute manner, there
derives first of all a non-being, under the form of a necessary accident or property. Of itself the quiddity does not exist; and in the
same sense we will have to say that the quiddity is neither one, nor
true, nor good.[62]

It is not easy to understand just how Avicenna conceived "absolute nature." His intention is to avoid pantheism, and yet he seems
inclined to identify with the divine Essence this finite nature, which
is imposed on thought with an absolute necessity.[63] On the other
hand finite being possesses a contingent existence, since it depends
on the creative activity of God; but here again we must get clear
on the meaning of the words. According to Avicenna, in God, the
necessary Being, everything is subject to necessity, even including
the creative act.[64] Hence, the contingence of created existence is reduced, ultimately, to a necessity, but dependently on God. This necessity *per aliud* (through something else) of finite existing being is
opposed to necessity *per se* (through itself), which is peculiar to the
quiddity of even finite being.[65]

Moses Maimonides (1153–1204) seems to have accepted this
thesis of the real distinction; on the contrary, Averrhoes (1126–
1198), the outstanding commentator on Aristotle, rejects it without
reservation.[66]

---

[62] *Op. cit.*, pp. 141, 8–11; p. 144.

[63] *Op. cit.*, pp. 84–91.

[64] *Op. cit.*, pp. 230 sqq.

[65] *Op. cit.*, pp. 156–180.—In an analogous way Avicenna distinguishes the
internal, absolute possibility (*scil.*, the absolute intelligibility which amounts
to the quiddity independently of every reference to a real or possible existence),
and the external or relative possibility, which implies the relation uniting the
quiddity to a cause, capable of making it exist. Cf. *op. cit.*, pp. 156–180.

[66] Averrhoes presents the theory of Avicenna as if the latter made a predicamental accident of existence, but this is not accurate. The Scholastics in turn
take up this interpretation of Averrhoes, and consequently even the champions
of the real distinction, for example, St. Thomas, declare themselves adversaries
of this thesis, supposedly Avicenna's.

Through the works of Avicenna the Christian Scholastics at the beginning of the thirteenth century came to know the thesis of the real distinction between essence and existence. Those who accepted it believed then that they found the same doctrine in the writings of St. Augustine and St. Hilary, and especially in those of Boethius and in the *De Causis*.

William of Auvergne (+1249), Bishop of Paris, is without doubt the first Latin Scholastic who made mention of the famous distinction, and admitted it. It is often difficult to establish with certitude what is the opinion of the authors of this period on this point, since it is not always easy to determine if "id quod est" (that which is) and "esse or id quo est' (to be or that by which it is) are to be taken in the sense of essence and existence, or rather (and this is the case most frequently) in the sense of nature (or perfection) and subject. For this reason there is no agreement about the opinion of Philip, the Chancellor (+1236), of Alexander of Hales, O.F.M. (+1245), of John de la Rochelle, O.F.M. (1200–1245). It seems indeed that in certain places of his works St. Bonaventure, O.F.M. (1221–1274) opposed essence to existence. It is the same with St. Albert, the Great, O.P. (1193/1206–1280) at least in some of his writings where he is yielding to the influence of Avicenna; in others he does not make mention of it, even in those places where one would expect him to do so.

In the same period there are authors who explicitly reject the said distinction: Alexander of Alexandria (in first half of the thirteenth century), Alexander Rufus (about 1250), the anonymous author of the *Summa Philosophiae*, and above all Siger of Brabant (+1281/84), the famous Master of the faculty of Arts at Paris, who on this point drew his inspiration from Averrhoes.

From the simple reading of the works of St. Thomas Aquinas we cannot resist the impression that the Angelic Doctor is a defender of a non-logical distinction between existence and essence in every creature, material and spiritual. Undoubtedly, to justify this opinion it would not be necessary to insist too much on the expressions used by him; for in the matter of distinctions the terminology had not yet sufficiently crystallized.[67] It is certain, however, that the theory

---

[67] It is thus that the expressions "non est idem secundum *rem*," "secundum *rem* differt," "est additio *realis*" designate the logical, virtual distinction as well as the non-logical distinction. The expression "realis distinctio" is not met with in St. Thomas. We find "realis compositio" once to indicate the composition of essence and existence, in *De veritate*, q.27, a.1, ad 8.

of participation, extended to the sphere of the "to be," the perfection of perfections, to which St. Thomas attached more and more importance, demanded between essence and existence a distinction which was not purely in the order of knowledge. What, then, is the attitude of the Angelic Doctor in this matter? How does he conceive being and the distinction between essence and existence which is related to being?

The meaning which one attaches to the substantive *ens* depends on that which one attributes to the word *esse;* for *ens* designates that which is, that which possesses *esse:* "ens dicitur quasi esse habens." [68] St. Thomas observes, and he refers to Aristotle on this point, that *esse* is not always used in the same sense: now it designates real being, now logical being. In this last case there is question of the copula of the judgment. Understood as real being, some use it to designate quiddity, essence, [69] but in this meaning St. Thomas opposes another to it, that of "actus essentiae (non actus secundus, qui est operatio) sed actus primus," "actus entis resultans ex principiis rei." [70] The Angelic Doctor shows himself little inclined to give to the

---

[68] III *Sentent.*, d.6, q.2, a.2; *II Gent.*, c.52; *Quodl.*, IX, q.2, a.3; XII *Metaphys.*, lect. 1 (edit. Cathala, n.2419); *Summa theol.*, Ia, q.39, a.3; q.45, a.4; q.65, a.4; IIIa, q.11, a.5, ad 3; q.17, a.2; q.18, a.2, ad 1; q.77, a.1, ad 4, etc.

[69] This is what Aristotle does. Cf. *supra*, p. 116.

[70] "We must know that *esse* is predicated in three ways: first, the very quiddity or nature of a thing is said to be, just as it is said that the definition is an *oratio significans quid est esse;* for the definition signifies the quiddity of things. In the second way the very act of the essence is said to be (just as *vivere*, which is the *esse* for living things, is the act of the soul), not the second act which is the operation, but the first act. In the third way that is said to be which signifies the truth of composition in propositions, and according to this *est* is called the copula. According to this it is in the intellect, composing and dividing as in its complement; but it is founded in the *esse* of the thing, which is the act of the essence." I *Sentent.*, d.33, q.1, a.1, ad 1.

"We must answer that according to the Philosopher, V *Metaph.*, *esse* is predicated in two ways: First, as it signifies the truth of a proposition, inasmuch as it is the copula; and thus (as the commentator says in this same place, text. 6) *ens* is an accidental predicate. And this *esse* is not in the thing, but in the mind which unites the subject with the predicate, as the Philosopher says in VI *Metaph.*, and hence there is no question about this *esse* here. Secondly, *esse* is predicated as something pertaining to the nature of the thing, inasmuch as things are distributed in the ten categories; and this *esse* indeed is in the thing as the *actus entis*, resulting from the principles of the thing, just as *lucere* is the act of something that shines. At times, however, *esse* is taken for the essence, according to which the thing is, because by *actus* the principles of things (such as potencies or habits) are wont to be signified." III *Sentent.*, d.6, q.2, a.2.

"To the second objection we must answer that *esse* is used in two ways: first, it signifies the act of existence, and secondly, the composition of a proposition,

word *esse* the meaning of quiddity or essence. In the first chapter of *De Ente et Essentia* he does not even list the term *esse* among the synonyms of essence; and in the passages where he brings out this signification of essence, he does it with a view to interpreting the texts which he cites, or to being able to answer certain objections.[71] Further, the role of the copula of the judgment is attached to *esse* taken in the sense of *actus essendi.* . . .[72] In the final analysis, it is this last sense which is fundamental.

Esse simpliciter, that is, "to be" without having to add to it any qualification, signifies to exist. That which is not, in this last sense, does not exist; strictly speaking, it is nothing. Hence, existence is that which is most fundamental in every thing; without it there would be nothing to say of any thing, since it would have no reality. That which exists, *ens*, has existence, possesses "to be," "habet esse." This "to exist" concerns in the first place the substantial principles, to which belong the peculiar nature and individuality of the existing subject. If this substance went by default, everything which the subject included would disappear.[73] To exist, *esse simpliciter*, is therefore nothing other than "to subsist," to exist in itself as a whole, as one being, as a *suppositum*, as an hypostasis, "substantia per se subsistens." [74]

which the soul discovers, while uniting the predicate to the subject." *Summa theol.*, Ia, q.3, a.4, ad 2. Cf. *Quodl.* IX, q.2, a.3.

[71] Cf. I *Sentent.*, d.33, q.1, a.1, ad 1; III *Sentent.*, d.6, q.2, a.2.

[72] Cf. I *Sentent.*, d.33, q.1, a.1, ad 1. St. Thomas distinguishes two intellectual operations, the formation of the concept, *apprehensio*, and the judgment, *judicium;* they are the beginning and the end of the activity of the intellect. The formation of the concept has reference to the quiddity, "respicit *quidditatem* rei"; the judgment has reference to the existence, "respicit *esse ipsius.*" (I *Sentent.*, d.19, q.5, a.1, ad 7). Every judgment is an affirmation, *scil.*, an affirmation of *esse*. Cf. *De Trinitate*, q.5, a.3; *Summa theol.*, Ia, q.85, a.1, ad 1; VI *Metaphys.*, lect. 4 (edit. Cathala, nn.1223-1225).—Confer A. Marc, S.J., "L'Idée de l'être chez Saint Thomas et dans la Scolastique postérieure" (*Archives de Philosophie*, vol. X), Paris, 1933, pp. 80-101.

[73] "For when the substantial form is introduced, a thing is said to become *simpliciter*, just as we say that man comes into being." *De principiis naturae.*—"For since man comes into being, not only is it true to say that man did not exist before, but it is true without qualification to say that he did not exist." I *Physic.*, lect. 12. "For when Socrates begins to be a man, we say simply that he begins to be." VII *Metaph.*, lect. 1, (edit. Cathala, n.1256).

[74] "*Ens* is predicated as something having *esse*. This, however, is only substance, which subsists." XII *Metaph.*, lect. 1 (n. 2419). Cf. X *Metaphys.*, lect. 3 (n.1979). "*Esse* properly belongs to that which has *esse*, and is subsistent in its *esse*." *Summa theol.*, Ia, q.45, a.4. Cf. IIIa, q.11, a.5, ad 3.

Finite being subsists according to its nature. This being taken in its totality is the "suppositum" which exists, the "ens quod habet esse," the being which possesses *esse*. Nature is only one element belonging to the structure of this being; it is an internal principle by which the subject exists, "quo subjectum est." [75] Similarly, substance is a principle by which a thing exists, unless we understand the word in the sense of *suppositum*.[76] A fortiori, the substantial form is not, as such, the subject of the *esse*, but a principle by which a thing is.[77]

It is in the framework of this conception that St. Thomas interprets the Aristotelian adage "Forma facit esse," the form makes the

---

Esse belongs to substance absolutely and first of all (*De ente et essentia*, c.1; *De Veritate*, q.21, a.5); *proprie et per se* (*De Hebdom.*, c.II; *Summa theol.*, Ia, q.45, a.4; q.39, a.3); *simpliciter et per seipsam* (VII *Metaph.*, lect. 1, n.1248; *Summa theol.*, IIIa, q.11, a.5, ad 3; *De Malo*, q.3, a.2, ad 3); *principaliter et maxime* (VII *Metaph.*, lect. 2, n.1274; X *Metaph.*, lect. 4, n.1331; XII *Metaph.*, lect. 1, n.2417). The reason for this is that it exists in itself, "quia subsistit."

St. Thomas takes delight in stressing this point. Thus it is that all the articles which treat of the unity of the existence of Christ, "utrum sit unum esse in Christo?" commence with the same affirmation of the principle: "The subsistent being is that which possesses *esse*, as belonging to that which is." III *Sentent.*, d.6, q.2, a.2, (1254–56). "*Esse* . . . is attributed to that which properly and truly possesses *esse*, or which is; and thus it is attributed only to substance, which *subsists per se*." *Quodl.* IX, q.2, (1256).—"*Esse* pertains to the *hypostasis* . . . as to that which has *esse*," *Summa theol.*, IIIa, q.17, a.2 (1272). —"*Esse* properly and truly is said of the subsistent *suppositum*." *Quaestio disputata de unione Verbi incarnati*" (1272).—Confer L. De Raeymaeker, "De betekenis van 'esse' volgens de H. Thomas van Aquino," in *Tijdschrift voor Philosophie*, t.VIII, 1946, pp. 423–429.—The problem of "suppositality" will be treated later on, in Chapt. VIII, pp. 240–247.

[75] "For the subsistent being is that which has *esse*, as something belonging to that which is, although it belongs to the nature or the form, as something belonging to that by which a thing is. Hence neither the nature of the thing nor its parts are properly said to be, if *esse* is taken in the aforesaid way (*scil.*, as *actus entis*, and not as essence, nor again as copula). Similarly, neither the accidents are said to be, but the complete *suppositum*, which exists, affected by all these accidents." III *Sentent.*, d.6, q.2, a.2. Cf. *loc. cit.*, ad 1; *Quodl.* IX, q.2; *Summa theol.*, IIIa, q.17, a.2, corp. and ad 1; *Quaestio de unione Verbi incarnati*.

[76] "In one way substance is called the quiddity of a thing which the definition signifies. . . . Now this substance the Greeks call οὐσίαν, which we can call essence. In another way substance is called the subject or the *suppositum*, which subsists in the genus of substance." *Summa theol.*, Ia, q.29, a.2. Cf. X *Metaph.*, lect. 3 (edit. Cathala, n.1979).

[77] "Forms do not have *esse*, but the composites have *esse* through the forms." *Summa theol.*, Ia, q.65, a.4. "(Form) is called *ens* on account of this that through it something exists." *Summa theol.*, IIIa, q.17, a.2. Cf. Ia, q.9, a.2, ad 3; II *Gent.*, c.54.

existence; [78] a being can be found in possession of existence, only if it
is such a reality, only if it contains a determined quiddity. Now it is
the substantial form, which is the principle of determination, the
actus [79] of the fundamental quiddity; and this is why in every material reality, hylomorphically composed, prime matter is necessarily
united to the form as a complement,[80] which is indispensable for the
constitution of a substance capable of being the subject, receptive of
esse.[81] It is only in this well defined sense that form can be called the
principium essendi, the principle of existence.[82] It goes without saying that prime matter, which St. Thomas conceived as a pure potency
and not as an inchoative act, has no relation to the *esse*, and it participates in existence only by reason of its actual union with the form.[83]

Esse can also be considered *secundum quid* (according to a certain
point of view), from the aspect of accidental determinations, *esse
accidentale*. Now, in reality, an accident rests on substance as on its
principle of individuation; hence, it presupposes the existence of this
latter, *esse simpliciter*. Undoubtedly, accidental determinations are
real, and they can therefore be considered from the point of view
of *esse;* since, however, they rely on substance, and therefore on the
existence of the *suppositum*, their reality is not fundamental or first,
but comes in the second place. Accidents have *esse secundum*, and
this is not subsistence, the "esse by which a thing subsists"; [84] or the
esse superadditum, added, namely, to the *esse* of the substance and

---

[78] "The substantial form, however, gives the *esse simpliciter*." *Summa theol.*,
Ia, q. 76, a. 4; cf. a. 6.

[79] "The form through itself makes the thing to be in act, since by its essence it
is act, nor does it give the *esse* through some medium." *Summa theol.*, Ia, q. 76,
a. 7.—"*Esse* belongs *per se* to the form, which is *actus*. Hence matter actually
acquires *esse* by this fact that it acquires the form." *Ibid.*, q. 75, a. 6.

[80] "Form is said to be a *principium essendi*, because it is the complement of
substance, whose act is *ipsum esse*." II *Gent.*, c. 54. "The soul in Christ gives
esse to the body, inasmuch as it makes it actually animated, which is the same
as giving it the complement of nature and of the species." *Summa theol.*, IIIa,
q. 18, a. 2, ad 4.

[81] "Through the form the substance becomes the proper subject of that which
is *esse*." II *Gent.*, c. 55. Cf. *De Spiritualibus creaturis*, q. 1, a. 1; III *Sent.*, d. 6,
q. 2, corp.; *Summa theol.*, Ia, q. 42, a. 1, ad 1.

[82] II *Gent.*, c. 54.

[83] "In the nature of corporeal things matter does not *per se* participate in *esse*
itself, but it does this through the form." *De spirit. creaturis*, q. 1, a. 1. "(Matter)
has *esse* in act by means of the substantial form, which makes (*facit*) the *esse
simpliciter*." *Summa theol.*, Ia, q. 76, a. 6; Cf. q. 75, a. 6.

[84] *De ente et essentia*, c. 7.

dependent on it; [85] or the *esse secundum quid* [86] or *esse aliquid,* that is, they do not possess *esse simpliciter.*[87] An accident is not a being, a *suppositum,* any more than substance is; "it does not have *esse* but by it something, the *suppositum,* exists." [88] Besides, it is not according to its accidental determinations that the *suppositum* exists in itself, that it has *esse* or, strictly speaking, "exists," but according to its nature or substance. And if it is true to say that the fact of existing according to a substantial nature (for example, that of being a man) is opposed to the fact of not existing at all, "non esse simpliciter," and not merely to that of not being a man,[89] it is altogether otherwise with the fact of possessing such an accidental determination, since of itself accident always presupposes real substance.[90] The disappearance of the substance carries in its train the disappearance of the existence, of the very subsistence of the *suppositum,* and it is equivalent to the disappearance of all the reality which the *suppositum* carries with it.[91] On the contrary, the suppression of an accidental determination

[85] *IV Gent.,* c. 14.

[86] *De principiis naturae.*

[87] *In De Hebdomadibus Boethii,* c. 2.

[88] "The accident does not possess *esse,* but by means of it something is, and on this account it is said to be an *ens,* just as whiteness is said to be an *ens,* because by it something is white. And the same reason holds for all non-subsistent forms." *Summa theol.,* Ia, q. 90, a. 2. Cf. Ia–IIae, q. 55, a. 4, ad 1; IIIa, q. 11, a. 5, ad 3; IIIa, q. 17, a. 2; IIIa, q. 77, a. 1, ad 4; III *Sentent.,* d. 6, q. 2, a. 2; *Quodl.* IX, q. 2, a. 3; *Quaestio de unione Verbi incarnati.*

[89] Cf. *supra,* p. 128, note 73.

[90] "That to which an accident comes, is an *ens* complete in itself, constant in its *esse;* and this *esse* naturally precedes the accident which comes on later, and therefore an accident coming on later, by its conjunction with that to which it comes later, does not cause that *esse* in which the thing subsists, and through which it is an *ens per se;* but it causes a certain secondary *esse,* without which the subsistent thing can be understood to be, just as something first can be understood to be without the second." *De ente et essentia,* c. 7.

[91] "For what becomes a man, not only previously was not a man, but it is simply true to say that he was not. When, however, man becomes white it is not true to say that he did not previously exist, but only that previously he was not such." I *Physic.,* lect. 12.—"To be white is not *esse simpliciter* but *secundum quid.* This is evident from the fact, that when he begins to be white, we do not say that he begins to be *simpliciter,* but that he begins to be white. Hence it is evident that to be a man signifies *esse simpliciter,* but to be white signifies *esse secundum quid.*" VII *Metaph.,* lect. 1 (edit. Cath., n. 1256)—"There is a twofold *esse, scil.,* the essential or substantial *esse* of a thing, as, e.g., to be a man, and this is *esse simpliciter.* There is, however, another accidental *esse,* as, e.g., for man to be white, and this is *esse secundum quid.* . . . When the substantial form is introduced a thing is said to become *simpliciter,* just as we say, man comes into being or man is generated; when, however, an accidental form is

is not at all equivalent to the suppression of existence altogether, since it is not identified with the suppression of the substance, and since on the contrary it presupposes the reality of this substance, and therefore also the subsistence of the *suppositum* itself. And so the accidental *esse* is not *esse* unqualified, but an *esse aliquid,* for example, *esse album.* Also, we cannot translate it by "to exist," (a term which does not admit such qualification: we exist or do not exist, we do not exist white or black) but by "being in such or such a manner," for instance, being white. The reality of the accidents, their participation in existence, their *esse,* comes from their union with substance, just as the reality of prime matter, its participation in the subsistence of the *suppositum,* comes from its union with the substantial form. "The subject gives *esse* (existence) to the accident, because the accident does not have *esse* except through the subject." [92]

Strictly speaking, therefore, the term *esse* signifies "to exist" in the sense that we say that a being exists in itself, that it subsists, that it

---

introduced, a thing is not said to become *simpliciter,* but to become this." *De principiis naturae.*

St. Thomas insists on an analogous consideration beginning at least with the *Summa contra Gentiles,* every time that he treats the question, "whether there is one esse in Christ?" The Word of God existed already before being man. This "esse simpliciter" cannot therefore be dependent on the human nature of Christ; consequently this nature, while being of the substantial order, is not the reason of the subsistence or the *esse,* but only of the *esse homo.* (Cf. IV *Gent.,* c. 49.) And what is added to the *esse simpliciter* of the Word is a "new relation of the personal *esse,* which existed before the human nature," (*Summa theol.,* IIIa, q. 17, a. 2), "because the person of the Son of God was before the humanity which was assumed" (*Quaestio de unione Verbi incarnati*), so much so that we have reason to speak of a secondary *esse,* although it is not an accidental *esse.*" (*Ibid.*) This is pretty much the same as when we speak of an *esse secundum quid* in regard to accidental realities.

And thus St. Thomas succeeds in neatly delimiting the mystery of the person of Christ; in the natural order the existence is nothing more than that which corresponds to the whole substance. (*Esse homo* for a man is the same thing as *esse simpliciter;* and to cease to be a man, for a man, is nothing other than to cease to exist. Cf. the texts from St. Thomas already cited in this note). In the supernatural order, on the contrary, the human nature of Christ, substantial as it is, does not bring with it existence *simpliciter,* since this human nature has been assumed into the Person of the Word, already subsisting, and it has as its effect that the Word should be man, and not simply that He should be: here is the whole mystery. See why St. Thomas is led to speak of an *esse secundarium* in regard to the human nature of Christ. In *De Ente et Essentia,* c. 7, he had already used the expression *esse secundum* in an analogous sense, to designate the *esse accidentale,* but later for this he had regularly substituted *esse secundum quid* to indicate the accidental reality.

[92] *De principiis naturae.*

has an *esse*.[93] *Esse* and *ens* cannot be treated as synonyms, since there exist many beings, *entia*, every one of which is defined by its quiddity, nature, essence. How can we make the relation, uniting the essence and existence of a real being more precise? St. Thomas sees here a relation of potency to act.

In his first works the Angelic Doctor expresses himself as follows: [94] If we take the term *esse* to express real being, without doubt we can use it to designate the essence—and this is done at times—but it is better to reserve it to indicate the act which corresponds to this essence, that is, *actus essentiae*.[95] The act of which there is question in that case is by no means an action, an accidental act, "the second act which is the operation," but the first act, an act which is on the level of substance, of that, namely, which is the most fundamental in the

---

[93] St. Thomas establishes a distinction between *ens simpliciter* and *ens secundum quid*, just as he distinguishes *esse simpliciter* and *esse secundum quid*. *Ens simpliciter* designates substance, in the sense of a *suppositum*, which is *absolute* and *per prius, simpliciter* and *per seipsam, principaliter* and *maxime, proprie* and *per se*, i.e. it has *esse;* it is subsistent *in esse suo*, that is, in its own to be.
Ens secundum quid designates the accident which is real only dependently on the subsistent reality, i.e. *per substantiam, per posterius, secundarie;* and which ought rather to be called *ens entis*, i.e., a reality which belongs to a subsistent being. "Accidents are called *entia*, not because they are, but rather because something is by means of them." XII *Metaph.*, lect. 1 (Cathala, n.2419).
St. Thomas expresses himself in the same way on the subject of essence: "(Essence) is truly and properly in substances, but in some way and *secundum quid* in accidents." As a matter of fact, every subsisting reality contains an essence, "in as far as through it and in it an *ens* has *esse*." *De ente et essentia*, c. 1.
[94] See the texts cited above, p. 127, note 70.
[95] In I *Sentent.*, d.33, q.1, a.1, ad 1, St. Thomas adds the following: "The act of the essence (just as *vivere*, which is the *esse* for living things, is the *act of the soul*), not the second act, which is the operation, but the first act. Hence, he compares the relation of essence and existence, to that of substance and accident; the vital activity, *vivere*, is an accidental determination, of which the soul, the principle of life, is the substantial foundation: "it is the accidental act of the soul." But every comparison limps: the *esse* is by no means "the second act which is the operation," as is the vital activity. On the contrary, *esse* is the *actus primus*, i.e., an act in the order of substance.
As regard the Aristotelian adage "*vivere* is the *esse* of living things," St. Thomas observes that the term *esse* is not to be taken in the sense of existing without further qualification, but that it designates the reality inasmuch as it possesses a specific degree of perfection by reason of the formal principle which it contains. "*Vivere* is a kind of *esse*, specified by a special principle of being." III *Sentent.*, d.6, q.2, ad 1. Cf. *De anima*, quaestio unica, a.1, corp. We have already said (*supra*, p. 130) in what sense St. Thomas calls the substantial form, *scil.*, the principle of specific perfection, the *principium essendi*. In the adage quoted, *esse*, therefore, is considered on the side of its union with the nature or the quiddity.

being.[96] This act of real being, "esse in re," belongs to the nature of the subsistent being, and it results from the internal principles which constitute this nature, just as an act derives from the potency corresponding to it, for example, as activity derives from the *suppositum:* "Sicut lucere est actus lucentis." [97]

In his last works St. Thomas uses similar expressions: Accident differs from substance and is added to it; in the same way the *esse* of a being differs from its essence and is added to it. Assuredly, it would be a mistake to consider this *esse* as a predicamental accident; really, it is situated on the plane of substance and not on that of accidental activity, and it is, so to speak, the constitutive principles of the essence itself which constitute the *esse*.[98]

St. Thomas therefore distinguishes essence and existence, and he reduces their union to that of potency and act. Further, he strives to make their relations more precise by comparing them to those which obtain between potency and act along the line of activity; hence, the examples which he gives (to live, to illumine) and the verbs which he uses (to result, to be constituted). Still, he never fails to emphasize how the case of essence and existence differs from the others: existence is not in any way a predicamental accident; [99] it is not on

---

[96] The principle of pure potency, *scil.,* of total determinability, is called prime matter, i.e. matter or determinability in the fundamental or substantial order. In this sense we could call the substantial form the first form. Similarly, *esse* is called *actus primus,* i.e., that which corresponds to the quiddity of the being, to the substantial principles (i.e., matter and form) which constitute its fundamental essence, its substance.

[97] "*Esse,* which pertains to the nature of a thing, is spoken of as it is distributed in the ten categories. And this *esse* indeed is in the thing, and it is the act of a being that results from the principles of a thing, just as *lucere* is the act of something that shines. Sometimes, however, *esse* is used for essence, according to which the thing is, because by *actus* their principles (as potencies and habits) are wont to be signified." III *Sent.,* d.6, q.2, a.2. Cf. *Quodl.* IX, q.2, a.3: "*esse* resulting from these things, from which the unity of the thing is integrated." There is question here of the nature or the substance in opposition to the accidental principles. The nature is the reason of the specific perfection and of the individual identity of the *suppositum,* and by that same token it is the reason of the substantial unity of this being; on this nature the *actus essendi,* or the *esse,* confers existence.—Cf. *Quodl.* II, q.2, a.3, ad 2: "*esse* . . . being not as an accident, but as the actuality of every substance whatever."

[98] "For the *esse* of a thing, although it is something other than its essence, is not to be understood as if it were something superadded by way of accident, but as if it were something constituted by the principles of the essence. And therefore this name (*scil., ens*) which is conferred by the *esse* itself, signifies the same thing as the name which is conferred by the very essence" (*scil., res*). IV *Metaph.,* lect. 2 (edit. Cathala, p. 187, n. 558).

[99] "The opinion of Avicenna was that *unum* and *ens* always predicate an

the plane of action, but on that of substance, or nature, the fundamental principle of action. Activity is *actus secundus,* whereas existence is *actus primus.* Nevertheless, it would be inaccurate to say that existence is an internal principle of substance, as is the substantial form which is a quidditative act; on the contrary, the act of a being, *esse,* is distinct from the substance. That is to say, in material beings, *esse* is distinct from the substance composed of prime matter, the principle of individuation, and of substantial form, the principle of specific perfection; and it is to this substance, taken in its entirety, that there corresponds an *esse* as an act to its potency.

Such is the conception which St. Thomas develops from his first writings. From the start he likewise insists on the transcendental character of the idea of being, *ens,* appealing to the authority of Avicenna and Aristotle. This idea is the first of all ideas, it is implied in every intellectual operation, and it applies to all reality.[100] It is not a generic concept, as Aristotle has well shown, since it cannot receive any extrinsic complement. Nevertheless, the Stagyrite had failed to say how such an idea, the most universal of all, could still acquire any determination whatsoever. St. Thomas examines this question, and he solves it as follows: The determination, not being able to come from the outside, ought to be found on the inside. It is merely an "explicitation" consisting in expressing the modes of being which the idea of being already contained, but implicitly.[101] The distinction of

---

accident. . . . This, however, is not true. . . . And so I say that the substantial *esse* of a thing is not an accident; . . . strictly speaking it is not an accident. And as for what St. Hilary says, I say that accident in a broad sense is said to be everything which is not a part of the essence, and such is the *esse* in created things; for only in God is the *esse* His essence." *Quodl.* XII, q.5, a.5.—"The question *an est* is different from the question *quid est.* Hence, since everything which is outside of the essence of a thing is called an accident, the *esse* which answers to the question *an est* is an accident." *Quodl.* II, q.2, a.3. Cf. *De potentia,* q.5, a.4, ad 3; X *Metaph.,* lect. 3 (edit. Cathala, n.1982).

[100] "*Ens,* however, and essence are the first things conceived by the intellect, as Avicenna says in the beginning of his metaphysics." (*De ente et essentia,* prooemium). "That which the intellect first conceives as most known and into which it resolves all its concepts, is *ens,* as Avicenna says in the beginning of his metaphysics." *De Veritate,* q.1, a.1. "*Ens* comes first in the conception of the intellect, because everything is cognoscible in as far as it is in act, as is said in the ninth book of the Metaphysics. . . . Hence *ens* is the proper object of the intellect; and thus it is the first intelligible, just as sound is the first thing audible." *Summa theol.,* Ia, q.5, a.2. "That which first comes into our apprehension is *ens,* whose understanding is included in everything whatsoever any one apprehends." *Summa theol.,* Ia–IIae, q.94, a.2.

[101] "*Ens* cannot be a genus. In this respect some things are said to be added

being and its modes, therefore, makes it possible to safeguard for the idea of being its transcendental character, while we leave room for the development of ideas, which forces itself on us with such evidence.

St. Thomas exercised his subtlety very especially on this point, above all in the course of the last ten years of his life. Under the influence of Neo-Platonic writings [102] the Angelic Doctor takes pleasure in bringing to light the fact that *esse* is the fundamental perfection, the universal value.[103] Thereafter, he will call *esse* not only act, actuality, complement, but also perfection, good, the formal element, and he will emphasize quite insistently that *esse* is this perfection in all things without exception.[104] This conception of being St. Thomas expresses as his very own; "this which *I call esse*" he opposes strictly to those who see in the idea of being only the most abstract and the poorest of all ideas.[105]

---

to *ens*, in as far as they express its mode, which is not expressed by the name of *ens* itself." *De Veritate*, q.1, a.1. Cf. *De principiis naturae; I Gent.*, c.17, c.25; *De Potentia*, q.3, a.16, ad 4; *Summa Theol.*, Ia, q.3, a.5; III *Metaph.*, lect. 8 (n.432); V *Metaph.*, lect. 9 (n.889).

[102] Notably, the *Institutio theologica* of Proclus, and his *De causis*, which St. Thomas had had occasion to study more closely.

[103] Cf. Joseph De Finance, "Être et agir dans la philosophie de saint Thomas" (*Bibliothèque des Archives de Philosophie*), Paris, 1945, pp. 111–118 (L'excellence de l'*esse*).—Étienne Gilson, "Le Thomisme. Introduction à la philosophie de saint Thomas d'Aquin." (*Études de philosophie médiévale I*), 4th ed., Paris, 1942, pp. 41–51.

[104] "*Esse* is the complement of every form." *Quodl.* XII, q.5, a.5.—"*Esse* is the actuality of every form or nature." *Summa theol.*, Ia, q.3, a.4.—"The perfections of all things belong to the perfection of existing." *Ibid.*, Ia, q.4, a.2. "*Esse* itself is the most perfect of all things; . . . *actus;* . . . *actuality* of all things." *Ibid.*, Ia, q.4, a.1, ad 3.—"The *esse* of any thing whatever is something good and likewise a perfection." *Ibid.*, Ia, q.20, a.2. "The *esse* is that which is more intimate and more profound in anything, since it is the formal element with respect to everything in the thing." *Ibid.*, Ia, q.8, a.1. Cf. *Ibid.*, q.3, a.4; *De divinis nominibus*. Already in I *Gent.*, c.28, we can read: "All the nobility of everything belongs to it in proportion to its *esse*."

[105] In *De potentia*, q.7, a.2, object. 9, the idea is expressed that *esse* is that which is most imperfect and the least determined. "Besides, that which is most imperfect must not be attributed to God, who is most perfect. But *esse* is most imperfect, just as prime matter; for just as prime matter is determined by all the forms, so *esse*, since it is most imperfect, has to be determined by means of all the proper predicaments. Therefore, just as prime matter is not in God, so neither ought *esse* to be attributed to the divine substance."

St. Thomas answers that, on the contrary, *esse* implies every perfection. Three times he declares that it is in this way that he intends to understand *esse*. "To the ninth objection we must reply that 'this which I call *esse*' is the most perfect of all things, and this is clear from the fact that act is always more perfect

If perfection is found on the side of existence as well as on that of quiddity, if existence is a good, a value, nothing prevents us from applying fully the theory of participation to the domain of being itself. There are degrees of being; different beings participate in existence according to the measure of their essence. The fundamental principle of ontology is brought to light: existence is the first act, the unique source of all participation; existence does not participate in anything, but everything participates in existence.[106] This development of the doctrine of St. Thomas, in particular the fact of emphasizing *esse*, understood as the value of being, in which all reality participates, likewise betrays itself in the way in which the Angelic Doctor presents the relation of essence and existence.[107]

Under the influence of Avicenna, St. Thomas grounds himself principally, in the beginning, on considerations of the logical order. For "whatever is not of the concept of essence or quiddity, comes from

---

than potency. But any designated form whatever is not understood to be in act, except through this that it is placed in existence. For humanity or 'fire-ness' (*igneitas*) can be considered as existing in the potency of matter, or in the power of the agent, or even in the intellect; but that which has *esse*, is rendered actually existing. Hence it is evident that 'this which I call esse,' is the actuality of all acts, and on this account it is the perfection of all perfections. Neither must we understand that to that which I call *esse*, something is added which is more formal than it, determining it, as act determines potency; for the *esse* which is of this kind, is other in essence than that to which it is added as something to be determined. But nothing can be added to *esse* which would be extraneous to it, since nothing is extraneous to it except *non ens* which cannot be either form or matter. Hence, *esse* is not determined by something else as potency is by act, but rather as act by potency. For in the definition of forms the proper matter is placed in the place of the difference, just as when it is said that the soul is the act of the physical, organic body. And in this way this *esse* is distinguished from that *esse*, inasmuch as it belongs to such or such a nature."

[106] *De anima*, a.6, ad 2; *De malo*, q.16, a.9, ad 5. In regard to the Neo-Platonic list of perfections, *scil.*, to be, to live, to think, cf. I *Sentent.*, d.8, q.1, a.1, sol. *Ratio* of Dionysius: q.2, a.2; d.17, q.1, a.2, ad 3; III *Sentent.*, d.30, q.1, a.2; *De potentia*, q.7, a.2, ad 9; *Summa theol.*, Ia, q.4, a.2, ad 3; Ia–IIae, q.9, a.5, ad 2. According to St. Thomas, *esse* is the supreme perfection, and it is therefore superior to life and intelligence, but living beings (*viventia*) and a fortiori, beings endowed with intelligence (*intelligentia*) surpass in perfection those which exist, devoid of life and intelligence (*existentia*). In this last case there is no question simply of the perfection of being, but of a very inferior degree of participation in being, *scil.*, of a degree inferior to those which life and intelligence carry with them. These last represent also degrees of participation in being, which is the fundamental and universal value.

[107] A study of the arguments of St. Thomas in favor of the distinction between essence and existence has been made by Cornelio Fabro, C.P.S., "*La nozione metafisica di partecipazione secondo S. Tomaso d'Aquino,*" Milan, 1939, pp. 215–250.

outside and forms a composition with essence." [108] Or again, "If, however, quiddity is not *esse* itself, it must have acquired *esse* from another." [109] Likewise: "Whatever exists in a genus, has a quiddity differing from *esse*." [110] At other times, he advances the principle which enunciates the unicity of every simple perfection, *perfectio separata*.[111] Time and again he begins with the fact that all finite reality is caused, to conclude from it that the being which it possesses is a received being; [112] only the subsistent Being is uncaused.[113] In his first writings he had already observed, now and again, that if two beings resemble each other, at least one of the two must be composite on the plane of this resemblance.[114] This consideration opened the way to the doctrine of participation. Beginning with 1266 especially, St. Thomas regularly relies on participation in the value of being to conclude to the distinction between essence and existence in every finite being.[115]

---

[108] *De ente et essentia*, c.5 (c.4 of Roland-Gosselin's edition). Cf. II *Sentent.*, d.3, q.1, a.1; *Compendium theologiae*, c.11.

[109] I *Sentent.*, d.8, q.5, a.2, corp.; q.3, a.2; q.4, a.2; d.19, q.2, a.1. *De ente et essentia*, c.5; II *Sentent.*, d.3, q.3, a.1, ad 4; d.37, q.1, a.1; *De Veritate*, q.8, a.8; *Quodl.* IX, q.4, a.6; II *Gent.*, c.52, arg. 3, 4, 5; *Summa theol.*, Ia, q.3, a.7, ad 1; q.4, a.3, ad 3; *De causis*, lect. 4.

[110] I *Sentent.*, d.8, q.4, a.2, The third rather subtle reason is Avicenna's; d.19, q.4, a.2; *De Veritate*, q.27, a.1, ad 8; I *Gent.*, c.25; *Summa theol.*, Ia, q.3, a.5; *Compend. theol.*, c.14, *Item* (Omne quod est in specie); *De spirit. creaturis*, a.1, ad 10.

[111] I *Sentent.*, d.8, q.4, a.1, ad 2; I *Gent.*, c.28; *De Causis*, lect. 9; *Compend. theologiae*, c.15, *Item; Comment. in Evang. Joannis*, c.3, lect. 6.

[112] *De ente et essentia*, c.5; *De Veritate*, q.8, a.8 (This attributes the argument to Avicenna).

[113] II *Gent.*, c.52, arg. 3, 4, 5.

[114] I *Sentent.*, d.48, q.1, a.1, sol.; II *Sentent.*, d.16, q.1, a.1, ad 3; *Summa theol.*, Ia, q.4, a.3, ad 3.

[115] II *Gent.* (1259), c.52. St. Thomas here appeals implicitly to participation, considered in the dynamic order, *scil.*, *a primo agente* (by the first agent).

In the commentary on the *De Hebdomadibus* of Boethius (1257–58) for the first time St. Thomas makes an explicit appeal to participation outside of every consideration of causality. The same manner of procedure is found, later, in *Summa theol.* (1266), Ia, q.3, a.4; q.75, a.5, ad 4; VIII *Physic.* (1268), lect. 21; *De Causis* (after 1268), lect. 4 and 9; *De malo* (1268), q.16, a.3; *De spirit. creaturis* (1266–68), a.1; *De anima* (1269–1270), a.6, ad 2; *Quodl.* II (1270), q.2, a.3; *Quodl.* III (1270), q.8, a.20; *Quodl.* XII (1271–72), q.5, a.5; *Comp. theol.* (1271–73), c.68; *De substantiis separatis* (1272–73), c.3, cc.5–9.

The composition of the finite and the infinite in every reality other than the One (according to Proclus and the book *De causis*), that of *esse* and the *forma* (according to the *De causis*), that of *esse* and that which is (according to Boethius), have all been interpreted by St. Thomas in the sense of a composition of essence and existence.

If we take these observations into account, notably the manner in which St. Thomas compares the composition of essence and existence to that of substance and accident, and the development which he gave to his doctrine in the sense of a philosophy of participation, it is not at all possible to admit that the distinction of essence and existence of the finite being could be reduced, according to him, to a distinction of the logical order.. There must be question here of a composition of reality itself.

This conclusion is forced upon us all the more, if we consider the attitude which St. Thomas took in the controversy of universal hylomorphism. The Scholastics found themselves generally agreeing in the affirmation that no creature, material or spiritual, can be simple. They cite in this connection the text of Boethius: "In everything that exists except the First, there is this and this." [116] Already in the twelfth century this was the opinion of Gilbert de la Porrée,[117] of Peter Lombard, and of many others. In the 13th century, notably under the influence of the theories of Avicebron, a goodly number of authors tried to interpret this non-simplicity in the sense of a hylomorphic composition.[118] An angel, as well as a material creature, would then be composed of prime matter and substantial form. St. Thomas set himself resolutely against this doctrine; [119] according to him prime matter is the substantial principle of passivity and of quantity, so that there is no sense in speaking of "spiritual matter," [120] from the moment that we admit that a spiritual being is not passive

---

[116] *De Trinitate*, c.II (P. L. 64, col. 1250).

[117] Gilbert de la Porrée introduces the expression "id quo est."

[118] Notably Alexander of Hales and St. Bonaventure, O.F.M., Roland of Cremona, Richard Fishacre and Robert Kilwardby, O.P., and the secular priest Gerard of Abbeville.

[119] I *Sentent.*, d.8, q.5, a.2; *II Sent.*, d.3, q.1, a.1 and 4; d.17, q.1, a.2; *De ente et essentia*, c.5 (edit. Laurent, p. 122); *Quodl.* IX, q.4, a.6; II *Gent.*, c.50, 51, 93; *De potentia*, q.9, a.1; a.3, ad 5; *De malo*, q.16, a.1, ad 18; *De spir. creaturis*, a.1; a.8, ad 14; *Summa theol.*, Ia, q.50, a.2, a.4; q.76, a.2, ad 1; *De unitate intell.*, c.7; *De substant. sep.*, cc.7, 8; *Summa theol.*, IIIa, q.77, a.2.

[120] Aristotle calls the object of mathematics "intelligible matter" "ὕλη νοητή" (*Metaphysics* VII, 10, 1036 a9; VIII, 4, 1045 a34). Plotinus carried the notion of intelligible matter to the ontological plane of the ideas (*Enneads*, II, 4, 3; 4, 5; 4, 16; 5, 3; III, 8, 11). It is on him that Avicebron depends, and it is also to Neo-Platonism that the Augustinian notion of "spiritual matter" attaches. (St. Augustine, *De Genesi ad litt.*, V, 5; VII, 6, 7, 9, 17). The doctrine of spiritual matter is likewise found in the *De unitate*, a work of Gundissalinus (12th century) which was for a long time attributed to Boethius. St. Thomas already had recognized that this ascription was false: "It is not Boethius', as the style itself indicates." (*Quaestio de spirit. creaturis*, a.1, ad 21).

and that it has no quantity.[121] When it was objected to the Angelic
Doctor that in this case he had to admit that an angel is a simple being
—which would be erroneous, since simplicity is a divine prerogative
—he rejected this conclusion, by laying down that, even though an
angel does not contain hylomorphic composition, it is none the less
composed of that "which is" and of "*esse* by which it is," of essence
and existence.[122] There is no reason whatever to believe that St.
Thomas considered this composition of essence and existence to be
less real than that (namely, matter and form), for which he substituted it.[123]

Moreover, a good number of St. Thomas' immediate disciples are
convinced champions of the real distinction, and some of them affirm
that on this point they are merely harking back to the thought of the
Master. Finally, certain contemporaries of St. Thomas, who declared
themselves adversaries of the real distinction explicitly attributed to
him this doctrine. This is notably the case with Siger of Brabant.[124]

How does it happen, then, in the 20th century that some have been
able to doubt that the Angelic Doctor had ever admitted the real dis-

---

[121] Unless you would wish to call any potency whatsoever by the name of
matter, as St. Thomas observes: "but this is not said properly according to the
ordinary use of words." *De spir. creaturis*, a.1, corp., *in fine*. Cf. II *Sent.*, d.3,
q.1, a.1, c.*in fine; Quodl*. IX, q.4, a.6.

[122] *De ente et essentia*, c.5; II *Sent.*, d.3, q.1, a.1; *Quodl*. IX, q.4, a.6; II
Gent., c.52; *De spir. creaturis*, a.1; *Summa theol.*, Ia, q.50, a.2; *De substantiis
separatis*, cc.4–6.

[123] Cf. Corn. Fabro, C.P.S., "Circa la divisione dell'essere in atto e potenza
secondo San Tomaso," *Divus Thomas* (Piacenza), t. XLII, 1939, pp. 529–552.
Idem, "Un itinéraire de S. Thomas. L'éstablissement de la distinction réelle entre
essence et existence," *Revue de Philosophie*, t. XXXIX, 1939, pp. 285–310.

[124] Siger of Brabant writes that Thomas of Aquin follows a middle path between the real identity of essence and existence and the real distinction advocated
by Avicenna, i.e., according to the thesis attributed to Avicenna by the Latin
Scholastics: existence is an "accident." He presents the theory of St. Thomas
as follows: "*Esse* is something added to the essence of the thing, not pertaining
to the essence of the thing; not that it is an accident, but it is something added,
constituted by the essence or by the principles of the essence." Siger de Brabant,
Quaestiones in Metaphysicam, q.Ia post Prol. Cf. F. Van Steenberghen, "La
composition constitutive de l'être fini," *Revue néoscolastique de Philosophie*,
t. 41, 1938, pp. 508–518.
As a matter of fact we read in the Commentary of St. Thomas on the fourth
book of Aristotle's *Metaphysics* (edit. Cathala, p. 187, n.558): "For the *esse*
of a thing, although it is other than its essence, is not to be understood as something superadded by way of accident, but it is, as it were, constituted by the
principles of the essence. And therefore this name, which is imposed by the *esse*
itself, signifies the same as the name which is imposed by the essence itself
(*scil., res*)."

tinction betwen essence and existence in the creature? [125] This is the reason. In 1276, two years after the death of St. Thomas, one of his disciples, Giles of Rome (1247–1306), of the Hermits of St. Augustine, published a work entitled *Theoremata de esse et essentia*, to set forth and defend the thesis of the real distinction between essence and existence.[126] He there states that it is his intention to treat of the problem with precision and method, because up till then everybody had neglected to do so; and he insists on the special importance of this question, in particular in theology. The theory which he proposes and justifies at length, is given as a new solution; between essence and existence there is a real distinction, "a distinction between thing and thing." Essence and existence are inseparable, yet they are two things, "duae res"; in material realities, composed of matter and form, the "to be" is a third thing.

The work of Giles of Rome provoked a very spirited reaction at the University of Paris. Henry of Ghent, master of theology, particularly set himself against this novelty.[127] In a very short time there appeared a fairly considerable number of writings, entitled *Quaestiones de essentia et esse;* a bulky literature treated of this problem, and the thesis of the real distinction became one of the most controverted points of Scholasticism, and it has remained such even to our day.

Would not Giles of Rome be the inventor of this real distinction?

---

[125] Max Limbourg, S.J., *De distinctione essentiae ab existentia theses quattuor,* Ratisbonae, 1883.—J. M. Piccirelli, S.J., *Disquisitio metaphysica, theologica, critica de distinctione actuatam inter essentiam existentiamque creati entis intercedente, ac praecipue de mente Angelici Doctoris circa eandem quaestionem,* Naples, 1906. M. Chossat, S.J., in *Dictionnaire de théologie catholique* (Vacant et Mangenot), t. IV, art. "Dieu," (sa nature selon les scolastiques), col. 1151–1243, especially col. 1180.—Fr. Pelster, S.J., *Acta congressus thomistici,* Rome, 1925, p. 26; "La quaestio disputata de S. Thomas De unione Verbi incarnati, sa date et son importance," *Archives de Philosophie,* vol. III, cah. 2, *Études sur S. Thomas,* Paris, 1925; Thomas de Sutton, O.P., *Quaestio de reali distinctione inter essentiam et esse* (*Opuscula et textus, series scholastica*), Münster, 1928, Introductio, p. 8; Review of Roland-Gosselin's "De Ente et Essentia de saint Thomas d'Aquin" (Le Saulchoir, Kain, 1926), in *Scholastik,* t. III, 1928, pp. 265–266.—P. Descoqs, S.J., *Archives de Philosophie,* vol. IV, cah. 4, *Bibliographie critique,* Paris, 1927, pp. 132 sqq. "Sur la division de l'être en acte et en puissance d'après S. Thomas," in *Revue de Philosophie,* t. XXXVII, 1938, pp. 410–429; *Sur la division . . . Nouvelles précisions, op. cit.,* t. XXXIX, 1939, pp. 233–252, 361–370.

[126] Edg. Hocedez, S.J., *Aegidii Romani Theoremata De Esse et Essentia.* Text preceded by an historical and critical introduction (Museum lessianum, section philosophique, n. 12), Louvain: 1930.

[127] Cf. Edg. Hocedez, S.J., "Le premier quodlibet d'Henri de Gand" (1276), *Gregorianum,* t. 9, 1928.

Some have thought so.[128] It is a fact that on the point of the real distinction St. Thomas never encountered any opposition in his life time. Would this not be because he never taught this thesis? For, hardly had Giles of Rome made his point of view known, when a violent attack was unleashed against him. Furthermore, Giles never appeals to his master, Thomas of Aquin,[129] but pretends to set forth an original work. His adversary, Henry of Ghent, likewise declares that the thesis is new. The camp of the disciples of St. Thomas is divided; one part defends the real distinction and some of them attribute it to St. Thomas; another part is opposed to it, and others finally refuse to commit themselves.[130] At the beginning of the 14th century authors continue to speak of "Giles' distinction" to designate the real distinction between essence and existence; it is only considerably later that they will call it the *Thomistic* distinction.

How are we to account for these facts? First of all, we must remark that St. Thomas did not devote any *opusculum* or any question to the examination of the problem in its entirety. The reason is that the subject was not brought up explicitly; but he constantly speaks of it in its applications. He expresses himself with great reserve; essence and existence are never called two things, nor is it ever said explicitly that the thesis of the real distinction is one of the pillars of the philosophical and theological system. Hence we can understand why a goodly number of the Angelic Doctor's disciples had not at first grasped all the import of the problem and even why they needed time and study in order to disengage the genuine thought of the Master. Moreover, it was only towards the middle of the 14th century that unanimity was established on this point in the Thomistic school.[131] Since then, the real distinction between the real principle

---

[128] This, notably, was the opinion of M. Chossat, *op. cit.*

[129] This fact has its importance, for in his writings on the unity of the substantial form, which appeared in 1277 and 1278, he sets himself down as a convinced champion of St. Thomas' theses on the matter.

[130] Cf. M. Grabmann, in *Acta Hebdomadae thomisticae*, Rome, November 1923, pp. 139 ff. In 1925 in the *Acta primi Congressus thomistici*, Rome, p. 262, he made the statement: "At first I thought it more probable that Thomas did not teach the real distinction, on account of the dissension among his disciples. Afterwards, however, I came to be persuaded that he really held this opinion, considering especially the doctrine of St. Thomas' first disciples. I have already set this forth at the time of the 'Thomistic Week,' and today I confirm the same opinion: It is historically evident that St. Thomas taught the real distinction."

[131] At the beginning of the 14th century Hervé of Nedellec rejects the thesis of the real distinction. He is, none the less, an admirer of the Angelic Doctor and it was he who as general of the Dominican Order worked for the canoniza-

of existence and the principle of essence in the creature is considered the fundamental thesis of Thomistic philosophy.[132]

Giles of Rome succeeded in rendering the problem explicit; he propounded the question vigorously and insisted on the capital importance of this doctrine, not only in philosophy but also and especially in the realm of theology. He even asserted that no dogmatic truth whatever can be developed as it ought, if account is not taken of the thesis on the real distinction. These last assertions were assuredly novel, and they provoked opposition in the faculty of theology. The question of the real distinction was immediately studied seriously, and in a short time different opinions were propounded.[133]

Giles proposed a clear, clean-cut thesis, and expounded it methodically; it was, however, wanting in subtlety. Hence it provoked lively opposition immediately, and the controversy about the real distinction has clung to Giles' formula all too naturally and for such a long time. St. Thomas, who had rejected the opinion attributed to Avicenna, according to which existence in a creature is an accidental principle, would without doubt have likewise refused to subscribe to the formula of Giles. For he would not have wished to call the existence of the creature a thing (*res*), for only the subsistent subject is a thing; *ens* designates the same reality as *res*.[134] Constituent prin-

---

tion of St. Thomas (July 18, 1323). He secured likewise the teaching of Thomism in the Dominican houses of study. A decree of the general chapter of the Order, held at Metz in 1313, provides as follows: "that no Brother by reading, determining, answering, should dare openly to hold the contrary of what is commonly believed to be the opinion of the aforesaid Brother (Thomas)." It seems, therefore, that Hervé himself, the adversary of the real distinction, did not think that this was commonly considered in his time as one of Thomas' theses.

[132] Cf. N. Del Prado, O.P., *De veritate fundamentali philosophiae christianae*, Fribourg (Switz.), 1911.

[133] Giles of Rome himself observes in his *Quaestiones de Esse et Essentia:* "I reply by saying that on this point there are various opinions. Although now *for a long time* there have not been many opinions of the theologians on this point, still some great men have proposed without hesitation that in creatures *esse* and *essentia* do not really differ. We, however, hold the opinion that they are really distinct."

[134] "This name (*scil., ens*) which imposed by the *esse* itself, signifies the same thing as the name imposed by the essence itself (*scil., res*)." *In IV Metaphys.*, lect. 2, (edit. Cathala, p. 187, n.558).

On the subject of the double meaning of the word "res" and of the relation to be placed between "res" and "ens," St. Thomas writes: "The name 'res' is taken in two ways. *Simpliciter* 'res' is said to be that which has an *esse ratum et firmum* in nature, and it is thus called 'res,' because the name is used inasmuch as it has a certain quiddity or essence. 'Ens,' however, is used inasmuch

ciples have no reality outside of their correlation to each other; *esse* does not signify a being or a thing, but that by which the subsistent being exists. "Esse non est ens, sed est quo ens est." [135]

In the camp of the adversaries of the real distinction, various opinions have found favor. Some admit at most a distinction of pure reason between essence and existence: Siger of Brabant (+1281/4) and the Averrhoists; Godfrey of Fontaines (+1306), Hervé of Nedellec, O.P. (+1323), Peter of Auvergne (+1304), John Duns Scotus, O.F.M. (*circ.* 1267–1308), Durandus of Saint-Pourçain, O.P. (+1334).

James of Viterbo, O.S.A. (*circ.* 1255–1308), and at times, Nicholas Trivet, O.P. (beginning of the 14th century), distinguish essence and existence as the abstract and the concrete.

Henry of Ghent (+1293) in his first *Quodlibet* (1276) introduces a new distinction, *distinctio secundum intentiones:* [136] this is not a real distinction or a purely logical distinction, but a logical distinction founded on the relation which binds the finite being to the creative Cause. Richard of Middleton, O.F.M. (*circ.* 1249-after 1294), proposes practically the same solution, but notices besides, a second relation, that of existence and essence, thanks to which the existence makes of the essence a subsistent reality or an hypostasis.

Alexander of Alexandria, O.F.M. (+1314), admits a logical distinction "under a variety of aspects." Francis Suarez, S.J. (1548–1617), discovers between existence and essence merely a distinction of reason with a foundation, because they answer to two different questions about this being: "*Is* it?" and "*What* is it?" We have said above that the conception which Suarez makes his own in regard to the idea of being, necessarily excludes all analogy of proportionality from this idea. [137] He does not admit that existence is a perfection

---

as it has an *esse*, as Avicenna says, *Metaphys.*, tract. I, cap. VI, distinguishing the meaning of 'ens' and 'res.' But since 'res' is knowable on account of its essence, the word 'res' has been transferred to mean everything which can fall under knowledge or the intellect, inasmuch as 'res' is derived from 'reor, reris.' And in this way we speak of 'res rationis,' which do not have an *esse ratum* in nature, and negations and privations can also be called 'res,' just as they are called 'entia rationis,' as the Commentator says in IV *Metaphys.*, comm. 2." II *Sentent.*, d. 37, q. 1, a. 1, sol.

[135] "Just as we cannot say that *currere* itself runs, so we cannot say that the *esse* itself exists." *In librum De Hebdomadibus*, lect. 2, *explanatio.* "Esse itself is that by which substance exists, just as running is that by which a runner runs." *Summa theol.*, Ia, q. 50, ad 3; cf. q. 75, a. 5, ad 4.

[136] Cf. Jean Paulus, *Henri de Gand*, "Essai sur les tendances de sa métaphysique" (*Études de philosophie médiévale*, XXV), Paris: 1938, pp. 220–237.

[137] Cf. *supra*, pp. 49–50.

properly so called; hence he cannot admit a participation on this level.[138] The Suarezian theses on the analogy of being and the real identity of essence and existence of particular being follow logically from this.

Dominic Soto, O.P. (1491–1560), calls the distinction between existence and essence a "distinction deriving formally from the nature of a thing, or really and formally, and not as one thing from another." If we recall the way in which he understands the real distinction, namely, as that which exists between separable elements [139]—this is the definition, by the way, which all the adversaries of the Thomistic thesis give—we understand why he did not find an application of this distinction in the case of essence and existence. It is probable that his opinion is not too far removed from that of St. Thomas.

In present-day Scholasticism the controversy continues between Thomists and Suarezians. Too often representatives of the Thomistic school have yielded to the facile but exaggerated conception of Giles' distinction. On the other hand, their adversaries have not succeeded in stating precisely just what is the real foundation, sufficient for their "virtually founded" distinction.

If we take our stand on metaphysical ground, on the value of being of concrete reality, we cannot escape the Thomistic thesis of the distinction between essence and existence. The two fundamental affirmations, that of the existence and that of the individual mode, which together express adequately particular being, that is, the subsistent being which participates in the value of absolute being, can be grounded only on two real principles, whose correlation forms the internal structure of this particular being.

The nominalistic theories espoused by decadent Scholasticism were very deleterious for metaphysics, which they undermined fundamentally. In particular, they tended to stigmatize as fruitless every search for a real internal structure whose principles had to be, by definition, inaccessible to empirical knowledge. Now both the rationalistic and empiristic currents of modern philosophy, at their origin, came under the influence of these ideas. Little wonder, then, that these modern philosophers in general refused to appeal to the internal compositions of particular being, and especially to that of essence and existence to offer an explanation of reality.

---

[138] It is significant that the term "participation" does not appear in the list of root-words in the index of Suarez' *Disputationes metaphysicae.*

[139] Cf. *supra,* p. 113.

And yet the question of essence and existence was forced on Spinoza, who solved it by some sort of distinction.[140] At first sight this fact does not fail to surprise us, since the Spinozistic system is a monism, and the Scholastics believed that they could find in the distinction (either real or virtual) between essence and existence a justification of their metaphysical dualism. Still, on considering it more closely, we notice that in Spinoza's system also this distinction comes into play only in as far as there is question of limitation and multiplicity, and that it disappears as soon as the infinity of substance appears on the scene.

According to Spinoza the human intellect, inasmuch as it is limited, is bound up with the imagination, and it considers the objects of the world as so many distinct and finite things, as particular modes of being; but in truth these are not subsistent beings. In point of fact subsistence implies that the essence contains in itself the principle of its existence, so as to be truly by itself and to subsist in complete independence. Now, finite modes do not exist in this case; since they are finite they are not everywhere or at all times; hence, they are not necessarily, and it is not contradictory to conceive them as not existing, but as possible. In other words we must distinguish in them the state of possibility and that of their actual realization, of their presence in the temporal order, that is, their essence and existence. Further, as they take their place in the series of the finite modes, they are bound together mutually, the one dependent on the other, the one caused by the other. In a word, their presence in time is founded on a causal relation.

Man, however, is in a position to disengage himself from the imagination which takes limited and abstract views of the world. He is able to understand that the series of the finite modes is wholly contained within bona fide and infinite being, that is, in the unique Substance, whose essence it is to be, and consequently, to exist in everything, everywhere and always. This Substance cannot be conceived as possible; it exists necessarily. It maintains everything in existence by its immanent omnipresence; nothing can exist outside of it. From this transcendent point of view we understand that the necessity of this Being envelops everything absolutely (included

---

[140] Cf. B. Spinoza, *Ethica ordine geometrico demonstrata*, p. I, prop. 24, 28. English translation by R. H. M. Elwes, in "Chief Works of B. De Spinoza," London, 1883–4, Vol. II. Confer Alb. Rivaud, "Les notions d'essence et existence dans la philosophie de Spinoza (*Bibliothèque de Philosophie contemporaine*) Paris, 1906.

here is the series of the finite modes), and that the subsistence of these modes is merely pure appearance. The modes are founded on, and every distinction is effaced in infinite Nature; the opposition between possibility and reality, between essence and existence, disappears in the fundamental unity of pure Being.[141] For Spinoza, therefore, essence and existence do not designate principles of being; the meaning he attributes to them, comes near to that which the non-Thomistic Scholastics as well as the majority of modern philosophers give to them, namely, the two correlative states of the possibility and the actual realization of things.

The rebirth which metaphysics enjoys in contemporaneous philosophy, has brought attention back to the problems of ontology, and especially to the problem of the relations of existence and essence.[142]

[141] The Indian school of Avaita (Shankarâchârya, circ. 788–820) which allies itself to Brahmanism, maintains likewise that the world is real only because it is identified with the absolute, Brahma. Limitation and multiplicity derive from a potency, Mayâ, the great sorceress, who dwells in the heart of reality. They are only an illusion, an effect of ignorance, of imperfect knowledge, Avidyâ. Whoever places himself at the true point of view of the absolute, Brahma, enters into possession of the full wisdom, Vidyâ, which makes Mayâ and Avidyâ disappear and this man enjoys the beatific vision of all things in the perfect simplicity of Brahma.

[142] In attaching itself to the apprehension of the "essences," while putting the "existence" of things in parentheses, the phenomenology of Edmund Husserl has drawn attention to the distinction to be placed between the two terms, essence and existence. Husserl does not take the word "existence" in the sense of value of being, and besides he does not make its meaning precise, contenting himself with neglecting it altogether, thanks to his "phenomenological reduction." The question, however, arises precisely of finding out if we can make abstraction from existence, and in what sense it would be permissible to do this.
As we have established above, it is not possible not to take into account existence, understood as value of being, for the essence can only be understood as a mode of being. But if we take the term "existence" to signify the state of effective actualization of a being, in opposition to the possibility, we are not justified in declaring that it can be separated mentally from the essence of a thing, before having established that this latter (scil., essence) is a contingent reality, and that there is no contradiction in considering it as non-existing, i.e., as purely possible.
Max Scheler used the phenomenological method in the domain of values. He went beyond the phenomenology of Husserl to end in realism, and he understood the importance of a realistic ontology. He did not find time to write this ontology, but yet he formulated some theses which he counted on putting at its base. (Cf. "Vom Ewigen im Menschen," p. I. Die religiöse Erneuerung, Leipzig, 1921; 3rd edit., Berlin, 1933, pp. 112 ff.). Among these theses: there is a real distinction between essence and existence in finite beings ("an ontological distinction, one rooted in the being of things themselves and not in our intellect"); and also, the logical distinction between essence and existence in God ("it is only relative to our knowledge, to a knowing subject"). Cf. op. cit., p. 118.

We will confine ourselves to pointing out the solutions on which Nicolai Hartmann and Louis Lavelle insist; the first rejects the real distinction between essence and existence, and the latter accepts it after a fashion. It is quite interesting to examine the reasons which have inspired these two.[143]

Hartmann studied the problem at length, and the solution which he proposes is not wanting in originality.[144] He takes the word essence (*Sosein*) in its concrete signification: that which is the individual reality. After having examined successively all the ontological, logical, and gnoseological arguments which have been brought forward in behalf of a real distinction between essence and existence, he concludes that all these proofs are inconclusive. It is, however, important to note that Hartmann calls that distinction real which exists between separable elements.

On the other hand, he thinks that essence and existence (*Sosein* and *Dasein*) ought to be distinguished as two inseparable moments or aspects. Of its own nature essence is neutral in regard to two opposed states of being, possibility and reality, for these states do not enter into the definition of the essence. And yet it is quite necessary that the essence be either ideal or real, as must be the existence itself, and this precisely on account of the relation which unites it to existence. This latter on its part is always related to a determination, to an essence.

The relation between the two concrete, distinct but inseparable, moments of the individual reality can be conceived as a relation of "identity which is constantly displaced in the complexus of the order of being," [145] so as to explain both the identity and the disjunction of essence and existence.[146] This double aspect of things flows from the

---

[143] We could study other systems and there discover conceptions which, to a certain point, tend to tie up with the traditional theory of essence and existence, understood in the sense indicated above. It is thus that René Le Senne, not finding himself satisfied with a purely dialectical system, i.e., with a philosophy of determinations or essences (e.g. with the system of Octave Hamelin), turns resolutely towards existence as given in human experience, and there discovers "value, i.e. the absolute." It is in this sense that he speaks of a "double Cogito" (Cf. *Obstacle et valeur*, Paris, n.d. 1935; pp. 193 ff.) which reveals at once the distinction and the solidarity of the fundamental and absolute value, manifested by the existent "I," and of the individual determination of the "ego," which is related to other terms.

[144] Cf. *Zur Grundlegung der Ontologie*, Berlin, 1935, pp. 88–150.

[145] "Eine fortlaufend verschobene Identität im Ganzen des Seinzusammenhanges." *Op. cit.*, p. 133.

[146] ". . . identity and distinction of the moments of being." L. c., p. 166, n. 14.

limitation of the things considered. In fact, every thing which occurs in reality, is there (*es gibt*); it possesses existence (*Dasein*). Besides, it occurs in such a determined manner and in no other; it has a "taleity" (*Sosein*). By reason of its "taleity" individual reality is in relation with another thing; or rather, it forms part of another thing, it belongs to it. For example, this tree is there; it has existence (*Dasein*); inasmuch as it is there, it is this determined tree which is found in such a forest. Its "taleity" is no other than of the forest; for if this tree were not in the forest, it would not be such as it is. In other words, by reason of its limitation the tree is joined to a larger group.

By considering different things successively we see their limits being constantly extended. For example, such a leaf is there, but it exists as a leaf on such a branch; this latter is there, as the branch of the tree; the tree is there, as a tree of the forest, etc. We pause at each object barely for an instant, only immediately to continue our inquiries; these pauses are merely provisional, they never serve as the final term.

We can run through this series of objects in two opposite ways. In the one and the other we encounter the same disjunction of essence and existence, which by turns escape from each other and then overtake each other again, and thus they constantly resume the same game of pursuit. Let us revert to the example just used: The leaf is there, it exists; it is there because it has a *taleity;* but this *taleity* is that of the branch, and therefore the branch itself must also exist. This branch must have a *taleity* which belongs to the tree, and so the tree must be there, etc. In the other direction: The tree exists, it has a determined *taleity,* it exists such as it is, among other reasons because this branch is there. In its turn this latter exists, and it appears such as it is, with its *taleity,* especially by reason of the leaf which is there, etc.

Suppose that we could contemplate at a single glance the whole gamut of reality. Then we should rise superior to this duality of existence and essence (*Dass* and *Was, Dasein* and *Sosein*), and we should get to perfect identity. Existence has to do with the thing considered in itself, in an absolute manner, it *is;* essence has to do with the relativity of this same thing. It is such in a group; as such, it helps to make the other, and in the last analysis, the group, exist. But the whole of reality exists in itself, absolutely, without referring its "taleity" to any other thing.

What are we to think of Hartmann's thesis? The meaning which he attributes to the terms "essence and existence" comes very close to that which the Thomistic school gives to them. These terms designate distinct, but inseparable moments of concrete reality: essence is not to be taken in an abstract sense, it signifies the individual "taleity." Essence is not opposed to existence as the ideal sphere is opposed to the real; both of them are correlatives in the ideal as well as in the real sphere.

Hartmann is correct in thinking that the essence manifests the relativity of things. We can only grasp it by placing ourselves at the point of view of a complexus in which we consider the relation of one thing and another. This is, moreover, the point of view which we must take; for nothing can occur in isolation outside the order of being.[147] In real multiplicity Hartmann sees only parts; the disjunction of essence and existence is a function of the knowledge which we get of a partial complexus. As the whole of reality cannot be referred to some other thing, the consideration of this absolute whole coincides with that of the complete being, where no distinction between essence and existence is any longer manifested.

And yet the real order is not composed merely of parts. Hartmann neglected to take account of participation. There are subsistent beings, they are many; no one of them is the whole of reality; however, each one of them is a complete whole and not merely a part of a subsistent whole. Consequently, in the study of reality we ought to halt at each of these beings as at a complete and definite whole. As these beings are finite, since each one of them is not the whole of reality, they are defined by their mode of being, their "taleity" or essence; and this definition is by no means provisional; it expresses a definitive, internal, constitutive "taleity" of the being in question. The distinction between essence and existence is therefore not a function of a partial view of reality; it forms the fundamental structure of particular being.

Without doubt we run up against the problem of reconciling subsistence and finitude; but here precisely is the problem of the participation in being, of the one and the many, of the absolute and the relative. And so once more we see how imperative it is to make the terms of the problem precise. There is question of explaining not any kind of multiplicity, but a multiplicity of subsistent beings, and it

---

[147] Cf. *supra*, pp. 26–27.

is only in relation to this multiplicity that the question of the distinction of essence and existence is raised. Hence, we must before all else strive to establish the fact that subsistent beings exist, that the value of being gives rise to a participation in the true sense of the word.

Louis Lavelle admits the personal and subsistent character of the ego and its fundamental distinction from the non-ego; he professes a philosophy of participation and he lays down the thesis of the correlation of essence and existence in every finite being. There are multiple beings, for particular beings are inscribed in the realm of being, each one tracing its limits there. They are not, strictly speaking, parts of the whole of being—a thing which would imply pantheism; they are participations, for being is entirely present in every one.[148]

To understand this we must lay stress on activity. Being is essentially an act and not a passive bulk; and because there are many acts, it is necessary to admit that there are many beings. The act signifies the interiority, the intimacy of being, intellectual and free initiative, both in itself and by itself. It is by its act that each individual being is affirmed, established, traces the limits of its domain, and is distinguished from the others.

In every individual being we must distinguish existence and essence. Existence can be understood in a threefold sense: it is being in as far as it is manifested to others, or again in as far as it rests on being; but it is especially (and this meaning is presupposed in the

---

[148] "Being is not at all a sum of its parts. It is the common principle which allows each one of them to be detached from it in order to contribute to the formation of the whole, while receiving from it the initiative by which it will be able to subsist. Thus we will never encounter being separated from particular beings. In each one of them being is wholly present." Louis Lavelle, "De l'insertion du moi dans l'être par la distinction de l'opération et de la donnée," in *Tijdschrift voor Philosophie*, III, 1941, p. 726.

"If I restrict myself to saying that the being which is peculiar to me, is a being which I receive, and which is not at all co-extensive with total being, but which nevertheless is not heterogeneous in relation to it, the unity of the whole is safeguarded, but then pantheism threatens us."

". . . If the total Being envelops in itself all the particular beings, the infinite Act, which is a pure liberty, can become an act participated in, only if it gives to all consciousnesses the faculty of being separated from it, in order to be constituted themselves, thanks to an act which is peculiar to them. Participation here is the foundation of independence, in place of abolishing it." L. Lavelle, "Être et acte," *Revue de métaphysique et de morale*, 43e année, 1936: pp. 204–205.

two others) "the act itself by which I break away from being with a view to finding in it my essence." [149] "Essence is what gives to each thing its intimate nature and its perfection." [150] "Our essence is the best part of ourselves; it is always inseparable from the act by which we seek to coincide with it." [151]

The distinction between essence and existence is later than that which we designate by the term being. For it is being which "constitutes their unity, not their synthesis as if they could in some way precede it; but it is the principle in which they appear as opposed, the one to the other, as soon as the analysis or the participation has commenced." [152] "Being then is the indivisibility of essence and existence, that is to say, the existence of the essence, or the essence taken in its actuality and not in its possibility." [153] "There is between the two terms a sort of reciprocity, since every existence is the existence of an essence, and since we cannot posit an essence without positing at the same time its existence, at least as essence." [154] The characteristic of every individual being is "to dissociate essence and existence in order to unite them." [155] Its existence is limited; "it must be continually sacrificed, precisely in order to acquire an essence. In taking on its essence the ego assumes according to its powers its responsibility not merely in regard to itself, but in regard to universal being." [156] For individual being is truly itself only in the measure in which it is free and detached from the others; its individuality, its inscription in being depend therefore on the act by which it is affirmed and by which it realizes its interiority. This act "is a step which permits us precisely to make the discovery of the essence, and

---

[149] L. Lavelle, "La dialectique de l'éternel présent: De l'Acte" (*Coll. Philosophie de l'esprit*), Paris, 1937, p. 101.

[150] *Ibid.*, p. 103.

[151] *Ibid.*, p. 105.

[152] *Ibid.*, p. 92.

[153] *Ibid.*

[154] *Ibid.*, p. 93. We see that essence and existence are opposed on the same plane, and that Lavelle does not distinguish them as "that which can be" and "that which is." "The univocity of being has rendered us the service of obliging us to surmount the opposition between possibility and existence, since we would not know where to place the essence, if we did not place it in being. And so if we regard existence as being only the character of the things which are, we must say that there is always an existence of the possibility, i.e., of the essence." *Op. cit.*, pp. 92–93. Cf. what we said about the ideas of Nicolai Hartmann, *supra*, p. 150.

[155] *Op. cit.*, p. 94.

[156] *Ibid.*

up to a certain point to constitute it." [157] "Existence is, if you wish, this real and even actual aptitude which I possess to give my essence to myself by an act which it depends on me to accomplish." [158] Still, the essence is not the effect of the act, no more than it is its support; for it is the act "which constitutes the very reality of the essence." [159]

The relation of existence and essence, then, will be reduced at bottom to that of being and of act. Now in every individual being the terms of this relation are inseparable and irreducible; being is for this act a datum which goes beyond it infinitely, and against which it collides both in itself and outside of itself, since the individual being is no more responsible for its own birth than for the existence of the external world. On the other hand, as soon as the act is seen really registered in being, it transcends its own peculiar limits and feels itself in possession of an infinite virtuality. And thus "act and being, both of them infinite, pursue each other without truce, always going beyond each other, and never succeeding in overtaking each other, much less in embracing each other." [160] We must posit this correlation of being and act "to render the entrance of the individual into the world possible." [161] And yet the act, while not coinciding with being, does not belong to the domain of non-being; even in finite reality the act is being, and being is act in this sense that in all these consciousnesses it is the being which is actualized, and it is the act which penetrates into the nature of the being.

When we apply this to the whole and no longer to an individual being, the relation of being and act is resolved into an essential identity.[162] God is pure Being and He is pure Act. Similarly, it is legitimate to say that God "is merely existence, since everything in Him is actual, and He actualizes everything that is. We can also say that He is only essence, since there is nothing exterior to Him, and He gives its interiority to everything." [163]

As we see, Lavelle considers essence as being a mode of being, as the reason of the individuality, the limitation and the infinitely nu-

---

[157] *Ibid.*

[158] *Op. cit.,* p. 95. "Existence has meaning in us only to permit us not to realize an essence posited for the first time, but to determine it by our choice and to coincide with it." *Ibid.*

[159] *De l'Acte,* p. 68.

[160] "De l'insertion du moi dans l'être par la distinction de l'opération et de la donnée," *Tijdschrift voor Philosophie,* III, 1941, p. 720.

[161] *Ibid.,* p. 732.

[162] *Ibid.,* p. 723.

[163] *De l'Acte,* p. 108.

merous relations which cling to this individual being and all the
others. Essence and existence constitute a real correlation; and Lavelle treats this problem, as all the others, from the angle of action.
Undoubtedly, the mode of existence, the individuality of the particular being, is affirmed and developed in the autonomous acts which
characterize the becoming of this being; but does it suffice to consider
them inasmuch as they are conscious and free acts in order to grasp
their whole nature? Lavelle himself lays down some restrictions here:
"The act is a step which permits us precisely to make the discovery
of the essence, and up to a certain point to constitute it." [164] It is the
act "by which I disengage myself from pure being, and from which
nevertheless I borrow the power which I put to work in order to become in some sort the origin of myself." [165] For the ego itself is a
datum for the act and it is "infinitely richer than the consciousness
which we have of it." [166] "It is as if the ego were never revealed to
itself except in part, and paradoxically, had to be posited as exterior
to its own subjectivity." [167] The reason for this is that "at the opposite
side of the creative act, we never draw our own peculiar being from
nothing but from simple possibility, which is itself a real possibility,
unceasingly offered to our clutches by the divine generosity, a possibility whose usage alone is left to us." [168] And therefore the plane of
the individual essence is extended beyond conscious and free subjectivity; the interiority of the act has an ontological foundation which
consists in a possibility or a real potency. This fundamental potency
is a pure gift of God; we do not constitute it, but we have the usage
of it, and in so far we can freely actualize it.

To understand the significance of the correlation of being and act
in Lavelle's system, we must take these last remarks into account.
The subsistent being, in particular the ego, is revealed to us by human experience and constitutes the object of reflection. We get at it
in as far as it manifests itself, hence in its activity, in the real act by
which it asserts its presence in expressing its concrete nature, its
individual essence. Here, first of all, we lay hold of a correlation of
essence and existence, but we cannot limit ourselves to seeing in
conscious acts personal decisions, by which we freely trace the limits

---

[164] *De l'Acte,* p. 94.

[165] *De l'Acte,* p. 101.

[166] "De l'insertion du moi dans l'être par la distinction de l'opération et de la
donnée," *Tijdschrift voor Philosophie,* III, 1941, p. 730.

[167] *Ibid.,* p. 731.

[168] *Ibid.,* p. 728, note. Cf. *De l'Acte,* pp. 269–274, 341–342.

of our being by impressing a direction on the course of our life. For our liberty is itself limited to the usage of that real potency of being which has been bestowed on us, and of which we ourselves are not the source.

We will say, therefore, that this usage is merely a modification of a mode of fundamental being, of a nature; and this is why essence in its first meaning (the correlative term of the real principle of being), itself implies a structure, that of a mode of substantial being, or nature, and of accidental principles, active and passive, such as free will. We shall make an analysis of this in the following chapter, devoted to the dynamic order of being; meanwhile, it remains true that Lavelle has emphasized, quite correctly, the fact that the correlation of act and being is implied in every finite subsistent reality, and that in the Infinite, on the contrary, these terms must essentially coincide.

II. STRUCTURE ALONG THE LINE OF THE MODE OF BEING

MATERIAL PRINCIPLE AND FORMAL PRINCIPLE

1. The Problem of Multiplicity in One and the Same Species

The complexus of beings includes various groups, combining all the beings of the same species. Is the specific unity of these multiple terms bound up with an internal structure, analogous to the ontological structure which lies at the bottom of the unity of the many in the order of being? [1] Before solving this problem we must get clear on its data. First of all, are there beings of the same species? How are we to establish this fact?

By its activity the nature of reality is manifested. If then there exist beings whose activity is defined in the same way, we must conclude

---

[1] We do not have to treat the whole philosophical problem of material being. It is under the jurisdiction of the philosophy of nature, of cosmology and psychology. We are restricting ourselves here to examining it under one of its fundamental aspects, *scil.*, the question of the one and the many on the plane of specific perfection, i.e., the question of the individuation of the material being, in as far as it is parallel to the question of the one and the many on the plane of transcendental being, and which can from this fact throw some light on the fundamental metaphysical problem and on the conception which must be formed of the structure of being. Later on it will also be seen that the hylomorphic theory, by which we finally solve this question, can be utilized in the study of the activity and the causality of beings.

from this that the nature of these beings is of the same species. Now this is especially the case with human beings.

It is possible for us to give a precise definition of man, because by an act of reflection we grasp directly our conscious acts, and so we can define them exactly by indicating their natural orientation, their formal object. Man is at one and the same time a material and spiritual being, a rational animal; he is a corporeal reality, endowed with life of the soul, whose superior activity has as its formal object transcendental value, being and the good. There exists a number of men, beings who, while being corporeal have at their disposal spiritual forces which develop on the plane of transcendental value. These men have a specifically similar nature, since they exercise an activity which is defined by the same specific or formal object; they belong to the same species.

To indicate the mode of concrete being of a being which is specifically similar to others, it will then be necessary to note what it has in common with these others, and what belongs to it as its own. To say what this being is, is to indicate its specific nature and its individual notes; and then the question arises: what is the relation between these two elements and what is the foundation of each of them?

The specific nature of man is known to us at the end of an inquiry which proceeds by way of abstraction, disclosing successively the different aspects of human activity. Man has at his disposal physico-chemical forces, as everything that is material; he reacts as a whole living being just as plants do. He achieves unity of psychical life as do the animals; he develops his personal perfection in the conscious and autonomous life of the spirit. These different degrees of activity are added up and complete one another; they are grounded in one and the same human activity, and their synthesis permits us to define the specific perfection, the nature of man.

However, the specific definition does not indicate fully what a real man is, for it does not include that which characterizes the individual as such. We might believe that it is sufficient to add an individual aspect to the different aspects already considered, but this is not true. The individual difference does not constitute the prolongation of the line of the determinations which constitute the specific perfection. To bring this point home it suffices to note that these determinations form an ascending series of degrees of perfection, and that the individual difference is not in any way added as a superior degree.

The perfection of the plant surpasses that of inorganic matter; that of the animal is superior to the perfection of the plant, and psychical energy is of a different order from the powers of vegetative activity; the perfection of the spirit transcends that of the animal, and the spiritual faculties are not reducible to sense functions. But if the plant is more than inorganic matter, and the animal more than a plant, and man more than an animal, we cannot say that the individual human being is more than a man, that he is a superman. For to the individuality there does not belong any power or faculty which is not proper to the whole human species.

Hence, the individual difference relatively to the species is in a very different relation from that which unites the specific difference and the genus. Whereas the specific difference prolongs the line of the generic perfection, the individual difference neither increases nor diminishes in any way the specific perfection. What, then, is the role of the individual difference? It provides the particular being with the special mode according to which this being possesses the specific perfection.

The multiplicity of the individuals of one and the same species constitutes a case of participation. Man in the concrete is a man, whole and entire, and he is only that; he is a complete man, not merely half a man. And yet, he is not the whole of man; he is not identified with all human reality, since there exist other men besides himself. In a word, man in the concrete is an individual who forms a part of the whole of humanity. On what title is he contained therein? Strictly speaking, it is not in the role of an integral part, since he is a complete man. Humanity does not itself form one subsistent being, an immense organism whose various organs men would constitute; it is rather a unity of order whose elements are the human persons who exist and act by themselves. And so, man forms a part of humanity in virtue of every individual, a subsistent element, which participates in the perfection of man, which possesses completely this perfection but in a particular fashion, according to an individual mode. The fact of being an individual human being supposes necessarily that there exist or can exist other individuals of the same species; and this fact implies, of itself, that there is a humanity, an order or ensemble of men. Man in the concrete is not identified with humanity, no more than he is in the proper sense of the word, a part of humanity; he is this man here, distinct from that one over there, in one and the same ensemble. Therefore, the individual belongs to humanity by reason of his whole reality. The social character is identified with the individual character of man in the concrete; the one and the other bring out that it is of the essence of man to participate in human perfection by virtue of being a complete and subsistent person.

2. The Proof of the Non-Simplicity of the Particular Being Which Participates in a Specific Perfection

Just as participation in being implies a structure comprising the two principles of existence and essence, so also participation in specific perfection, which is effected on the plane of the essence, supposes that the essence itself consists of a structure of two principles, of which the one is the real reason of the essential or specific perfection, and the other the real reason of the individual mode which affects this perfection. These two are the principle of specification and the principle of individuation. Now this structure of the essence ought to be real, since participation in the specific perfection, which is not a mere mental viewpoint but a reality, demands a real foundation.

We might hesitate to admit this, because we lay hold of the specific aspect of beings by abstract knowledge; but we must determine precisely the relation of this abstraction and the apprehension of the individual mode of the concrete subject. There are different steps in the development of abstract thought; they are situated on the lines which proceed from the most remote genera down to the species. To arrive at a definition of what a being is, we consider successively its different aspects, we line up the various degrees of perfection which it manifests, and we make a summary of them. It is thus that we end up with the specific perfection, which is the ultimate term to be attained; we define a being by indicating the species to which it belongs. The indication of the genus or of the specific difference would furnish only an insufficient definition; that of the species provides a perfect definition.

Now abstractive knowledge must stop definitely at the species, since beyond it there is nothing more to abstract. We might be tempted to believe that there is reason to take into account the individuality, so as to line it up on the same level as the generic and specific aspects; that, de jure, this individual aspect could be abstracted just as well as the others: and that de facto, if we did not grasp it by our abstractive reason, this would be due to the weakness of this human reason. This way, however, of looking at the matter is inaccurate. The knowledge of the specific aspect is abstract, because it makes abstraction from the individual mode of the reality; we could not conclude from this that this individual mode is, in its turn, an aspect which we could grasp by abstraction, that is, by making an abstraction from the specific aspect. The individual mode is, of itself, the concrete mode, for reality is concrete, individual; and if we could grasp the abstract by abstracting it from the concrete, this would be as senseless as grasping the concrete by abstracting it from the abstract! By adding the abstract to the abstract, we will never get to the concrete; the individual mode is not found in the prolongation of the line which binds the genus to the species. In an altogether different way is the individual mode related to the specific perfection, as has been shown above.

Consequently, particular being gives rise to a twofold knowledge, that of the specific perfection and that of its individual difference. The one is not reducible to the other, for abstract knowledge reaches its full development in the knowledge of the species, and it could not be developed any more in the same line, and so neither could it get to the individual mode. In a given reality there is that which can be abstracted, and that which necessarily resists abstraction. In this regard reality itself, taken in its totality, presents a double character: it is not simple, it contains the real reason of the specification, and that of the individuation.[2] Participation in the specific perfection, and the real relativity which binds the subsistent individuals together in the whole species, require a structure in the essence of every individual.

The whole internal structure of particular being consists in the correlation of its constituent principles, and the reality of these principles is reduced entirely to that of their correlation. Each one of these principles is a transcendental relation ("ordo ad alterum") whose corresponding principle is the term, so that in the definition of the one the other is always mentioned. This is why the character peculiar to the one is communicated directly to the other, since each one is what it is only by reason of its relation to the other. In other

---

[2] "That by which Socrates is a man can be communicated to many; but that by which he is this man, can be communicated only to one. If therefore Socrates were a man by that by which he is this man, just as there cannot be many Socrates, so there could not be many men." St. Thomas Aquinas, *Summa theol.*, Ia, q. 11, a. 3.

words, each principle is the reason of a character which manifests itself in the whole particular being.[3]

By reason of the principle of specification this whole being (and
not merely one of its parts or one of its principles) possesses such
specific perfection; and by reason of the principle of individuation
this whole being (and again not merely one of its parts or one of its
principles) possesses such an individual mode of existing in the
species.

A constitutive principle of being does not exist in itself; it is not a
subsistent being, it has reality only through the structure which contains it. That is why, in truth, it is not the internal principle of existence, but the whole subsistent being (the structure comprising all
the principles) that exists. The internal principle of essence is not
a particular finite being, but the whole subsistent being (the ensemble of the principles) is particular and finite by reason of the
essence.[4] Similarly, the essential principle of specification is not
specifically determined, just as the essential principle of individuation
does not have an individual mode of existence. Rather, the whole
subsistent being participates in such specific perfection in a distinctive and individual way, by reason of the principles of specification
and individuation which it contains and whose correlation forms its
essence.[5]

3. The Hylomorphic Structure of the Essence of the
Material Being

To make more precise what these two internal principles of essence
are, we can observe that the principle of specification is the real internal reason of the whole essential determination of the being under consideration. We call this the fundamental, formal principle or

---

[3] Cf. *supra*, pp. 104–106.

[4] Cf. *supra*, p. 107.

[5] Speaking of the being and of the becoming of the principle of determination
or "form," St. Thomas expresses himself as follows: "The form is said to be or
to be an *ens*, because by it something is. . . . The form, properly, does not become, but it is that by which something becomes. . . . That which becomes,
is not the form but the composite, which becomes from matter and not from
nothing. And it becomes from matter inasmuch as matter is in potency to the
composite itself, by this that the matter is in potency to the form. And thus it is
not correctly said that the form 'becomes' in the matter, but rather that it is
educed from the potency of the matter. . . . That which becomes is the composite, not the form." *De potentia*, q.3, a.8.

the substantial form,[6] the reason of the degree of perfection according to which particular being subsists in itself (by the principle of the corresponding existence) and according to which it participates in the value of being. In scholastic language every principle of determination is called an act. The principle of individuation is not the reason of any new degree of perfection, but of the individual mode which affects the degree of perfection (and this latter is determined by the form) of such a being which is being considered. Since this principle is not the reason of any degree of perfection or determination, we call it a principle of indetermination. Nevertheless, it is not purely negative: this would have no meaning at all; as a transcendental relation of which the form is the term it participates in the formal determination; it receives the form, and is therefore of itself a principle of receptivity, of determinability. This is why we call it a potency, a potential principle. As the substantial form is the real internal reason of all the fundamental determination of particular being and as the corresponding principle of individuation cannot be the reason of any further determination, this principle is a pure potency. In opposition to the substantial form we call it prime matter, the fundamental or substantial material principle.

Prime matter cannot exist, not even for an instant, without being actually united to the form;[7] in fact, no being can be real without being determined in itself, without being determinately distinguished from every other, without being one being. Now prime matter is not a source of determination, but it is the reason of the particular way in which the essential determination of such a being is realized. This is why prime matter cannot exercise any function, if it is not in connection with the substantial form, the source of this determination. It can exist in relation with the internal principle of existence and be made a participant in being only as a relation of which the form constitutes the term, that is, in virtue of the determination which the form communicates to it.

In a particular being only one single substantial form can exist.[8]

---

[6] In general we call "form" in scholastic language, every principle of determination, every "act." The term applies, before all else, to the domain of the quiddity or essence (substantial or accidental): it is predicated less often of the act of existence.

[7] "Matter acquires *esse* actually in as far as it acquires the form." *Summa theol.*, Ia, q.75, a.6. "Through the form the substance becomes the proper subject of that which is the *esse.*" *Contra Gentes*, II, c.55.

[8] Cf. *Quodlibetum* XI, q.5, a.5; *Contra Gentes*, II, c.58; *De Anima*, aa.9, 11; *Summa theol.*, Ia, q.76, aa.3, 4.

Beings differ one from the other by reason of their essence, of their determined mode of being. It is the substantial form which is the real principle of this essential determination, and by reason of it the essence is in correlation with the principle of existence. Now this correlation forms the fundamental structure of a subsistent being; and so a multiplicity of forms brings with it an equivalent multiplicity of particular beings.[9]

4. Objections Against the Theory of Hylomorphism

Objections have been raised against this conception of hylomorphism, according to which prime matter, pure potency, would be the principle of individuation of beings of the same species, whereas the substantial form would be their principle of specification. These objections correspond exactly to those which have usually been made against the thesis of the distinction of the real principles of existence and essence, and they tend to show that on the basis of this real distinction it is impossible to form any idea of matter or form which would be free from contradiction.

And first of all our opponents argue: To exercise a function of individuation prime matter would itself have to be determined antecedently. The internal determination of prime matter ought therefore to precede, at least logically, the exercise of its function of individuation. Now, if we must conceive matter as determined, even abstracting from the relation which binds it to the form, it possesses its own peculiar determination independently of its union with the substan-

---

[9] We might suppose that if there are many substantial forms in one and the same being, they would fit into each other in such a way that they would be related one to the other, and only the last one would be related to the *esse*. Then we would have to ask ourselves on what this distinction would be founded, *scil.*, this distinction between two species of forms, those which are the modes of being and those which, properly speaking, are not such modes. As a matter of fact, we would distinguish in one and the same being as many real forms as we could distinguish aspects to abstract, *scil.*, generic aspects and the specific aspect. But we have shown above that these aspects indicate the stages which our abstractive reason traverses in order to acquire progressively a complete knowledge of the formal perfection of particular being. The result of these successive efforts is wholly contained in the definition of the species, and there is no cause to admit in the being a real structure which would be parallel to the structure of this abstractive movement of our knowledge. There is really only one substantial form, but it is virtually multiple (Cf. *supra*, pp. 156 ff.). On the contrary, the knowledge of the specific perfection and that of the individual difference are irreducible, and there ought to correspond to these a correlation of two real principles, which form the structure of the essence of particular being.

tial form. Hence, it is itself an act and not a pure potency; it is in act not by reason of the form, but it is an act in its own right.

As regards the substantial form, the objection is raised that if the form is conceived as individuated and limited by the matter, this implies that antecedently to its being united to matter and hence before exercising its function of specification, it was universal and unlimited. Does this mean a logical universality and illimitation, such as characterize the abstract concept which is applicable to an indefinite series of subjects? Assuredly not! Who would, then, dream of maintaining that the real essence of a being can be composed of a real pure potency and of an abstract notion? Does this imply, on the contrary, the universality and illimitation of a real form? Then it would be necessary to hold that prime matter proceeds to carve out individual and limited forms; but no one can see any meaning in such an affirmation. One does not escape the necessity of admitting that the form is in itself individual and that it is such by reason of itself, independently of its relation with prime matter. It is therefore perfectly superfluous to appeal to the individualizing function of this matter.

This line of argumentation, just as that which was directed against the real distinction between the principles of essence and existence, rests on the idea that every principle which enters into the constitution of particular being must be considered in two ways: first in itself and then in its relation with a corresponding principle. If this were true, it would be necessary to admit really, that the principle considered in itself already possesses all that is attributed to it by reason of its relation with a second principle; the intervention of this latter would appear perfectly useless. But this conception cannot be defended: the principles which constitute particular being are transcendental relations; they are essentially in correlation, the one with the other; they have meaning or reality only in the structure which they form. We are therefore not allowed to speak of prime matter otherwise than in relation with the form; we can never consider it outside of its union with the form, abstracting from the determination which it receives from this form. Similarly, the form has meaning only in relation to matter, and it can be conceived only from this angle.[10] Hence, we can say nothing of it without tak-

---

[10] "Matter according to its proper definition is *ens in potentia*." *Quodlibetum*, III, q. 1, a. 1. "*Esse in potentia* is nothing other than to be ordered to the act." *De Malo*, q. 1, a. 2.

ing into account its relation with the real principle of pure potency, without having regard for its individuation by matter.

To make the whole significance of this theory of individuation more precise, we must take into account the consequences which flow from it in the sphere of activity. In the following chapter, it will be shown that to the fundamental hylomorphic structure of the individual being there corresponds on the plane of action a structure of quantity and quality, of passivity and activity. Individuals of the same species belong to one and the same material order; they are situated in time and space, each one with relation to the others; and their individuality bears the profound imprint of these temporal and spatial relations as much in their origin as in the exercise of their activity.

5. The Spirituality of the Human Soul, and Its Individuation by Matter

The definition of man carries with it a twofold element, the genus "animal" and the specific difference "rational," of which the one indicates the material aspect, and the other the spiritual aspect of one and the same individual human person.[11] The substantial form of man is therefore the fundamental reason of a perfection which on the one hand is corporeal, measured by time and space, and on the other transcends material conditions. In analyzing the spiritual aspect of human actions, we can come to recognize here a natural orientation towards an eternal existence, natural because it rests on the formal object and the nature of the faculty of action. Individual man survives the disintegration of the body; he is immortal, and he is

---

"Form is nothing other than the act of matter." *Summa theol.*, Ia, q.105, a.1. "From the matter and form there results one thing, no extraneous bond binding them together." *Contra Gentes*, II, c.58: *Adhuc.*

[11] St. Thomas quite insistently emphasizes substantial unity, and this is why he admits only one substantial form in every being, even when there is question of a human being. The substantial form of man is the soul, which while being spiritual, is individuated by the substantial principle of matter, just as every form which by its union with prime matter goes to make up one substance. For this reason the substantial unity of man is not less than that of material things. On the contrary, as St. Thomas remarks, we could say that this unity is stronger: "The *unum* that results from an intellectual substance and corporeal matter is not less than that which results from the form of fire and its matter, but perhaps stronger, because the more the form surpasses matter, the greater unity will be effected from it and the matter." *Contra Gentes* II, c.68.

called on eternally to pursue an existence not subject to the conditions of organic life in this world.

This means, first of all, that the substantial form of every man (we
call it the soul, because it is the fundamental principle of life) constitutes in union with matter the human essence; it is individuated
within the species, owing to this relation which binds it to matter;
and it is the reason of the corporeal determination, of the corporeity
of the human being. But then this corporeity does not exhaust all the
riches of perfection of which the soul is the principle; for this soul
is likewise the source of a spiritual life and it can exist and act, even
without being actually united to prime matter, without actually exercising its function of principle of corporeity and of organic life.

In its existence separated from matter does the soul lose its individuality, since it is matter which is the principle of individuation?
Not at all. The principle of individuation is not alone in being individual; it is the entire particular being which is individual by
reason of this principle. The substantial form is stamped in itself with
the individuality which is peculiar to the complete being, since it
enters into the fundamental structure of this being, since it is a
transcendental relation of which the prime matter is the term. When
the fundamental structure of man, essence—existence, is separated
from prime matter, it does not cease to carry the individual stamp
which characterized it before. For its substantial form does not cease
to be a formal principle, since it is completely oriented towards
matter, and is defined by this relation with the material principle.

Between the separated souls, therefore, there obtains a distinction
which is not formal, not specific, not founded on the form alone,
considered absolutely, but on the form considered in its relation with
prime matter. In the last analysis the individual difference traces its
root to this matter.[12] Even in its separated state, the human soul remains, at least virtually, a principle of corporeity and of organic
life. The separated soul is by no means an angel, a pure spirit, whose
essence contains merely an absolute form, with no relation to another essential principle.[13] While being a spirit, this soul is virtually

---

[12] "For not every diversity of forms effects a diversity in the species, but
only that which is in accordance with the formal principles or the essence of
the form." *Contra Gentes* II, c. 81.—"The difference of form which derives only
from the different disposition of matter, does not effect a diversity in the species,
but only a numerical diversity." *Summa theol.*, Ia, q. 85, a. 7, ad 3. Cf. *De
potentia*, q. 3, a. 9, ad 7; *In epistolam ad Romanos*, c. 5, lectio 3, *Ad hoc autem*.
[13] An angel, considered as a pure spirit, must be conceived as unique in its

material; for not only does it bear within itself the fruits of its past union with matter, but by definition it remains always and essentially capable of being united with the material principle. Its peculiar mode of possible union, its special orientation towards the material order, constitutes its individuality, and places it in the class of human beings.[14]

6. Historical Notes

From the time of the ancient Greeks, philosophers have discussed the problem of the individuation of material beings, and for a long time they reduced the philosophical problem of the one and the many principally to the question of the multiplicity of individuals in the species.[15] To solve this problem they always believed they had to appeal to two explanatory principles, that of the unity and that of the multiplicity. The whole problem was to find out how these principles had to be conceived.

Plato appealed, on the one hand, to the subsistent idea, and on the other to matter-space. The reflection of the idea in the different parts of space is at the root of the multiplication of the individuals

species: "Every angel is its own species." The angels can be distinguished only by formal differences, since their essence is identified with their form. This thesis St. Thomas professes without the least hesitation.

[14] "And although its individuation depends on the body as on its occasion (*occasionaliter*) for its beginning, since it does not acquire an individuated *esse* except in the body whose act it is, still it is not necessary that, if the body is destroyed, this individuation should perish. For since (the soul) has an absolute *esse* from the time that it acquired an individuated *esse,* and this from the fact that it became the form of this body, this *esse* always remains individuated. And therefore Avicenna says that the individuation and multiplication of souls depend on the body for their beginning but not for their *end." De ente et essentia,* c. 6 (edit. Laurent, n.116, p. 188). "Souls are indeed multiplied inasmuch as bodies are multiplied; still the multiplication of bodies will not be the cause of the multiplication of souls." *Contra Gentes,* II, c. 81.—"Hence, a multitude of souls, separated from the bodies, follows indeed upon the diversity of forms according to their substance, because the substance of this soul is other than the substance of that soul; still that diversity does not proceed from the diversity of the essential principles of the soul itself, nor is it according to the different essence of the soul itself, but it is according to the different commensuration of souls to bodies. For this soul is commensurate with this body, that soul with that body, and similarly for all souls. Such commensurations, however, remain in the souls even when the bodies perish, just as their substances remain, seeing that they are not dependent on the bodies for their *esse." loc. cit.*

[15] We explained above how it is that the problem of the one and the many on the plane of transcendental being, took such a long time to be raised. Cf. *supra,* pp. 115–145.

of one and the same species. But there is no substantial union between the idea and material space; and besides, the idea itself is unique and subsistent, and it is only its image which is multiplied in the matter.

Aristotle rejected this extreme dualism. Material reality belongs indeed to being, and every individual, this man here, is substantially one being. Hence, every one possesses necessarily in his own substance his own principle of specification as well as his principle of individuation: the idea or form, and the prime matter. Every individual contains therefore a hylomorphic composition.[16]

The Aristotelian theory of individuation was taken up in the Middle Ages, as much by the Arabian philosophers (Avicenna, 980–1037, and Averrhoes, 1126–1198), as by a goodly number of Christian Scholastics, for example, William of Auvergne (*circ.* 1180–1249), Bartholomew, the Englishman (*circ.* 1225 at Paris), Alexander of Hales, O.F.M. (+1245), Jean de la Rochelle, O.F.M. (+1245), St. Albert the Great, O.P. (1196/1206–1280), St. Thomas Aquinas, O.P. 1224/5–1274), Siger de Brabant (+1281/84), etc., but it was elaborated in very different ways.

From this theory Averrhoes concludes to monopsychism: the human soul (both the agent and the passive intellects) is unique, for it does not carry with it any matter, and hence does not include any principle of individuation which would allow a multiplicity of individuals in one and the same species. This doctrine was strenuously attacked by the majority of the Christian Scholastics, notably by St. Albert the Great and St. Thomas Aquinas. Siger of Brabant gave an exposition of the Averrhoistic thesis in his teaching at Paris; he appears to have admitted it for a while, but later on he attacked it.

The Angelic Doctor drew all the consequences of the doctrine of the individuation by matter, both in philosophy and in theology. According to him the human soul, which is spiritual, is individuated by matter even after the death of the human body. An angel who is a pure spirit, is necessarily unique in its species.[17] Quantity, an accidental principle which has its substantial reason in prime matter, also enters into the individuation of bodies, but in a subordinate way, dependently on the prime matter; for an accident can never play a substantial role. Thus we must understand the individualizing role

---

[16] Cf. *Metaph.* XII, c.9, 1074 a33; V, c.6, 1016 b 32; VII, c.8, 1034 a 5–8; c.9, 1035 b 30; X, c.3, 1054 a 33; c.9, 1058 b 5.

[17] "But there are as many species as there are individuals, as Avicenna says explicitly." *De ente et essentia,* c.5 (edit. Laurent, p. 135).

of *materia quantitate signata* (matter, signed or signated by quantity).

Certain Scholastics struck out along other paths. St. Bonaventure, O.F.M. (1221–1274), who considers matter as the principal reason of the individuation, attributes a role also to the form. Godfrey of Fontaines (+1303) and James of Metz, O.P. (*circ.* 1300) ascribe the principle of individuation to the form alone.

Others refuse to raise the problem of individuation. They content themselves with observing that only an individual reality can exist, and that it must necessarily be composed of principles which are, all of them, likewise individual. Roger Bacon, O.F.M. (*circ.* 1214–1292/94) adopted this attitude at a certain stage of his career, and this opinion was shared by John Peckham, O.F.M. (+1292), Richard of Middleton, O.F.M. (+1300/08), Peter of Trier, O.F.M. (end of the 13th century), John of Naples, O.P. (+1330), Durandus of Saint-Pourçain, O.P. (+1334), Peter Aureolus, O.F.M. (+1322), William of Ockham, O.F.M. (*circ.* 1300–1349) and all the nominalists, and much later by Francis Suarez, S.J. (1548–1617). The same thesis was taken up by Leibnitz (1646–1716).

The doctrine, put forth by John Duns Scotus, O.F.M. (*circ.* 1267–1308), has a certain affinity with this last point of view: the reason of the individuation is the *haecceity*, the mark of individuality which characterizes the whole being in all its constitutive principles. This being is composed of *this* form and *this* matter. The *haecceity* is a formality or real determination which we must distinguish from the generic and specific aspects; there exists between all these determinations a formal distinction which derives from the very nature of reality, a *distinctio formalis ex natura rei*.

The Thomistic doctrine does not in any way deny that everything which exists is necessarily individual in all its principles, formal as well as material. At the same time, however, it maintains that a problem arises in regard to the multiplicity of beings in one and the same species, as well as in regard to the subject of the multiplicity of beings on the transcendental plane. It likewise holds that an explanation can be found only in a correlation of real principles. Still, the solution of the question does not lie in an exaggerated formalism, which pretends to find in reality the exact replica of the logical structure of abstract knowledge. The formal or virtual distinction is of the logical order, and it does not answer directly to a parallel distinction in reality; nevertheless, it rests on an internal and real structure of the nature of the being, for it implies a specific order, containing many individuals. This last requires a real double source to assure to the complete reality of every individual its specific perfection and individuality.

The Thomistic solution of the problem of individuation of material beings is grounded on a determined conception of hylomorphism: the matter is a pure potency, the substantial form of every individual is unique. Matter and form are essentially correlatives, and the hylomorphic structure is real only by reason of a principle of existence distinct from this structure.

Francis Suarez, (1548–1617), admits as does St. Thomas, the pure potentiality of the matter, and the unicity of the form; but on the other hand, he is opposed to the real distinction of essence and existence. The material essence, composed hylomorphically, is really identical with the act of existence; and so the matter as much as the form is an entitative act. Suarez does not see why it would be contradictory to say that prime matter could exist, while being completely separated from the form. But immediately there arises the problem of the substantial union of the hylomorphic composite: if the matter is existent in itself and likewise the form, and if they can exist separately, what is the internal principle of their substantial union? This principle is neither the matter nor the form nor merely the conjunction of the one and the other; it is a mode of union, implied in the substantial composite.[18] But does this opinion offer anything more than a mere verbal solution?

In Thomism this problem does not arise, because the constituent principles are conceived as correlations; they have no meaning except from the viewpoint of their synthesis, and there can be no question of appealing to any other reason to explain their union. "From matter and form an 'unum' arises, with no extraneous bond to rivet them together."[19] Besides, matter, a pure potency, is not of itself related to the principle of existence; it can have this relation only by reason of its reference to the substantial form. For all that exists must be quidditatively determined. From every point of view the unity of the individual is solidly established on the internal cohesion of its structure.

---

[18] "The union of matter with the form is something substantial, and it is not the matter nor the form nor the composite, but it is implicitly involved in the composite." Francis Suarez, *Disputationes metaphysicae,* dist. 34, sect. 4, n.34 (edit. Vivès, Paris, t. 26, p. 378 a).

[19] *Contra Gentes* II, c.58: *Adhuc.*

CHAPTER VII

THE DYNAMIC ORDER OF PARTICULAR BEING

I. BEING AND BECOMING

THE ONTOLOGICAL STRUCTURE OF BEING IN BECOMING

1. The Correlation of Potency and Act

ACCORDING to the testimony of science matter is subject to constant motion, and life carries with it an immanent development without surcease. Becoming reigns supreme in the whole domain of human experience, whether internal or external. Heraclitus was quite right in observing that everything is in flux, πάντα ῥεῖ, that everything changes and, in fact, that nothing "is," in this sense that nothing ever reaches a point where it is fixed definitively in its term.

Two questions can be raised à propos of all reality: *is* it? and *what* is it? For the things of our world of experience we will answer this last question by saying that they are things in motion. The study of becoming is therefore on the plane of that of *quiddity* or essence.

The motion of the objects of the external world can be verified only from the outside. On the contrary, in myself I observe becoming as a fact that is lived, with which I am identified and which burgeons into consciousness; I lay hold of it as from within, a fact which permits me to note its characteristic and essential traits.

Becoming always signifies the passage from one term to another. Such is local motion, the transfer necessary to go from one place to another; such also is qualitative motion by which, for example, colors change their shade, and sounds their pitch, sensations are transformed, and ideas are developed.[1] In all becoming at least two

---

[1] "In every change it is necessary that there should be something identical, common to both terms of the change. . . . For by the name of change and

170

determined points come into play, of which one is attained after the other, but in connection with the first. Becoming implies the many but also unity; it is a synthesis, an order, one becoming. It is not enough that one determination should present itself after another, in order that there may be a becoming; if we restrict ourselves to draining a glass of water and then filling it with wine, we have not by this very fact changed water into wine. Becoming demands an essential bond between the two terms of the change; both of them, the one after the other, must determine the same subject intrinsically.

The synthesis of the two terms is made in the real unity of the subject. If I pass from one idea to the other the whole reality of this becoming is reduced to the real subject which I am, since it is I myself who change when I am affected successively by these two determinations. The subject of the becoming, therefore, extends to the two terms and it embraces them in its unity. It preserves its identity all through the change; it perdures.

Further, in the subject the terms of the changes are linked together in a particular fashion. They have formally a point of contact, for the first term plays a role in the production of the other term, and the second term prolongs the first by modifying it. For example, I have such and such a thought. It does not appear to me as *the* thought without further qualification; it is only this thought here and now, and it is distinct from every other which could likewise present itself. The thought which comes to my mind appears, therefore, as relative to others; it belongs to an order of thoughts. I can pass from one to the other; in other words, a change can be produced in my mind. Consequently, the active determination of the mind is bound up with a determinability; when I find myself in the act of thinking of such an object, I am at the same time in potency to think of such other object, and the second act will be bound to the first by the fact that in the first I am already really in potency to attain to the second act. Becoming, therefore, implies the permanent identity of a subject whose determinability is actuated successively in different ways.

transition there is designated that something identical is different now from what it was before." St. Thomas Aquinas, *De potentia*, q. 3, a. 2, corp. Cf. *loc. cit.*, ad 1, ad 4; *In libr. Sententiarum*, II, dist. 1, q. 1, a. 2, obj. 2; *Contra Gentes* II, c. 17 Praeterea; *Summa theol.*, Ia, q. 45, a. 2, ad 2. Confer Henri Bergson, *L'Évolution créatrice*, 20e édit., Paris, 1917, pp. 1 and 323 ff.

Every term of the becoming is relative to the other terms of the same order. It is distinct from them, and is therefore limited. As a finite act, it is bound up with an ulterior determinability, with a potency which remains directed towards other acts. In other words, it is individuated because it is received into a potency. At every stage of its evolution the subject participates in a new way in a specific perfection, according to the measure in which the potency contained in it is actuated. All becoming implies, therefore, a structure of potency and act; the successive acts which come to determine the subject in motion arise from and are grounded in the broad determinability of the subject which remains. Whatever changes acquires a new "taleity" and becomes other than it was, but only in a relative way, that is, within the limits of the potentiality which remains; and that which changes never ceases to remain the same determinable subject, but relatively, that is, its new determination must be taken into account.

This structure is as real as the being in becoming. The determination and the determinability are at every instant concrete properties of the real subject, considered in its entirety. They are irreducible, for they are opposed as the positive and the negative. What is determined is such, and not otherwise. The same subject considered as determinable can become other, while just now it is such as it is. It is not enough to say that the determinable subject does not possess such or such determination (this would be simply negative); we must add to this that it has really a positive disposition for this determination, that it is in potency relatively to this determination. Undoubtedly, at this moment it is only potency, and this is why it has not yet attained the determination in question, and in so far it is undetermined. Being in becoming, therefore, is at once determined and undetermined; it is a synthesis of act and potency.

Potency and act are principles of being, transcendental relations. Just as becoming they have to do with one and the same real being. It would be altogether futile to maintain that one part of what is in motion changes, while the other part remains; for then motion would have to do only with the first part, and not with the other, and the problem of the non-simplicity of the being in the process of becoming would therefore remain unanswered.

Potency and act of the being in motion have meaning only if we consider them as correlations. The definition of this act must mention the potency, which is its principle of individuation and limita-

tion; the definition of the potency must mention the act, to which it
is related as to its principle of determination. From the correlation
of potency and act in the being in becoming it follows that their
structure is wholly and entirely subject to change, that is, this being
which remains always determinable, in potency, is determined in
itself by its successive acts. It also follows that this same being,
unceasingly determined, remains always determinable in itself, but
the fundamental reason of the determination of the whole subject
is the principle of act, and the reason of the determinability is the
potential principle.

Since the potentiality of the being in becoming is determined, and
therefore modified, by gliding through successive acts it impresses
a direction on the change. The potentiality which is preserved during
the course of the evolution of the subject is not oriented towards any
and every act whatsoever, but towards such a particular determination which is adapted to what is actually present; the becoming
takes place according to an order. The structure of this becoming,
the correlation of potency and act, impresses on it a regular course
and secures for it an internal unity. For example, in my memory
which endures and is constantly developed just as everything living
is developed, the past acts on the present, and the present moment
prepares for the future. At the present moment the memory acts
dependently on the work which it has put forth in the past, and its
present activity sketches the outlines of its future action. Never are
the various moments of a change, of everything which takes place in
the course of time, interchangeable; every one of them occupies the
only place which can belong to it, exactly as the years roll on in a
fixed and invariable order. Becoming implies the internal and ordered unity of the different moments which succeed one another.

In every finite reality multiple changes are effected in various
directions, and the structure of a being is complicated in proportion
to the number of its lines of development.

2. The Fundamental Structure of Substance and Accidents

The particular being, the subsisting reality of the finite subject, is
subject to motion, and the permanent subject includes in its duration the various terms of the change which affects it. When I take a
walk I do not cease to be the same person all the time of my stroll;
after as before my consciousness reveals to me the same ego. In the

course of my walk my identity is maintained: I have not become an other, you or he. As a particular being, as this man here who is distinct from every other, and who therefore must be called a being in himself, a substantial reality,[2] I have remained exactly the same. Nevertheless, I have undergone a change, for in truth it is I myself who have taken a walk. Now to walk is to move, to be changed; my whole self has been in motion, and therefore my whole self has undergone a change. Since this change has not penetrated into the substantial identity of the conscious being which I am, it

---

[2] Among the ancients the word "substance" had, in the current language, a material meaning which it always preserved, *scil.*, goods, riches, inheritance, property. It is with this meaning that it is found in the Latin translation of the Bible. The following use it in the same sense: Tacitus, Quintilian, the jurists of the 12th and 13th centuries, as also St. Jerome, Prudentius, St. Gregory the Great, and others. The word is used also to designate a sediment, more or less solid, in a liquid. Cf. *Psalm* 68, v.2.

Seneca (2–66) gives the word *substantia* a philosophical meaning; he gives it the meaning of material reality, i.e., of reality without further qualification, corresponding to the Greek "ὑπόστασις" in the language of the Stoics, in opposition to the term *emphasis* which designates an appearance, an empty apparition. Quintilian (1st century) put the term *substantia* in relation with *ousia*, the first of Aristotle's categories. In the sense of *ousia*, it is found in Tertullian (160–240), in the Latin version (4th century) of the works of St. Irenaeus of Lyons, in Marius Victorinus (4th century), and in St. Augustine. He writes: "For instance, essence, which in Greek is called *ousia*, and which we more commonly call substance." (*De Trinitate*, Bk. V, 8, 9; P. L. XLII, 917). Frequently a relation is established between the word *substantia* and the verbs *substare, subsistere*, and it is then given the meaning of a substratum. Cf. Curt Arpe, *Substantia* in *Philologus* (Leipzig), t. 94 (N.F. 48), 1940, pp. 65–78.

In the course of the dogmatic controversies, especially those of the 4th and the following centuries, the term *substantia* became equivocal, because writers put it in relation to the Greek word "ὑπόστασις." This latter they had opposed after some time to *ousia*, for which up to then it had often been a synonym, and to which they had given the meaning of "person."

The Scholastics prefer to give to *substantia* the meaning of *essentia,* and they frequently put us on guard against possible misunderstandings on account of the Greek term ὑπόστασις. Thus Ulrich of Strasbourg writes as early as the 13th century: "The noun, *substance*, is equivocal. It is used there . . . according to the usage of the Latins who, as St. Augustine says in the same place, take substance in the same sense as essence. When however it is said that person signifies substance, since this name was used by the Greeks, it is evident that it signifies that substance on which the Greeks imposed this name, and this is substance which is *hypostasis*." (This unedited text is cited by J. De Ghellinck, S.J., "L'entrée d'essentia, substantia, et d'autres mots apparentés dans le latin médiéval, *Archivum* "Latinitatis Medii Aevi" (*Bulletin du Cange*), t. XVI, 1941, p. 110; "Essentia et substantia. Note complémentaire," *ibid.*, t. XVII, 1942, pp. 129–133.)

At the time of Scholasticism's full-bloom, writers generally distinguished *substantia* and *subsistentia*, and this last word had then the meaning of person. On the subject of the signification of the terms *hypostasis* and *subsistentia*, cf. *infra*. pp. 241–242.

must be that I have become other without becoming an other, that my being, therefore, has undergone in its subsistent reality a non-substantial modification.

This non-substantial change of the subsistent being indicates the presence in this latter of a non-substantial determinability, of a real potency directed towards real acts, which do not modify the substantial identity itself, and which, therefore, do not correspond to any potency strictly substantial. From this it follows, first of all, that the being in becoming includes the structure of substantial and of non-substantial principles or accidents; and then, that these accidental principles carry with them principles of the order of potency and principles of the order of act.

Becoming is the passage from one "taleity" to another, from a first determination to a second, from one positive term to another positive term. Becoming never terminates in nothing; otherwise it would get nowhere. Whatever does not go anywhere never moves; consequently, change does not have to do with being, as being, for being is not opposed to non-being. It is not possible to get inside of being, no more than it is possible to get out of it, since being is transcendental. Being cannot be changed into non-being, nor can nothing become being. Creation is not, strictly speaking, a change or a becoming, no more than annihilation would be such. Becoming, therefore, always has to do with particular being considered in its "taleity," in its *essence*.

Consequently, we must admit that besides the substantial determination which endures and is maintained throughout the change, there are accidental determinations which the change affects. We will say, therefore, that besides substance or the substantial essence there are accidents or accidental essences.[3] We cannot really confound this question "What is this being?," or, "What is its mode of

---

[3] St. Thomas uses the expressions *essentia substantiae*, and *essentia accidentis*. Cf. *Summa theol.*, IIIa, q. 77, a. 1, ad 2.

The Angelic Doctor observes that the term *substantia* is taken at times in the broad sense of quiddity or essence, and that then it can be applied equally well to accidents. "*Substantia* is used in two ways, as is evident from *Metaphysics* V, text. 15. For in one way substance is used, inasmuch as it signifies the content (*rationem*) of the first category; and this is either the form or the matter or the composite, which is in the predicament *per se*. In another way substance is used for that which signifies "quid" in all things, just as we say that the definition of a thing signifies the substance of a thing; and in this way whatever is said positively, no matter in what genus it is, is substance or has substance." II *Sentent.*, d. 37, q. 1, a. 1, sol.—Besides, St. Thomas notes that if *substantia* is taken often in the sense of *quidditas*, it signifies at times *suppositum*. Cf. *supra*, p. 129.

substantial being?" with this other question: "What is it besides?" or, "What is its mode of accidental being?" The mode of substantial being is essence par excellence, and the term "essence" designates this in the very first place, for the accidental determination is only the accidental modification of the substantial mode of being. When the term "essence" is used to designate accidental realities, we express this clearly; for example, we will ask in what do the quality, quantity or the relations of a being essentially consist.

Substance and accidents are the constitutive principles of being, transcendental relations. Their whole reality consists in their correlations; they have meaning only in the structure which contains them. Since they are correlatives, both of them stamp with a concrete character the whole reality which contains them. There cannot, therefore, be any question of conceiving substance as an immobile or inert substratum, on which or around which motion takes place which by itself would have nothing to do with the fundamental reality of the subject in becoming.[4] Undoubtedly, particular being rigorously preserves its fundamental identity all through its changes; consciousness bears witness to this: I am and I remain always the same all through the course of my life. But on the other hand, to live is to move oneself (*vivere est sese movere*); life is a constant evolution. Not for one instant do I hold myself aloof from such evolution; it would be nonsense to pretend that my life unfolds itself around me without touching me. On the contrary, this evolution takes place in me; it is I who live, it is I who change.

The structure of substance and accidents is the ontological foundation of these data of experience. It is a structure: substance is a principle of substantiality which has to do with the whole being, including the accidents. Hence, accidental becoming participates in the substantial reality, it belongs to it and it finds in it its principle of individuation. Every moment of my life is completely my own; it is carried along, animated, individuated by my substance, and it would be inconceivable that it could change from this subject or that it could in any way belong to another person. And vice versa, the accidents are principles of the becoming of particular being,

---

[4] ". . . since, however, *fieri* belongs only to the composite, whose property also is the *esse* (for "forms" are said to be not as subsistent, but as that by which the composites are). Hence, they are said also to become, not as if they themselves were produced, but by the production of the composites, which are changed by the transformation of matter from potency into act." St. Thomas, *Quodlibetum* IX, q.5, a.11.

considered in its complete reality, including the principle of substantiality. Consequently, substance takes part in the change which it individualizes. Every one of my actions really exists in me and through me; it is in them that I live and exist.

The correlation of substance and accidents can therefore never be broken up. We cannot conceive them outside of their mutual relation. The substance of particular being has meaning only as a relation to the accidental becoming, and the accidental order has meaning only as a relation to the substance. Hence it follows that the distinction between substance and accidents cannot be verified by experimental methods. There are no means to separate the accidents in order to uncover the substance and to verify its reality, no more than we can isolate the accidents in order to study them outside of the relation which orients them towards substance.

Many authors seem to consider the existence of accidents as an empirical fact which it suffices to verify; and they strive to prove merely that it is necessary to admit the reality of a substance, placed outside of these accidental data. This is a mistake. What is given in experience is the real, particular being, and not the accidents. It must be proven that this being carries with it a structure, containing both accidents and a substance. The reality of these accidents, which are the constitutive principles of particular being, cannot be revealed by methods of observation any more than can the reality of the substance. On the other hand, we cannot prove that there are accidents in this being without proving by the same means that there is a substance, and reciprocally, since substance and accidents are real correlative principles. It is not easier, therefore, to get to the accidents than to recognize the substance; we must admit them together as distinct principles or indeed reject their real distinction.[5]

---

[5] The Scholastics found in certain truths of the supernatural order, notably in the dogma of the Holy Eucharist, a confirmation of their philosophical theory of substance and accidents. In the Holy Eucharist the accidents of bread and wine are separated from their substance; a fortiori it must be admitted that they are really distinct from substance. As a matter of fact, the Council of Trent teaches that in the consecration of the Sacrifice of the Mass "there takes place a conversion of the whole substance of bread into the Body, and of the whole substance of wine into the Blood of our Lord Jesus Christ, the species only of bread and wine remaining." (Sess. XII, can. 2, Denzinger–Bannwart, *Enchiridion Symbolorum*, n. 884.) The theory of the real distinction of substance and accidents permits us therefore to express this dogma adequately, and such theological application in a matter so important argues assuredly in favor of this scholastic doctrine.

It would be quite another thing to wish to establish the philosophical value

3. Objections Leveled Against This Structure

These considerations suffice to show that the objections which some bring against the theory of substance lack foundation, at least if we understand this theory in the sense we have just set forth. These objections always presuppose that we are justified in considering substance and accidents separately. Substance, it is said, is conceived as a complete and finished reality; otherwise, how could it be the substratum of the accidental order? And accidents must possess their own peculiar determination, since they help to determine substance. But thus we see ourselves forced to set up a separa-

---

of this theory by starting from theology. It would be necessary to prove, first of all, that the terms used by the Council of Trent are not to be taken merely in the usual sense of the words, but that they must be given the technical significaction which scholastic philosophy, and even such a definite scholastic school, attributes to them. It would be necessary, in particular, to show that the words "species of bread and wine" must be understood exactly in the philosophical sense of the accidents of bread and wine.

Furthermore, if in the Holy Eucharist the accidents of the bread and wine are separated from their substance, and on the other hand they present all the appearances of ordinary bread and wine, we must not conclude from this that in the things which common experience confronts us with, we get directly to the accidents and not to the substance, and that only the reality of this substance, in opposition to that of the accidents, demands strict proof before we can admit this substance.

As a matter of fact, we must take into account transubstantiation. This is something altogether different from the simple suppression of the substance of the bread and of that of the wine, since it is a *conversio* of these substances, terminating in the Body and Blood of our Savior, which it renders present under the species of the bread and wine. These species remain real only in connection with this transubstantiation and with the real presence of our Savior in them. Thanks to this their reality can "subsist" as if the proper principle of substance were still present, and this is why this reality appears to us to be that of ordinary bread and wine.

On this point an analogous case can throw light on this matter. The Thomists admit that the human nature of Christ, while being deprived of its own proper *esse*, exists by reason of the *Esse* of the divine Word, to whom this nature is united hypostatically. No one ever dreamed of concluding from this that, since the human nature of Christ is real without being effectively united to its own proper *esse*, and since on the other hand our Lord in the course of His life on earth seemed to be similar to other men, our daily experience permits us to verify only the nature or substance of men, and that their *esse* could be admitted as real only if we have demonstrated its reality by means of discursive reasoning.

What experience gets at, is the particular being. This being consists of a structure of essence and existence, of substance and accidents; i.e. a metaphysical structure, which must be demonstrated and of which no principle is, as such, ever a datum of experience.

tion between being and becoming, and consequently between being and life in living things. Substance is and remains the same; the accidents become, they change, by them life is developed. And yet, it is nonsense to maintain that the substance of a living thing does not live, does not become, since it forms the permanent substratum of the stream of life. Consequently, we must admit that substance is itself in a state of becoming; we must therefore attribute to it what was considered as belonging properly to the accidents.

Similarly, it is nonsense to maintain that the stream of life is not, that it does not have consistency. We must, therefore, admit that accidents have in themselves what it takes to be real; in other words, we must attribute to them what was declared to be proper to substance. In a word, we cannot without contradiction separate the idea of substance and the idea of accident, since the definition of the one mentions what is proper to the other, and reciprocally. A fortiori, our adversaries conclude, there can be no question of admitting a real distinction between substance and accidents.

These objections are untiringly rehearsed in modern philosophy. They contain a grain of truth, but they do not fall in line with the sane concept of substance. Once the correlation of substance and accidents is established these objections lose their efficacy.

In virtue of its real principle of substantiality a being demands existence in itself, as a particular being, "ei competit esse in se, subsistere." [6] But this principle is likewise a substance in the etymologi-

---

[6] "Since *ens* is not a genus, this very thing which is *esse*, cannot be the essence of the substance or the accident. Hence, the definition of substance is not "ens per se sine subjecto," nor the definition of an accident "ens in subjecto"; but rather, it belongs to the quiddity or essence of substance to have an *esse non in subjecto*, but to the quiddity or essence of an accident it belongs to have an "esse in subjecto." *Summa theol.*, IIIa, q. 77, a. 1, ad 2. Cf. *Sentent.* IV, d. 12, q. 1, a. 1, sol. 1; *Quodl.* IX, q. 3, a. 5, ad 2; *Summa theol.*, Ia, q. 3, a. 5, ad 1.

The principle of substantiality is not identified with the principle of existence, but it is in correlation with this latter, just as in the line of quiddity it is in correlation with the accidental principles. We can, therefore, conceive the case where a substance would not be effectively united to its own proper principle of existence. This is the way in which the Thomists express the mystery of the Person of Christ: the human nature of our Lord exists, not by its own proper *esse*, but by the divine *Esse* of the Second Person of the Blessed Trinity. However, this nature or substance remains none the less a particular nature, a transcendental relation, oriented towards its own proper *esse*. This is why, in place of saying that substance is "that which is in itself," we say more more accurately, "substance is that to which it belongs to be in itself." Furthermore, these expressions are elliptical, and we must understand them as follows: that which is or subsists, is the particular being, by reason of a principle of existence which corresponds to a mode of substantial being.

cal meaning of the word, *sub-stare;* it is the substratum of the accidents, that is, it is in potency to receive further accidental determinations. The first meaning is not to be separated from the second: the principle by reason of which the being demands existence in itself is precisely that by reason of which it is determinable in an accidental manner. For the principle of substantiality, which is wholly the principle of individuation of the accidents, is a transcendental relation of which the accidents are the term; and this is all that it is.

Accidental becoming determines the subsistent being, it is added to the latter: *accedit substantiae.* It belongs to a particular being which in virtue of the principle of substantiality demands existence in itself. It belongs to an accident to be related wholly to the substance, *ei competit inesse substantiae,* and thus to participate in the existence of the particular being: *ejus esse est inesse.* We must avoid considering substance as a complete and subsistent being to which the accidents would come to be added from the outside. Substance is a principle of substantiality; it is not identified with particular and subsistent being, since this last ought likewise to include accidental principles. The accidents are, just as much as substance, constitutive principles of particular being. They are received into the substance as into the potential principle which individuates them; they participate in the correspondent existence and they borrow their reality from it.[7]

This is why every one of the accidental principles does not have its own principle of existence; there are not as many accidental

---

[7] The accidental principles being really distinct from the substance, we can conceive the case where these accidents would not be effectively united to their substance. In this way the theologians commonly express the mystery of the Holy Eucharist: by transubstantiation the substance of the bread and that of the wine are changed into the Body and Blood of our Lord, while the accidents of the bread and wine remain, and our Lord is rendered present in them, without these accidents becoming properly the accidents of Jesus Christ. These accidents remain, nevertheless, accidental principles, transcendental relations, completely oriented towards their substance, and by this reference to their own substantial principle they remain individuated. This is why, in place of saying that the accident is "that which is in a substance," we say more accurately: "An accident is that to which it belongs to be in a substance." It is proper for it to be related to the substance as to its subject of inhesion and therefore of individuation.

We can draw a comparison with this case, which is of the supernatural order, *scil.,* that of the human soul which naturally survives its actual union with matter, and which continues always to be a formal principle, a transcendental relation, individuated in virtue of its reference to the material principle. Cf. *supra,* p. 165.

principles of existence as there are accidents. For there can be only one principle of existence in a particular being.[8] We must not forget that every constitutive principle is a transcendental relation which is related to the other principles and which communicates to them, by this thorough-going relation, the peculiar character of which it is the reason; every principle imprints a particular stamp on the whole subsistent being.[9] The principle of existence is the reason of the subsistence of the whole structure of particular being which includes accidental principles as well as substance. Similarly, the principle of substantiality is the reason of the fundamental "taleity" in virtue of which the particular being is distinct from every other reality and is directed to one peculiar existence; and this essential and distinctive character stamps the accidental order as well as that of substance and existence.[10] Similarly, too, the accidental principles are the reason of a becoming which concerns the particular being in its entirety, and in which its whole ontological structure as well as every one of its constitutive elements participate.

4. Historical Notes

Aristotle was the first to formulate explicitly the distinction between substance, οὐσία, and accidents συμβεβηκότα; but he treated the question especially from the logical viewpoint. After the example of the Arabians, the scholastic authors developed the theory on the ontological plane. In the 13th century it was unanimously admitted that in particular being there is a real distinction between substance and accidents; [11] the Schoolmen were even strongly inclined to exaggerate the distinction and to admit without qualification the separability of these elements.

St. Thomas Aquinas, however, took pains to refine his ideas on this

---

[8] "There is also a certain creature which does not have *esse in se*, but only in another, just as prime matter, any form whatever, or the universal; for *esse* does not belong to anything except it be something particular subsisting in nature." St. Thomas Aquinas, *I Sentent.*, dist. 8, q.5, a.1.

[9] Cf. *supra*, pp. 104–106.

[10] The same remark holds good for prime matter and the substantial form, which are the constitutive elements of the essence. The matter individualizes the whole particular being, the form gives all of this latter its specific determination.

[11] "Whatever may be said of the faculties of the soul, no one save a mad man (*insanus*) ever thought that the habits and the acts of the soul are its essence." St. Thomas Aquinas, *De spiritualibus creaturis*, a.11, ad 1.

point. An accidental principle according to him is not a being, but it is that by which a thing is, the real reason in virtue of which the particular being is determined in such or such an accidental fashion. The accident has not in itself its principle of individuation; it is individuated by the substance which receives it. Similarly, it cannot be conceived outside of the relation by which it is referred to the substance.[12] Substance, *id quod est,* could not on its part, be conceived outside of its role of substratum, without its reference to the accidents; for it is only by the union of substance and accidents that the complete particular being exists.[13]

Decadent Scholasticism forfeited the meaning of ontological structure. It considered every non-logical distinction as a real distinction between things, *inter rem et rem.*[14] On this pattern William of Ockham . O.F.M., conceived the distinction between substance and accidents.[15] Undoubtedly, he grants that in the natural order these elements are inseparable; they are nevertheless real objects which are defined separately, and it would be impossible to deduce from the consideration of one the existence of the other,[16] since the first is not in the second. Considered in itself, every one of these elements is therefore complete and finished, and if it enters into relation with others this relation is superadded to its own reality. Nicholas d'Autrecourt (*circ.* 1338) defended the same thesis, but with more logic and insistence. No one, he says, has ever been able to verify empirically the existence of material substances, no more than any one has ever been able to demonstrate their reality. The soul is the only substance which is accessible to us, since it manifests itself to our consciousness.[17]

---

[12] In regard to the relation between the accident and the *esse* according to St. Thomas, cf. *supra,* pp. 130–132.

[13] "The faculties of the soul are accidents as well as properties. Hence, although we may understand what the soul is without these faculties, still it is not possible or intelligible for the soul *to exist* without these." *De anima,* a. 12, ad 7.

[14] Cf. *supra,* pp. 65–66.

[15] "In creatures there cannot be any distinction whatsoever outside of the soul, except where there are distinct things." William of Ockham, *Summulae in libros Physicorum,* p. 1, q. 14.

[16] Cf. Erich Hochstetter, *Studien zur Metaphysik und Erkenntnislehre Wilhelms von Ockam,* Berlin, 1927, pp. 139–143.

[17] "Aristotle never had evident knowledge of any substance other than his own soul, understanding substance as a certain thing, other than the objects of the five senses and our formal experiences. And this is true because he would have had knowledge of such a thing before all reasoning,—which is not true, since they do not appear intuitively, and even rustics would know such things to exist.—Neither are they known from reasoning, *scil.,* by inferring from things

In the course of the scholastic renaissance of the 17th century, Francis Suarez, S.J., tried to free himself from nominalism in order to renew an intimacy with the tradition of Scholasticism in full-bloom, and in particular with the doctrine of St. Thomas. On the problem of substance and accidents he does not faithfully hark back to the conceptions of the Angelic Doctor. Accidents, he teaches, differ from substance and they find in it their substratum; and yet they have in themselves the reason of their own individuation,[18] and it is not impossible that certain accidents, for example, quantity, should pass from one substance to the other while remaining the same individual reality.[19] These remarks make us wonder just what difference there is ultimately between substance and accidents; substance is the subject which receives the accidents, but before exercising this function of substratum, it exists in itself as a subsistent reality. The accidents on their part are individual realities, things, before being received into the substantial subject. Why then could we not call them beings? Suarez remarks, as a matter of fact, that being can be predicated absolutely and without qualification of the accidents.[20] And so there arises the problem of the unity of the particular being: what is the foundation of the unity of a being composed of many things? What is the bond which unites substance and accidents? Suarez makes an appeal to a mode of union, *modus*

perceived that they exist before all discursive reasoning, because from one thing it cannot be inferred that another thing exists, as the conclusion placed above states." J. Lappe, "Nicolaus von Autrecourt, sein Leben, seine Schriften" (*Beiträge zur Geschichte der Philosophie des Mittelalters,* B. VI, H. 2, Münster, 1908, pp. 1–13, and 1*–8*).

[18] Cf. Fr. Suarez, *Disputationes metaphysicae,* dist. 5, sect. 7, n. 3. This thesis corresponds to that which Suarez defends on the subject of the individuation of material beings. The matter and the form are concrete, and therefore individual realities, and there is no cause for seeking a reason of individuation which would be extrinsic to them save the efficient cause which produces them. Suarez does not see the significance of the problem posed by St. Thomas, just as, besides, he does not see the significance of a parallel problem, *scil.,* that of the distinction of the real principle of existence and that of the essence. This problem is that of the limitation or the individuation of the particular being by its principle of *taleity.* As a matter of fact, these problems have no meaning if the constituent elements of a being are conceived as absolute things, and not as transcendental relations.

[19] "Although it is probable that numerically the same accidents do not remain in the thing generated as were in the thing corrupted, the opposite still seems more probable as regards the quantity and the dispositions." *Op. cit.,* d. 14, s. 3, n. 38.

[20] "*Ens* can be predicated absolutely and without qualification of the accident." *Op. cit.,* d. 32, s. 2, n. 18. This St. Thomas denies explicitly; cf. *supra,* p. 133.

inhaerendi, which is added to the accidents to fix them in the substantial subject; [21] but this is a purely verbal answer. At bottom, the problem is insoluble because it is only a pseudo-problem, resulting from an inexact conception of the structure of particular being. In the Thomistic system such a difficulty could never be raised, since the elements of the real structure, in this case substance and accidents, are there conceived as mutual relations. They have meaning only in relation to their union; they are therefore united without our having to make an appeal to some superadded bond, *nullo vinculo extraneo ea colligante.*[22]

Non-scholastic philosophers of the modern era reject the real distinction between substance and accidents. Actually it is to the concept of substance, bandied about by decadent Scholasticism, that they are opposed, but they do not know any other concept than this; and the identity which they establish between the activity and the complete reality of the being does not allow them to make a stand against insuperable difficulties. This was, first of all, the attitude of Descartes (1596–1650),[23] who speaks of things or of substances.[24] Between a substance and the attribute which makes us know it [25]

---

[21] "For in the accidental form, to be actually in another is, as it were, the ultimate term or mode of such form in regard to its existence. For an accident, although by force of its existence it is apt and prone to inhere, still it is not actually inhering merely by force of its existence, but it needs a special mode of inhering which is, as it were, the ultimate term of its existence." *Op. cit.,* d. 34, s. 4, n. 24.

[22] St. Thomas uses this expression in regard to the hylomorphic composite, but it applies literally to the present case. Cf. *Contra Gentes,* II, c. 58: *Adhuc.*

[23] "The constituent elements of the idea of substance such as Descartes had received from the scholastic instruction at La Flèche, were the same as are met with in Suarez but stripped of the subtleties of the Spanish Jesuit, and reduced to a rough sketch where the difference between the Thomistic and the Suarezian substance was no longer sensible." R. Jolivet, *La notion de substance,* Paris, 1929, pp. 128–129. Cf. Étienne Gilson, *Index scolastico-cartésien,* Paris, 1913, pp. 275–281.

[24] "But what is it therefore that I am? A thing which thinks, that is to say, a thing which doubts, which understands, which conceives, which affirms, which denies, which wills, which does not will, which imagines, and which senses." *Lettre à . . .* (6 *mars,* 1638), édit. Adam–Tannery, t. II, Paris, 1898, p. 38. Cf. "IIᵉ Méditation"; *Réponses aux troisièmes objections,* t. IX, Paris, 1904, p. 136.

"Now I frankly avow that to signify a thing or a substance . . . I have availed myself of terms as simple and as abstract as I could." *Op. cit.,* t. IX, p. 135. "I knew that I was a substance." *Discours de la méthode,* 4ᵉ partie (t. VI, p. 33).

[25] "But if after this we wished to strip this same substance of all its attributes which make us know it, we would destroy all the knowledge which we have of it, and thus we could in truth say something of substance, but all that we

there is not a real but only a logical distinction.[26] Thus it is that
material substance is nothing other than extension, and spiritual
substance is not really distinct from thought.[27] The other properties
of matter and spirit are merely modifications of these substantial
attributes.

This point of view is not without difficulties. What becomes of
the unity of the thinking substance during the succession of the acts
of thought? If all matter is reduced to extension how are we to explain the transient activity of material things? Where are we to find
the fundamental unity of man, if he is composed of a corporeal substance and of a substance which thinks?

The occasionalism of Nicholas Malebranche (1638–1715)—which
consists in denying activity to matter, under the pretext that everything is created by the Power of God [28]—and his ontologism, which
refuses to see in the spiritual activity of man a bona fide conception
of human thoughts, and which reduces this activity to a pure contem-
plation of the divine ideas,[29] cannot suffice to solve these difficulties.[30]

---

would say of it would consist merely in words, whose meaning we would not
conceive clearly and distinctly." *Réponses aux quatrièmes objections,* t. IX, p.
173. Cf. *Les principes de la Philosophie,* 1e partie, ch. 60, 63, t. IX, pp. 51, 53.

[26] Descartes does not recognize any other real distinction than the distinction
between things. "The real (distinction) exists properly . . . between two or
more substances. . . . There are two sorts of modal distinction, *scil.,* the one
between the mode which we have called manner (*façon*) and the substance on
which it depends and which it diversifies; and the other between two different
manners (*façons*) of one and the same substance. . . . Finally, the distinction
which is made by thought, consists in this that we at times distinguish a substance from any one of its attributes, without which nevertheless it is not possible for us to have a distinct knowledge of it. Or it consists in this that we strive
to separate from one and the same substance two such attributes, by thinking of
the one without thinking of the other." *Les principes de la Philosophie,* 1e partie,
cc. 60–62, t. IX, pp. 51–53.

[27] "But even though every attribute is sufficient to make us know substance,
there is nevertheless one in every substance which constitutes its nature or its
essence, and on which all the others depend. For example, extension or length,
width and depth, constitute the nature of the corporeal substance; and thought
constitutes the nature of the substance which thinks. For everything else besides which can be attributed to body, presupposes extension, and it is only a
dependence on this which is extended. Similarly, all the properties which we find
in the thing which thinks, are only different manners of thinking." *Op. cit.,* ch. 53,
p. 48.

[28] Cf. Nic. Malebranche, *Entretiens sur la Métaphysique,* 7e Entr., V et XIV.
(edit. of Arm. Cuvillier in Bibl. des textes phil., Paris, 1945, pp. 209, 222). *Recherche de la Vérité,* 1. VI, 2e partie, ch. 3 (edit. of Paris, 1871, t. IV, p. 325).
Cf. *Éclaircissements sur le traité de la nature et de la grâce,* 1r éclairciss.

[29] Cf. *Recherche de la Vérité,* 1. III, 2e partie, chap. 6, (t. III, pp. 398 ff.).

[30] Arnold Geulincx (1624–1669), professor at Louvain and later at Utrecht,

The fact remains that it is impossible to ground matter and spirit, the two constitutive substances of man, in one and the same substantial unity. Neither is it explained how the activity of spirit, which unfolds itself in various acts, is reduced to the reality of one and the same spiritual substance; [31] and finally it is not without reason that Leibnitz thought that if material substance is not truly active, we must conclude from this that strictly speaking it does not exist at all.[32]

Benedict Spinoza (1632–1677) severs the Gordian knot of the metaphysical problem by reducing all reality to one unique substance. This infinite being possesses an infinity of properties, of which only two are known to us, extension and thought. The objects which we perceive are merely modifications of these attributes and their reality is not distinct from the eternal substance.[33] In this pantheistic conception the activity and the responsibility of finite persons are definitely compromised and the infinite Being becomes the receptacle of contradictions.

G. W. Leibnitz (1646–1716) grasped the whole importance of the problem of substance, and all during his life he strove to solve it.[34]

---

had already proposed the doctrine of occasionalism. *Opera Philosophica, Metaphysica vera*, Pars III, Quinta Scientia. "Fortis est ille creator seu motor." (edit. J. P. N. Land, La Haye, 1892, t. II, p. 19). *Annotata ad Metaphysican*, ad pag. 192 (pp. 291–293) and ad pag. 195 (pp. 297–298).

[31] Confer Nic. Malebranche, *Réflexions sur la prémotion physique*, c. X (édit. Œuvres complètes, Paris, 1837, t. II, p. 387. Cf. *Réponse à la troisième lettre d'Arnauld*.

[32] G. W. Leibnitz, in *Acta eruditorum*, Leipzig, 1698 (edit. C. J. Gerhardt, *Die Philosophischen Schriften von G. W. Leibnitz*, t. IX, Berlin, 1880, p. 515). Cf. *Lettre à Hoffmann*, 27, IX, 1699 (edit. J. E. Erdmann, Berlin, 1840, t. 1, p. 161, a).

[33] Spinoza's monism is implicit in these two definitions:
"By cause of itself, I understand that whose essence involves existence, or that whose nature cannot be conceived except as existing."
"By substance I understand that which is in itself, and is conceived through itself; that is, that whose concept does not need the concept of another thing by which it ought to be formed." *Ethica more geometrico demonstrata*. Pars prima, defin. 1 et 3.
Spinoza deliberately turned away from the Cartesian conception of substance. He formulated Descartes' definition as follows: "By substance we understand that which needs only the concursus of God in order to exist." *Renati des Cartes Principiorum philosophiae* pars II, def. 2 (edit. Carl Gebhardt, t. I, Heidelberg, 1923, p. 181). According to this conception of Descartes, it is not substance but the divine Being distinct from every finite substance, which is the fundamental reason of all reality.

[34] ". . . substance, whose knowledge is the keystone of the vault of philosophy. This is the difficulty which has embarrassed Spinoza and Locke so much."

Pantheism appeared to him to be a profound mistake, and occasionalism in his eyes was merely camouflaged pantheism. On the other hand, Cartesian mechanism seemed indefensible to him, and he opposed to it his monadology, conceived as a pluralistic dynamism.[35] He pushed this dynamism to the extreme, to the point of denying all passivity to matter, and he likewise developed the most complete pluralism by availing himself of a theory of continuity, constructed on the pattern of infinitesimal calculus.

Leibnitz ran up against the problem of the communication of the monads, a problem which was for him very difficult to solve after having defined substances as congeries of monads, beings endowed only with immanent activity, but yet hermetically sealed and without windows. He searched for the solution in the universal order of the monads, an order which must be grounded on their nature and ultimately on God, the author of their being and their order. There exists a pre-established harmony of the substances which finds its reason in God.[36]

As its author understands it, monadology is a metaphysical doctrine, not an empirical one,[37] for Leibnitz considered it as certain that

---

Lettre du 22 mars 1714 (edit. C. J. Gerhardt, *Die Philosophischen Schriften von G. W. Leibnitz,* t. III, Berlin, 1887, p. 567).

[35] "The monad is nothing other than a simple substance, which enters into the composites; simple, i.e., without parts. And there must be simple substances, since there are composites. For the composite is nothing other than a heap or *aggregatum* of the simples. Now, where there are no parts there is neither extension, nor figure, nor possible divisibility. And these monads are the veritable Atoms of Nature, and in one word, the elements of the things." *Monadologie,* n. 14, t. VI, Berlin, 1885, p. 607.

"The monads have no windows by which any thing could either come in or go out." "The change in every monad is continual." "From this it follows that the natural changes of the monads come from an internal principle, since an external thing cannot influence its interior"; "an internal principle which effects the change from one perception to another." *op. cit.,* nn. 7, 10, 11, 15, pp. 607–609.

[36] "I have said that we can imagine three systems to explain the commerce which obtains between the soul and the body, i.e., first, the system of the influence of one on the other, which is that of the schools, taken in the popular sense, and which I believe impossible according to the Cartesians. Secondly, that of a perpetual surveillant who reproduces in the one that which takes place in the other, in pretty much the same way as if a man had been charged constantly to bring into agreement two faulty watches which of themselves would not be capable of keeping together; and this is the system of occasional causes. Thirdly, that of the natural agreement of two substances, such as would obtain between two very exact watches." *Lettre à Basnage,* 1698, *op. cit.,* Vol. IV, p. 520.

[37] "A monad is an atom of substance, and it is a metaphysical point." *op. cit.,*

a physical system, such as that of Descartes, leads inevitably to ulterior problems of a metaphysical nature. And yet this monadology raises more questions than it solves. Among others, how are we to explain the fundamental unity of beings such as man, who is composed of a number of monads? Leibnitz began by appealing to the theory of the "dominating monad" [38] which quite soon appeared to him as insufficient; and reflection on these difficulties led him more and more to Scholasticism.[39] The theory of the "substantial bond" which he proposed hesitatingly towards the end of his career, bears resemblances to the ideas of the Scholastics. It is a principle of metaphysical unity, which is distinct from the monads [40] to such an extent that there is no contradiction in its being separated from them; [41] a principle, moreover, which reduces the various monads to the unity of one and the same being.[42] But how are we to understand this thesis? Every monad is a substance; the substantial bond is one of these likewise, and all of these substantial unities can be separated

Vol. IV, p. 511. "They are not parts but foundations, not ingredients but requisites of the phenomena." Vol. II, pp. 262, 270.

[38] "Animal or corporeal substance, which the Monad, dominating over the machine, makes one." t. II, p. 252. Cf. *loc. cit.*, pp. 305, 306, 482.

[39] "My doctrine, therefore, of the composite substance seems to be the very doctrine of the peripatetic school, except that it did not admit the monads, but I add these with no detriment to their doctrine. You will hardly find any other difference, even though you strain your mind." t. II, p. 511.

"You will be surprised that I pretend to rehabilitate in some fashion the philosophy of the Schools, so decried in the opinion of many. . . . But the same principles of mechanics and the laws of movement spring in my opinion from something superior which depends rather on metaphysics than on geometry, and which the imagination would not be able to get at, although the mind conceives it quite well."

Système nouveau pour expliquer la nature des substances (première rédaction), Vol. IV, pp. 471–472.

[40] "This union (of the soul and body) is a thing of metaphysics, which does not change anything in the phenomena." Vol. VI, p. 45.

"(This bond) differs from the Monad, because it realizes the phenomena; the monads, however, can exist, although they are not bodies, but only phenomena." Vol. II, p. 519. "It consists in primitive active and passive force from which arise both actions and passions of the composite, which are grasped by the senses, if more than the phenomena is placed in existence." Vol. II, p. 518. "And that will be what they call prime matter and substantial form; and it will be necessary that the accidents of the composite be its modifications. These indeed are transitory but the composite substance itself will endure equally as well as the dominating Monad." (t. II, p. 486).

[41] "This substantial bond is a bond naturally, not essentially. For it requires monads, but it does not essentially involve them, since it can exist without monads, and the monads without it." (t. II, p. 516).

[42] "From many substances there arises one new (substance)." (t. II, p. 438).

and exist separately, even after they have been united. How then can they be founded in one single being? To solve this problem Leibnitz would have been obliged to revert to the Thomistic conception of metaphysical structure.

Just as Cartesianism, so English empiricism borrowed the notion of substance from decadent Scholasticism. John Locke (1632–1704) who received at Oxford a training in the philosophy of Ockham, considered substance as the unknown substratum which we suppose must be found under the qualitative data of things in order to support them.[43] But while declaring substance as unknown, he admits it as real, both in material things as well as in spiritual beings.

George Berkeley (1685–1753) develops this empiricism in an idealistic sense: material things are only subjective representations of the minds; they have no substance.[44] On the contrary, personal consciousness puts us face to face with the substance of our spirit, and with the reality of its functions of knowledge and will.

David Hume (1711–1776) pushed empiricism to the limit, and derived phenomenalistic conclusions from it. The concept of substance has no intelligible content; it is not possible to distinguish the substance of things from the immediate data which these things furnish us, for in this case it would have to be possible likewise to separate them from this substance. But if we make an abstraction from these data there is nothing left to know.[45] What we call substance is only a collection of the data which we consider as constant, because we can discover them at will in our experiments. The ego is not a privileged instance; it, too, is merely a flux of impressions and feelings, which through memory we gather up into a pe-

---

[43] "The idea, then, we have to which we give the general name of 'substance,' being nothing but the supposed, but unknown, support of those qualities we find existing, which we imagine cannot subsist *sine re substante,* 'without something to support them,' we call that support *substantia;* which according to the true import of the word, is in plain English, 'standing under' or 'upholding.' *An Essay concerning Human Understanding,* Book II, c. 23, n. 2 (edit. London, 1880, p. 209).

[44] "Their *esse* is *percipi;* nor is it possible they should have any existence out of the minds or thinking things which perceive them." *Principles of Human Knowledge,* p. 1, n. 3 (edit. A. C. Frazer, Oxford, 1901, t. 1, p. 259).

[45] "We have no impression of self or substance, as something simple and individual. We have therefore no idea of them in that sense."

"Whatever is distinct is distinguishable; and whatever is distinguishable is separable by the thought or imagination. All perceptions are distinct. They are, therefore, distinguishable and may be conceived as separately existent, and may exist separately, without any contradiction or absurdity." *Treatise of Human Nature,* Book I, appendix (edit. Oxford, 1896, pp. 633–634).

culiar and "substantial" unity.[46] This conception of Hume reappears
in the positivism of the 19th century, for example, in England in the
writings of John Stuart Mill and in France in the works of Hip-
polyte Taine.[47]

It is, nevertheless, easy to see that to explain reality it is not enough
to appeal to a multiplicity of data. These latter present themselves
as clustered together, as unified; whence comes this unity? And in
particular, what does the unity of the current of conscience hold on
to? What is its real principle? Hume understand only too well that
this was a real problem, and he declared honestly that he felt himself
unable to answer it.[48]

---

[46] "The idea of substance must therefore be derived from an impression of
reflexion, if it really exists. But the impressions of reflexion resolve themselves
into our passions and emotions; none of which can possibly represent a substance. We have therefore no idea of substance distinct from that of a collection of particular qualities, nor have we any other meaning when we either
talk or reason concerning it."

"The idea of a substance as well as that of a mode, is nothing but a collection of simple ideas, that are united by the imagination, and have a particular
name assigned them, by which we are able to recall, either to ourselves or others
that collection." *Op. cit.*, Book I, p. I, sect. 6, p. 16.

"We readily suppose an object may continue individually the same, though
several times absent from and present to the senses; and ascribe to it an identity,
notwithstanding the interruption of the perception, whenever we conclude that
if we had kept our eye or hand constantly upon it, it would have conveyed an
invariable and uninterrupted perception. But this conclusion beyond the impressions of our senses can be founded only on the connexion of cause and effect;
nor can we otherwise have any security, that the object is not changed upon us,
however much the new object may resemble that which was formerly present
to the senses." *Op. cit.*, Book I, p. III, sect. 2, p. 74.

"Setting aside some metaphysicians of this kind, I may venture to affirm of
the rest of mankind that they are nothing but a bundle or collection of different
perceptions, which succeed each other with an unconceivable rapidity, and are
in a perpetual flux and movement." *Op. cit.*, Book I, p. IV, sect. 6, p. 252.

[47] Cf. J. Stuart Mill, *System of logic ratiocinative and inductive*, London,
1843, Book I, c.3, paragraphs 6, 7, 8. As regards the unity of our conscious life,
it would rest on a substance whose nature escapes us.

H. Taine expresses himself as follows: "The essence or nature of a being is
the indefinite sum of its properties." *Le positivisme anglais*, Paris, 1864, p. 35.
"The ego . . . does not contain anything outside of its events and their connections." *De l'Intelligence*, Paris, 1870, t. I, p. 383. "We think that there is
neither spirit nor body, but simply groups of present or possible movements,
and groups of present or possible thoughts. We believe that there are no substances at all, but only systems of facts. We regard the idea of substance as
a psychological illusion." *Le positivisme anglais*, p. 114.

[48] "In short there are two principles which I cannot render consistent; nor is
it in my power to renounce either of them, viz., that all distinct perceptions are
distinct existences, and that the mind never perceives any connexion among

Kant (1724–1804) attempted by means of criticism to solve the difficulties which had been suggested to him in good part by reading the works of Hume. He retains the idea of substance, but merely as a subjective category which leads us to synthesize the successive data of experience around a permanent and solid nucleus. It is in a synthetic a priori judgment that we express the substance of the objects.[49] Substance, therefore, has no ontological value; it teaches us nothing about the nature of reality. Furthermore, if we attribute to it the traditional realistic meaning, we find ourselves driven into a corner by antinomies both in regard to the soul and in regard to the body.[50]

To solve these philosophical problems Henri Bergson (1859–1941) appealed to the intuition of reality, such as is given to us in the lived experience of our conscious activity.[51] Reality appears to us there in

distinct existences. Did our perceptions either inhere in something simple and individual, or did the mind perceive some real connexion among them, there would be no difficulty in the case. For my part I must plead the privilege of a skeptic, and confess that this difficulty is too hard for my understanding. I pretend not, however, to pronounce it absolutely insuperable. Others, perhaps, or myself upon more mature reflexions, may discover some hypothesis, that will reconcile those contradictions." *Treatise of Human Nature*, Book I, appendix, p. 636.

[49] "Our apprehension of the manifold of appearances is always successive, and is therefore always changing. Through it alone we can never determine whether this manifold, as object of experience, is coexistent or successive. For such determinations we require an underlying ground which exists at all times, that is, something abiding and permanent, of which all change and coexistence are only so many ways (modes of time) in which the permanent exists. And simultaneity and succession being the only relations in time, it follows that only in this permanent are relations of time possible." *Critique of Pure Reason*, First Division (i.e. Transcendental Analytic), Book II, Chapter II, section 3, 3, *First Analogy*; N. K. Smith's translation, pp. 213–214.

[50] *Op. cit.*, Second Division (i.e. *Transcendental Dialectic*), Book II, Chapter II; N. K. Smith's translation, pp. 384–484.

[51] In this method we must see more than a simple empirical description of facts. This is what Bergson himself observes in emphasizing the difference to be placed between his conceptions and the "stream of thought" theory of William James. "This is tantamount to saying that the 'stream of thought' is of an essentially psychological nature, and that my duration (*durée*) is more metaphysical. I understand by it that it is at the root of all reality, that it is common to us and to things. . . . The analogy between the views of James and my own, although real, is therefore less striking here than people at first believed, and it masks a fundamental difference." *Lettre du 23 août 1923, in Études bergsoniennes.* "Hommage à Henri Bergson" (1859–1941), Paris, 1942 (new printing of the special number of the *Revue Philosophique*, août 1941). Floris Delattre, *Les dernières années d'Henri Bergson*, p. 10.

constant becoming. Life is a vital current and its unity is that of the current.[52] We should be mistaken in distinguishing here immobile moments between which the change would stretch. The intellect which represents becoming to itself as formed of congealed and parcelled out blocks to which motion would be added, sees itself forced to spread underneath an inert "substance" which links the disjointed parts together. But it is impossible for this artificial construction to give us an accurate knowledge of the becoming which is constantly flowing on.[53] In fact, the unity of that which becomes is not found outside of the becoming, for reality is not in itself a stranger to motion. This unity is nothing other than real duration; that which lives, endures, preserves itself in being developed; that which preserves itself, is no different from that which lives and is developed. That which lives, therefore, belongs to the real in itself, to subsistent reality; we can call it a substance, provided that we do

[52] Cf. *L'Évolution créatrice*, 20e édit., Paris, 1917, pp. 3 ff., 325 ff.

[53] "But as our attention has distinguished and separated them artificially, it is indeed obliged to reunite them by an artificial bond. It imagines thus an amorphous ego, indifferent, immutable on which the psychological states (which it has erected into independent entities) would be strung or unstrung. Where there is a fluidity of fading nuances which encroach upon one another, it perceives glaring colors and, so to speak, solid colors which are juxtaposed as the various pearls of a necklace. It is forced then to suppose a string, not less solid, which would hold the pearls together. But if this colorless substratum is unceasingly colored by that which covers it, it is for us in its indetermination as if it did not exist, for we perceive precisely only what is colored, i.e., our psychological states. In truth, this substratum has no reality; it is for our consciousness a mere symbol designed to recall to it unceasingly the artificial character of the operation by which attention juxtaposes one state to another, where a continuity unfolds itself. If our existence were composed of separate states, of which an impassible ego had to make synthesis, there would be no duration for us, and one psychological state which remains identical as long as it is not replaced by the following state, does not endure either. It would be fatuous, therefore, to align these states alongside of each other on the ego which sustains them; these solids strung on another solid will never make up the duration which flows. As a matter of fact, what we thus obtain is an artificial imitation of the interior life, a static equivalent which will lend itself better to the exigencies of logic and language, precisely because we will have eliminated real time from it. But in regard to our psychical life, such as it unfolds itself under the symbols which cover it up, we readily perceive that time is its very stuff.

"Furthermore, there is no stuff more resistant or more substantial. For our duration is not one instant which replaces another; there would then be nothing but the present, no prolonging of the past into the actual, no evolution, no concrete duration. Duration is the constant progress of the past, which gnaws into the future, and which swells up as it advances. From the moment that the past grows unceasingly, it also preserves itself indefinitely." *Op. cit.*, pp. 3–5; (English translation, pp. 3–4).

not distinguish it from life, the whole of which is developing unceasingly.[54]

Bergson's descriptions bring out into strong light the double character which stamps the whole reality of being in becoming; this being changes and yet it preserves its identity: it perdures. But how
can we stop at our verification of this? How can we refuse to search
for what reality requires in order to be able to perdure? And as a
simple reality could not present the double character which becoming carries with it, we must indeed wonder how the non-simplicity of
this reality must be conceived, and what is the ontological structure of being in becoming.

Louis Lavelle likewise would put us on our guard against the
theory of substance as a support. Being, he says, is always act, and
although in finite being act and being do not coincide, they are
nevertheless in correlation. It is being which is actualized, and it is
the act which penetrates into the nature of being. There is, therefore,
no being which is not intrinsically affected by act, and there is no
substance which would be merely an inert substratum. "It is because
the act is one that the subject is one. The apparently unfathomable
mysteries of metaphysics are born of these subjects in which an
idolatrous propensity realizes the abstract idea of permanence, and
which (as we easily see) are impervious to all intelligibility and incapable of any efficacy." [55]

And yet finite being does not posit itself altogether autonomously;
it is not an act that is entirely free; it does not create itself. Its act
consists in the free usage which it makes of a real potency which has
been given to it, and of which it itself is not the source.[56] In this
case, however, we must distinguish in the order of acting the act
itself and the real potency to which it corresponds. This fundamental potency is what the Scholastics call substance or nature,

---

[54] "Previously Bergson protested against those who wished to make of him
one who denies substance. 'They might just as well (says he) ascribe to me
the denial of the *ego*, which I have spent my life in studying. I reject an ego-
thing, i.e., an immobile ego, and in a general way a substance which would be
an inert and undefinable support. But to define substance and the ego by their
very mobility, this is not to deny them, no more than we deny the themes of a
symphony, which are likewise an essential mobility." A. D. Sertillanges, *Avec
Henri Bergson*, Paris, 1941, p. 37.

[55] L. Lavelle, "De l'insertion du moi dans l'être par la distinction de l'opération et de la donnée," in *Tijdschrift voor Philosophie*, III, 1941, p. 735. Cf. *De
l'Acte*, Paris, 1937, p. 67: "The act is itself without support and without effect."

[56] Cf. *supra*, pp. 153–155.

and the faculties which are accidents emanate from it. There is no difficulty in admitting these as really distinct principles, provided that we do not forget that they are real correlations, forming together a structured being.[57]

II. THE ACCIDENTAL ORDER

Substance: The Active Principle, the Subject, the Final Cause of the Accident

All accidental reality belongs to a particular and subsistent being. It does not come from the outside as a foreign element which would be tacked on to this being merely by an extrinsic bond; it really forms a part of it, and is found there as in its subject of inhesion, and since it is an element of accidental becoming it arises and is developed in the being which it affects.

Becoming bears witness to the activity of the finite being, for we speak of activity wherever something is produced; and this is indeed the case with becoming. As it is in one and the same being that the becoming takes place and is therein wholly comprised, it is indeed this being itself which is changed, modified, and which acquires new determinations, while preserving its substantial identity. We must, therefore, consider the principle of substantiality, the fundamental reason of the identity of the being, as the active principle[1] of the accidental modifications. In this sense we generally call it the "nature" of the being.[2] As the whole course of accidental be-

---

[57] The American non-scholastic authors, e.g., Muirhead, D. W. Prall, J. Loewenberg, A. S. Murphy, Pepper, Dennes, V. F. Lenzen, who recently examined the question of substance, have not raised the true metaphysical problem, as Augustine J. Osgniach, O.S.B., has shown quite well.

Cf. *The Analysis of Objects of the four principal Categories, An historical-critical Analysis in the light of Scholastic Philosophy*, New York, 1938, pp. 137–174.

[1] It is better to call it "active principle" rather than "efficient cause," because this latter term designates, in general, the extrinsic efficient cause, i.e., the being which is the cause of that which is produced in an other being.

[2] The term "nature" (in relation with the Latin *nasci*, to be born) signifies, therefore, the fundamental, substantial reason of the activity of the being. One is impelled by his "nature," (we say); one acts according to his "nature." Often the word "nature" is used as a synonym of the words "essence" and "quiddity." It is thus that we ask: what is the nature of this being, i.e., of this substantial reality? But also: what is the nature of this quality, quantity, or relation, i.e., of this accidental reality?

St. Thomas distinguishes the following meanings of the word "nature": "The

coming unfolds itself in the reality of the subsistent being whose identity is attached to the principle of substantiality, this substantial reality is actuated by it, and it is the final principle of it. The accidental determination, therefore, has its active principle in the substantial being, and it finds therein its subject of inhesion as well as its purpose.[3]

Every being acts conformably to its nature; it finds there the rule and the measure of its development. Since accidental becoming is the active expression of the substantial determination of the perfection peculiar to a being, it is by this means that we endeavor to determine the nature of this being.

A. STRUCTURE OF THE ACCIDENTAL ORDER

1. Quality, Activity

Accidental becoming implies an accidental structure of potency and act. The principle of determination, which is the accidental act, comes to determine a potency just as every other actual principle does. This potency must be an accidental potency, for the passage from a substantial potency to the act would necessarily constitute a substantial change, a transformation of the substance. It is, therefore, not enough to have an accidental act; there must also be a potency of the same order to form the ontological foundation of the accidental becoming of a being.[4] This potency can be designated, in

---

name "nature" is spoken of in many ways, as Boethius says in the book *De duabus naturis et una persona Christi*. For first, "nature" is used inasmuch as it refers commonly to all beings, inasmuch as nature is defined as everything which can be grasped in some way by the intellect. Secondly, in as far as it belongs only to substances; and thus nature is said to be that which can act or be acted upon. Thirdly, nature is said to be that which is the principle of motion or rest in those things in which it is *per se*, and not merely accidentally. Fourthly, the specific difference informing everything, is called nature." *II Sentent.*, d.37, q.1, a.1, sol.

[3] "The subject is compared to the accident in three ways. First, as offering it a support; for the accident does not subsist *per se*; it is, as it were, propped up by the subject. Secondly, as potency compared to act; for the subject is put under (*subjicitur*) the accident as a kind of potency under the act, hence accident is called a form. Thirdly, as a cause in regard to its effect; for the principles of the subject are the principles of the accident *per se*." *De virtut. in communi*, a.3. "The subject is the cause of the proper accident, i.e., the final cause, and in a certain sense the active cause, and also the material cause, in as far as the subject receives the accident." *Summa theol.*, Ia, q.77, a.6, ad 2.

[4] Cf. *supra*, pp. 175–176.

a general way, by the name of faculty. It is the real reason on account of which a particular being, fully determined in its substance, remains none the less determinable in an accidental manner.

By accidental becoming particular being acquires a new quality; while remaining substantially this being here determined by its substantial form, it is modified in "such" a manner. That is, it is determined by a form or an accidental principle of "taleity," by a "quality." The faculty, just as the act which corresponds to it, is found in the line of quality.

2. *Quantity, Passivity*

In the material being whose substance is composed of a potential principle and an active principle, that is, matter and form, accidental becoming must present a structure, corresponding to this hylomorphic composition, since becoming is only the active expression of the substantial perfection. This is the reason why it includes not only a principle of activity, the faculty directed towards action, but likewise an opposite principle, that of passivity. It is therefore by a natural necessity that the action of material things is penetrated by passivity. Undoubtedly, the faculty of these things is in itself determined, oriented towards such a formal object, but this natural orientation while being determined in certain respects, remains nevertheless determinable. This is to say that it suffers a lack of intrinsic perfection and that it is exposed to outside influence to fill up this void. A material thing passes over into action only by the help of another; it must get an impulse from the world that surrounds it. In their activity material things always hold together; they complete and sustain one another mutually. The active element of material becoming resides in the quality, and the passive element in the quantity.

Quantity is bound up with extension, with the exteriority, the continuity of the parts. The unity of a being here loses its strength, for every extended reality in space is divisible; the parts which are there united are in potency to be separated. This is a source of weakness, for things extended in space are physically dependent on one another; in other words, they are subject to the physical laws which govern the cosmos. Material things form a continuous mass, inert and passive, weighted down with bonds which bind them one to the other. To put itself in motion a physical thing must be moved by another; to pass over into action it must be pushed into action. Action and passion are always found united in the same active process. Material force spreads itself out in moving from one point to the other. The activity of every portion of matter is intrinsically dependent on that of the others, and it is developed within the framework of the external stimulus which it undergoes unceasingly.

3. The Bond Between Quality and Passivity. Space and Figure. Time and the Line of Evolution. Situation in Time and Space: Here and Now

Every particular being is being (*ens*) by reason of the real principle of existence which its structure includes; it is this being here (*res*), distinct from every other by reason of its principle of substantial essence. When there is question of a material reality its degree of specific perfection is bound up with the substantial form, whereas its individuation is connected with prime matter. Considered in its accidental development, every particular being includes a qualitative determination (*quale*); if there is question of a material reality, it is, besides, a thing extended in space (*quantum*).

The correlation which is established between quality and quantity corresponds to that which unites form to matter in the substance; it is a reflection of this latter in the accidental order. The two terms of this relation are irreducible, really distinct, but they are united to such an extent that it is impossible to define the one without mentioning the other. Quality and quantity form a complexus of transcendental relations; their correlation is a structure of act and potency. Prime matter is the substantial principle of individuation; quantity plays a corresponding role in the accidental order. Material activity is individuated, measured and limited by passivity.

Consequently, it is impossible for quantity to exist without its union with quality; it would not have the minimum of determination required for existence. And it is equally impossible for a material quality to exist without its union with quantity; for then it would lack individuality. Matter, extended and quantified, is always determined in such or such a way by reason of the quality which is found there; and matter, active and qualified, is individually this thing here by reason of the place which it occupies in space. The in-

terpenetration of quality and quantity in one and the same individual thing imposes on it determined dimensions, a characteristic
figure, which manifests its nature; for example, it is the external form
of such an animal or such a plant, or the various crystalline forms.

Material activity implies a qualitative becoming which must be
developed in the continuity of space, since it is bound up with quantity. It traverses successively different parts of space; it is a movement which goes on in the continuity of time. And just as the becoming of a particular being always carries along with it its individual
qualitative stamp, every material reality is developed according
to a rhythm which is peculiar to it. It expresses, so to speak, its nature within the graphic curve of time which it traces, and there it
fixes the traits of its history; animals, plants and all things, each one
of them has a duration which is peculiar to each one.

Every material reality is bound up with those which surround it,
by reason of its extension in space. It is impossible to extract it from
the physical order and to isolate it, for it is precisely the fundamental
principle of quantity which is the reason of its individuation. Consequently, this thing is wholly dependent on its relations with the
surrounding realities; we can indicate it only by giving it a situation (*situs*), by indicating its place in time and space, in other words,
by determining where (*ubi*) and when (*quando*) it presents itself,
at what distance it is from the other moments of time and the other
portions of space. In order to speak of what happens in the material
order we must determine precisely where and when it takes place.[5]

4. The Structured Unity of the Faculties

It is a fact of experience that the development of a finite being
is not simple; for example, our study of man establishes the fact that
human activity is directed at one and the same time towards many
irreducible formal objects. The active determinability of man carries
with it, therefore, a structure; it is not made up of a simple potency,
but it includes a whole complexus of faculties. As a matter of fact,

---

[5] Time and space form the general framework including all the lines which
the development of things must follow. A material fact, therefore, always presents a mechanical aspect; it is realized in a local motion. It is this point of view
which the modern physical sciences have chosen in their researches; they strive
to measure the facts, to define the *hic et nunc* of every datum, by determining
minutely its mechanical relations with the others.

we must distinguish the physical and physiological forces from those of the psychical order, and these latter include organic energies and spiritual faculties. These last are the intellect, oriented towards being, and the will, whose formal object is the good, willed as good by reason of the value which we recognize in it. All these forces and faculties of man are related to one another in different ways, and they correspond to one another as act and potency. The complexus of these active principles furnishes the picture of the various developments by which man expresses the riches of his substantial perfection of being, and by which he untiringly pursues the full expansion of his nature.

Thanks to his spiritual faculties, the human being transcends the material and organic order; on the other hand he has at his disposal material forces, but we can never lose sight of the fact that his activity, which forms a complicated structure, remains fundamentally one, as he is one human nature. The superior faculties are united to the organic forms by a natural and therefore harmonious relation. As the spiritual soul is the substantial form of the human organism, and is individuated itself by the substantial matter, the spiritual operation animates human activity entirely, and it carries in itself the individual stamp which the accidental principle of quantity imprints on it. And furthermore, internal experience bears witness to the fact that, on its side organic and sentient life is introduced into the unity of consciousness, and that it there participates in the higher life of the ego. There is a profound distinction, but not a chasm, between the so very different elements which go to make up human activity; they compenetrate one another and are grounded in one and the same development.

5. *The Faculties and the Habits*

The faculties (which are potencies directed towards action) are qualities; those which are spiritual are withdrawn from the determinism of matter and they develop themselves freely. They are flexible and docile powers which we can guide, educate, and "form," by imprinting on them a firm disposition, a permanent orientation, a tendency to be developed in such a direction rather than in such other. Such internal modification of the faculties increases their efficacy; action becomes more sure and more supple, more agreeable and easier. In scholastic language this stable disposition is called a *habitus*.

There are innate habits which spontaneously incline the faculty to express itself in a determined direction, for example, to recognize the first principles of thought ("habitus" of principles) and of moral action ("synderesis"). Others are acquired, either rapidly or after repeated acts. Habit, a stable disposition which determines the faculty in itself, is capable of being developed and of becoming stronger. It would not be necessary to conceive its growth as a quantitative enlargement, resulting from the adjunction of new parts, but it should be thought of rather as a qualitative maturation. For the faculty is a quality and its internal modification must, therefore, be of the same order.[6] And yet the spiritual element of human activity is always bound up with an organic element, and the qualitative development of the spirit never ceases to be translated in some way into the life of the organism. The spirit animates the human body and imprints its stamp upon it, just as the spirit itself borrows from its relation with matter the individuality which characterizes the whole being.[7]

---

[6] It was principally in regard to the increase of Christian charity that the Scholastics raised the problem of the development of the habits. St. Thomas Aquinas defends with a good amount of decision the thesis of the qualitative increase. Cf. *I Sentent.*, dist. 17, q.2, a.2; *Summa theol.* Ia–IIae, q.66, a.1; q.24, a.5; *De virt. in communi*, a.11.

Henri Bergson attempts to show that life and becoming are of a qualitative nature, and that they cannot be measured by quantity. Pierre Duhem has insisted likewise on the fundamental distinction which we must put between quality and quantity. "A large quantity can always be formed by the addition of a certain number of small quantities of the same species. There is nothing similar to this in the category of quality. Assemble in one vast convention as many mediocre geometricians as you will be able to encounter; you will never have the equivalent of an Archimedes or a Lagrange. Stitch pieces of dark red cloth one to the other; the result obtained will never be bright red. . . . Every degree of a quality has its own individual characteristics, which render it absolutely heterogeneous to other degrees, more or less intense. A quality of a certain intensity does not contain, on the title of an integral part, the same quality of less intensity; it does not enter, on the title of a part, into the composition of the same quality rendered more intense. . . . Diderot asked facetiously how many snowballs were necessary to heat an oven; the question is embarrassing only for one who confuses quality and quantity." *La théorie physique*, Paris, 1906, p. 205. Cf. *ibid.*, pp. 179–180.

[7] It is, therefore, not so surprising that it is possible by the study of human behavior to measure in a certain sense the spiritual element by passing through the organic element. We understand by this fact the signification of the quantitative study which is made in psychology of certain superior functions, e.g., by the use of the metric scale of intelligence. Cf. Arthur Fauville, "Psychologie scientifique et psychologie philosophique," *Tijdschrift voor Philosophie*, II, 1940, pp. 626–627.

6. Relation: Logical and Real Relations. No Real Distinction Between the Relation and Its Qualitative or Quantitative Foundation

The elements of all plurality are related the one to the other to form a whole, as much in the logical order as in that of reality. Ideas are not merely stacked up in our mind, they are organized according to rules. Every idea has a content of signification in virtue of which it holds on to the other ideas; it is related to them logically, it is a moment of the logical course of ideas, of the discursive life of reason. The different ideas are combined among themselves; they form an order because of the logical relations which bind them together. In reality there exist likewise distinct unities which go to make up an order, by reason of the relations which really bind them together. For example, material individuals are united in one and the same species, and all beings together form the order of being. It is in the activity of beings that we see these relations manifested.

Every particular being possesses in itself its existence; it is an "in-itself," but it is finite and therefore it is related to a reality situated outside of its own limits. This relation with something outside of itself does not suppress its own subsistent reality, its "in itself-ness"; on the contrary, it is necessarily connected with it. The particular being is wholly marked with this relativity, since it is wholly finite, and its activity bears witness to this by its whole structure. For example, the series of faculties by which man is developed in multiple directions implies a series of relations, just as varied, through which he is inserted into the order of being. By knowledge, striving, and feeling, by all the energies which he has at his disposal, he is related and bound up with the others. We can classify these relations according to the faculties in which they arise: the relation of knowing and of known differs from that which binds the subject of an appetite to an object because their foundations differ. Spiritual faculties unite beings differently from the way in which organic and material forces unite them, because the relations which derive from quantity profoundly modify the qualitative relations which spring from activity.

Finite reality is characterized, therefore, by its relativity. Relations are really encountered in beings (*esse in subjecto*) and they relate these beings really to others (*esse ad terminum*) on the basis of the substantial nature and of the accidents of quantity and quality which derive from this nature. The question arises for us to discover whether this relativity finds its reason in an ontological acciden- tal principle, i.e., the real predicamental relation which would be really distinct from the principles of quality and quantity, its immediate foundations, and a fortiori from the principle of sub- stantiality.

We must give a negative answer to this question. Every par- ticular being *is*, and it is *this;* we must admit the fundamental struc- ture of the real principle of being and of that of the substantiality. This last principle, by reason of which the being is an "in-itself" dis- tinct from all other reality, is a principle of individuation exercising a function of limitation. Now limit implies a relation between the adjacent domains which it separates, in such wise that the substantial reason of the limitation is at the same time the substantial reason of the relativity. The limitation of the being brings in its train the limitation of its action; if we must distinguish the principles of exist- ence and of substance, we must a fortiori distinguish the principles of existence and of action. The activity of the finite being is at the bottom of tendency, and it is developed in an accidental structure which is really distinct from the substance. Accidents are, therefore, the principles by reason of which particular being is determined in its action. These principles are merely accidental modifications of the mode of substantial being, that is, of the fundamental limiting function. Hence the relativity which characterizes this function ex- tends inevitably to these accidental principles. This is the reason that quality and quantity also imply relativity, since they are, by means of substance, principles of a limited determination of the perfection of being, just as substance itself is such a principle.

On the basis of substance, quality and quantity form the on- tological reason of the limitation of particular being, of its belong- ing to the order of being, and consequently of its relation to the beings which this order includes.

7. The Categories

Along the line of quiddity several predicates can be applied to reality: such a thing is red, such other is heavy; here is a man, a mountain rears its crest down there. In every age philosophers have striven to classify these attributes, but Aristotle has provided us

with a celebrated classification of the categories [8] or of the supreme
"genera," called by Boethius (480–525) the predicaments of being.
At times [9] he reduces them to ten categories, of which the first indicates substance and the other nine the different accidents.[10]

Pythagoras and Plato before Aristotle, and the Epicureans, the
Stoics, and Plotinus after him interested themselves in the same
problem.[11] St. Augustine, Boethius, and the Scholastics took up the
Aristotelian categories, but Descartes, Christian Wolff, and John
Locke proposed a new classification.[12] In the philosophy of Kant
the problem takes on a new meaning; the categories are the fundamental concepts of the pure understanding, "Stammbegriffe des
reinen Verstandes," subjective forms of thought, whose content is
furnished by the data of sense experience.[13] Present-day philoso-

---

[8] The term is borrowed from juridical language, where it has the meaning
of accusation, i.e., of a declaration serving to express how the accused must be
judged. Aristotle used the word to indicate the most general attributes, which
express what must be thought of their "inferiors," scil., of the subjects of which
they are predicated. The first book of the Organon of Aristotle is entitled "Kate-
goriai," and it treats of the supreme genera of being.

[9] Categor., c.4, (edit. Bekker 1 b 26–27); Topic., I, c.9, 103 b 22–23.

[10] Substance, quantity, quality, relation, where? when?, action, passion, posture, habitus. In Greek: οὐσία, ποσόν, ποιόν, πρός τι, ποῦ, ποτὲ, ποιεῖν, πάσχειν,
κεῖσθαι, ἔχειν.

[11] The Greeks of the classical period thought more of the finite than the
infinite in the sense of "undetermined," and they placed the odd above the even.
Pythagoras divided reality into two series of 10 groups, the good and the bad,
scil., the finite and the infinite, the odd and the even, the one and the many,
the right and the left, the masculine and the feminine, the immobile and the
mobile, the straight and the crooked, light and darkness, the good and the bad,
the square and the right angle. In the Sophist, 254 d, Plato enumerates the five
following classes: being, the same, the other, rest, motion. The Epicurean, Lucre-
tius, in his De rerum natura libri sex presents the following series: "intervals,
ways, connections, weights, tracts or regions ('plagae');—concurrence, motion,
order, posture, figure." Among the Stoics, the following classification found favor:
substance, quality, mode, relation. Plotinus distinguishes in the intelligible
realities the five categories of Plato; in the sensible world: substance, relation,
quantity, quality and motion. Cf. Enneads VI, 1, III, c.3.

[12] Descartes and Spinoza distinguish substance, attribute, and mode. Leibnitz
practically adopts Aristotle's list: substance, quantity, quality, activity, passivity,
relation. Christian Wolff proposes the following: beings, essentials, attributes,
modes, extrinsic relations. John Locke reduces all things to the following classes:
substance, mode, relation.

[13] Kant tries to draw up the list of the categories starting with the classifica-
tions of the forms of judgment. He divides judgments into four classes, each of
which contains three subdivisions: quantity (general, particular, singular);
quality (affirmative, negative, infinite); relation (categorical, hypothetical, dis-
junctive); modality (problematic, assertoric, apodictic). To these divisions he
attaches his twelve categories: unity, plurality, totality; reality, negation, limitation; substance, causality, interaction; possibility, reality, necessity.

phers are still pushing their inquiries in this direction, and a number of them are still concerned with this problem of the categories.[14]

Assuredly, Aristotle's classification of the categories which was drawn up experientially, and which consequently applies to material realities, has enjoyed signal success. We have here a series of supreme genera, the first eight of which deserve our special attention.[15] These categories can be considered both from the logical as well as from the ontological point of view. In this latter case, we must ask what are the categories whose irreducibility is such that it denotes a real distinction.

Proof has been given above that in the particular being a real distinction obtains between substance and accidents; hence there is question of metaphysical categories. Among the accidental categories, we must first of all retain quality; it includes especially the various faculties and their "habits." In material beings quality is really distinct from quantity.

The three categories of substance, quality, and quantity indicate the mode of fundamental (substantial) being and the modifications (qualitative and quantitative) which affect it. They imply the limitation of the particular being, and consequently its relativity. All three are, therefore, by definition categories of relativity, because they are categories of particular being. Hence it follows that there is no reason to reserve a special category for relativity. The Aristotelian categories *ubi, quando, passio-actio, situs, habere* and others which we might add to them, emphasize the complicated system of relations of every kind which bind finite beings together, while they develop qualitatively in their spiritual faculties and qualitatively and quantitatively in their organic and material powers.

How does it happen that particular beings which are subsistent entities are wholly included in the order of beings, and are therefore penetrated with relativity in all their elements? What is required for a being to be a being and to be finite? On what ultimately is the structure of finite being based? Here once again we have the fundamental problem of metaphysics.

---

[14] To cite only a few names: Fr. Schleiermacher, H. Lotze, J. Fr. Herbart, Ed. von Hartmann, J. H. von Kirchmann, Chr. Sigwart, A. Rosmini, Ch. Renouvier.—We can read a brief historical survey of the problem of the categories in "Geschichte der Metaphysik" (*Geschichte der Philosophie in Längsschnitten*, Heft 2), by Max Wundt, Berlin, 1931, pp. 93–119.

[15] The last two, *situs* (to be standing, seated, lying down, etc.) and *habere* (to be clothed, armed etc.), as categories are devoid of interest.

The categories permit us to classify the attributes, taken in the order of essence or quiddity. They do not include the attribute "being." Aristotle was the first to observe that being transcends every category since it belongs to the categories to indicate the modes of being, the fundamental mode being that of substance. From this he concluded to the analogy of being; [16] but he did not succeed in posing in a precise way the metaphysical problem of the relation which binds being to the categories, that is, being and essence or quiddity. We have treated this question above: there is in every finite being a real distinction between the principle of existence and the principle of essence; [17] along the lines of this last we must distinguish further the principle of substantiality and the accidental principles.[18] They form a metaphysical structure, a correlation. The essence or the mode of being consists in a transcendental relation whose term is the real principle of existence. Every explanation of the domain of essence, that is, of the domain of the categories, therefore, will have to be grounded ultimately on being. Consequently, becoming, tendential activity, the accidental development of finite being demand an ontological explanation.

B. The Ontological Signification of Active Becoming

1. Becoming: A Tendency to Possess Oneself in the Order of Being. Consciousness of Self and Objective Knowledge

What is the meaning of the active evolution of a being which is continually being developed along the line of the categories, all of them stamped with a relation to the other beings? Why and how is this relativity expressed in the activity of particular beings? At the bottom of every metaphysical explanation we must place the identity of beings; being is only itself, it is radically attached to itself. A particular being is not a part of being, but an ontological whole, substantially complete, existing itself, a subsistent being.[19] In the ego it affirms itself as such, actively taking possession of itself.

This active possession is manifested in consciousness, which is a recollection, a return on oneself, an immanence, a consciousness of self. It consists in knowing oneself, in willing oneself, in being at-

---

[16] Cf. *supra*, pp. 52–53.
[17] Cf. *supra*, pp. 99–104.
[18] Cf. *supra*, pp. 173–177.
[19] Cf. *infra*, pp. 240–247.

tached to oneself, in possessing oneself. It is oriented towards the con-
servation and affirmation of self, towards free and autonomous action,
towards repose and enjoyment in the full dominion over oneself.

And yet the affirmation of self holds good only on the basis of the
affirmation of being; the ego has consistency only because it is and
is rooted in the absolute of being. On the other hand, as there is
question of a particular being which subsists by its participation in
the value of being, it is not possible that in the consciousness of self
the affirmation of being should be reduced to that of the ego. As a
matter of fact, the value of being must be met with in the beings
which exist or can exist outside of the ego, since every participation
implies multiplicity. Hence to know oneself in all truth, particular
being must grasp its individuality and therefore know its limits; it
must recognize that it is one being among many others; it must see
itself, but in the place which it occupies in the complexus of realities;
it must localize itself exactly in the order of beings. When it becomes
conscious of itself and grasps itself as being, it places itself at a
transcendental and absolute point of view, in order to affirm that
it participates in the value of being, as do all the others in the order
of beings. Finally, to know oneself is to lay hold of all reality from
one's own personal point of view.[20]

In addition to knowledge, conscious activity contains the will,
tendency, love. In order to be truly solid the deliberate will to maintain oneself, to love oneself and to enjoy one's perfection must be
founded on a will, a tendency, a love, an enjoyment which embraces
everything [21] since consciousness of self would be vain if it were not
sustained and animated by the absolute of the consciousness of
being.

Conscious life is an activity that is immanent, retiring within itself, incommunicable at least in a direct way; it is nothing other than
the acting ego. If I lay hold of myself only in a conscious activity
which makes me appear as a member of the order of beings, it is alto-

---

[20] "The most profound originality of every ego resides precisely in this power
by which in every point of the universe, it lays hold of an original consciousness
of this Whole in which it is placed, and which in some manner ought to take
place in it in its turn. This it does by revealing itself to it under a unique, privileged perspective, by discovering to it the relations between its parts, which
have meaning only for it, and of which it is always in a sense the artisan and the
creator." L. Lavelle, "Être et Acte," *Revue de Métaphysique et de Morale,*
43rd year, 1936, p. 195.

[21] Cf. J. Peters, C.SS.R., *Liefde* (*Wijsgerige grondbegrippen,* 15), Ruremonde-
Maaseik, 1946, p. 61.

gether necessary that the other beings which this order contains, should likewise appear to me. In myself, in the immanence of my conscious activity, I get to them and recognize them as others distinct from myself, objects that are not reducible to the active subject which I am. Objective knowledge, in all necessity, takes place along the path of conscious recollection by which the subject enters into himself to possess himself such as he is. It is the immanent fruit of conscious and personal activity; it derives from the autonomous power (free from every physical bond) of spiritual consciousness which transcends matter and passivity. It springs from what the Aristotelian tradition calls the agent intellect, from intelligence, a vital immanent activity, which itself conceives the *verbum* which it understands.

Objective knowledge is an enrichment, a completion, an enlargement of the knowing subject, since it is the other, that is, the non-ego situated outside of the subject, which appears to this latter and which is there integrated into the personal life of this finite subject. Particular being strikes out beyond its limits; it breaks, so to speak, the bonds of its own peculiar finite reality. It rises above itself even to the point of laying hold of the infinite, since it brings home and assimilates all the rest, all the other to itself. "It becomes in some sense everything." [22] And yet the ego does not in any way lose its

[22] "A thing is found to be perfect in two ways; one way is according to the perfection of its *esse*, which belongs to it according to its own species. But since the specific *esse* of one thing is distinct from the specific *esse* of another, hence in every thing created there is as much lacking to such a perfection found in every thing, as something more perfect is found in the other species. The result of this is that the perfection of any thing whatever, considered in itself, is imperfect, being only a part of the whole perfection of the universe, which arises from the perfections of the individual things, mutually associated together. Hence in order to apply some remedy to this imperfection, some other mode of perfection is found in created things, according to which the perfection, peculiar to one thing, is found in another; and this is the perfection of the knower, inasmuch as he is knowing. The reason for this is that a thing is known by the knower, inasmuch as the thing known is in some way in the knower; and therefore it is said in III *De anima* (comm. 15, 17) that the soul is in some way everything, since its nature is (*nata est*) to know all things. And according to this mode it is possible for the perfection of the whole universe to exist in one thing. Hence, this is the ultimate perfection at which the soul can arrive, according to the philosophers, that the whole order of the universe and its causes be described in it; and in this also they have placed the last end of man." *De veritate*, q. 2, a. 2.

"Every substance is as an entire world and as a mirror of God or indeed of the whole universe, which it expresses each one in its own fashion, in pretty much the same way as one and the same city is represented differently according to the different situations of him who observes it. Thus the universe is in some fashion multiplied as many times as there are substances, and the glory of God

own identity. This enrichment takes place by an accidental assimilation; this becoming is a self-development, a manifestation of life, self-motion. How are we to explain this immanent enrichment? Ontologically, it is grounded on participation in being.

What participates in the value of being is completely inserted in this order of participation, the order of transcendental being, and it does not contain anything which is conceivable outside of this order. Consequently, it is by its whole reality that a particular being is bound to the other beings; its subsistence keeps step with a relativity which binds it completely to the order of being, to the other particular beings, and just as these latter to the principle of unity which is the foundation of this order. It belongs to metaphysics to study this problem of the one and the many, of subsistence and belonging to another, of the absolute and the relative.

If it is true that by reason of its real participation in being, every particular subject truly possesses this perfection of being and bears witness to its absolute value, it is not less true that for this same reason (that it possesses this perfection only by participation) it bears witness to the order of being, that is, to the other beings which go to make up with it the orderly complexus of reality. What is not pure, subsistent Being, *Esse purum,* but is defined by a finite essence, a particular mode of being, implies necessarily the possibility of other particular beings, and therefore an order of beings. This is the reason why every particular being is related to the others, and it is related to them by reason of its very nature, by reason of the manner in which it subsists. It is related to them ontologically, with absolute necessity, by the whole reality which it contains. This relation to the others is therefore by no means adventitious; it is rooted in the depths of nature. The reality of particular being is inseparable from the relativity which radiates from it in every direction; in its very subsistence it is identified with the cluster of relations through which it is inserted in the ontological order.[23]

is likewise increased by just so many entirely different representations of His work." Leibnitz, *Discours de métaphysique* (ed. Henri Lestienne, Paris, 1929, p. 37).
   [23] "One object cannot be distinguished from the sum of the relations which unite it to all the others. It is, so to speak, their intersection; and the sum of these relations is confounded in every point with the cluster of possibilities which allows every individual form to be and to be inscribed in the universe by a participation which, de jure, is total, but, de facto, is always incomplete and unfinished. There is its veritable essence." Louis Lavelle, "De l'insertion du moi

Consequently, as soon as a particular being succeeds in seeing itself clearly such as it is, it seizes in itself this real relation to all things, and by this very fact it possesses, from the angle which is peculiar to it, a view of the whole order of being. As a matter of fact, this real relation, this orientation towards things, implies an intentional presence of these things in the subject. For every relation is what it is only by reason of the term to which it is related; it borrows from it its real meaning; it possesses this term in its own manner, *quodammodo*, since it signifies and announces it. Similarly, every being, because it is a particular being carries in its own peculiar reality, in an intentional manner the whole order of being. In the measure in which a being becomes more perfectly conscious of itself it distinguishes more and more the infinitely variegated nuances of its intentionality, and there it lays hold of in a strictly personal fashion the unlimited riches of the whole order of being.[24] The development of consciousness of self and that of the knowledge of the order of beings are perfectly correlative.[25]

2. In Man, the Enfeeblement of the Immanence of Becoming by Reason of His Connection with Transient Activity

Why does man not find himself forthwith in possession of explicit knowledge of what is concealed implicitly in his transcendental idea

---

dans l'être par la distinction de l'opération et de la donnée," *Tijdschrift voor Philosophie*, III, 1941, pp. 723–724.

"Subjugated in being by their limits, they (*scil.*, individual beings) seek to make themselves equal to it by their operation." *Ibid.*, p. 726.

[24] We could make applications of this general doctrine to the knowledge which the separated soul considered in the natural order enjoys.

[25] In an interesting study ("Impliciete intuitie," *Tijdschrift voor Philosophie*, I, 1939, p. 84–105) D. M. De Petter, O.P., has brought to light perfectly the fact that the objective and real value of all abstractive and discursive knowledge is founded on an intellectual apprehension of the concrete and existing reality, as such, i.e., as being. Nevertheless, this apprehension is confused, and in so far, insufficient; and as we have consciousness of this insufficiency we must conclude from this that the conscious idea of being is related to some adequate contact of the knowing subject with reality on the purely ontological plane. This real contact which the idea of being succeeds in expressing only in a confused way, Father De Petter calls an "intuition," by reason of its concrete and existential character; but it is an intuition which is only "implicit," since far from its constituting an act of knowledge on the level of consciousness it is a real element of the ontological order, implied in every act of human knowledge.

It is this real contact, this "intentional, ontological presence," essentially required by all conscious life, which we are endeavoring to bring out with precision here.

of being? Because he is not a pure spirit, but a being at once spiritual and corporeal.

Every corporeal substance contains a principle of essential indetermination; on the plane of substance, prime matter is a pure potency, a fundamental principle of determinability.[26] This is the reason why the activity of bodies is characterized by passivity, that is, a body acts only dependently on a complementary actuation which it receives from the bodies that surround it. It is only within the framework of this influence, submitted to passively, that it itself enters into action; material action is always a re-action, an action which unfolds itself within the limits of a "passion."[27]

Man's nature is material; his substance carries with it a hylomorphic composition. All his activity bears the seal of his physical dependence, relatively to the things which surround him. His knowledge is before all else an experience, a contact with present realities, with the ego-in-the-physical-world. Undoubtedly, man is not merely corporeal, he is also spiritual; and this is the reason why this contact is conscious. But as spiritual as he is he always remains corporeal, and thus all his activity, even including his spiritual operations, remains dependent on the material conditions of his being and his acting. His intellectual and voluntary acts themselves take place in a succession of time, that is, within the framework of the material data of experience and organic reactions.

It would be inaccurate to speak of an intellectual knowledge and a sensible knowledge of man, if by this we understood two complete operations. There is only one human activity of knowing, just as man, substantially one, constitutes only one subject of knowledge. But this knowledge is not simple; it carries with it a structure, just as the substance of every man contains a hylomorphic composition. This knowledge is at once sensible or organic, and intellectual or spiritual. The sensible element and the intellectual element are never separated one from the other; they form a correlation: they are transcendental relations which are defined by this correlation, and they exist only in the equilibrium of the structure which they form by their union. The influence which they exercise, the one on the other, is not that of an extrinsic causality similar to the action of one being on another; on the contrary, it is comparable to that which every transcendental relation exerts on the complexus of the

[26] Cf. *supra,* p. 161.
[27] Cf. *supra,* p. 197.

structure which contains this relation; for example, essence, existence, substance, accidents, intellect, will. We have consciousness of the organic character of our knowledge because this latter carries with it a spiritual element; and on the other hand, this knowledge considered in its intellectual development, never ceases to be related to the material data of experience, because its real structure always includes principles of the sensible or organic domain.

The explicitation of the idea of being by making use of the riches which it contains, that is, the determination of the various modes of being which the ontological order embraces, can therefore never be made outside of a human experience which takes place in time. It is effected only in the measure in which, under the influence of physical agents, man acquires in his operative potencies themselves the complement of determination which he lacks by reason of his material passivity. As soon as this material condition is realized his cognitive activity goes over into action; on the other hand, it *re-acts* by reason of its sensible elements, and it is developed within the spatio-temporal framework of experience. On the other hand, by reason of his spiritual elements this cognitive activity (the agent intellect) acts autonomously by going beyond all spatio-temporal relativity and by placing itself at the point of view of transcendental being, that is, at the point of view of the absolute, in one word, that of truth.

An analogous relation unites the instincts and free will. When the intellectual element of knowledge acquires a certain degree of development, there ensues a clarity of consciousness sufficient to allow man to determine himself with full knowledge. Man then impresses upon his existence a peculiar orientation; he succeeds in dominating, up to a certain point, his instinctive tendencies and in freely directing them to the attainment of his own personal last end.

3. In Animals, Plants, Inorganic Matter: Progressive Degradation of Individual Unity and of Its Individual Becoming

The analysis of human activity can throw some light on material things. From this point of view, as we pass from animal life down through the realm of vegetative life to the mineral world, we can verify a progressive diminution of ontological unity. In the world of inorganic things it is quantity which prevails, and activity there is bound up quite closely with local motion which goes on indefinitely in the universe. A plant is already on a plane of higher organization; it possesses a typical, external form and its own duration; it reacts as a whole, and before disappearing it perpetuates itself by giving birth to organisms that are specifically similar, destined to follow a path of similar development. As regards the animal organism, it possesses greater cohesion; it is more supple and mobile, less attached to the surrounding world, and its behavior presents a certain resemblance to the conduct of man, both in its individual reactions and in those of its collective life.

To sum up, the cohesion of the material universe is maintained along the continuous lines of the movements which traverse it. Life which penetrates the clods of matter fashions various organisms; and these latter, seizing upon material forces, turn them to their own advantage. This life develops into innumerable and diverse ramifications, but its victory over matter is never definitive. No organism resists for a long time the external pressure which weighs heavily upon it; it itself is soon to disintegrate. Life is maintained only by change and by unceasingly producing new organisms, which are always as fragile as they are ephemeral. Nowhere in the vegetative and animal world do we encounter the fundamental unity of a subsistent being. Man alone, who has access to conscious life, possesses the indivisible unity of the ego, the autonomy of a personal existence. While living in matter he is in a position to disengage himself from the determining law of the universe, thanks to a spiritual life which is fully immanent. The activity of the plant and of the animal is hardly more than a shadow of that which man manifests in his thoughts, his willings, his feelings. Man alone in the world has the power to achieve his personal liberty by conquest through the conscious apprehension of the absolute identity of being.

III. BEING AND THE GOOD

The Sphere of Values

1. The Good Is That Which Pleases, That Which Constitutes a Term and an End, That Which Is Agreeable. The Good Is Order

The metaphysical study of the activity of being causes the problem of the good or of value to arise. In current parlance the term "good"

designates, first of all, that which pleases, the agreeable feeling
which we experience, as well as every factor capable of provoking
this feeling. For example, we find that such a particular food has an
exquisite taste, that this particular music soothes the ear, that such
an event produces an excellent impression: all of this is "good."

That which is agreeable attracts us, and on the other hand all that
meets with our desires pleases us. By stretching the meaning of the
term "good," we call that good which responds to any psychical
need whatever and even to every tendency, whatever it may be, conscious or otherwise. *Bonum est quod omnia appetunt;* the good is
that towards which everything tends.[1] In this sense the good satis-
fies the tendency, it makes it cease by satisfying it, by giving it a term,
an end; the good is the final term. And just as the tendency follows a
direction necessarily, and is oriented towards a determined term, the
good which is at the end of a tendency is likewise the end of it, the
term envisaged, the end to be attained. *Bonum habet rationem finis.*
The intermediate terms, the means which lead to the end, participate
by this same token in the goodness of the end, and they also will be
called goods.[2] "The good is diffusive of itself": the goodness of the
end communicates itself to the means.[3]

In attaining to the end pursued the active being finds its completion, its perfection. This end is adapted to it, it agrees with it; see
why it is a good that is desirable.[4] The end and the tendency, therefore, are bound together by a relation of agreement; they belong to
one and the same order; but if the reason of the goodness of the end
is found in this adaptation we must admit that the other term of the
same relation, the subject of the tendency, possesses a corresponding adaptation, and that it deserves likewise to be called "good." As
a matter of fact that which is directed towards a final complement,
which betters it by completing it, already possesses in itself an initial

---

[1] "When it is said that 'the good is that which all things seek,' this is not
thus understood as if everything good is sought by everybody; but in this sense,
that whatever is sought, has in itself the form (*rationem*) of goodness." *Summa
theol.*, Ia, q.6, a.2, ad 2.

[2] *Ibid.*, Ia, q.5, a.6.

[3] This particular application of the Neo-Platonic adage: "Bonum est diffusivum
sui," does not exhaust its full meaning, as we shall see later on.

[4] "The good is defined by an appetition, but this latter presupposes an agreement, for a being only desires what agrees with it. It is not because I desire it
that health agrees with me, but I desire it because it agrees with me." Th.
De Regnon, S.J., *La Métaphysique des causes d'après saint Thomas et Albert le
Grand,* 2nd ed., Paris, 1906, p. 376.

goodness. And therefore the source and the term of the tendency are both good; the activity of the tendency unfolds itself entirely on the plane of the good, because it is naturally oriented by reason of the relations of agreement which bind the terms together.

Finally, the good is that which agrees, that which is according to rule in order. Goodness is order: the terms ordered are bound together by mutual relations, they complete each other, they form an harmonious unity. They are good.

Thus, the constitutive principles of a particular being are adapted, the one to the other, in order to form an undivided whole, so that the perfection and the harmony of the complexus radiate through all the parts and manifest its goodness. Thus, too, particular and subsistent beings are bound to one another by relations and so form an order. Nevertheless, their relations are numerous and diverse, some superficial, and others profound. We must, therefore, inquire into their fundamental goodness which is attached to the most profound relations, to the most radical order.

2. Ontological Good Formally Concerns Active Being. It Is Transcendental. Ontological Evil Is Impossible. The Good Consists in the Perfection of the Act of Being; Quidditative Acts (Substantial and Accidental) Individualize It and Measure It. The Idea of Good Is Analogous

The fundamental order is that of being, since it embraces all things and the whole reality of every one of these things. Fundamental goodness is, therefore, ontological goodness, which belongs to being inasmuch as it is being. Now, the ontological order implies necessarily the activity of beings. As we have explained above,[5] every being is active in virtue of its nature; this activity binds it to all the other beings, and maintains it as solidly established in the ontological order. Transcendental good, therefore, formally concerns active being.

Nothing can withdraw itself from the law of the identity of being; everything is necessarily in order in this regard; it is good from the ontological point of view. This means that good is a transcendental, just as being is;[6] they are convertible. Hence it is that ontological

---

[5] Cf. supra, pp. 205–207.
[6] Cf. Summa theol., Ia, q.5, a.3; De veritate, q.21, a.2.

disorder, ontological evil, is nonsense, a pure nothing of being and of thought.

It is true that the goodness of every particular being is limited as is its reality, but we should be wrong in concluding from this that this being is evil in the measure in which it is not infinitely good. By reason of its nature every particular being possesses its existence in an individual fashion, which distinguishes it from every other; but always it *is* in the proper sense of this word; it truly participates in the perfection of being. This is why it occupies the place that comes to it in the order of being; because it is in a relation of agreement with the other beings, it is perfectly in order, entirely good. Without doubt, it possesses its individual stamp, and it is not as the others are, but we cannot say that these other modes of being are wanting to it, and that their absence constitutes in it a privation of perfection and of order. This absence is not an evil; [7] on the contrary, it is part of order that these modes are foreign to it. Leibnitz, therefore, is wrong in calling the absence of infinite perfection in a finite being a "metaphysical evil." [8]

---

[7] Cf. *Summa theol.*, Ia, q. 48, a. 3; cf. *supra*, pp. 30–31.

[8] "We can take evil metaphysically, physically, and morally. Metaphysical evil consists in simple imperfection, physical evil in suffering, and moral evil in sin." Leibnitz, *Essais de théodicée*, 1e partie, paragraph 21.

Martin Heidegger emphasizes with some insistence the negativity, which according to him would characterize being itself, existence such as is revealed to us in our consciousness, notably in anxiety. Our existence is oriented towards its destruction, not by reason of some external factor but by itself; it carries in itself the germ of death; it is this germ, it is a "Sein zum Tode" (being unto death). Cf. *Sein und Zeit*, 3rd edit., Halle a.d. S., 1931, pp. 235 ff. In this conception being would be ontologically in default; it would be intrinsically evil because it is limited in its entire reality, and because in itself it is non-being, death, nothing.

"Negativity is omnipresent in being. It assails being at its beginning; it assails it in its end that is already pre-existing. . . . It assails it in a present which it dominates only halfway. It is anchored at the heart of its structure in anxiety. Being is, therefore, infected with a fundamental and irremediable culpability, if it is true that culpability is in negativity." A. De Waelhens, *La philosophie de Martin Heidegger*, Louvain, 1942, p. 163.

To quote Heidegger himself: "In der Struktur der Geworfenheit sowohl wie in der des Entwurfs liegt wesenhaft eine Nichtigkeit. Und sie ist der Grund für die Möglichkeit des uneigentlichen Daseins im Verfallen, als welches es je schon immer faktisch ist. *Die Sorge selbst ist in ihrem Wesen durch und durch von Nichtigkeit durchsetzt.* Die Sorge—das Sein des Daseins—besagt demnach als geworfener Entwurf: das (nichtige) Grundsein einer Nichtigkeit. Und das bedeutet: *das Dasein ist als solches schuldig,* wenn anders die formale existenziale Bestimmung der Schuld als Grundsein einer Nichtigkeit zurecht besteht." *Sein und Zeit*, p. 285.

We must conclude that the goodness of a being is measured by the perfection of its act (or determination), as St. Thomas Aquinas says. Every being is fundamentally good, and it clings to itself, because by the act of being which is peculiar to it it is fixed in the absolute of the synthesis of being. That is why every being is borne naturally to the love of itself in the order of beings; but the mode according to which it possesses the perfection of being depends on its quidditative determination, that is, on the principle of substantiality to which the principle of being is riveted, or according to the consecrated expression, "in which the principle is received," and by which it is individuated. The substantial form, the act in the order of the substantial essence, determines the specific perfection of the particular being; it fixes the measure of its natural goodness and hence also the level and the rhythm of its activity. For the finite being acts according to its nature; it expresses its substantial determination in the operations which come to actuate its multiple potencies, with a view to participating always more and more in the absolute perfection of being.

The idea of the transcendental good is analogous, as is the idea of being. Since the mode of being varies from one reality to the other, the ontological goodness of beings is never the same absolutely but always analogically. Every reality occupies its particular place in the order of being. Substantial goodness is the source of accidental operations, by which particular being succeeds in developing itself by involving the other realities in its evolution. The more perfect a being is the wider is the field of its activity; the terrain of operation of the animal is more extended than that of the plant, and the range of the spiritual faculties infinitely surpasses that of the organic powers, since it embraces absolutely everything.

This thesis, on which Heidegger's system rests is erroneous. The finitude of particular being is not a metaphysical evil because it is not a negativity, an absolute nothing. It is the negative facet of individuality, which is positive. By reason of this individuality every particular being is bound up with the others, and it is in the order, the harmony of beings, that it must be understood. It is quite true that, considered alone, finite being cannot be explained; isolated, it would be absurd. For in this case its limitation would be an absolute negativity; but it is not isolated. Its limits, indeed, are positive, since they are relative, relative, namely, to the other beings. (This being here is not that one there, i.e., it is this one here over against that one there.) These beings are in the order; they sketch the special and ineffable mode according to which such a being "participates" in the absolute value of being. In other words, they constitute its essence, by providing the measure of the ontological goodness of particular being.

As a matter of fact, by its spiritual activity particular being aims to possess in a manner which is peculiar to it, the whole order of being. Intelligence has as its formal object, being; it looks out, therefore, on the complexus of everything there is, and it is in a position to grasp its ontological goodness. This is why the will, which corresponds to the intellect, is not restricted to pursuing this or that particular object, but its tendency is oriented towards everything which possesses goodness, no matter on what title.[9] The transcendental outlet of his spiritual activity makes man capable of desiring all good; never will he stop definitively at the possession of a limited good. Only the infinite good, which the whole order of being carries with it, can satisfy the appetitive power of human nature.

3. The Good and Value. The Worth of Values. The Affective Perception of the Sphere of Personal Values

The term "value" as authors generally understand it in contemporaneous philosophy, has the same meaning as the scholastic expression *ratio boni*. It designates the reason why anything is good.[10] Value is that which does not allow us to be indifferent, that which deserves to be known, sensed, willed, or desired.[11] There are nu-

---

[9] For this reason man can act through altruism or egoism; he can strive for the good of another and his own good; he can be solicitous for others besides himself. Man is capable of loving some one, and of loving him more than he loves himself, if he finds in him a value which surpasses his own value. This is why he can love God above everything. The animal does not act either through altruism or egoism; and it is not capable of friendship or love, because it does not recognize the good, as such, and it cannot therefore lay hold of the good as a personal motive for action. The animal is determined by its nature to act in such or such a manner.

[10] And so we are led to distinguish the *good* (*ratio boni*) or value, and the goods, i.e., the things which are good, which embody a value.

[11] The present-day philosophy of values is concerned chiefly with the manner in which man discovers values. Generally it admits an original experience in which the affective (emotional) life plays the principal role. Max Scheler especially steered research in this direction. He strove to show that values appear to us exclusively as objects of a sense faculty, which is as intentional and as objective as "representative" knowledge, but which is distinct from this latter, and fundamentally opposed to it. Neither intelligence nor the senses will ever make us discover a real value. For example, the simple definition of love will not teach very much to him who has never loved. It is certain that value appears to us concretely only in as far as we "live" it, and in as far as we sense it penetrating our life of feeling. We have consciousness of the strength of our appetitive activity which draws us on, and which makes us ascribe to things and to persons a "signification," a value, which we do not explain to ourselves by the intellect.

merous values and it belongs to their nature to be ordered: some of them are worth more, the others are worth less. The problem then is to estimate such data at their value, and to avoid confusing them or inverting their places in the hierarchy of goods. Thus it is that we must distinguish the substantial or fundamental value which is a personal value for every being endowed with spiritual life; and also that which is attached to the ulterior (accidental) development of beings. This development is effected in a variety of ways, according to various faculties: to each of these there must correspond a group of goods, a sphere of values. There is a distinction between the order of biological values and that of intellectual values, between the order of aesthetic values and those of moral, religious, juridical, social, and economic values.

Human activity is nothing other than bringing into relief the substantial and personal foundations of man, following the lines of reference which bind each person to other beings. By this activity man aims to assimilate the values which these other beings embody, to be enriched by them, to enjoy them. And since he is not the creator of the universe no more than he is the cause of his own individual nature, he can develop normally only by conforming himself to the order of the goods which he discovers. These goods and their hierarchy are imposed on him; they have worth, and their worth is the norm of his activity. This worth is grounded, in the last analysis, on being which is the fundamental value; besides, the first principle of human activity is to "acquiesce" in being, in the absolute.

4. Moral and Physical Evil

Beings are good. Every thing is such, conformably with its nature; its natural tendency is good and the same is true of the end which corresponds to it. Is this not to plunge into a naive optimism? Is this

---

And yet the intellect is not absent from this experience, for our psychical life does not allow itself to be shut up in compartments. This is the reason why reflection can be exercised on these data. Undoubtedly, the intellect finds itself just as little capable of penetrating all the secrets of psychical data and of the values which correspond to them, as it is incapable of understanding completely physical data; but we must not conclude from this that it is condemned to silence. It will even be able to define with more penetration these internal data, which are nearer to it, than it succeeds in grasping the foundation of physical phenomena.

not to reject even the possibility of evil, which nevertheless no one dreams of denying? The question arises as to the meaning that must be given to "evil."

Evil is the contrary of the good. It is not merely the absence of some good—a pure negation—but the privation of a good, the absence of that which ought to be, of that which is required de jure. Evil is the lack of conformity to rule; it is disorder. Absolute or ontological evil is altogether impossible, since the law of being suffers no exception. Ontological good is transcendental; inasmuch as it is being everything is good, nothing escapes from the law of the identity of being. If therefore evil has any meaning, it can only be on the basis of the ontological good, which is present everywhere.[12] Evil can have meaning only as relative evil, in relation to a subject which is good, in as far as it is being.[13] This is what we mean by saying that it has a material cause, a subject of inhesion. And thus, in every case it presupposes the limitation of being, the structure which is composed of the principle of existence and of that of "taleity"; and it could only be found on the plane of the *taleity*, and not on the level of being, considered in its transcendental character.

The substantial "taleity," the foundation of the individuality of the particular being, is directly and entirely a mode of being; it cannot deviate from its relation to the principle of being. It is a determined mode of being, neither more nor less, under the penalty of otherwise suppressing all the reality of the subject under consideration. As such, it is a participation in being; it is in order, it is good.

Evil, therefore, can only occur in the accidental order, and can concern only the active development of finite being. This development takes place in a determined direction, and it is the nature, the substantial principle of activity, which is its norm. Consequently, evil consists in an abnormal development, in an irregularity of activity.

Where and how does such a disorder become conceivable? It goes without saying that it cannot come into being in a natural and necessary evolution, since nature in itself is good. In order that it may

---

[12] Metaphysical pessimism is, therefore, a radical error, nonsense. Disorder cannot get to the plane of being, of the absolute, and therefore not to the plane of the absolute, creative cause. This is why the goodness of God and that of the order created by God can in no instance be held in check by the bad actions which creatures would place.

[13] Similarly, we have seen above that nothing (non-being) can have meaning only as relative non-being. Cf. *supra*, pp. 56–57.

become possible, it is necessary that between the nature of the particular being and the fruit of its finite activity there should be interposed a free will, which allows this being to direct *ad libitum* the course of its operations. It is only in the moral order, the order, namely, of the autonomous activity of finite being that evil, disorder, could be introduced.

Man is a being who can do evil. His activity (as we have shown above) consists in assimilating to himself, in a personal way, the forms of the other beings, and in being enriched by their values. In order that this activity may run off in a normal way, it must be regulated according to the order of beings and according to the hierarchy of goods; for man himself forms a part of this order and he is, therefore, not its master. If a man, while using his autonomous power, refuses to submit himself to this natural law of his development, and decides to direct himself in an opposite way, he will deviate from the normal line of his evolution and deliberately introduce disorder into his own life. Never will he in this way be able to arrive at the full expansion of his being; in the measure of his liberty he will miss his end; he will lose his soul.

It is true that he could never prevent himself from pursuing some good. As a matter of fact, the formal object of every will is the good as such, that whose value the agent has recognized; and it is manifestly impossible to act otherwise than by means of one's faculties or to free oneself from their natural orientation, from their formal object. This is the reason that every action is necessarily good, at least in some way, *secundum quid;* but he who at the same time refuses to conform himself to the hierarchy of goods, he who inverts the order of values, exercises an operation which, all things considered, is fundamentally bad, *simpliciter mala.* For example, when he looks for sensible enjoyment which corresponds to his tendencies, he pursues a good; and yet if he does this at the expense of a higher good which the normal development of his life demands, he does evil, for while thus obtaining some advantage, he creates in himself a real disorder.[14]

---

[14] In the moral order, which has to do with free activity, disorder can present a number of differences. The evil which turns man formally from his last end attacks the very foundations of his personal life. Other faults merely shackle the ascent of life without formally breaking the bond which unites man to his end. This is the difference between mortal and venial sin. The one and the other cause a disorder in moral life, but there is more than a difference of degree between them. Their resemblance is purely analogical.

A being which acts freely is a subsistent and autonomous entity, complete in itself; it possesses value in itself. It pursues an end which is peculiar to it and which is, therefore, definitive, ultimate, the full expansion of its person. Consequently, we must look at it from the point of view of this last end, in order that we may pass adequate judgment on the value of a human action. Every action which under this relation would be affected with a disorder, must be definitively condemned as being evil, as *simpliciter mala*.

We are likewise wont to speak of physical evil, namely, suffering, maladies, death. In what sense can we do this? The answer to this question depends entirely on the conception which we form of natural things, and in particular of living bodies.

When we say that a plant or an animal suffers some harm, we understand thereby that this organism, considered in itself, has been shackled in its development, a phenomenon which surely constitutes an evil from the point of view of this organism. But does not this judgment rest on a one-sided consideration of reality? When there is question of passing a judgment on the value of a living body are we justified in isolating it from the complexus of things? On the contrary, would it not be necessary, before all else, to take into account the universe of which it forms a part?

As soon as we have verified the fact that an object is completely dependent on what surrounds it, that it is only a part of a whole, we are in no wise disturbed at seeing it undergo profound modifications. Not for an instant, to say the least, do we see in this an evil for this object, because we do not conceive the idea of judging events entirely or principally from its point of view. For example, if there is question of chemical transformations we do not in any way deplore the fact that certain combinations disappear to make place for others. On the contrary, all of this appears to us to be in order, and we strive to follow the regular course of things with a view to formulating the law of this evolution of matter.

But as soon as we observe in organized matter, in particular in animals, a spontaneity and a behavior which recalls, even remotely, the conduct of man, we are inclined to recognize here subsistent beings and to judge from their isolated point of view the events which affect them. Now, a more painstaking examination of the data tends to establish the fact that this subsistence is extremely relative, that it is more apparent than real. We will not expatiate here on these questions which have to do with the philosophy of nature; suffice it to observe that on the testimony of experience an animal never gives any proof of true liberty. It acts through instinct and we are correct in not holding it responsible for its reactions. The animal does not act personally, by itself; it does not subsist, but it forms an element which belongs to a more comprehensive nature; it is a part of the material world, and this is why its whole reality is subject to the law of the physical universe. Consequently, it is not a being which is capable of pursuing its own proper good, but a fragment of the universe in which there is realized, at the same time as in all the other things, the harmony of the complexus. Hence, we will conclude that it is from the point of view of the complexus of the universe that we must judge the evolution of the animal, and not from the point of view of this organism, taken in isolation.

If living bodies are nothing but forms of temporary organization which constitute transitory phases of the evolution of organic life, it is normal that they end by disintegrating and making place for other combinations of matter. Their death is the normal end of their existence, since it is only a moment of the perpetual becoming of matter, the passage towards a new state: "Corruptio unius generatio alterius." All things considered the death of the organism, therefore, belongs to the order of things; "est simpliciter bonum": [15] it is good without qualification.

In fact, it is principally in regard to man that the problem of physical evil arises. Undoubtedly, the human organism, as that of the animal, is subject to the physical laws of the universe; it is therefore exposed to the accidents of matter, and it ends in death. But, unlike the animal, man is also endowed with spiritual life. Matter and spirit are united in him in one and the same substance, for sense activity and intellectual operations are here grounded in one simple consciousness, and they belong therefore to one and the same ego. What is more, every man who has consciousness of his corporeal state considers his body as being truly "his," his "personal" body.

The distinctive mark of a person, as we have shown above,[16] is to pursue his own personal good as a last end. Consequently, man is

---

[15] We cannot linger here on the question of the suffering of the animal: that would lead us too far afield; still we cannot forget that since we do not ascribe personality to the individual animal we must deny it consciousness, properly so called, i.e., consciousness of self. In this case the suffering of the animal is fundamentally different from that of man, and the difficulties which it presents from the point of view of the problem of evil, are diminished by just so much.

[16] Cf. *supra*, pp. 220–221.

directed towards an immortal life; he is called to a permanent possession of himself. Now, it is a fact that man feels himself inclined to
make this tendency to the indefinite preservation of his personal
life bear also on the organic life of his body. As a matter of fact, he
is apt to judge that death comes to interrupt brutally the course of
his existence and his activity; he dreads sickness which can lead to
death; he turns aside from suffering which is disagreeable, and which,
pushed to a certain degree, jeopardizes his health. And yet, would
it be reasonable to maintain that all damage to the body constitutes
an injury done to the personal good of man? The question is a com-
plex one, and to arrive at a solution, we must lay down certain distinctions ahead of time.

Moral evil is an evil in the proper sense of the word; physical
evil, considered in the animal, is not truly a disorder, in this sense
that it is conformable to the law which governs the whole universe.
When there is question of man we must observe that he freely dis-
poses of his body, at least to a certain degree, and that he can therefore interfere personally with the course of material phenomena. I
take a walk, I displace objects, I make use of physical energy, as
soon as I decide to act in this way.

There is a goodly number of men all of whom have this power
at their disposal, and the decisions of the one do not necessarily
agree with those of the other. It can happen, therefore, that I collide
with the action of another, and that by this fact I suffer some injury
to my body, a physical evil. In this case two things must be noted: on
the one hand, what happens to me is in agreement with all the physical and biological laws, and in so far it does not constitute any disorder; this is not a physical evil. On the other hand, however, that
which happened, could not have happened, since it is the consequence of a free decision; and just in so far there is question of a
contingent event. If it runs counter to my legitimate desires it is
natural for me to bristle up against it, and I am inclined to call it an
evil. From this we must conclude that in the measure in which it is
reasonable to see here an evil which should not have been inflicted
upon me, there is a relation to a free will, and the disorder is found
in this will and not in material nature. The physical event of which
there is question, enters perfectly into the physical order, but it
manifests a moral disorder which affects the liberty of man. At bottom, there is question of a moral evil.

If we could rule out of our life all the evils which men inflict on us, and if we could, further, do away with all the evils which we have to bear through our own fault (and those which are the consequence, for example, of the passions which we have failed to curb, of an unwholesome regimen which we have followed, of unreasonable hopes which we nourished, etc.), the majority of physical evils, in any event those which are the most painful for us, would indisputably have disappeared. In other words, it is with moral evil, with disorder properly so-called and for which man is himself responsible, that we collide as soon as we try to get clear on the problem of physical evil. The fact remains that we experience a spontaneous aversion for the death of the body and everything connected with it, sickness and suffering. We turn away from it as from an evil.

This reaction is good and efficacious, since it makes us take protective measures which are laid down for the preservation of life. But here once again, all things considered, is there any question of an evil?

If death were to bring in its train the annihilation of the human person, it would be a catastrophe whose ineluctable character would justify the most radical pessimism; but it is not possible that it should be such. For man feels himself borne inevitably towards the absolute, and hence towards the eternal; and this orientation of his activity is by no means the product of a fantastic desire or of a personal and free decision, but it can fittingly be called a natural tendency. In other words, it is a tendency which attaches to the fundamental essence of man's reality, and which therefore is bound up with the fundamental law of the human being. As a matter of fact, the formal object which translates the nature of the spiritual activity is the transcendental, that is, being and the good; as it goes beyond all limit, it produces in man's conscious life a need for the infinite. Every personal step of man rests on this ineradicable tendency, and it draws from it its eternal value.

In the light of these truths we can discover the meaning of life and of death. The existence of the living organism is temporal, but it is the introduction to an eternal life. The moment of death far from putting an end to personal life, constitutes the passage from a transitory state of life to another which is the definitive state. In this perspective death no longer appears as an evil; on the contrary, it acquires a most important positive value.

It is to man's interest, endowed as he is with reason and liberty, to take into account the organization of nature, with a view to determining for himself a rule of conduct. It belongs to him to have dominion over himself and to make use of his instinctive reactions for the purpose of arriving at his personal end.[17] And since the life of man in this world is good, in spite of its precariousness, precisely because it leads through death to eternal life, the means for man to be assured in the beyond of equilibrium and the normal expansion of his personality, is to conform himself in this world to the laws of nature and to rest all of his personal activity on them.[18]

A number of problems arise on the subject of evil, notably in regard to its causes. This is not the place to examine these, but it was sufficient in this present chapter to get a clear notion of evil, and to determine its degree of intelligibility. From the various considerations which have been made it follows, first of all that evil, a privation of the good, is a disorder; then, that metaphysical evil, a disorder relatively to being, is nonsense; and finally that if we can speak of physical evil only in a very relative and provisional sense, moral evil on the contrary has a definite meaning, and it can occur in free activity, in particular in that of man.

---

[17] Stoicism insisted on the necessity of man's leading a reasonable life conformed to the order of nature, with a view to achieving the full development of his powers and the most profound happiness. But these views, lofty as they may be, are accompanied always by a certain sentiment of melancholic resignation, in the measure precisely that they are not bound up with considerations of the life beyond the grave. If death puts an end to our personal life, inevitably from our point of view it is evil which has the last word. In this case the attitude, proclaimed by Epicureanism appears more logical; as all life ends in death, all our efforts lead ultimately to nothing. Why, then, should we not avail ourselves, according to our lights, of the few moments which we chance to have at our disposal?

[18] In treating of the question of evil two errors are often made. First of all, some overestimate the value of the animal, exaggerating the resemblance which exists between the animal and man. Undoubtedly, they do not ascribe a spiritual life to the animal, but they consider it, nevertheless, as a subsistent being having value in itself just as man has. Then it becomes impossible to justify the physical injuries and especially death to which the animal naturally must submit. On the other hand, others underestimate the value of man, not emphasizing sufficiently his transcendence in relation to the material world. These latter, it is true, attribute to man a spiritual soul, but they forget, none the less, to insist on a supremely important consequence which flows from this, i.e., eternal survival after death. Now, if we are confined within the narrow horizon of a temporal life, it is not possible to attribute a positive value to death which comes to put an end to this existence. Only from a broader point of view, that of immortality, does death appear as a good, inasmuch as it assures the entrance into eternal life, which constitutes a decisive advance over the state of life in this world.

5. *Historical Notes*

The problem of the good has always exerted a profound influence on the development of philosophical theories. In opposing the 'world of immutable ideas to that of the sensible and mobile realities, Plato passed judgment on their value; in the first world everything is perfect and completed, whereas in the second there are only things doomed to constant becoming, which will never attain to final completion, the fullness of being, repose in perfection. Hence springs an irrepressible tendency of the human soul, which is in touch with the world of ideas, to free itself from the corruptible body and to withdraw itself from the humiliating conditions of matter.

Aristotle set himself against this extreme dualism. According to him there exists, undoubtedly, an immaterial reality, Pure Act, but that does not prevent the reality of this world from belonging truly to being; for the nature of every thing is fully determined, it contains in itself an "idea" or "substantial form." This perfection of the nature of things forms the foundation of their becoming which belongs to the accidental order, and which is directed towards a determined end by reason of the substantially perfect nature from which it proceeds. Nevertheless, the substance of material things likewise contains "prime matter," a principle of determinability and therefore imperfection. This is the reason of the contingency of natural phenomena. Now, in the measure in which facts contain the element of contingency they are not amenable to order, to the necessity of law, and they can no longer form the object of a scientific study, for order alone is intelligible.

Aristotle does not fail to observe the singular and transcendent character of the human intellect, but he does not succeed in defining it in a sufficiently clear-cut way so as to draw from it the precise consequences in regard to personal survival. These obscurities do not fail to encumber his ethics, which is otherwise profoundly human and reasonable.

The Stoics went even farther: all reality whatsoever is reduced to that of our material universe, and here reigns perfect order; for here everything is subject to an inescapable law. Man is in a position to recognize the perfection of this order, and the only good attitude which he can adopt is to allow himself to be guided by reason in order to conform himself stoically to the exigencies of the laws of nature.

Epicureanism which likewise bandied about an out-and-out materialism, maintained on the contrary that everything at bottom is contingent, and that there is no natural and necessary law. Hence, they left everyone free to act as it seemed good to him. Neo-Platonism harks back to the dualism of Plato, and it sees in matter the source of every evil, physical and moral; hence it endeavors to lay special emphasis on ascetical and mystical doctrine and methods.

In this matter of good and evil Christianity has provoked a profound change of ideas. At the very basis of the truths of Christianity lies the dogma of God, who is unique, the creator of all things, exercising universal providence; hence, all reality, even the most lowly, is good. Undeniably, there is evil in the world, sin, moral evil, but man is responsible for it. Physical evil likewise finds its origin here; it is the chastisement imposed by God on sinful humanity, and it constitutes at the same time a means of expiation and reparation. All things considered, so-called physical evil is a good, since it conduces towards re-establishing order; sin alone ought really to be called *the* evil.

The Fathers of the Church and the Greek ecclesiastical authors, notably Origen, St. Gregory of Nyssa, and the Latins, especially St. Augustine, plumbed the depths of the problem of good and evil. They did make unsparing use of Greek philosophy, especially Plato's conceptions and those of the Stoics and the Neo-Platonists, but they always brought into vivid relief the fundamental goodness of all reality, even material reality, the personal responsibility of every man, and the internal struggle which man must wage in order to practise virtue. On this basis they constructed a far-reaching ascetical and mystical doctrine.

St. Augustine studied particularly the nature of evil, and he did this with a view to combatting Manicheism, to which he had adhered for some years, and which admitted the dualism of a good God and an evil god. According to St. Augustine evil never possesses a positive nature; it is a negative element, a privation. "Mali enim nulla natura est; sed amissio boni, mali nomen accepit." [19] "Quid est autem aliud quod malum dicitur, nisi privatio boni?" [20]

These ideas of St. Augustine had a decisive influence on the Chris-

---

[19] "For there is no nature of evil; but the loss of a good has received the name of evil." *De Civitate Dei,* c.9 (P.L. 41, col. 325).

[20] "But what else is that which is called evil, but the privation of a good?" *Enchiridion,* c.11 (P.L. 40, col. 236).

tian Middle Ages,[21] during which the Scholastics elaborated the moderate doctrine of the transcendental good. Alexander of Hales (+1245), drawing his inspiration also from the philosophy of the Arabians, had already developed it, at the same time that he expounded his ideas on the other transcendentals.[22] St. Albert the Great (1196/1206–1280),[23] St. Thomas Aquinas (1224/1225–1274),[24] John Duns Scotus (*circ.* 1267–1308),[25] and Francis Suarez (1548–1617) [26] subsequently developed this doctrine more elaborately.

The theory of the transcendentals was taught by Christian Wolff (1679–1754),[27] who was influenced in more ways than one by Suarez, and thus it was that Kant came to learn this doctrine. Kant, however, adapted this theory to his own subjectivistic principles; [28] according to him the predicates "one, true, and good" do not designate attributes of reality as it is in itself, but they enunciate certain conditions of the knowing subject, which are found along the line of the Kantian category of quantity.

Kantianism introduced into modern philosophy a new dualistic

---

[21] Compare, for example, the formulae of St. Thomas Aquinas and those of St. Augustine. "Evil is not something existing, or some nature, but the very absence of good," *Summa theol.*, Ia, q. 48, a. 1. "It is the privation of good." *Ibid.*, Ia, q. 14, a. 10. "It is the defect of the good, which it is born to have and ought to have." *Ibid.*, Ia, q. 49, a. 1. "There is no evil by essence, or by participation." *Ibid.*, Ia, q. 49, a. 3, corp., and ad 4.

[22] According to Alexander of Hales there are three attributes of being: the one, the true, and the good. The unity, truth, and goodness of creatures are explained by their resemblance with God, the efficient, exemplary and final cause. Cf. *Summa theol.*, p. I, inq. 1, tract. 3, q. 1, *initio* (edit. Quarrachi, Vol. I, 1924, p. 112).

[23] "Although *ens, verum, bonum* are convertible according to the *supposita*, they are not so according to their *esse* and definition. For a thing is called *ens* by comparison with the efficient cause, true by comparison with the formal cause, and good by comparison with the final cause." St. Albert, the Great, *Summa theol.*, p. I, tract, 3, q. 15, membr. 1, art. 1, particula 2, assign. 4 (ed. A. Borgnet, Paris, Vivès, Vol. 31, 1895, p. 194). Cf. L. De Raeymaeker, "Albert le Grand, philosophe. Les lignes fondamentales de son système métaphysique," *Revue néo-scolastique de Philosophie*, 35th year, 1933, pp. 14–19.

[24] *De Veritate*, q. 1, a. 1. The theory of the transcendentals of St. Thomas differs considerably from that of St. Albert the Great.

[25] *Opus oxoniense*, I, dist. 8, q. 3, n. 19 (Lyons, 1639, t. 5, p. 729).

[26] *Disputationes metaphysicae*, disp. 4–11.

[27] *Philosophia prima sive Ontologia*, 2nda edit., Frankfort and Leipzig, 1736, paragraph 169, p. 138.

[28] *Critique of Pure Reason*, First division (Transcendental Analytic), Book I, Chap. 1, section 3, paragraph 12; N. K. Smith's translation, pp. 118–119. We must recall that Kant attached new meanings to the terms transcendent and transcendental in his own system.

conception, that of pure reason and practical reason. Pure or theoretical reason synthesizes sensible data in reducing them to the
unity of the knowing subject. Further, it strives to comprehend cosmological phenomena by attaching them to a spiritual order; but all
this in vain, because this operation is effected outside of every contact with the real, and therefore it remains a purely formal operation.

Nevertheless, our moral life opens up another way to knowledge.
It is a fact that every exercise of the will is subject to the internal
law of a categorical imperative, and according to Kant's way of
thinking this fact implies freedom and postulates the existence of
God and the soul. Thanks to action, therefore, we are in a position to
know noumenal reality; we get to it not as an intuitive datum nor
as the logical conclusion of a ratiocination of the theoretical order
(which would be based on an understanding of the nature of things),
but as a postulate of practical reason, of the consciousness of willing. The good, which is the rule of human action, is therefore defined as the "conformity to duty." It is exclusively from the subjective
and formal element of obligation, and not from the matter of the
action, that the act of willing borrows its goodness.

The influence of this dualistic conception on contemporaneous
philosophical thought has been extremely profound, and especially
does the whole current of the philosophy of values attach to this
dualism. The representatives of this current are wont to oppose being
to value. The term "being" looks then to the fact of existence, and
is applied to everything which can be encountered in reality, to
everything which is in a position to furnish a content of representation. Things which "are" manifest themselves in experience, individually in sense experience, and they constitute the determined objects of intellectual operations. On the contrary, value is the rule
which is worthy of being applied, the law which fixes that which
"ought to be," the norm of the facts. Value itself, therefore, can never
be considered as a fact; it is not an existent thing. There are things
which embody values, but there are no values which are things.
What characterizes value is not being but the "ought to be," the
"worth"; (in the moral order they call it obligation). Contemporaneous philosophers who give themselves to the study of values find before them an extremely extensive field of inquiry, since they have
had to distinguish very different orders of values, notably biological,
aesthetic, moral, religious values, etc.

Herman Lotze (1817–1881) was the first to conceive a philosophy of values, founded on the opposition of being and of worth (*Seinsol-len*). He interpreted the world of Plato's ideas in the sense of a sphere of objective values in relation with the mind.

In Germany the philosophy of values was developed in different ways and on different planes. There was, first of all, the psychological current which drew its inspiration from empiricism, and which tended to identify value and the feeling of value, or even the object which provoked this feeling. Lotze himself seems at times to express himself in this sense. This current is represented by Wilhelm Schuppe (1836–1913), Theodore Lipps (1851–1914), A. von Meinong (1853–1931), Christian von Ehrenfels (1850–1932), Theodore L. Haering (born in 1884), and W. Gruehn.[29] In this conception the distinction between fact and value is reduced to a minimum, for value participates in the relativity of fact; but in this case how can value be considered, strictly speaking, as the norm of facts?

The philosophical school of Baden, represented by Wilhelm Windelband (1848–1915), Heinrich Rickert (1863–1936), Emil Lask (1875–1915), Jonas Cohn (born in 1869), Bruno Bauch (1877–1942), and Leonore Kühn,[30] strove to emphasize vigorously the normative and absolute character of value, and this to the point of identifying without further qualification value and worth (*Sollen*). Value is nothing other than the ideal, universal and necessary worth, independent of us, absolute. Hence, there is good reason to distinguish three domains; that of the existent beings, of real facts; secondly, that of values, which are not real things but objective norms, holding for everything and every one in a universal and absolute way; and finally, that of morals and civilization, which are the fruit of human action. As a matter of fact, because of this action, being is impregnated by value, and from this union of a real matter and an ideal form there springs the sense (or meaning) of the facts; to the chaos of the real there succeeds an axiological order, in which objects occupy the place which belongs to them, and by which transitory phenomena acquire an eternal signification. Thus we get to the true, as soon as we think of what ought to be thought of; we achieve the good when we do that which ought to be done; and we realize the beautiful in producing that which ought to be an object of aesthetic enjoyment.

Nevertheless, if we suppose that value ought to be reduced en-

---

[29] Cf. his *Das Werterlebnis*, 1924.
[30] Cf. *Die Autonomie der Werte*, 2 vols., 1926 and 1931.

tirely to the pure ideal form of "worth," we should have to admit that it is unique and always the same; and would that not be the same as rejecting every differentiation and the whole hierarchy of values? This theory has indeed been espoused by a good number, notably Max Scheler (1874–1928) and Nicolai Hartmann (born in 1882). This is the reason why they think that "worth" is not the essence of value, but is rather only a property of it. They reject Kantian formalism: value is not reducible to an ideal "form," but is rather constituted by an objective "matter." Every value is a quality (and not a simple relation) under the same title that color and sound are qualities. Still, it is not a physical thing, no more than it is an act or a state of the psychical order. Value cannot, therefore, be grasped by the senses or comprehended by reason; it is not a datum that can be represented or an object that can be conceived. We discover it only by means of our affective activity, and by this we must not understand the subjective state which is feeling (*Gefühl*), but the operation of the emotional sense (*Fühlen*), which is just as objective as the external senses and reason, and which therefore cannot be reduced to these two. This function of affective perception is therefore subjective only in as far as it is an activity of the subject, as are the power of representation and reason; but in as far as it is a cognitive function, it is intentional and looks to an objective value, just as the other avenues of knowledge.

The axiological domain comprises a multitude of values. In perceiving them we recognize their hierarchy right away: some of them appear to be better than others. At the same time we feel that they are forced on us as a norm, that they are "valid"; for example, the moral values oblige us to act in such or such a manner.

In this conception, the dualism of being and of value is pushed to the extreme. Being is accessible to rational knowledge and value is not; it is amenable to an intentional, but yet an irrational activity. Thus, our intentional functions operate in two different directions: they proceed from the activity of one and the same subject, and they are unified in their source, but this subject is not capable of reducing to a fundamental unity the two objective spheres which it gets at, that of being and that of value. The categories of being and those of value are patently irreducible. And yet, if things are "so to speak penetrated with values," as Max Scheler maintains,[31] and if conflicts could ap-

---

[31] *Der Formalismus in der Ethik und die materiale Wertethik*, 2nd ed., Halle a.d. S., 1921, p. 17.

pear between values and reality, as Nicolai Hartmann admits,[32] must we not conclude from this that there are points of contact between the two spheres and that a larger and more fundamental domain embraces both of them? Perhaps it is difficult or impossible for us to make the nature of the principle of fundamental unity precise; but as soon as we understand that we must necessarily admit it, we can no longer declare it to be completely inaccessible. William Stern (1873–1938) made an effort towards unity by finally reducing value to being in the autonomous reality of a person.[33]

The distinction between being and value has been propounded likewise in French philosophy. Jules Lagneau (1851–1894) sets up an opposition between "to exist," taken in the sense of being able not to be, and "being," understood in the sense of necessary being. He thinks that neither the one nor the other can suffice, that the one and the other are subject to a higher law, and that it is necessary to go beyond them in order to discover fully autonomous, absolute reality. He discovers this absolute in thought, because it has no other law than itself, and it finds its consistency in its liberty. In the experience of its free activity thought verifies that which ought to be, value: it lays hold of the data of experience in an objective affirmation, and it furnishes them with their meaning and their absolute truth by locking them up in the pure form of necessity for which it itself serves as the foundation. It must be admitted, therefore, that the idea forms the foundation of being (this latter term being taken in the meaning indicated above), that law surpasses fact, that value is at the base of all reality.[34]

René Le Senne (born in 1882) does not reduce value purely and simply to liberty as does J. Lagneau; nevertheless, he does discover value in the will. Value affects concrete consciousness in a special way by animating and orientating the will.[35] Strictly speaking, value

---

[32] *Ethik*, 2nd ed., Berlin, 1935.

[33] "Only that which is in itself, can have meaning-in-itself. The question about the true value of self is also the question as to the true being." Cf. Wm. Stern, "Person und Sache," Vol. III, *Wertphilosophie*, 1924.

[34] "The absolute reality which we are looking for, is therefore neither existence nor being; it is value. . . . There is therefore a superior order of reality which consists neither in existence nor even in being. For to exist is to be able not to be, and to be is to be necessary; and this is not to be truly. For all the degrees of thought, value is truly the reality which thought affirms." J. Lagneau, *De l'existence de Dieu*, Paris, 1925, pp. 55–57.

[35] *Obstacle et valeur*, Paris, 1934.

has no determination which could form the object of a representation, and in this sense it is not possible to express it in terms of being.[36] It resides, nevertheless, in reality; and this latter, therefore, reveals to us a double source: that of value and that of the objects which value penetrates and envelops.

Gabriel Marcel (born in 1886) admits that there is an absolute value, which he identifies with being. It is more fundamental than intellectual values which are relative, since we can compare them among themselves and so evaluate them.[37] This absolute being cannot constitute the determined and objective content of our reason; it is situated outside of that which we can get at by solving problems, and in this sense it is non-problematical. It is a mystery which allows itself to be grasped, directly and obscurely, in a "faith." In this way every one knows himself and also the other (the "thou") and God.

At the opposite pole of these views, positivistic authors think that values are not at all irreducible to facts. Eugene Dupréel (born in 1879) especially maintained that values are themselves facts to be verified and to be studied by the methods of the empirical sciences. Values are infinitely numerous, and their consistency is precarious. Every metaphysical explanation is proscribed; there can be no question of recognizing an absolute value or of finding a unique foundation for the diversity of values.[38]

In the various idealistic and existential conceptions there is manifested the design to bring to light the independence of value by relation to being (taken in the sense of empirical reality), and even the absolute autonomy of value. We observe here a strong tendency to affirm that the apprehension of value is effected otherwise than in

---

[36] "Life therefore shows us always rushing about in pursuit of something of which we can say nothing, of an X outside of all that we are able to apprehend or contemplate. It is not an object, for an object is determined or determinable. The characteristic of this X is that it is outside of all determination, from which it recoils indefinitely." R. Le Senne, "La condition humaine et la métaphysique," *Études philosophiques*, Ghent, 1939, p. 48.

[37] "All evaluation is related to a possible exchange, and consequently has bearing only on that which is commensurable with something other than itself. . . .

"There is therefore value in this entirely relative sense only of that which is exchangeable, that is, in that which is for sale (*venal*).

"But love on the contrary has bearing on that which is unique, on that which has a common measure only with itself: the circle of love. . . ." G. Marcel, *Journal métaphysique*, 2e édit., Paris, 1927, pp. 135.

[38] Cf. Eug. Dupréel, *Esquisse d'une philosophie des valeurs*, Paris, 1939.

representative and conceptual knowledge. The domain of the rational, that of science, is that of the thing, of the determined object, of the datum of experience, but it is not the domain of value. This latter is found on the side of the affective sense, of liberty, of the will, of a certain personal faith.

It seems indeed that the opposition between theoretical reason and the will, between representation and emotion, and furthermore, between the empirical fact and its value, has been pushed too far; or at least, that after the requisite distinctions it had been necessary to strive to discover the fundamental unity, both on the side of the knowing subject and on that of the domains which the subject discovers by means of his various cognitive functions.

Quite à propos Edg. De Bruyne (born in 1898) insists on the indissoluble unity of knowledge and appetite. The affective element is never found isolated, he writes, no more than the element of knowledge; and this latter holds on to the primacy. We must reject exaggerated emotionalism, but we must just as much be on our guard against an intellectualism which would content itself with abstract knowledge. We apprehend values in every lived tendency, in every conscious operation, provided that we do not limit ourselves to considering these elements separately and abstractly. We must view them in their connection with the real person which we are; we must judge them in the light of the fundamental orientation of our whole being towards that which is capable of perfecting it. Value is found essentially bound up with the dynamism of being.[39]

The discovery and the study of values cannot be made outside of the knowledge of the data of experience, of real facts, of determined objects. On this point empiricism is right, but our study of true value can never produce any good result if we stop at data, taken as particular objects. For values have to do with order; and we must admit with the idealists that there is a priority of value on each object in particular. Finally, we must admit that every object must belong to the universal order of being in order to have meaning and to secure a place in reality. A particular object has value only by participation in the perfection of being; it holds good only in the network of relations which bind all things together on the level of transcendental being.[40] And therefore, to give an account of being,

---

[39] Cf. Edg. De Bruyne, *Ethica*, 3 vols., Brussels, 1934, 1935, 1936.
[40] Cf. Aimé Forest, "L'expérience de la valeur," *Revue néoscolastique de philosophie*, t.43, 1940, pp. 5–20.

taken in the sense of empirical reality, of particular and determined objects, we must recognize the presence of being understood as the absolute, the fundamental value, the supreme source of all "worth."

CHAPTER VIII

PARTICULAR BEING. VIEW OF THE COMPLEXUS

I. PARTICIPATION AND STRUCTURE

1. *Limitation, Individuality, Order and Participation*

THE examination of reality makes us discover numerous beings; they limit one another mutually, and by the same token they are related one to the other, they hold together. This limitation is not to be taken in the negative sense of a non-completion, of an imperfection, of an evil, but rather in the positive sense of an individuality, of the particular mode according to which a perfection presents itself in such a determined case. This mode is individual for it supposes other instances of it from which it is distinct; and by relation to these it is limited, since it does not include them in itself.

This meaning of the term "limitation" implies that of participation. Every one of these individual beings is a particular being, for it participates in an individual manner in a perfection; and this perfection it possesses wholly and not merely in part, but it possesses it in such a way that other modes of possession remain possible outside of its own mode. Consequently, in the same way in which it realizes its own perfection, this finite being forms a part of an order, of a complexus of individual beings which participate, all of them, in the same perfection.[1]

This participation appears, first of all, on the plane of being; there exist many beings, they are, all of them, but every one is defined and distinct from the others by its mode of individual being. This real participation is the objective foundation of the analogy of the idea of being.[2]

---

[1] Cf. *supra,* pp. 29–30.
[2] Cf. *supra,* pp. 44–46.

In the sphere of specific determination participation appears under a new form; there are truly individuals of the same species. Every one of them possesses in a particular way all the formal perfection common to all of them. This makes possible the formation of univocal, specific concepts.[3]

Limitation and consequently the belonging to a real order which participation brings in its train, determine in the particular being an evolution by which it tends to assimilate to itself in its own individual manner, the entire order in which it is found, and to which it also strives to adhere actively.[4] By the display of this activity particular being manifests in all its fullness the value of its participation in being and in the specific determination.

2. The Structure of the Finite. The Leitmotiv: Potency and Act

How must we conceive particular being in itself in order to give an account of the participation which characterizes it? We must conceive it as a being which is not simple, which implies a structure.

As a matter of fact, on the level of being, we must admit that every particular being manifests a value of absolute being, which is the same everywhere. On the other hand, all these particular beings differ among themselves, since they are many, and there is therefore, among them a difference that is non-absolute. Finite being consists in the correlation of a real principle of being, or of "absoluteness," and a real principle of "taleity," individuality, limitation, opposition, relativity. This structure must be admitted as real, since the characters which it is called upon to ground, are mutually irreducible.[5]

A similar situation presents itself in the domain of "taleity," or of essence, when there is question of beings which belong to one and the same species. They possess a "taleity" of being which is formally the same in all; and yet they are many and there is, therefore, a non-formal difference among them. Consequently, these beings present in the order of "taleity" a correlation of a formal principle of specific determination and a material principle of numerical individuation. This hylomorphic structure must be considered as real, since the

---

[3] Cf. *supra*, pp. 155–157.
[4] Cf. *supra*, pp. 205–209.
[5] Cf. *supra*, pp. 99–104.

characters of which it is called upon to give an account, and which affect particular being in all its reality, assert themselves as altogether irreducible.[6]

Active evolution which the participation peculiar to finite being brings in its train, implies structures corresponding to those which have just been indicated. In fact, if particular being must tend actively to its own perfection, it must needs preserve all through this becoming its substantial identity; but at the same time it changes, the moments of its evolution are multiple and distinct from one another. In other words, being in the process of becoming manifests non-substantial differences. This dynamic structure is real under the same title as the structures of the static order to which it corresponds.[7]

On the accidental plane, structure is complicated according to the formal lines of evolution which being in the process of becoming follows. Accidental correlations will be more numerous in the material being, whose substance is itself composed hylomorphically, than in the spiritual being, whose substance is a pure form.[8]

Hence, wherever there is a real order (real multiplicity reduced to unity, limitation through participation) a real structure is implied in the terms which it contains. This structure consists every time in the correlation of two principles, of which one is the real reason of a determination, and the other the real reason of a determinability; the first is called act, and the second, potency. Act is a principle of perfection: potency is a principle of individuation, the reason of the particular mode according to which the being possesses the perfection in which it participates. Act is the reason of the resemblance which unites the terms of one and the same order of participation; potency is the reason of the differences by which these terms are opposed to each other, of the limits which separate them, and hence also of the relations which, while binding the terms together prevent them from becoming mutually identified.

The whole reality of the principle of act and of the potential principle consists in their correlation. They are defined completely by their mutual relations; the one cannot be conceived without the other.[9]

---

[6] Cf. *supra*, pp. 155–157.

[7] Cf. *supra*, pp. 173–177.

[8] Cf. *supra*, pp. 195–198.

[9] "Potency, inasmuch as it is anything, is spoken of in relation to act." *Quaestio de anima*, a. 13. Cf. *Contra Gentes* I, c. 20, "Et ideo melius"; *II De anima*, lect. 5, n. 281; *De unitate intellectus*, c. 1 (edit. Keeler, 1936, n. 46).— "For potency, according to what it itself is, implies a certain relation to act,"

Just as potency, so the principle of act is not a being, having a value in itself or being able to subsist; that which is and which acts, is not a principle of act or a principle of potency, it is rather the subsistent being, the whole finite being, the structure of potency and act.[10]

The theory of act and potency is the leitmotiv which recurs unceasingly in the study of the internal composition of particular being; it corresponds to that of participation. And just as it is indispensable to make as precise as possible the meaning of the terms limitation, individuality, order, and participation, so it is necessary to have a precise conception of the structure of finite being, a well-defined theory of act and potency, under penalty of otherwise running into incoherence every time we raise the question of the non-simplicity of finite reality. This is why we have endeavored to define as clearly as possible the elements of the structure of being, and why we have not hesitated to have recourse to it on the occasion of the study of every internal composition. The fundamental notion which we must hold on to, is that every structure is a correlation of the type of potency and act, and that the elements of the structure, potency and act, have no other reality than that of their correlation.

II De anima, lect. 6, n.304.—"Potency is nothing else than a certain order to act": *ibid.,* lect. 11, n. 366.—"For potency is not called an *ens* except in relation to act": *De substantiis separatis,* c.5.—"Since *esse* in potency is nothing other than to be ordered to the act": *De malo,* q.1, a.2.—"For potency is not defined except through act": *IX Metaphys.,* lect. 7 (edit. *Cathala,* n. 1846).—"Act, inasmuch as it is such, is referred to potency": *Contra Gentes* II, c.53: "Amplius, quod inest."—"For act and potency are spoken of in relation to each other": *Contra Gentes* I, c.22: "Amplius, Esse."—"For they are proportionate to each other": *Contra Gentes* II, c.73: "Ostensum est."

[10] "Many have fallen into error with regard to forms on this account that they pass judgment on them as substances are judged. This seems to come about from the fact that forms are designated in the abstract after the manner of substances, for example, as whiteness, virtue, or something of that sort. Hence, some following this way of speaking pass judgment on them as if they were substances." *De virtutibus in communi,* a.11.

"The whole Thomistic system is bound up with the concept of form, and every error with which the Thomists reproach their adversaries, derives from this that they represent forms to themselves as if they were things." P. Rousselot, S.J., "*Métaphysique thomiste et critique de la connaissance,*" *Revue néoscolastique de Philosophie,* 17th year, 1910, p. 480.

II. PARTICIPATION IN BEING AND PERSONALITY

1. Unity of Being and "Suppositality." The Completion of a Being and Its Incommunicability

Every participation implies a multiplicity of subsistent beings. If there could only be one being its manner of existence would be the only one possible; the perfection of this being would be complete and unique, and by that very fact all participation would be abolished. Consequently, participation in the value of being, and therefore also the structure of the principles of existence and essence which constitutes finite being, are necessarily presupposed by every other participation.

Every particular being is one being, an individual being, undivided in itself, complete in itself, yet divided, distinct from every other. It subsists; since it is a complete ontological unity it possesses in itself its own peculiar existence, and it is marked with the incommunicable seal of its individuality. In scholastic parlance it is called a "suppositum"; and generally by this note of incommunicability we define *suppositum*. We mean to signify by this that it is not merely a part which by its union with the other parts would form a whole, but that it is itself a "whole which is," a unity of being.

Incommunicability is only a negative expression of the totality which the Scotistic school prefers to emphasize.[11] The *suppositum* is a complete being, not a part of a being; it possesses in itself what it must have to exist. It is, therefore, not "assumed" into a subsistent whole, it is itself a whole; it is sufficient unto itself. Incommunicability is with reference to the totality what the second part of the traditional definition of unity, divided from all others, is to the first part, undivided in itself. The definition of *suppositum* is merely the definition of the one, applied to participation in the order of being.[12]

2. Person and Thing

By observing activity we succeed in recognizing the subsistence or the "suppositality" of a being. The subject which posits its acts

[11] Cf. Claud. Tiphanus, S.J. (1641), *Declaratio ac defensio scholastica doctrinae SS. Patrum Doctorisque Angelici de hypostasi et persona*, Pont-à-Mousson, 1634. (New edit. Paris, 1881.)
[12] For the participation in being, cf. *supra*, pp. 29–32.

by itself must possess in itself the means to exist; otherwise, how could it be active? That which acts is that which is: "Actions belong to *supposita*." By means of his conscious life the subsistence of a human being is revealed. This activity is deliberate, free, and independent; it is sufficient unto itself. We call it a "personal" activity; every man is a person.[13]

A person, therefore, is called a subsistent being, endowed with spiritual, conscious activity. Thus, Boethius (480–525) already had defined it, "naturae rationabilis individua substantia," an individual substance of rational nature.[14] The terms "individual substance" do not signify substance in the sense of a principle of individual substantiality, but the whole subsistent reality of the subject under consideration. This latter possesses a "rational nature," it is a being endowed naturally with reason. St. Thomas Aquinas formulates the same definition as follows: "Distinctum subsistens in aliqua natura intellectuali," a *suppositum* endowed with intellectual life.[15]

Modern contemporaneous philosophy has proven faithful to this conception, at least in this sense that it has continued to link the notion of personality with that of consciousness; [16] and experimental psychology has followed suit.[17] The authors who in the analysis of conscious life attribute more importance to the irrational factors than to reason, will be inclined to tie up personality principally with the life of the emotions. Thus, Max Scheler rivets personality to love, which he considers as the basis of every affective perception of values. In defining personality some writers refuse to appeal to the metaphysical elements which would be found outside of the conscious data; they adopt this attitude either on account of their con-

---

[13] Cf. *supra,* pp. 17–20.

[14] *De duabus naturis,* c. III.

[15] *De potentia,* q. 9, a. 4. Cf. *Summa theol.,* Ia, q. 29, a. 3; IIIa, q. 16. a. 12, ad 2. —"For only rational substances have dominion over their acts, so much so that they have the power to act and not to act; but other substances are rather acted upon than acting." *De potentia,* q. 9, a. 1, ad 3.

[16] For example, Descartes and Locke attach personal identity to the consciousness which we have of this identity. Christian Wolff proposes the following definition: "A person is said to be an *ens* which preserves the memory of itself, i.e., he remembers that he is the same *ens* which was previously in this or that state." *Psychologia rationalis,* Vol. II, sect. 4, c. 2, paragraph 741, Frankfort and Leipzig, 1734, p. 660. Kant took over this conception.

[17] Théodule Ribot explains his position as follows: "In psychological language we generally understand by person the individual who has a clear consciousness of himself and acts in consequence (of such knowledge). This is the highest form of individuality." *Les maladies de la personalité,* Paris, 1884, p. 1.

cern for method (this is the case with experimental science), or from reasons which spring from metaphysical agnosticism. Scholasticism has always been the adversary of agnosticism in philosophy, and the definition which it offers of personality has a metaphysical significance; it does not formally retain the conscious element, but the subsistent reality which is the foundation of conscious activity.[18] In scholastic language person [19] is also called hypostasis [20] or subsistent.[21]

---

[18] When we fail to distinguish psychological and ontological definitions, we run the risk of crashing into theological difficulties in the treatises *De Trinitate* and *De Verbo Incarnato.*

[19] In Latin *persona* signifies first of all a masque; then a figure, an image, an actor; finally, function, dignity, and likewise man as a juridical person. This last meaning was introduced under the influence of Stoicism, which spoke freely of the role which man played on the stage of the world. Cf., for example, Epictetus (1st century), *Enchiridion,* 17; *The Dialogues of Epictetus,* I, 29.

The same evolution is observed in the signification of the Greek term "πρόσωπον," which under the influence of Stoicism took on a juridical and philosophical signification.

In the 4th century, in the course of the Trinitarian controversies "πρόσωπον" was opposed to "οὐσία" and "φύσις," and *persona* was opposed to *natura;* for example, there is in God one "οὐσία, φύσις" or *natura;* and there are three "πρόσωπα" or *personae.*

[20] The Greek "ὑπόστασις" signifies what is placed underneath, as base, foundation; that which is deposited at the bottom of a vase, the lees, sediment; at times, mire, mud; or again, ambush, snares. For example, in Holy Scripture, Book of Kings, I, 13, 23, 14, 1, translated into Latin: *statio Philistiim;* a variant reading of 14, 1: *in substantiam allophylorum.* Figuratively, "ὑπόστασις" signifies the foundation of an affair, the subject of a discourse, the principles on which one rests; at times, strong conviction; more often presence of mind, hardihood, confidence.

The Stoics used the word in the philosophical meaning of substance. During the period of the theological controversies, especially the Trinitarian controversies of the 4th century and later, the word "ὑπόστασις," often used in the sense of "οὐσία," essence, took on the meaning of *person.* (In God there are three "ὑποστάσεις" and only one "οὐσία," and this is the meaning which it preserves in theology).

Mutius, in the 4th century, translated "οὐσία" by *essentia,* and "ὑπόστασις" by *substantia* and *hypostasis.* This last term, *hypostasis,* slowly crept into Latin theology and was commonly used during the period of Scholasticism's full bloom in the sense of *person.*

[21] Marius Victorinus, in the 4th century, uses *subsistentia* as a synonym for *existentia* and *substantia.* The word is found also in Rufinus (345–410). Boethius (480–525) translates the Greek "ὑπόστασις" by *persona* and *individua substantia;* and yet he employs this last word less than his contemporary Cassiodorus, 477–c. 570). The translator, Epiphanius Scholasticus of the same period, uses the word likewise in the sense of *person,* and he distinguishes it from *substantia.* The deacon Rusticus in the 6th century at times gives to the word *subsistentia* the meaning of *persona,* at times that of *substantia.* Pope John II in 582 uses it to signify *person.* We meet with it four times in the glossaries of the

Men are the only persons in this world. Purely material organisms do not subsist personally; their activity is never entirely disengaged from the necessitating pressure of their environment. They act by instinct; the spontaneity which they manifest is not liberty, their operations do not belong to them as their own. Animals and plants do not "act" by themselves; they "are" not, therefore, "in themselves." They are not persons but things, elements of the constant evolution of the universe.[22] In things the "distinct from every other" is never found perfectly realized; they are not "supposita" in the strict sense of the term. Nevertheless, animals and even plants manifest a relative unity, for every one reacts as a whole, and preserves for a time (sufficiently short) its typical form. We see in this a pale reflection of the personal unity and subsistence of man, and we treat them readily as *supposita*. We must, however, avoid confusing persons and things, and we must not lose sight of the fundamental difference which separates them.

3. *The Formal Constitutive Principle of Personality*

If every particular being comprises within itself a metaphysical structure, what is the formal constitutive principle of personality, the principle whose presence brings personality in its train, and whose absence does away with it?[23] This must needs be an "ontological" principle, since the difference which obtains between a reality which possesses incommunicability, and another reality which does not have it, has to do with the subsistence, the "being."[24]

Middle Ages in the sense of *person;* in the neuter plural it takes on a material signification. It is only very much later that the term *subsistentia* is accepted definitively in the philosophical language of the Middle Ages. Cf. J. De Ghellinck, "L'entrée d'essentia, substantia, et d'autres mots apparentés dans le latin médiéval," *Archivum Latinitatis Medii Aevi* (Bulletin du Cange), t. XVI: 1941, p. 110. In regard to the meaning of *substantia*, cf. *supra*, p. 174, note 2.

[22] Cf. *supra*, pp. 211–212.

[23] Historically, the problem arose from reflection on revealed Christian truth. The divine Being is one nature in three Persons; Christ possesses two natures, the divine and human, hypostatically united in one Person, the second of the Blessed Trinity. We must, therefore, distinguish nature and person: why are there in God not as many natures as there are persons? Why is Christ not a human person? In what does the ontological difference between nature and person consist?

[24] The Scotistic school and many other Scholastics think that personality disappears as soon as a real nature is "assumed" by a person, and that consequently it acts and exists dependently on the latter. Cf., for example, P. Descoqs, *Archives*

This ontological reason is the real principle of existence, by which the person exists. As a matter of fact, a reality is a being when it is complete in itself to the point of subsisting by reason of its own proper structure; otherwise it would only be a part. It is complete, it is "in act"; and it is complete with relation to being, it is "in the act of being." Now in the line of being the structure of a subsistent reality terminates in the principle of existence. Therefore, this principle is the formal constitutive principle of personality. Every reality which possesses this principle, enjoys existence in itself; it subsists.[25] A reality which is deprived of this principle, can exist only by reason of a source of being which does not belong to it; it exists in the being which contains this source, it does not subsist, but is assumed into another to which it is "hypostatically" united. In short, it is a real nature without being a person.[26] This doctrine of per-

---

de Philosophie, vol. V, cah. 1, "Thomisme et scolastique," Paris, 1927, pp. 72–73. But how are we to believe that ontological personality can be missing in a being, if nothing is wanting to the ontological structure of this being?

[25] We must conclude from this that man preserves his personality after the death of the body, since he continues to subsist in his soul. Besides, he continues to live and therefore to exercise an immanent activity: "actions belong to *supposita.*"

Two questions can be raised on the subject of man: *Is* he? and *What* is he? The first concerns the suppositality; Is he? i.e., does he exist; does he himself possess the internal reason of his value of being? Or rather is he only an element belonging to a subject which comprises in itself the reason of this value? We have explained that this real reason is found in the "principle of being," i.e., the *esse proprium.*

The second question concerns, on the one hand, the degree of being, or of specific perfection (whose real reason is called the substantial form, i.e., the human soul), and the other hand, the individuality in the species (whose real reason resides in the material principle, or prime matter).

Man survives the death of the body; in his soul his life goes on eternally. In this state of separated soul he continues to subsist; he does not cease to be a *suppositum,* a subsistent being, i.e., one which exists thanks to its own *esse proprium.* He possesses always his degree of being, his human quiddity, because this soul is a form, a substantial principle of determination; and he possesses this degree of being in an individual manner, because this form, namely, the soul, is a formal principle, which is real only in as far as it is a transcendental relation oriented towards its prime matter. This orientation which constitutes the formal principle completely, persists as long as the formal principle itself persists; it is, therefore, preserved when the soul is really separated from matter, so that the material principle never ceases to be the real reason of the individuation of the human person. Cf. *supra,* pp. 164–166.

We must be on our guard against confounding, as some so often do, the problem of individuation and that of suppositality.

[26] According to this theory we must say that the human nature of Christ does not exist by its own proper principle of existence, and therefore it is not a per-

sonality is in line with Thomistic principles, and St. Thomas seems to have professed it.[27]

Nevertheless, following Cajetan, a goodly number of Thomists think that the constitutive principle of personality must lie on the side of the nature, rather than on that of the existence. In order that a reality may be a person, its nature or its essence must be made complete by a mode of subsistence, to which there necessarily corresponds a principle of existence which is peculiar to it.[28] In the absence of such a mode this principle of existence must itself disappear.

This opinion seems to rest on this consideration that personal existence implies a special mode of existence, and consequently that this principle must be looked for along the line of the mode of being, of the "taleity" of the nature. This point of view is inaccurate, for the present case does not have to do with answering the question *quid sit?*, *what* is this reality?, but rather with the question *an sit?*, *does* it exist? Does it exist in itself, is it precisely that which subsists? Only that which subsists, *is:* the parts and the principles are not in themselves, but they exist in the subsistent reality with which they communicate, with which they are united, and to which they belong as constitutive elements or into which they are "assumed."

Cajetan refines his conception of the mode of subsistence by comparing it to the last point which terminates a line.[29] And yet, we

---

son; but it exists by the divine existence of the second Person of the Blessed Trinity. (This divine existence is not a "principle" of existence belonging to a structure, for it is identical with the divine nature, which is absolutely simple.) Consequently, the human nature of Christ is "assumed" by the second divine Person; it is united to the latter "hypostatically."

[27] The brief exposition, presented in the *Quaestio disputata De Unione Verbi incarnati*, art. 4, is at first blush reconciled with difficulty with the parallel passages of the works of St. Thomas, and it has given rise to controversies. See the author's *Metaphysica generalis*, 2nd ed., II, Louvain, 1935, pp. 426–440. Cf. what we said *supra*, p. 132.

The theory which we developed above was professed by Giles of Rome (*circ.* 1247–1316), and other immediate disciples of St. Thomas. John Capreolus sets it forth in his *Defensiones theologiae divi Thomae Aquinatis*, III Sentent., d.6, q.1 (Tours, 1904, Vol. 5, pp. 111–124). L. Billot, S.J., was one of the principal defenders of this in his *De Verbo incarnato*, 5th ed., Prato, 1912, pp. 75 ff.

[28] Cf. Rég. Garrigou-Lagrange, O.P., "La synthèse thomiste" *Bibl. française de Philosophie*, 3rd series, Paris, 1947, pp. 657–667.

[29] The mode of subsistence is "the ultimate *terminus,* and as such the pure *terminus* of the nature of the substance." "To terminate, as such, does not bespeak any causality." "This mode is not only outside the genera of extrinsic causes, but also outside the intrinsic causes, since it is related to the nature not in the genus of formal cause or in that of material cause, but as its terminus. . . . Nor is this an invention, but it has support from the *termini* of quantity; a point

cannot deny that this point forms a part of the line, and that it is not distinct from the line. Similarly, the nature which is a principle of limitation has no need of any mode which would serve to "terminate" it. It is, by definition, a "mode of substantial being," oriented by its whole being towards the real principle of being, which is the reason of the existence of the whole subject: an existence, to be sure, which is a "subsistence," since the principle of it is found in the very structure of particular being.

Cardinal Mercier thought he could attribute a special role to the mode of subsistence, as Cajetan had conceived it. In one being, the Cardinal says quite correctly, there can be only one principle of existence; but on the other hand there are in it many essential principles (quidditative principles), namely, substance and accidents. As one act can determine only one potency, substance and accidents must needs be united in such a way as to constitute only one subject of reception for the existential act. The mode of subsistence plays this role of unifying mode.[30]

This theory has no foundation, if it is true that we must conceive the constitutive principles as correlations; for in this case they are conceived only in the structure which they form, and there is no need to appeal to any bond which would be extrinsic to them.

The Thomistic conception, such as we have expounded according to Capreolus and others, and Cajetan's theory presuppose the distinction of the principle of existence and of the principle of "taleity" in the finite being. If we reject this distinction we must maintain either with the Scotistic school that personality is not connected formally with a principle of the structure of finite being, or else admit the opinion of Francis Suarez. This latter teaches (as does the Thomistic school) that personality is founded on a constitutive principle of finite being; and then (like Capreolus) that it is formally on the side of existence that we must look for it, and not on the side of the quidditative aspect of reality.[31] Suarez, how-

---

is the terminus of a line in such wise that it is not a cause of it." Cajetan, *III Summae Theologicae*, q. 4, a. 2, X (Editio leonina, Vol. II, Rome, 1903, p. 76 b). —Cf. J. J. Balthasar, *Mon moi dans l'être*, Louvain, 1946, 172–178: Historical notes on the subject of the "modus subsistendi," exposition and critique of Cajetan's theory.

[30] D. J. Mercier, *Métaphysique générale*, 7th ed., Louvain, 1923, 3rd part, chap. I, n. 152, pp. 313–317. Cf. J. J. Balthasar *op. cit.*, pp. 179–181: exposition and critique of Cardinal Mercier's theory.

[31] ("I say) . . . that personality is given to a nature in order that it may give it the last complement in the line of existence, or (so to speak) in order to com-

ever, cannot find it in the principle of existence itself, since he rejects the distinction between essence and existence. Furthermore, as
the nature or the essence cannot be identified with the person, he is
forced to admit a mode, *modus substantiae,* which serves to determine the existence itself, and to terminate it in such a way as to
make a subsistence of it.[32] This theory, which has been taken up by
only a few authors, contradicts one of the principles most solidly
established and admitted by most of the Scholastics, namely, that
the act of existence is in the line of ultimate act and is in no wise
determinable.

Whatever determines substance, outside of the act of existence,
can be conceived only as an accidental modification, which is therefore in the line of the essence or mode of being. The Suarezian "mode
of substance" which must "terminate" substantial existence is to be
rejected, just as the "mode of union" which is intended according
to Suarez to "terminate" the accident and to bind it to substance.[33] In
both cases solution is given to pseudo-problems which result from
an erroneous conception of the structure of particular being. If we
conceive the principles of this structure of the finite as correlations,
there is no need to appeal to modes of union to explain the unity of
the composite being. And neither is there any reason to reject as
contradictory the real distinction between the principle of "taleity"
and the principle of existence, the first being the reason of the
limitation and of the "individuality," and the second being the reason of the "subsistence" of particular being.

---

plete its existence in the line of subsistence. Hence, personality is not properly
the terminus or the mode of the nature according to the *esse essentiae,* but rather
according to the *esse existentiae* of that very nature." Suarez, *Disputationes
metaphysicae,* d.34, s.4, n.23 (Vivès, Paris, 1866, Vol. 26, p. 274 a).

[32] "In created things, *per se existere* or the *perseitas existendi* does not belong
to the nature formally by itself or by its existence, but by something real, and
that, really distinct from it and from its existence." Suarez, *De Incarnatione,* disp.
II, sect. 3, n. 10 (t.17, p. 443 b).—Confer J. J. Balthasar, *op. cit.,* pp. 184–193,
Exposition and critique of Suarez' modalism.

[33] Suarez himself made the comparison between the *modus unionis* of an
accident ("which is, as it were, the ultimate terminus of existence itself"), and
the *modus* of a substance ("by which ultimately the existence of a nature is
terminated, so that it may be in itself without dependence on anything supporting it"). Cf. *Disputationes metaphysicae,* d.34, s.4, n.24 (Vol. 26, p. 274 b).

PART III

THE CAUSAL EXPLANATION
OF
THE ORDER OF BEING

CHAPTER IX

PARTICIPATION AND CAUSALITY

THE PRINCIPLE OF CAUSALITY

1. Every Particular Being Is Dependent on a Cause, as Much in Its Existence as in Its Activity

CAUSALITY is bound up intimately with participation and it furnishes the ultimate explanation of it. Take the most fundamental participation, that of being; every particular being is a *suppositum;* it truly possesses the value of being, but it possesses it in an individual and incommunicable way. By reason of this individuality which keeps step with its limitation, it is related to other beings, which are at least possible. Therefore, by reason of everything which it contains, of its whole individual reality, it is included in an order of beings; in other words, every finite being is entirely an element of the order of beings, and it would never be possible to separate it from this order, to isolate it in any way whatsoever. Hence, we shall have explained nothing of particular being until we have offered an explanation of its belonging to the order of beings; and as a relation cannot be explained without its term, this means that it is not possible to give an account of a particular being without giving an account of the beings to which it is related. In a word, to explain a particular being we must offer an explanation of the all-embracing order of beings.

Now, evidently no one being taken in particular, constitutes by itself the reason that explains the order of beings, since it is in fact only a part, and as such it is distinct from the others and opposed to them. These latter are truly other than it, and they are outside of its limits; they are exterior to it. It is not what they are; it does not include what they comprise. In fact, every one of them is a *suppositum* stamped with an incommunicable individuality. This mu-

251

tual "exteriority" of particular beings is clearly manifested in the free activity of man: my decision belongs to me and I alone am responsible for it, and this responsibility is incommunicable, because the decision is entirely mine and it does not push any of its roots outside of me. Every other subject remains foreign to my ego. In the same sense every other particular being is exterior to the subsistent being which I am, and vice versa. One individual being cannot be the reason that explains another, no more than it can be rendered responsible for the free decisions of this other.

Consequently, the real adequate foundation of one particular being is not reduced to the reality of this one being; it extends beyond it, it is external to it. Every particular being, therefore, depends on a real extrinsic reason, on a cause; for by "cause" we mean a reality which exerts a positive influence on the existence or the mode of being of another reality.[1] Hence, every particular being is caused precisely because it is individual and finite.[2] Various questions arise on the nature of this cause and the relations which bind it to the other finite beings: for example, how and up to what point is it distinct from every other particular being, as well as from the complexus of these beings? These questions will be taken up later on.[3]

This complete dependence of the individual being is asserted likewise in the field of activity. As we have shown above finite being is developed indefinitely, fully, by becoming; unceasingly it becomes other, in assimilating in its own way other beings to itself. And since

[1] Aristotle uses the word cause, "αἰτία," in a broader sense; he designates by it not only a being which exerts influence on an other being distinct from the first (in which case there would be question of an *extrinsic* cause), but likewise every reality which enters into the constitution of a composite being, and which on that score really plays a role in the existence and the manner of being of this composite reality. (In this case there is question of an intrinsic cause.) In the language of today there is a tendency to reserve the word "cause" for extrinsic causes, and it is in this precise sense that we are using the word in this work.

Aristotle distinguished four causes, two of which are internal (*scil.*, the material and the formal, the two constituent principles of the internal structure of the finite material being) and two *external* (*scil.* the efficient and the final); and these remain distinct from the effect of their action. Cf. *Physic.* II, c.3, 195 a15; IV, c.1, 209 a21: *Metaph.*, I, c.3, 983 a25–33.

Later under the influence of Plato's ideas, a fifth cause was added to these, *scil.*, the exemplary cause, among others by L. A. Seneca, *Ad Lucilium epistolae morales*, Bk. VII, ep. 3, i.e., ep. 65 of the whole work (edit. O. Hense, Leipzig, 1898, p. 190).

[2] Cf. Fernand Van Steenberghen, *Ontologie* (Course published by the Higher Institute of Philosophy), Louvain, 1946, pp. 81–82.

[3] Cf. *infra, scil.,* Chapter XI.

a reference to these other elements of the real order is essentially implied in all the activity of the finite being, it is altogether impossible to explain this activity in any way, if we cannot give the reason of the other beings to which it is related. Hence, the real foundation which is the reason explaining the activity of the finite being, cannot be found in the mere reality of this being. It extends beyond it; this reason is a real extrinsic one. Particular being, in as far as it is active, is dependent on a cause, precisely because its activity is individual and finite.

2. In as Far as Man Belongs to a Species, He Is Dependent on a Cause, Both in His Human and Material Nature and in His Human and Transient Activity

We can make analogous considerations on the subject of the participation of material individuals in the perfection of one and the same species. By reason of the particular way in which the material individual possesses its formal perfection, it is limited by reference to other individuals that resemble it specifically. This is why it is essential to it to be referred to them, that is, to form a part of the order or the specific unity which the complexus of these individuals constitutes. Hence, it is impossible to explain any of these material beings without giving the explanation of the whole species to which they belong. Thus, we cannot offer an explanation of one individual man without explaining humanity.

Further, material species hold together, for they form together one all-embracing material order. No corporeal individual could be detached from the universe; the place which it occupies is inseparable from space, and the duration which it fills cannot be isolated from the time which, as it were, frames it. By reason of these necessary bonds with its surroundings, the material individual can be explained only by the whole universe. Consequently, considered as an individual human being, man requires an explanatory principle which is extrinsic to his own finite individual reality. As an individual, material man he depends on a cause, precisely because he is limited in the human species and in the universe.

This dependence, peculiar to the individual, material man, is revealed in human activity which is bound up with the transient action of the organism, even in his immanent operations. Now transient action is essentially a reaction in response to an influence, experienced from without; it is limited by the passivity of the individual which reacts ("quidquid movetur ab alio movetur"), and it is conceived only in the complete framework of the material universe which is governed by the system of physical laws. Consequently, the activity of the individual man, in as far as it essentially implies an organic element, cannot be explained without appealing to the real principle which explains the activity of the whole material universe. The real foundation which explains man's activity, therefore, extends outside of the reality of the individual man; it is a real reason, extrinsic to man. Man's activity, considered as such is dependent on a cause, precisely because it is individual and limited in the human species and in the material universe.

As such, the part is only conceived in, and is only explained by the whole. Similarly, if we take it as such, the element inserted in an order is only understood in this order, and it finds its reason in this order. Everything which exists by participation must, just in so far, be referred to the other individual terms which participate in the same perfection; and it constitutes with them one all-embracing complexus. This is why it is explained only with them, and why its adequate explanatory reason includes the reason of this entire order.

3. In a General Way, Whatever Is by Participation (hence, Whatever Is Finite and Whatever Implies a Metaphysical Structure) Is Dependent on a Cause

In a general way, therefore, we can formulate the following principles: "Whatever exists by participation, whatever belongs of itself to an order, whatever is finite, is by this very fact the effect of a cause." And since every finite being, considered as such, carries with it a real structure of potency and act, we can likewise formulate this principle: "Every composite being is a being that is caused." "Omne compositum causam habet." [4]

---

[4] St. Thomas, *Summa theol.*, Ia, q. 3, a. 7.—"Everything which belongs to something not inasmuch as it is that particular thing, belongs to it on account of some cause." *Contra Gentes* II, c. 15.—"If anything is found in some thing by participation, it must be caused in it by that to which that perfection belongs essentially." *Summa theol.*, Ia, q. 44, a. 1; Cf. ad 1; q. 3, a. 7; *Contra Gentes*, c. 18, Amplius; c. 22, Amplius, si esse.—Cf. Joseph Legrand, S.J., *L'univers et l'homme dans la philosophie de saint Thomas* (Museum Lessianum. Section philosophique, n. 28), Brussels-Paris, 1946, Vol. I, pp. 113–116.

The principle which affirms that all reality which begins to exist is dependent on a cause, is only an application of the general principle of causality just enunciated. Beginning to exist is a manifest sign of limitation; a beginning is intelligible only by reference to a real or possible preceding moment. The being which begins is therefore conceived in a temporal order which goes beyond this being, and of which it forms a part; it is conceived as a being, limited in time, and so it demands a cause by the very reason of its limitation.

4. Ontological Structure and the Principle of Causality

We can establish this principle of causality by bringing attention to bear directly on the real composition of particular being. Still, if we look at the matter more closely, the considerations we are thus led to make, do not differ one whit from those we have just set forth.

Every real structure of particular being consists in a real correlation, that is, in a harmony of transcendental relations, for instance, the correlation of the real principle of existence and the principle of essence, the hylomorphic structure, the composition of substance and accidents, etc. In each one of these structures the potential principle and the actual principle are really distinct, they are irreducible. Being distinct of themselves, they do not of themselves form a unity. Nevertheless, these principles are only conceived together, since they are correlative terms. Hence, there must be outside of them a real reason which makes them related, the one to the other, a reason which unites them; and since these principles have no reality outside of their correlation (for they are transcendental relations), this means that a reason is necessary to produce them. Consequently, everything composite is dependent on a cause.[5]

What is the exact meaning of this argumentation? A real union necessarily requires a real foundation, which in this respect excludes all opposition. Now transcendental relations which form the structure of particular being, are really and therefore radically distinct one from the other; they are by no means fused together in reality, since they are transcendental relations through and through, and therefore relative terms which of themselves are opposed to one

---

[5] "Things which are diverse according to themselves, do not agree in some one thing, except by means of some cause that unites them." St. Thomas, *Summa theol.*, Ia, q.3, a.7.

another. In as far as these terms are opposed, they cannot constitute a principle of unity.[6]

On the other hand, for this same reason that there is question of transcendental relations which are altogether relative terms, the constitutive principles of the structure of particular being can in no wise be conceived outside of their correlation; they are therefore united of themselves. Consequently, these principles which are necessarily united, do not contain in themselves the principle that explains their union; neither do they contain, therefore, the sufficient principle of their reality, since this latter is conceived only through their correlation. Hence, we must appeal to an external principle, to a cause, to explain the structure of particular being.

To grasp the exact bearing of this argument we must recall the precise meaning of the ideas of act and potency on which it is founded. Act is the principle of perfection; potency is the principle of the measure in which one participates in this perfection, of the particular mode according to which it possesses this perfection, of the limits within which it receives this perfection. Potency, therefore, is the principle of limitation, of individuation, and consequently also the reason of the opposition to the other terms in the line of the same perfection, the reason for belonging to an order of perfection.

The correlation of act and potency which constitutes the internal structure of particular being, is therefore the ontological reason of the external relations by which this being is bound to all the others which participate in the same perfection, and which form with it one and the same order of perfection, for example, that of being or that of species. And if particular being does not contain in itself alone the reason of its own peculiar structure, of its internal correlation, it is because it does not contain in itself alone the explanation of the whole order of which it forms a part by reason of this structure. Internal and external relativity of particular being are bound up together; they are two aspects of one and the same reality. It would be impossible to give an account of the one without explaining the other; they must have the same real foundation. Now it is impossible that this foundation should be a particular being: finite being can only be an effect, it proceeds from a cause.

---

[6] "Diverse things, in as far as they are diverse, do not form one thing." St. Thomas, *Contra Gentes* II, c. 41. Cf. *De potentia*, q. 7, a. 1.

5. *Historical Notes on the Principle of Causality*

Plato, Aristotle, Plotinus, and the Greek philosophers in general think that reality cannot be explained without the activity of causes. Only the skeptics called causality in question, and Sextus Empiricus towards the end of the second century, tried to prove that cause has only a subjective value; it is only a relation which the knowing subject establishes between two data—otherwise it is nonsense. In point of fact, if we suppose that the cause exists before the effect, or even that it exists at the same time as the latter, or again that it follows the effect, in these three cases we are driven into a contradiction.

In the Arabian philosophy of the Middle Ages, Algazel (1058–1111) denied that there were real causes in the world; and this moved Averrhoes (1126–1198) and Maimonides (1135–1204) to prove their reality.

In the period of Scholasticism's full-bloom, the problem at first passed by unnoticed. Nevertheless, especially beginning with the last years of the 13th century, difficulties were encountered on the subject of the universality of the principle: "Every movement has an external cause." In truth, do we not define life as immanent activity, as "sese movere"? But the nominalistic theories concerning the value of abstract knowledge threatened to ruin the foundations of metaphysics and put the principle of causality in jeopardy. If all knowledge must ultimately be reduced to mere empirical verification, how is it possible to establish the validity of universal principles? William of Ockham, O.F.M. (*circ.* 1300–1349), thinks that it is not possible to prove the principle according to which all movement must have an external cause. Peter d'Ailly (1350–1420) does not see how to justify the following principle: That which begins must have a cause. Before him Nicholas of Autrecourt (*circ.* 1338) attacked the principle of causality in general, reasoning as follows: The effect is not found in the cause, since it is distinct from the latter; hence, we shall in vain examine the effect in order to affirm its identity with the cause. The affirmation of the effect will never imply that of the cause. Nicholas of Autrecourt saw himself later on forced to retract his doctrine on causality; nor was he less quick to perceive the logical consequences of nominalism.

On more than one score is modern empiricism dependent on nominalism; it will therefore rehash its attacks on the principle of causality. John Locke (1632–1704), who received a nominalistic education, safeguarded nevertheless the principle of causality under this form: "Nothing comes from nothing," *Ex nihilo nihil fit*. David Hume (1711–1776), however, pushed empiricism to its extreme limits; consequently he denied that universal principles can be necessary, objective laws, and especially did he reject the principle of causality. According to him experience shows us successive facts, not the causes which produce effects. Further, I form for myself distinct, and therefore separable, representations of cause and effect; why then would it be contradictory that the effect should exist without the cause? Still, we have to explain how men are led to admit the principle of causality, and his explanation is a psychological one. Two facts which succeed one another regularly build up the habit in us of seeing them together, and thereafter when we see the one we expect the other; thus, we translate this impression by saying that the one brings the other in its train, that the first is the cause of the second. The principle of causality, then, carries with it a character of necessity, but it belongs to the psychological order. Undoubtedly, we do not explain in this way why all successions are not considered as causal series, for example, day succeeds night without being the effect of the latter. Still, the fact remains that Hume's theory was adopted by the empiricists of the 19th century, notably by John Stuart Mill.

In Kant's *Criticism* the principle of causality received a new interpretation; there it is pronounced to be necessary, but with a subjective necessity; for it is an a priori form of thought. This explanation was taken up by a number of philosophers, and it has exactly the value of Kantian subjectivism.

Henri Bergson attributes to the principle of causality only a subjective necessity of the *pragmatic* order; it is a principle conceived by the intelligence. Now this latter never gets to an adequate knowledge of reality, because it is modified by the interests of one's life, and because it pursues useful purposes. With a view to directing action, it immobilizes and breaks up into parts, in its representations and its ideas, the perpetual current of life and of all reality. It makes use of different processes, notably that of the principle of causality, in order to bind together the immobile segments which it has in a way fabricated, and also in order to give them a semblance of activity and of life.

The Neo-Scholastics have always been in agreement in admitting the absolute necessity of the principle of causality, but they strike out along divergent ways, as soon as it comes to justifying their point of view. These divergences are evinced in numerous controversies, which took place especially after a communication of Amédée de Margerie (1825–1905) to the International Scientific Congress of Catholics, held in Paris in 1888. Later, these controversies centered around an article of Jacques Laminne (1864–1924) which appeared in 1912 in the *Revue néoscolastique de Philosophie* of Louvain; likewise, since 1915 on the occasion of a work of Caspar Isencrahe (1844–1921) [7] who cast doubt on the validity of the principle of causality. This last controversy took place principally in Germany, but echoes of it were heard in other countries.

How do these thinkers try to justify the absolute validity of the principle of causality? [8] Some of them make an appeal to the deductive method, and by an analysis of concepts they strive to reduce the principle of causality to a more universal principle. They reduce it to the principle of sufficient reason,[9] or by using this latter as an intermediary, to the principle of contradiction,[10] or to the principle of identity.[11]

There are numerous others who consider the principle of causality as immediately evident and as irreducible to any other principle. In this case the explanation of reality rests on a double foundation,[12]

---

[7] *Über die Grundlegung eines bündigen kosmologischen Gottesbeweises,* Kempten, Munich, 1915.

[8] Some German Catholic philosophers consider the principle of causality as a postulate without a rational foundation. John Hessen (born in 1889) maintains that it can be denied without a contradiction, but that we cannot dispense with it if we wish to explain the real. Nevertheless, according to him there is no proof that the real is intelligible. Fr. Sawicki (born in 1877) and Arthur Schneider (born in 1876) express themselves in an analogous way. Very few authors admit an inductive justification of the principle of causality, as does Joseph Engert (born in 1882), and yet this seems to be Aristotle's and St. Thomas' opinion. Cf. an article by the translator in *The Modern Schoolman,* vol. XXII, no. 3, March, 1945, pp. 132–143.

[9] Bernard Franzelin, S.J. (born in 1868).

[10] E.g., Kaspar Nink, S.J. (born in 1885), and Th. Droege, C.SS.R. (born 1879).

[11] E.g., Rég. Garrigou-Lagrange, O.P. (born in 1877), Bernard Jansen, S.J. (1877–1942), Fr. Sladeczek, S.J. (born in 1889).

[12] A similar opinion was expressed in the seventeenth century by Leibnitz: "We must consider that there are two great principles of our reasonings: the one is the principle of contradiction which holds that of two contradictory propositions, the one is true and the other, false; the other principle is that of the determining reason. This means that nothing ever happens except there be a cause for

the principle of contradiction or that of identity and the principle of causality. Whereas the latter principle can be denied without a formal contradiction the first principle cannot be rejected without completely undermining the intellectual edifice, and consequently the principle of causality; for it is impossible to think and at the same time run counter to the principle of identity.[13]

Joseph Geyser (born in 1869) makes an appeal to the phenomenological method to solve the present problem. By the light of consciousness we see acts of our intellect and will being placed by us.[14] Reflecting on these concrete facts, and without making an analysis of concepts, we can according to Geyser, grasp the essential bond which obtains between "beginning to be" and "being a cause." It is of the essence of that which begins, to be in a relation of dependence on a cause, in such wise that it is impossible to begin to be if this is not dependent on a cause.[15]

What are we to think of these various opinions? It is not possible to ground the absolute necessity of the principle of causality on a purely inductive foundation. And yet, it is true that its justification can be given only in connection with experience; for only in an experience which puts us in contact with concrete and real being, do we lay hold of the value of being. Now this value of being is the soul of all absolute truth, and therefore the principle of causality itself ought to be reduced to the apprehension of being.

-----

it, or at least a determining reason, i.e., some thing which can serve as the reason, a priori, why that thing is existent, and why it is such rather than of every other kind." *Essais de Théodicée,* 1st part, n.44 (Gerhardt, Vol. 6, Paris, 1885, p. 127).

J. Laminne, however, writes: "Just as our mind is determined to affirm the irreducible distinction of being and non-being, so it is determined to affirm that every fact has its reason, and this subjective necessity corresponding to the objective truth of these principles, is nothing other than their evidence." "Le principe de contradiction et le principe de causalité," *Revue néoscolastique de Philosophie,* 19th year, 1912, p. 482. Cf. "Les principes d'identité et de causalité," *Revue néoscolastique de Philosophie,* 21st year, 1914–1919, pp. 357–364. P. De Munnynck, O.P., J. Bittremieux, R. Kremer, C.SS.R., answer Laminne. Cf. bibliography in the author's *Metaphysica generalis,* 2nd ed., Louvain, 1935, Vol. II, p. 468.

[13] This opinion is defended notably by Lorenz Fuetscher, S.J. (1894–1935), Pedro Descoqs, S.J. (1877–1946), J. De Vries, S.J., H. Straubinger, F. Budde, A. Heuzer, etc.

[14] Geyser fails to distinguish immanent activity from external causality. Later on (p. 265) we shall show that in this matter we cannot confound these without further qualification.

[15] Several others have espoused the same opinion, notably Oscar Herget, J. Santeler, L. Faulhaber, St. Zimmermann, L. F. Kahl-Furthmann.

The thesis which maintains that this principle cannot be deduced from the principle of identity or contradiction is true in the case where one would wish to restrict himself to abstract concepts. In fact, the abstract definition of specific or generic quiddity, for example, man is a rational animal, is, so to speak, closed in this sense that it does not mention any other being. The analysis of this definition will take from the contemplated reality only aspects not related to another being; it will therefore never make us discover the cause of the subject, since it is agreed that this cause is a being other than that which is defined. The analysis of the abstract quidditative identity cannot reveal causality. But the situation is altogether otherwise if we consider concrete being; its essence is identically a mode of being by which it is inserted in an order of beings, and if it is material, its essence carries with it a character of individuality which distinguishes it from other individuals, and binds it to the order of the species. The knowledge of particular concrete being, therefore, formally attains to the relativity of this being, to its belonging necessarily to an order of beings, and therefore also to its reference to the cause on which it depends.[16] The point of view of identity implies that of causality.

Geyser's phenomenological description has bearing on man's spiritual and immanent activity, which must not be confounded with external causality.[17] At any rate, suppose that we are examining in this concrete fashion a causal activity, properly so called. We shall be able to search for its beginning and its initial limit, and we shall emphasize the fact that this first moment is necessarily related to some other thing. As we have seen above,[18] the fact that a reality begins to exist is signal evidence of its belonging to an order, and therefore of its dependence on a cause. Again, in order to establish the absolute necessity of this causal relation, we must remain on the concrete level of the intelligibility of the order of being, and by that very fact we must understand that the principle of causality, formulated in terms of the beginning of a reality in time, is merely an application of the universal principle of causality, which is expressed in terms of limitation, as such.

---

[16] In this sense St. Thomas writes: "Although the relation to a cause does not enter into the definition of a being which is caused, still this relation follows upon those things which belong to its definition, because from the fact that something is an *ens* by participation, it follows that it is caused by another." *Summa theol.*, Ia, q.44, a.1, ad 1.

[17] Cf. *infra*, pp. 265–266.

[18] Cf. *supra*, pp. 254–255.

CHAPTER X

CAUSALITY IN THE WORLD

I. VARIOUS ASPECTS OF CAUSALITY

A. EFFICIENCY

1. Physical Causality Understood as a Material Structure Perceived by the Senses

To RENDER the nature of causality more precise we have to define the various aspects of it, as they present themselves to us in the world. In daily life, no one dreams of casting doubt on the influence of some things on others. No person hesitates to admit that one billiard ball can put another ball in motion by striking against it; that an automobile can crush a pedestrian; that man succeeds in harnessing physical energy so as to utilize it for his purposes. Undoubtedly these are facts, but a question suggests itself right away: What do we perceive of this causality in our external experience?

Now for a long time the majority of philosophers and psychologists have thought that it is impossible to verify the physical action of one object on another. David Hume, the chief representative of English empiricism of the 18th century, especially set himself up as the protagonist of this opinion, and he succeeded in getting this opinion accepted in scientific circles. In general, to establish this thesis the empiricists reason as follows: Sensation is necessarily bound up with a physical excitation of the sense-organs; likewise, we can perceive only stimuli, either simultaneous or successive, and this, in as far as they act on us. Consequently, it is not at all possible to have sensations which would represent the action of one physical object on another, since such action differs precisely from the action of these objects on our sense organs.

This point of view results from an atomistic interpretation of perception according to which sense knowledge would be composed of elementary reactions of the senses, in response to one and the same number of physical excitations. Thereupon these physical elements would be associated in various ways by the subject himself; and thus especially in a set of given conditions, they would be grouped into causal series. Now this psychological atomism does not accurately translate the process of sense knowledge. In reality experimental psychology establishes the fact that perception at first and always carries with it a structure, which is in no wise the result of an elaboration of the elementary data by the subject. To take only one example: the musical timbre [1] of a sound corresponds to the combined action of many physical stimuli which strike the ear and which rise, all of them, above the absolute threshold of hearing. And yet this timbre is not composed of an equal number of elementary sensations which would permit us to distinguish these stimuli. On the contrary, the reaction of the sense comprises only one sensation, characterized by a quality that cannot be analyzed, the timbre. Similar facts can be verified in the spheres of all the senses, and they tend to prove that sensation far from being a psychical echo in response to a simple physical stimulus, consists rather in a reaction which is characterized by the unity of an internal structure, by its form, corresponding to a group or a series of stimuli. Such structures correspond either to simultaneous stimuli or to successive stimuli; at times they take place in time, and then they present a dynamic character, for example, a melody; at other times they are static forms, for example, the figured passage of an arrangement.

Actually, certain dynamic structures have reference to what we call the physical action of things.[2] When the liveliness, the volume, the respective distance of a number of stimuli present certain determined relations, the sensations which they provoke, possess an original structure which we express by saying that one object exercises an action on another, that it pushes it, restrains it, draws it, repels it, cuts it up into pieces, crushes it, etc.[3] This physical causal structure

---

[1] The timbre is that quality of a sound which permits us to distinguish voices and musical instruments, even though they give out a tone of the same pitch and the same intensity; for example, the voice of a child and the voice of a man, the piano, the violin, the trumpet, etc.

[2] Cf. Albert Michotte, "La causalité physique est-elle une donnée expérimentale?" *Tijdschrift voor Philosophie*, Vol. III, 1941, pp. 290–328; "La perception de la causalité," *Études de Psychologie*, vol. VI, Louvain, 1946.

[3] Let us take the case of the motion which passes from one billiard ball to another. The first billiard ball rolls in the direction of the second; at a definite moment we have the impression that it is drawing near to it, and we apprehend

is a sensible datum, just as immediate as that of the musical timbre. To be sure, in noticing this fact we do not pronounce in any way on the ontological meaning of these physical phenomena.

2. *Physical Causality, in the Sense of a Regularity, Established by Experimental Methods*

The physical sciences strive to observe the stimuli and to measure their relations exactly, to determine precisely the physical foundation of the sensations. For example, analyze the physical factors of timbre. From this point of view the timbre itself, understood as a characteristic property of the sensation of hearing, does not any longer come under consideration. It is in the same way that one will study the physical forms of causality.

Scientific observation of objective data has revealed a remarkable physical regularity which is formulated in scientific "laws." These latter rest on the verification of recurrences, and they express the functional relations of the empirical data. Every time that fact "A" presents itself, fact "B" accompanies or follows it. Once these laws are established we can determine exactly what has happened or what is happening even beyond the limits of our own actual experience, just as we can likewise foresee what will take place in the future. It is superfluous to insist on the results which the various sciences have achieved by the systematic application of this method.

Such laws can be enunciated by saying that a situation "B" always follows situation "A"; that the first flows from the second, or again that the latter produces the former, that it is the cause of the former. That which takes place first, the antecedent, is then called the cause, and that which comes after, the consequent, receives the name of effect.

And yet the experimental sciences, which remain faithful to their exclusively empirical methods, have not refrained from pronouncing

---

both of them in one and the same sensible structure. The first ball continues its route and ends by colliding with the other which in turn is put in motion. Abruptly we remark in a new structure, that the second is withdrawing from the first. It withdraws more and more, and at a certain moment we have the impression that it has no more to do with the first; the bond is broken, the structure disappears. The perception of the putting in motion of one ball by the other, the perception of this "physical causality," is therefore attached to the fact that we see a brusque reversal of the structures. The first structure (one ball approaches the other) makes place all of a sudden for a different structure (the second ball withdraws from the first).

on the ontological nature of this physical causal nexus. Is there question of a causal relation in the philosophical meaning of the word? Do the consecutive situations belong to two beings, to two *supposita*, of which the one, being in such a state and observed in the first place, really produces in the other *suppositum* the state which we observe later? Or rather, are these two states merely two moments in the evolution of one and the same being? These questions do not enter into the limits of the empirical sciences, which are limited to determining with careful precision by the use of skillful measuring instruments, the relations which are produced among facts that can be verified.[4]

We must therefore refrain from calling that a philosophical cause which is a cause in the scientific and experimental sense of the word. This latter in no wise carries with it the denial of the first, but it is not identified with this first without further qualification. In speaking of causality the experimental sciences do not look to any other thing than a regular functional relation in the domain of facts, without in any way determining the metaphysical foundation, since their purely empirical methods forbid doing this. Assuredly, no one should be able to reproach the physicist for raising questions on the subject of the activity and the ontological nature of things, provided of course that this man of science knows that he is then getting out of the domain of experimental science, and that he is moving on an altogether different terrain, which is under the sovereignty of philosophy, properly so called.

3. Causality, as It Occurs in the Psychical Life of Man

The consciousness which we have of our immanent activity permits us to penetrate into our intimate life. There a vital impulse (élan) is developed which we direct towards personal ends; it is in our power to make free decisions, to regulate our intellectual activity, to govern our tendencies and our feelings, and to determine to a certain extent the behavior of our body. This activity cannot be called, in the strict sense of the word, a causality, for it is an immanent development which affects the acting subject himself; it is not an action which the active subject exerts on another being. It is thus not

---

[4] Cf. Fernand Renoirte, *Éléments de critique des sciences et de cosmologie*, (Course published by the Higher Institute of Philosophy), Louvain, 1945, pp. 105 ff.

merely with the action of the mind and the powers of the soul, but also with the action of the subject on his own body. For body and soul are not two separated beings: they form only one subsistent being, of which the soul is the substantial form, the principle which animates the body and makes it living. This is why the movements of the body are likewise immanent actions and why we have consciousness of them; we perceive them from the inside and we sense them as ours, as being the ego in motion.

The body, however, forms a part of the material universe from which it is inseparable. This is why all human activity presents a material aspect; it is transient at the same time that it is immanent.[5] Now transient activity is a reaction; it is provoked and measured by the physical stimulus which is exerted previously on the subject. It implies, therefore, a correlation of passion-action, and this latter merely translates into the behavior of this subject the quantity-quality correlation which forms the metaphysical structure of its accidental order.[6] On the other hand, man is a person, a subsistent being, who is distinct from the surrounding world as from another being. Consequently, the influence which the external world exerts on man is that of one being on another, and it is the same with the reaction of man on this world. In other words, in the two cases there is question of a causality, properly so called, of external causality. As human activity is always both transient and immanent, it always implies this factor of causality of which we have consciousness in the behavior of our body.

We have the impression of meeting analogous instances of causality outside of man, particularly in the animal world. Nevertheless, we cannot forget that even though the animal reacts as a whole it does not form a *suppositum*, completely subsistent, since from no point of view is its activity perfectly disengaged from that which surrounds it. The plant possesses still less spontaneity; it is rooted in matter and holds on to it tenaciously. In regard to inorganic matter it is difficult to decide if there are substantial unities and spontaneous operations there. Consequently, even the individual unity to which the higher species of animals attain, is merely a shadow of the subsistent unity of the human being; their vital operations are only a pale reflection of the spiritual actions, which are conscious and free, and peculiar to man. The fruit of their activity does not at

---

[5] Cf. *supra*, pp. 16, 20–22, 209–211.
[6] Cf. *supra*, pp. 196–197.

all resemble the civilizing efforts of man which transform the face of the earth and enrich it with values; and similarly the causality which we attribute to them presents merely a very distant analogy to the genuine causality which the human person exerts. It is incumbent on the philosophy of nature, cosmology, to render precise the degree of unity of the various realities which the world embraces; but in the hierarchy of things in the measure that we see their substantial unity tapering off, it seems less obvious to speak of their causality.

4. The Efficiency of the Cause. Efficiency and Participation. Analogy between the Cause and Its Effect

Before all else the cause is an efficient principle; it gives birth to, it produces the effect; it is the source of a new reality which is distinct from this latter. The effect, therefore, is not a part of the cause; to produce effects does not signify to distribute parts of itself and in so far to impoverish itself; [7] but the effect is a reality which results from the efficiency of the cause and which consequently participates in the perfection of the cause. The effect reproduces in a new and individual manner a determination which the cause possesses in its own right. Causality is understood only in terms of participation. If we do not admit this we cannot give any meaning to a real efficiency of beings. The doctrine of causality is an expression of optimism: being is good, and in so far it exerts its efficient causality by making other beings participate in its perfection. "Bonum est diffusivum sui": (The good is diffusive of itself).

There must, therefore, be a resemblance between the cause and its effect: "Agens agit sibi simile": (The agent produces something similar to himself). [8] And since the cause is the real, extrinsic principle of the effect, we shall say that the perfection of the effect must pre-exist in that of the cause. This does not mean that it pre-exists there in its individual reality, and that it is in some way contained there as in a sheath; for in this case the effect would no longer be produced by the cause, but at most its place would be changed by

---

[7] "To cause: this is neither to be enriched oneself, and above all, not to be impoverished. To cause is to give what one possesses without despoiling oneself. To produce an effect is essentially a gesture of magnificence and generosity." A. Hayen, L'intentionnel dans la philosophie de Saint Thomas, Brussels-Paris, 1942, p. 108. Cf. Contra Gentes, III, c.18, Item.

[8] This resemblance permits us, starting with the effect, to conclude to the nature of the cause, or at any event to know that the cause must possess at least a perfection corresponding to that of the effect.

the cause. It pre-exists there in the individual perfection of the cause itself. In reality, if the cause has the power (*virtus*) to produce this effect it is because its own perfection is participable by the effect, and in so far as it is the active source of participation, it must precontain (*virtualiter*) that which is derived from it.[9]

This is equivalent to saying that a being can only exert an efficiency in as far as it is in act of possessing the perfection in which the effect is to participate. Consequently all becoming is formally excluded from the action of the efficient cause, since becoming is the passage from potency to act, and since the cause can act only in as far as it is in act.

On this point observation of causality in the world could put us on the wrong scent, for causes are here subject to constant transformations; and yet we must observe that these transformations do not formally constitute causality. They are merely the conditions for its exercise. By reason of its quantity every material being is passive, undetermined, and it must submit to action from the outside, in order to acquire a determination which puts it in condition to act. To exercise causality the material being, therefore, must antecedently pass from potency to act, but only in virtue of this act can it produce an effect. Moreover, in acting on another being, the material cause actuates it and provokes on its part a reaction to which it submits in turn and which produces a change in it; but here once again, far from formally constituting causality, this change is only the consequence of the material conditions in which this causality is exercised.[10]

5. The Meaning of the Terms "Cause," "Condition," "Reason" and "Principle"

To anticipate misunderstandings let us make more precise some terms which are akin to that of cause,[11] namely, "condition," "princi-

---

[9] When the cause is of the same genus or the same species as the effect, St. Thomas calls it an univocal cause; otherwise he speaks of an equivocal cause (in the sense of analogous). Cf. *Summa theol.*, Ia, q.13, a.5, ad. 1.

[10] Aristotle observes quite correctly that change is produced in the being which submits to the action of the cause, and not in the cause itself: *actio est in passo*, i.e., the action is in the patient. In this adage the term "actio" does not designate the efficient action of the cause, but the effect of the efficiency. When *passio* is opposed to *actio*, the former term likewise designates the effect, but considered under another aspect, *scil.*, in as far as it flows from an extrinsic cause, whose being (in which the effect is produced) has undergone the action.

[11] For the meaning of the word "cause," cf. *supra*, p. 252.

ple," and "reason." In a very broad sense, we designate by the conditions of a being, all that this being demands in order to exist and to be such as it is. Hence, we must likewise count the external causes under this heading. In a more restricted sense the word "condition" signifies the same thing, but excludes external and internal causes; in reality this amounts to designating by this word "condition" all that is required in order that the causes of this being might be able to exercise their function. For example, material things act only under an external impulse; this impulse is the condition of their operation. Further, the matter on which these things are called to act at times must be put in a state capable of submitting to this action; this modification is an antecedent condition. Thus, certain foods must be prepared in order to be able to be assimilated. Finally it can happen that the activity of the causes is shackled by some obstacle, which must be removed before the causality can be exercised. For example, it is not possible that the rays of the sun should strike the retina of my eye if some one hinders them from penetrating to the place in which I am; at times it will be necessary to open or to clear the windows from obstructions, to permit me to see the light of day. This is a *conditio sine qua non,* an absolutely essential condition. Such is the strictest sense of the word "condition," that, namely, of "removens prohibens," removing an obstacle.

To fulfill the necessary conditions it will generally be necessary to exert a causality, to give an impulse to a material agent, to prepare foods, to remove a shackle: all this supposes the intervention of an efficient activity. Consequently the opposition which we place between condition and cause is only relative; it is bound up with a limited point of view where we take our stand in such a determined case. To obtain such an effect by the intervention of such a cause, it will first be necessary to realize such a condition. Undoubtedly the realization of this condition likewise demands the intervention of other causes; nevertheless, this last operation is called a condition in relation to its putting in operation such a particular cause which we wish especially to consider.

We must likewise distinguish cause and reason, since all reasons are not causes. We call a reason everything which illumines the mind, that which speaks to man's intelligence (or reason), that which explains anything and gives the reason for it. External causes are reasons for they explain the effect, but the external conditions and the internal principles of a reality likewise throw light on a thing, and they are so many reasons.[12] In the logical order the reason of the conclusion of a ratiocination is found in the premises.[13]

The word principle signifies whatever is first, or happens first. The cause is the principle of the effect, since this latter flows from the former. Moreover, in the order of knowledge it is legitimate to go from the effect back to the cause, and from this point of view the knowledge of the effect is the principle of the knowledge of the cause. Thus the applications of the term are countless, not only in the real order [14] but also in the logical order; [15] for example, in this last sphere the premises are the principles of the conclusion.

B. Finality

1. The Principle of Finality: Every Being Which Exerts Causality, Acts in an Orderly Manner, Namely, for an End

Every being is determined in its nature; it is therefore likewise determined in its activity of which nature is the substantial principle. If the action is determined, the effect of it will likewise be determined. This means that the action is directed towards a definite

---

[12] Of the divine Being we shall say that it has no extrinsic cause, and that it possesses in Itself its adequate reason.

[13] The term "reason" is used, therefore, as much in the logical as in the real order. The term "cause" applies generally only to reality.

Aristotle at times calls the premises the causes ($\alpha\iota\tau\iota\alpha\iota$) of the conclusion. Cf. *Post. Analyt.*, I, c.2, 71 b sqq.; c.13, 78 a 21-b 31; II, c.2, 90 a sqq.; c.8, 93 a 1-b 20; c.11, 94 a 20-b 26; c.16, 98 a 33-b 40; c.17, 99 a 35–99 b 8. *De Sophisticis Elenchis*, c.5, 167 b 21–168 a 16; *Rhetor.*, II, c.21, 1394 a 31.

Descartes writes in certain places: "the cause or the reason." *Réponses* aux 2es objections, axiome I (édit. Adam and Tannery, Vol. 9, Paris, 1904, p. 127); Spinoza also writes: "causa seu ratio." *Ethica*, I, prop. 11 (edit. J. Van Vloten and J. P. N. Land, 2nd edit., La Haye, 1913, Vol. I, p. 44.—Leibnitz at times identifies the two; cf. édit. Couturat, *Opuscules et fragments inédits de Leibnitz*, Paris, 1903, p. 471; and at times he distinguishes them: "causa seu realis ratio," (*ibid.*, p. 533).—Christian Wolff explicitly distinguishes them: "Cause and reason differ very much." *Philosophia prima sive Ontologia*, Frankfort and Leipzig, 1763, paragraph 71, p. 50.

[14] In the Most Holy Trinity the first Person is the real principle of the second Person and the first and second Persons together are the real principle of the third Person. By this we indicate the real origin while excluding all causality.

[15] The Scholastics distinguish the cause "ut quae" and the cause "ut qua." The first is the being which exerts causality, while the second is the internal principle which is the reason of the causal activity of a cause, *scil.*, the nature, the principle of substantiality, according to which the cause acts, or the faculty, the accidental active potency by which it operates.

term, or better that it is determined in itself by reason of its orientation towards a definite term. This term is therefore the reason of the action; it gives the action a meaning, for it specifies the action by imprinting a direction on it.

The effect is therefore not merely the final term, the end of the operation; it is above all the term to be attained, the final goal. The operation envisages it, pursues it, tends towards it, and it is determined in itself only by reason of this end to which it is directed, and by which it is attracted.[16] The operation depends on the end, the efficiency finds its reason, its meaning, in the end that is pursued.

To reject this doctrine it would be necessary to declare that the cause is independent of its end or purpose; but in this case an efficient operation would be adapted to any effect whatever. This is equivalent to saying that it would be undetermined, or in other words, that it would not exist. It stands to reason, therefore, that finality, the influence of the end or purpose on the operation, is an essential element of causality. "Quidquid agit, agit propter finem." (Whatever acts, acts for a purpose.) [17]

The law of finality is bound up with that of efficiency; the one and the other enunciate aspects of one and the same causal activity. The effect is a product; it depends on the operation, but the operation tends towards the effect, it is related to the effect, and in so far it depends on the effect. There is a reciprocal influence from the effect on the cause (in the order of finality), and from the cause on the effect (in the order of efficiency). The one does not occur without the other; [18] there is no efficiency without finality, neither is there

---

[16] "Whatever happens does not merely come from somewhere, but it goes somewhere. We conceive it as necessary that the cause comprises together with the reason of the origin, the reason also of the end whither its direction tends." Félix Ravaisson, *La Philosophie en France au XIX⁰ siècle*. Paris, 1884, paragraph 36, p. 254.

[17] Cf. Rég. Garrigou-Lagrange, O.P., "Le réalisme du principe de finalité" (*Biblioth. franç. de philosophie*, 2nd series), Paris, 1932, pp. 95–121.

[18] "The problem of final causes has been enunciated under this picturesque form: The bird has wings and it flies. Does it fly because it has wings, or does it have wings in order to fly? In the first alternative, the wings are efficient causes: the flying is the result of their action. In the second, the wings are a means, and the flying is an end.

"This formula of the problem is not happy; it makes us believe that efficient and final causes exclude one another, that we must choose the one or the other. Now the champions of final causes admit, as do the mechanists, that the evolution of nature is the effect of active causes, but they think that in order that the active causes may be determined to produce their effect, there must be final causes

any finality without efficiency: together they form the causal relation.

2. The Effect Envisaged Must Pre-exist in the Cause under the Form of an Idea. The Ultimate Foundation of the Effect Is an Intellect. Non-rational Beings Are Not the Adequate Reason of Their Activity

A problem suggests itself: How can the agent undergo the influence of the effect of which he is the author, in the very operation by which he produces the effect? As that which does not exist cannot exert any influence, it must be admitted that the effect exists before its own realization: a thing which can happen only under the form of an ideal pre-existence. The cause is determined to act in this connection by the idea of the end or goal to be attained.

Every efficient cause contains in its own way, *virtualiter,* the perfection of its effect, since this latter is formally only a real participation in the determination of its cause.[19] It seems now that every cause must contain, antecedently, the concrete and distinct outlines of its effect, since this effect is the end, the good to be attained, and since the end concretely gives the agent a purpose in drawing him to itself, and in thus impressing on him a determined direction. The efficient cause, therefore, must apprehend its end or purpose, must comprehend its good, must have knowledge of the term to be attained in order to be able to act.

Not any representation whatsoever of the final term is sufficient; there must be knowledge of the term as an end to be realized, as a

---

besides." Card. Mercier, *Métaphysique générale* (Cours de philosophie, II), 7th ed., Louvain, 1923, n. 237, p. 481.

"The term of an intention is a thing to be realized. Now, on the one hand, to realize some thing is the property of the efficient cause; the operation ceases when the effect exists; the effect realized is the goal, the term, the end of the operation. On the other hand, the being realized is precisely the being to be realized, i.e., the term of the intention. Hence, the intention and the action are united in one and the same term. Thus the end is the bond between the intentional and the efficient order, and consequently it belongs to both orders. In the efficient order the end is the goal of the operation, *finis in re;* but antecedently it was in the intentional order . . . the purpose of the operation, *finis in intentione.* Once realized this end is an effect which admits a cause, for it has been achieved by the operation; to be realized, it is a *cause,* for it determines the operation." Théod. de Regnon, S.J., *La Métaphysique des causes d'après saint Thomas et Albert le Grand,* 2nd ed., Paris, 1906, pp. 367–368.

19 Cf. *supra,* p. 267.

good to be desired. It is the goodness of the end which the cause must apprehend formally; in other words, the term of the operation must be an object of the will, and therefore it must have previously been understood in this way by the intellect. Finality implies a cause endowed with intellect.

There exists a world of material things, devoid of all knowledge or having only sensible representations at their disposal. These things exercise an activity and produce effects; but since they cannot form for themselves an idea of the terms which they pursue, they cannot of themselves account for the orientation of their operations. We must conclude from this that these material agents are not the adequate causes of the effects which they produce, and that all material causality rests necessarily on an intellectual activity which orders and guides it. "Intellectus est ordinare." The material world postulates one or more intellects which direct its operations towards a definite term.

3. The Internal Finality of a Being. The Finality of the Material Universe. The External Finality of Material Things

The nature of a being, its operation and its effect are ordered the one to the other. The determination of nature is expressed in the operation and this latter can only terminate in an end or purpose which is adapted to it. Such is the natural law of the particular being: every being acts according to its nature, according to its mode of being. The determination of the being is translated into that of action, and it ends with the determination of the effect produced. Now the determination of action is nothing other than its internal finality, the presence of the end as a principle of orientation, of tendency. Internal finality, therefore, is an absolute exigency of every being.

The universe is a whole, whose material parts have, as such, neither subsistence nor liberty properly so-called. They are and they operate only as parts, dependently on the whole complexus. They do not pursue any end which is peculiar to them, and the internal finality which is found in every one of them has meaning only as an element of the thoroughgoing internal finality of the universe.

Man, on the contrary, in as far as he is spiritual and subsistent, knows and pursues his own good; he tends towards an end which is personal to him. Besides, he is material, he forms a part of the universe; but thanks to his spiritual activity he possesses a certain mastery over his body, a fact which permits him to exert a personal action on the things that surround him. He will be able, therefore, to avail himself of them, to employ them as means, directed to the end which he proposes to attain, to insert them in the order of his own personal finality. To the internal finality of things there is to be added in this way external finality which is based on the former, since it uses the former and since it is bound up with an internal personal finality.

4. Chance in Relation to Material and Intellectual Causes; in Relation to a Limited Sphere and to the Order of Being

On the plane of being finality excludes chance; for everything there is intelligible, everything there has its sufficient reason for being. What meaning, then, could we give to the word chance? We call that "chance" which is produced without having been intended in any way by the cause. For example, we meet a friend by chance if the meeting occurs unexpectedly. Whoever discovers a treasure for which he was not looking, finds it by chance.

What takes place by chance always supposes the intervention of certain causes, each of which pursues its own end. Thus, in the case of the fortuitous discovery of the treasure: the person who hid the treasure placed a deliberate action, directed towards a precise end; the person who later set himself to dig in that very spot likewise pursued a definite end. From the meeting of these two purposive operations there results the discovery of the treasure.

It must be observed that precisely this meeting is fortuitous; this takes place without any prevision and is not subject to finality. But what precisely is this meeting? It does not represent anything outside of the two operations which have just been noticed, and it would be false to believe that it would be added to them as a third element. Each of the two operations comes to an end at a point foreseen, and this point happens to be the same for the one and the other. Hence, it merely remains to explain how it is possible that they could thus meet each other and under what conditions this is effected.

In the material world it is natural that forces meet each other, because they are operative in one and the same place. If there is question of purely material operations they will not give any play to chance, because they belong to one all-embracing system where everything runs off in a natural order. But when free agents come on the scene, fortuitous meetings must occur. Really, each of these free agents pursues his own personal goal, and his operations take place in an order which is independent of the other agents. And as they all live in the same material world, and as they can make use of the same objects, they run the risk of meeting and colliding with one another.

These meetings are fortuitous in this sense that one of the free causes cannot foresee what the other will do; hence, it cannot know ahead of time all the events which are going to happen. The multiplicity, consequently, and the limitation of the personal and free systems which exercise their activity on the same stage of the world, make fortuitous effects inevitable. From this we can conclude that if there exists a perfect Being endowed with a universal knowledge, which extends not merely to all things of the universe but likewise to all free persons, nothing could escape His knowledge, and hence nothing could appear to Him unforeseen and fortuitous. There can be no chance in regard to perfect knowledge. This Being: is He possible and does He exist? This question still remains to be answered.

C. Exemplarity

The purposiveness of every efficient operation can, in the last analysis, be explained only by the intervention of an intelligent cause, who knows the end or purpose as such, that is, by one who understands its value. The intelligent being acts under the light of knowledge; he executes his decisions under the direction of the idea which he forms for himself of the work to be realized; in a word, he acts conformably with his ideas. The idea therefore exerts an exemplary causality; it is the model according to which the agent regulates his action: "id secundum quod aliquid fit." Two important aspects of causality, namely, finality and exemplarity, are, therefore, formally connected with the intellectual character of the adequate cause; the agent is attracted by the goodness of the effect to be achieved, on condition that he knows this goodness, that he forms an idea of it for himself. On the other hand, the ideal representation which he has conceived of the term to be attained, guides him in the realization of his work. To execute his plan he has a perfect right to make use of a model already realized; but in this case it is only by means of the knowledge which he has of this model that this latter can act on him. It is as an idea that the model is an exemplary cause.

The fundamental cause of what occurs in the world or outside of it cannot therefore reside in material reality; it must be found in one or more personal beings endowed with activity of the mind. A person possesses himself, lays hold of himself in the clarity of conscious thought; he himself organizes his own existence and he directs himself towards his own peculiar purpose or end. He acts by himself and he is a subsistent being. See why, ultimately, it is a person who is in a position to cause, to make another being participate in his own perfection.

II. THE ORDER OF CAUSALITY

1. Coordination and Subordination (Essential or Accidental) of Causes from the Point of View of Their Efficiency

The universe is an order of active things; to understand the meaning of this, we must take into account the connection and the hierarchy of causes. Experience bears witness, first of all, to the fact that there is a coordination of causes from the point of view of their efficiency. Two horses are harnessed to a chariot; the one and the other can be considered as a partial cause of the movement of the vehicle, and together they are its total cause. In truth, each one does his part and is the total cause of what he produces, at least in this sense that he can act, exercise a traction, even if the other does nothing. To be sure, to make the chariot roll along they must unite their efforts and pull together, but this is because all the parts of the vehicle hold together. Their efforts, therefore, must be adapted one to the other; they must be coordinated.

The coordination of causes generally keeps step with their subordination. For example, a crew of sailors is on a boat; the boat is carried along by the water; the water covers the ground, etc.; or again, on a nail, driven into a wall, there is suspended a clothesrack on which a hat hangs. In these cases there is a coordination of elements: the one does not do what the other does, each one has the disposal of its own efficiency and does its part, and therefore we must add the different effects produced in order to obtain the total result. But besides, there is a subordination of one element to the other, since the efficiency of each one actually depends on that of elements which precede it; if the preceding element is defective, that which follows ceases to act. For example, if the wall crumbles, the nail comes out, the clothesrack falls to the ground. It is always thus in the world: one material thing can act only in the measure that it is pushed or supported by that which precedes and surrounds it.

We must be on our guard against confusing essential subordination with what is called accidental subordination; the first is a subordination properly so called, of the action of one cause to the action of another: it has to do with these two causes in as far as they are in the act of causing. If therefore the first cause does not act on the second (which is subordinate to the first) at the precise moment or point when the second cause is supposed to act, the action of this second cause will not be produced. For example, a penholder will not write letters if no one uses it for writing.

In the case of accidental subordination, the subordination is not produced formally along the line of the action which we consider at this moment, but it touches the agent from another point of view. It constitutes, therefore, an indispensable condition ("a conditio sine qua non") of the action under consideration. For example, in order to be able to take a walk at this moment, we must be alive; this supposes that we have been born of such parents, that these latter in their turn have had such parents, etc. There is here a real subordination, but it does not touch directly the present action of taking a walk. The death of our parents and of all our grandparents in no way hinders us from taking a walk at this moment, because their actual cooperation is not required for this action. In this case, the subordination has no essential bearing on the present action; it has to do with a condition of this action, with the past origin of the being which acts at this moment. This is the reason why this subordination, altogether real and indispensable as it is, is called accidental.

Instrumental causality is a typical example of the essential subordination of a series of causes. The principal cause and the instrument which it employs are, both of them, real principles of one and the same effect, which however they do not touch in the same way. For example, I am writing with a pen; without my intervention the pen would not write; without the pen, I could not write, at least not in this particular way. My activity cannot take the place of that of the pen, and I cannot replace this instrument by any other whatsoever, for example, by a hammer or a plough. Hence, the instrument plays an active role which is peculiar to it (*virtus instrumenti*). On the other hand, it goes without saying that the pen cannot supplant my intervention, and that I play an active role which is personal to me. Consequently, there is a cooperation of these two causes; their actions are added together to produce one common result.

This cooperation keeps pace with a subordination of one of these causes to the other: essential subordination, which formally concerns the two actions.[20] In writing I use a pen, I make use of it as an instrument, I insert my action in an order which looks to the realization of an end which I personally determine. I utilize the pen, I use it as a means suitable for obtaining the end which I have proposed to myself to attain. It is I, therefore, who direct the instrument; I am the principal cause and the instrument is the secondary or subordinate cause; it is I who impose on it the end to be obtained, and I will be responsible for this end. It is I who write, not the pen, but I write by means of the pen. The instrument is engaged in an operation which goes beyond it; under the conduct of the principal cause it realizes more than it could do all alone. To write letters is something quite different from making marks which have no sense. The efficacy (*virtus instrumenti*) which is proper to the instrument is raised to a higher plane, because it is completed by a transitory disposition (*virtus instrumentalis*) which the principal cause impresses on it during the whole duration of the common operation.[21]

In instrumental causality properly so called, the principal cause is a person, who pursues his own peculiar purpose and who is, consequently, capable of utilizing other realities and directing them to his own personal end. Man, at once corporeal and spiritual, is a person who must always make use of material forces to realize his aims; his personal action is inserted in a constant evolution of the material universe and it imprints on it unceasingly a human value.

---

[20] This is why the Scholastics call the instrument a *movens motum*, i.e., a moving cause, but one which is itself moved by another cause. Cf. Joseph Legrand, S.J., *L'univers et l'homme dans la philosophie de saint Thomas*, Brussels-Paris, 1946, Vol. I, pp. 121–128.

[21] This transitory disposition is called by St. Thomas *virtus fluens* (at times especially in his first works, *intentio fluens*), and it is opposed to the permanent powers of the agent. Cf. A. Hayen, *L'intentionnel dans la philosophie de saint Thomas*, Brussels-Paris, 1942, pp. 107–119.

Thus, for example, he employs material means to express the personal content of his conscious life; he creates symbols, material realities to which he attaches a signification. Attitudes and movements of the body, gestures, words, writings, all help to make known his thoughts, feelings, tendencies, decisions. These signs are instrumental causes, "intentional" inasmuch as man, the principal cause, attaches a meaning to them, and inasmuch as he inserts them in that way in a human order, directed towards his personal ends.[22]

2. Coordination and Subordination of Causes from the Point of View of Finality

Efficiency is inseparable from finality, for every action is intrinsically determined. Besides, if the efficient causes are coordinated and subordinated, this order must, before all else, have to do with the ends pursued. What, then, is the order of the ends or purposes?

Suppose we examine man's action. Every limited end which man pursues leaves a place open to other limited ends, which the first does not include; and it is, therefore, possible to pursue a number of purposes at one and the same time. For example, the man who distributes alms places an act which leads naturally to some result (*finis operis*), the alleviation of misery; and the author of this act can determine this end precisely (*finis operantis*). But more than this, he can by this same act pursue other ends, such as the practice of charity, of detachment, or some other virtue; he can intend to obtain certain advantages (*finis qui* or *finis cujus gratia*), and at the same time he can propose to make a friend profit by this alms (*finis cui*). The end which he has decided to pursue he might wish for by reason of the value which it embodies (*bonum honestum*) or again on account of the pleasure which it procures for him (*bonum delectabile*). If he pursues many purposes at once he can either arrange them in juxtaposition without giving the preference to any one, or he can arrange them in a hierarchical order, by giving more importance to one rather than to the other. In this last case, there will be primary or principal ends, and secondary ones; but they are all ends properly so called, because each is pursued for itself by reason of its intrinsic and peculiar value, and because no one is, as

---

[22] For example, a will is an efficient instrumental cause, creating rights and duties, inasmuch as it is the material expression of the will of the testator, which, moreover, is sustained by the will of those who hold power in society.

such, considered as a means made use of with a view to an end, nor in this respect is it entirely subordinated to this latter.

From the point of view of finality we must envisage not only the juxtaposition and coordination of ends, but also their subordination.

If we consider the universe we may wish to be able to make precise the place which every particle of matter occupies in the complexus of the cosmos, the function which each organ exercises with a view to the good of the organism of which it is a part; the activity which every living being is called on to exercise for the good of the species to which it belongs; the role of every species of living things and the manner in which one serves the other. We should see how plants rely on inorganic matter, and animals on plants, and how finally man orders everything for his own good. This would be a pyramid of ends or purposes, of which the spiritual good of the human person would form the apex.

Whatever may be true of this universal order, which natural philosophy ought to strive to discover, among the individual realities of this world man is the only being who enjoys a personal independence, and who can pursue his own end by utilizing all the material forces at his disposal. In human activity we can, therefore, observe a subordination in the order of finality: man uses means to attain his end. As such, these means borrow their goodness from the end towards which they are directed; the goodness of the end communicates itself to the means. "Bonum est diffusivum sui," "Goodness is diffusive of itself." [23] Nevertheless that which plays the role of means with respect to a limited end, always possesses in itself an intrinsic goodness (*bonum honestum*), and besides, it can at times constitute for the subject a certain value of pleasure (*bonum delectabile*). To this double goodness, then, there is to be added the goodness of the means, as such (*bonum utile*), the value which accrues to it by reason of its reference to the end.[24] It is therefore pos-

---

[23] This formula, of Neo-Platonic origin, was used before the time of St. Thomas for the order of efficient causality. The Angelic Doctor reserved it almost exclusively for finality. Cf. J. Péghaire, "L'axiome 'bonum est diffusivum sui' dans le néoplatonisme et le thomisme," *Revue de l'Université d'Ottawa*, II, 1932, special sect., pp. 5*–30*.

[24] We observe that there is an analogy between the relation of the means and the end in the sphere of finality, and that of the instrument and the principal cause in the order of efficiency. In the instrument we must distinguish efficiency proper (*virtus instrumenti*) and the efficiency which is communicated by the principal cause (*virtus instrumentalis*). In the means we must distinguish the goodness proper to this object (*bonum honestum* and *bonum delectabile*) and

sible to desire this object not only as a means, but also and at the same time by reason of its intrinsic value, as an end.

3. Coordination and Subordination of Causes from the Point of View of Exemplarity

Finality keeps step with exemplarity because both of them are connected with the mind; there will therefore likewise be an order of the exemplary causes.

Men who come to some agreement in order to conceive a plan of action coordinate their ideas. If one of them inspires the others he subordinates them to him in the order of exemplarity. But here, no more than in every other order, man is, strictly speaking, not a creator; he depends on his time, his milieu, his education, his experience, his reading. His mind must elaborate the data of experience and avail itself of the work of others in order to be able to end with personal results.

4. Total Subordination of Finite Causes

From every point of view the active centers of the universe unite in systems of coordination and subordination; but the dependence of one with respect to the other is never complete, since every finite cause carries with it an element which is peculiar to it, which is outside of the limits of the others and which no other could procure. Similarly, the effects of the hierarchy of causes are added to each other in order to form a complete result.

The principle of metaphysical causality, established above, asserts that every finite being depends on a cause because it is finite; consequently, in its whole reality this being is dependent on a cause, and this dependence extends likewise to the causality which it exercises. In this case, however, we must admit a total subordination of the finite cause, a subordination which excludes all coordination. The finite cause really acts, and yet complete as it is in itself the action here comprised and peculiar to it, is completely the effect of a higher cause, so much so, that it cannot from any point of view add anything to the action of this higher cause. How then must we conceive this absolute foundation of all activity and of all being? This question we must now answer.

---

that which is communicated to it by the end, and which makes a means of it (*bonum utile*).

CHAPTER XI

THE ABSOLUTE FOUNDATION OF BEING

I. THE EXISTENCE OF THE CREATIVE CAUSE

1. The Infinite Being, Absolute Foundation of the Order of Beings. The Proof for the Existence of God and the Infinite Series of Causes. The Transcendence and Immanence of the Absolute, Creative Cause. Creation, Contingence, and Pure Possibility

WHETHER we undertake the study of being directly or indirectly, one and the same fundamental problem always arises. We meet this problem in the first revelation of being; we find it in the study of first principles, of the finite and the infinite, of truth and possibility, of the categories of being, of the relativity which all finite activity implies, of causality.[1] This problem results from the radical opposition of two characters which mark the existence and the activity of every particular being, the absolute element of its value of being, and the relativity of its mode of individual being. To pose this problem with precision we must define its terms exactly. This is what we set ourselves to do all through the preceding chapters.

We have emphasized on various occasions the fact that participation in the absolute value of being which is found in all finite reality, and likewise that analogy properly so called which is inseparable from the transcendental idea of being, show with evidence that the complexus of particular beings constitutes an order absolutely unique.

Participation in being affects through and through the reality of that which is finite, just as the analogy of the idea of being concerns all concrete and individual reality; and this is the reason why every particular being carries with it an internal structure, as much in the

---

[1] Cf. *supra*, pp. 31–32, 38, 54–55, 60, 73–74, 86–87, 89–94, *etc.*

sphere of existence, namely, the principles of essence and existence, as in that of activity, that is, the principles of substance and accidents. This second structure, by the way, is merely a corollary of the first. This is equivalent to saying that the synthesis of all beings in a unique order is by no means superficial, and that it is not founded on any adventitious and accessory reference, which is to be added to a more profound reality already constituted. Quite the contrary. This synthesis has to do with everything that reality contains, even including what is most individual and intimate to this reality. In other words, that which unites beings is in no wise distinct from that which forms the reality peculiar to themselves; or again, that which every being is in itself is precisely that which unites all of them in an absolutely unique synthesis.

Consequently, as has been established above, there cannot be any question of explaining a finite being by itself, if abstraction is made from all the rest, since, as it seems to us, it cannot exist or be conceived outside of its union with other beings. The adequate reason of one particular being is identified with the reason that explains the whole order of finite beings.

Furthermore, it is evident that no particular being can constitute the fundamental reason of the whole order of beings, and this precisely on account of the individual and incommunicable character of the different beings which participate in the absolute value.[2] We would only be dodging the problem if we restricted ourselves to verifying the coexistence of finite beings in the universe. For if it is true that they are distinct one from the other, in as far as they are particular beings, it would be senseless to maintain that it is their multiplicity which formally constitutes the reason of their unity.[3] Now, as we have just recalled, this unity which is at first forced on us as a fact and as an incontestable truth, far from being adventitious, envelops and penetrates all reality through and through, since it is impossible (with an impossibility which admits of no exception) that a reality is ever found isolated, disengaged from the bonds which unite it to the other realities in the order of the value of being. Consequently, there is nothing more real than this unity; it rests therefore on a real foundation. The whole question is to know

---

[2] Cf. *supra*, p. 251.

[3] "For diverse things, inasmuch as they are diverse, are not united." St. Thomas, *De potentia*, q.7, a.1. Cf. *Contra Gentes*, II, c.41; I, c.18. "Before all multiplicity we must posit unity," *Summa theol.*, Ia, q.44, a.1.

precisely in what the real fundamental reason of the unique order
of beings consists.

This reason—can it be called the "fundamental substance?" We
must get clear on the meaning of the words. We have established
above [4] that the substance of particular being is the active reason and the principle of individuation of the becoming of this being.
The acts and the states of one finite being, for example, my efforts,
my feelings, my thoughts, are grounded, all of them, on the reality of
this finite being (in this case, myself), since they happen to coincide
exactly in one and the same substance or nature, in one and the same
active source which imprints on them its individual stamp. This
means that substance is the principle of individual identity and of
limitation on the plane of the value of being; [5] it is related to the
principle of existence, as potency to its first act, [6] and it demands,
therefore, of itself that the reality which it grounds, should be a *suppositum*, a subsistent being, comprising a structure which includes
its own peculiar principle of existence (its "esse proprium"). [7] And
just as this particular being possesses its own existence, [8] that is, it
exists in itself by reason of its internal structure, so it possesses likewise as its own the activity which proceeds from it. It acts by itself, and it develops by reason of the principles of its own structure,
"Actiones sunt suppositorum": Actions belong to *supposita*. [9] It is not
the hand which strikes, nor the head which bows, nor the intellect
which lays hold of a truth; we express ourselves accurately only by
saying that it is I who strike with my hand, it is I who bow my head,
who understand by means of my intellect. It is always the *suppositum*, the subsistent being, which is the subject of attribution of the
activity.

If, therefore, while preserving the proper meaning of the words,
we wish to call the fundamental reason of the order of beings the
deep-seated and unique "substance of all reality," the relation which
binds this fundamental reason to all things must be conceived according to the model of that which binds the substance of particular
being to its accidental development. Now, in this case it would be
necessary to deny that particular being is the subject of attribution

---

[4] Cf. *supra*, pp. 175–176, 194.
[5] Cf. *supra*, p. 107.
[6] Cf. *supra*, p. 133.
[7] Cf. *supra*, p. 244.
[8] Cf. *supra*, p. 129.
[9] Cf. *supra*, p. 241.

of its activity, since this latter would have to be referred to the fundamental substance as to its own proper subject; and it would likewise be necessary to deny that the free act of one particular being is fully independent of the being of every other particular being, since all these acts would exactly coincide in one and the same subject, the "fundamental substance." In other words, we should be in flagrant contradiction with immediate data; for nothing is more certain than the reality of my living and active ego, the subject of its own development, the source of free actions, of actions which are fully independent of the activity of every other particular subject.[10] As soon as we are forced to attribute a principle of substantiality to every particular being, we can no longer admit that particular being is related to the fundamental reason of all things in the same way that the activity of this particular being is related to it. If we speak accurately, the fundamental reason of all reality cannot be called the substance of things; on the contrary, we must distinguish it from the substantial reality of these things here.

The real foundation which is distinct from that of which it forms the foundation, is called a cause; the fundamental reason of beings will be called their fundamental cause. As this latter is not to be confounded with the reality of particular beings, it is, in this precise sense, an extrinsic reason, and not at all an immanent principle of these things. And yet, we must with extreme care avoid establishing a chasm between beings and their fundamental cause. It is not wrong to say that every particular being is more impregnated with the active influence of this cause than it is filled with its own substance, since this latter, wholly immanent as it is, does not offer the full reason either of the existence or of the action of particular being.[11] Besides, no one finite being is in a position to "solidify" itself to the point of being self-sufficient and of ever being able to detach itself, in any way whatsoever, from its fundamental cause. In reality, limitation and relativity, which all participation in the value of being implies, are formally the reason of the dependence of particular being with regard to the fundamental cause. Now, this reason permeates it completely, since everything which it contains is individual, and therefore finite and relative. Consequently, it is in a truly exhaustive way that it is dependent; it is such in its duration just as much as in its origin, in its extrinsic relations as in its sub-

---

[10] Cf. *supra*, pp. 13–22.
[11] Cf. *supra*, pp. 251–254.

sistent structure, in its activity as well as in its existence, in its intimate life and its free acts no less than in its natural and instinctive tendencies.

We must conclude from this that the fundamental cause is the absolute cause; for if particular beings are truly dependent in every respect on this cause, by the very reason of their finitude and their relativity, this cause could not absolutely depend on them in any respect. It is the cause of the whole order of finite beings, but not at all an element of this order; it is the source of all participation, but it itself does not exist by participation. It is disengaged from all external relativity and all limitation; it is the absolute, infinite Being.[12]

The fundamental cause, completely independent, is the perfectly adequate reason of everything, both from the point of view of efficiency and from those of finality and exemplarity. Its activity is withdrawn from every exterior condition; and so it does not depend either on any pre-existing matter to be transformed, or on the co-operation of another cause, for example, on an instrumental cause, or on a plan to be realized, or on a good to be achieved, or on an end to be pursued or on a means to be made use of. In one word, it is God, the Creator, the Cause absolutely free.

Absolute or creative causality, therefore, implies the contingency of the whole order of particular beings: what God produces, He could have not produced, and every creature must be conceivable as purely possible.[13] On the contrary, the divine Being is not contingent, since He cannot depend on any condition. It would be a contradiction to conceive Him as non-existent and yet as possible. He possesses in Himself the adequate reason of His existence; it is by nature, by definition, necessarily, that He exists. What He is, He must be by Himself, and not dependently on another. The absolute foundation of reality, the cause infinitely free, is by that same token the necessary Being.[14]

---

[12] For the idea of the infinite and its relations to the ideas of absoluteness and unicity, cf. *supra*, pp. 69–74.

[13] Cf. *supra*, pp. 93–94.

[14] In human activity we oppose the free act, which is personal, to the instinctive operation which proceeds from nature necessarily. It is not in this sense that the word necessary is used, when we say that God is the necessary Being. The divine necessity is not imposed from anything outside of the divine Being, and it is not a blind law which weighs on Him. It has no other reason than God Himself; it rests on His complete independence. It signifies that nothing, no person, conditions the existence of God, and that this existence could not,

In this way everything is explained. In point of fact, if all individual beings coincide perfectly in their unique total and absolute reason, they flow from the same source, they are riveted to the same principle; and this is why they all bear witness to the same absolute value of being, and why they are necessarily united in the same order of beings. The unshakable consistency, common to all of them, is bound up with the absolute Cause which envelops and penetrates them completely with its all-powerful fecundity. Every particular being is a pure gift of the Absolute, on which it depends completely, and it cannot do otherwise but reveal, in the measure of its reality, the value of being of the absolute principle in which it participates. This necessity is identically the same for all: behold the reason why the transcendental idea of being implies an analogy.

It will not be altogether devoid of interest to try to see just why the question of the infinite series of causes often enjoys so much importance in the elaboration of the arguments designed to prove the existence of God.

Finite causes are ordered among themselves; they form several series; a definite effect depends on a cause which is itself dependent on a second cause, and this last on a third, a fourth, etc. Every one is real; it exerts its peculiar activity and it brings about a result. And yet no one cause is the complete reason of its effect, since it is itself the term of a causal operation, so much so that its own activity is conditioned by the latter causal operation. The complete reason ought to contain the sum of all the causes and conditions; to obtain this sum it would be necessary to add up all the operations of the finite causes of the series being considered. This is why we are often inclined to think that the whole question boils down to knowing if this series must be finite or if it can be infinite. In the first case it has a first term, which could be explained only by a cause which is distinct from the finite elements of the series; the first finite term would be the effect of an infinite cause. On the contrary, if the series did not have a first term every cause would find in a preceding finite cause its explanatory reason, and at no moment should we have need to go out of the series and to appeal to an infinite cause. Many authors, therefore, go on striving to prove that an infinite series of

---

therefore, under any hypothesis, go by default. This absolute necessity is an aspect of the absolute independence or liberty of God. The absolute necessity and the absolute liberty of God transcend the opposition of the relative necessity and the limited liberty in man.

causes is nonsense, at least if there is question of causes essentially subordinated.

We have explained already [15] why every solution of this problem of the infinite series remains very doubtful; but this has little bearing on the present question, for we must not push our inquiries in this direction. Undoubtedly, a finite cause is really active and produces a real effect; but in metaphysics, there is question of knowing if such a cause is the adequate reason even of part of its effect. If we must answer "No," it becomes altogether useless to appeal to a second finite cause, a third, an indefinite series, since all of them would be in the same condition. No one among them would adequately explain the least effect, and all of them together would explain nothing, since zero multiplied as much as you would wish, still equals zero. Now, as we have seen above, the negative answer is forced on us: a finite reality is dependent on a cause, simply because it is finite. Its activity which is assuredly real, depends completely on a cause, since it is wholly and entirely finite. By itself a finite cause offers a reason neither for its whole effect nor for a part of this effect; by itself it offers a reason for nothing, since it can in no wise exist by itself, but only by the creative action of an infinite cause. It is therefore the whole order of finite causes, the whole network of their operations and the whole complexus of their effects which depend on an absolute principle. Outside of this relation of complete dependence this order is not, and it is incapable of producing anything.

There is, therefore, no necessity of getting mixed up with the series of finite causes with a view to ending at the first term and to mount by means of it to the creative cause, basing our proof on the principle that "everything which begins to be, is an effect of a cause." Without doubt, the beginning of a reality is a proof of its dependence on a cause; but in continuing to exist the finite being does not cease to be finite. Now, any limit whatsoever of a subsistent being is a reason for its causal dependence. Hence, to conclude to the existence of a creative cause, it seems preferable to base our argument on the actual limitation of particular being, rather than to pass through a series of causes about which it is difficult, if not impossible, to prove that it must have commenced in time.

These remarks can help us to make the nature of creative causality more precise. The infinite cause does not include any limitation, or any extrinsic relativity. It cannot form part of an order or enter into

---

[15] Cf. *supra,* pp. 71–72.

a series. It is not accurate to say that it "differs" from another cause as this being differs from that which is in the same line or on the same plane. In this respect, it is preferable to state that the infinite is not opposed to the finite, since they are not of the same order; they are diverse.

It would therefore be a mistake to consider the creative cause as the first of the causes, to put it at the head of a series of finite causes. Undoubtedly, we commonly call it the "First Cause"; but here again we must understand this expression accurately. This first Cause is not followed by a second, a third, fourth, etc. If we call it "first" all the other causes ought to be called "second," whatever they may be, material or spiritual, principal or instrumental, whether considered in the order of efficiency, or finality, or exemplarity. The second cause is distinct from the first Cause as the finite and relative cause is distinct from the infinite and absolute cause; every creature is finite and relative to others; its causality is "second," that is, it is completely subordinated to creative causality which alone is absolutely and uniquely the first.

The creative cause is, therefore, transcendent in relation to finite causes; it does not belong to the order of second causes, since it is the absolute source of them. But these latter can in no wise be separated from this source even for a single moment, under the penalty of otherwise being nothing. The transcendent cause, therefore, penetrates unceasingly even down to what is most intimate in its creatures; it is in them without being confounded with them, and this immanence is only one aspect of the transcendence of the divine, creative causality.

2. The "Ontological" Argument of St. Anselm, Descartes, and Leibnitz

These reflections permit us to pass judgment on the proof for the existence of God, called since the time of Kant the "ontological" argument. St. Anselm formulates it as follows: [16] I understand by

---

[16] "It is one thing to have an object in the intellect, and another to understand that this thing exists. When the painter conceives his work he has it in his mind, but he does not yet apprehend the existence of what has not yet been realized; but after he has painted it he has it in his intellect, and he also understands the existence of what he has now created. The fool himself ought to agree that there is at least in his intellect some thing than which a greater cannot be conceived, since, when he understands it he comprehends it, and since

the word "God" the most perfect being that can be conceived. This being must exist, for it is more perfect to exist than not to exist. The most perfect being possible is therefore not merely an idea, but also an existing reality.

Descartes reasons in this way: [17] That which I recognize clearly

that which is comprehended is in his intellect. But certainly that than which nothing greater can be conceived, cannot exist only in the intellect. As a matter of fact if it existed only in the mind, we could conceive it as being also in reality: and this would be superior. Hence, if that than which nothing greater can be conceived, is only in the mind, that than which nothing greater can be conceived is some thing than which something greater can be conceived—a thing which is certainly impossible. Beyond any doubt therefore, there exists some thing than which nothing greater can be conceived, both in the intellect and in reality.

"And it exists so really that one cannot even think of its non-existence. We can, as a matter of fact, conceive some thing which it would be impossible to think of as non-existent, therefore superior to that which we could think of as non-existent. This is the reason why if that than which nothing greater can be conceived, can be thought of as not existing, this same thing than which nothing greater can be thought of, is not that than which nothing greater can be thought of—a thing which is contradictory. Thus that than which nothing greater can be conceived exists so truly that we cannot even think that it does not exist. And this, this is Thou, oh Lord, our God. Thou, oh Lord, my God, dost therefore exist so really, that Thou couldst not be thought of as not existing; and this is justice. If any mind, as a matter of fact, could conceive some thing better than Thou, the creature would take precedence over the Creator and would judge his Creator—a thing which is perfectly silly. In truth, everything which is other than Thou alone could be conceived as not existing. Thou alone hast being, most truly of all and the greatest, because all that which is other (than Thou) is not as truly, and does not therefore possess the least being. Why, then, has the fool said in his heart: 'There is no God,' when it is so evident to the reasonable mind that Thou dost exist more than all else? Why, if not because he is silly and foolish?" St. Anselm, *Proslogion*, cc. 2, 3; (P.L. vol. 158, pp. 227–228). English translator's version.

[17] Cf. *Fifth Meditation* (edit. Adam and Tannery, Vol. 9, Paris, 1904, pp. 50–56). "But now, if from this fact alone that I can draw from my thought the idea of any thing, it follows that all that I recognize clearly and distinctly to belong to this thing, really belongs to it, can I now draw from this an argument and a demonstrative proof for the existence of God? It is certain that I find in me His idea, i.e., the idea of a being sovereignly perfect, no less than those of any figure or any number whatsoever. And I do not know less clearly and distinctly that an actual and eternal existence belongs to His nature, than I know that all I can demonstrate of any figure or any number, belongs truly to the nature of this figure or this number. And thus, although all that I have concluded in the preceding Meditations were not found to be true, the existence of God ought to pass in my mind at least for as certain, as I have thought up to now all the truths of mathematics, which have to do only with numbers and figures: although in truth that would not seem at first to be entirely evident, but it seems to have some appearance of sophism. For having been accustomed in all other things to make a distinction between existence and essence, I easily persuade myself that existence can be separated from the essence of God, and that thus we can conceive God as not actually being. But nevertheless, when I think of

and distinctly to belong to the nature of a thing, must be affirmed of it. Now if I examine carefully what God is, I recognize that existence must belong to Him, since the divine Being is conceived as the infinitely perfect Being, and since existence ought to be classified among perfections. We must therefore admit that God exists.

Leibnitz understood that it would be necessary, antecedently, to show the intelligibility or the possibility of the being whose nature implies existence; [18] consequently, he sets himself to complete the argument in this way: [19] If the being whose essence it is to exist is possible, he exists necessarily. Now this being is possible. As a matter of fact, the definition of the most real being or of the most perfect being includes only one positive element, namely, infinite existence. But a contradiction results only from the opposition of a positive

this more attentively, I find evidently that existence can no more be separated from the essence of God than that the sum of its three angles, equal to two right angles, can be separated from the essence of rectilinear triangle, or that the idea of a valley can be separated from the idea of a mountain. And thus there is not less repugnance in conceiving a God (i.e., a being, sovereignly perfect) to whom existence is wanting (i.e., to whom some perfection is wanting) than to conceive a mountain which would have no valley." (Translator's version.)

[18] Cf. *De la démonstration Cartésienne de l'existence de Dieu du R.P. Lami, Mémoires de Trévoux,* 1701.

[19] "By perfection I mean every simple quality which is positive and absolute, or that which expresses without any limits whatever it does express. But a quality of this kind, since it is simple, is therefore irreducible and indefinable. . . . Hence, it is not difficult to show that all perfections are mutually compatible, or that they can be in the same subject. For let the proposition be of this kind: A and B are incompatible . . . ; it is evident that it cannot be demonstrated without breaking down the terms A and B, either one, or the other, or both. For otherwise their nature would not enter into the ratiocination, and the incompatibility of all other things could be demonstrated just as equally as the incompatibility of A and B. . . . It could, however, be demonstrated about them, if it were true, because it is not true *per se;* but all propositions are necessarily true or demonstrable, or they are known *per se.* Therefore, this proposition is not necessarily true. Or it is not necessary that A and B should be in the same subject; therefore they cannot be in the same subject; and since we can reason the same way about any other qualities of this kind, therefore all perfections are compatible. Therefore, there is or there can be understood a subject of all perfections, i.e., the most perfect Being. Hence, it is evident that it (this most perfect Being) also exists, since existence is contained among the number of perfections." Leibnitz, *Fragment relatif à Spinoza. "Quod Ens perfectissimum existit"* (1676) (edit., C. J. Gerhardt, *Die philosophischen Schriften von G. W. Leibnitz,* Berlin, Vol. VII, pp. 261-262).

"Thus God alone or the necessary Being has this privilege that He must exist, if He is possible. And as nothing can hinder the possibility of that which does not contain any limits, any negation and consequently any contradiction, that alone suffices for us to know the existence of God *a priori." Monadologie,* n.45 (Vol. VI, p. 614). Cf. *Nouveaux Essais,* IV, 10, paragraph 7 (Vol. V, pp. 418-419).

and negative element; therefore, there is no contradiction to be discovered in the case given. Consequently, God is conceived of as possible.

What ought we to think of this argument? St. Anselm combines the idea of the most perfect being and that of the necessary being. He supposes that we distinguish different beings, some of which are more perfect than the others; and that thus we are led to conceive the Being which is the most perfect of all. He supposes, in the next place, that we distinguish the contingent, which is able not to exist, and the necessary, which cannot be purely possible but which must exist. He strives to show that the most perfect being is the necessary being. These two presuppositions are not subjected to an examination. First of all, St. Anselm does not ask himself in what sense it is permissible to speak of different beings. He does not take any notice of the hypothesis of metaphysical monism.

Neither does he ask himself if every being is not equally necessary, in which case the contingent would not be conceivable; on the contrary he admits, without any further exposition, that everything which is distinct from the most perfect being is contingent.[20] Nevertheless, if everything were equally necessary, would we not be forced to admit that all reality contains in itself the reason of its existence; and finally that all things coincide in one and the same nature, since they would be regulated by one and the same natural law?

Suppose that we fall in with the opinions of the man on the street, who considers the existence of distinct beings and of beings of different perfection as an evident fact, then we will be brought to admit also that certain beings manifest an equal perfection. But then the question arises of knowing if the same case does not present itself in the matter of the highest perfection. Actually, why must we admit a priori that supreme perfection can be encountered in only one being? Why would it be impossible for many beings to attain equally to the most exalted degree of perfection?

The negative answer which is commonly given to these last questions, stems from the fact that supreme perfection is identified with infinite perfection. It must, however, be remembered that confusions can result on the subject of the infinite; [21] there is no question, in this connection, of the sum-total of perfections which the entire and, in this sense, the unlimited order of finite beings represents, but of the

---

[20] Cf. the extract from Chapter 3 in the text cited above, p. 290.
[21] Cf. supra, pp. 69–74.

unlimited perfection of one and the same Supreme Being, from whom the complexus of finite beings is really distinct. Must supreme perfection be identified with infinite perfection, understood in this last sense? St. Anselm does not speak explicitly of this infinity of perfection. Hence the question remains: Is not the supreme degree of perfection, which is distinct from the inferior degrees, necessarily finite just as much as these inferior degrees, since we conceive it as being opposed to them? Do not these two, perfect being and infinite being, exclude each other mutually as square and circle do? And if such is the case, why cannot this supreme degree of perfection be realized in many beings?

St. Anselm's reflections, therefore, do not offer any solution to the problem of God. They do not prove to what we must subscribe, whether to monism, to dualism of the Being sovereignly (and perhaps infinitely) perfect and of the other beings, or to a pluralism of supreme beings, equally perfect and opposed in one and the same order, to beings of a lesser degree of perfection.

Descartes did not bring any light to bear on these points. He contented himself with affirming neatly just what the divine nature is: God is the perfect being whose essence implies existence, so that we must define Him as the subsistent Being.

Leibnitz discovered, quite correctly, that this definition could not be admitted without justification. He observes that a definition which includes only one element cannot imply a contradiction; to have a contradiction we must have at least two things which collide with each other; but the definition of the divine nature includes only existence without limitation, infinite existence. These considerations of Leibnitz are assuredly ingenious, but the question precisely is whether such a definition enunciates only one element. If every being were necessarily finite, the qualification "infinite" would remain foreign to it in all cases, and the expression "infinite being" would imply a formal contradiction. Experience teaches us that finite beings exist: just in so far is it certain that there is no contradiction between the idea of a subsistent being and the idea of finite. What then are the grounds for maintaining that the same thing must be affirmed of the ideas of subsistent being and of the infinite, of the negation of all limitation of this being? St. Thomas, discussing St. Anselm's argument, had already observed that the nature of God is known to us only a posteriori, passing, namely, through finite beings; we have no direct knowledge of the divine

Being, and hence we cannot affirm anything a priori of His nature or of His existence. See why the ontological argument, in as far as it is an a priori argument or *e simultaneo,* is not conclusive. Undoubtedly, this line of reasoning contains a germ of truth, but we do not see that the conclusion flows from it with certitude, because a good foundation of the premises has not been established. What is more, this could only be done a posteriori.

People sometimes censure the defendants of the ontological argument for passing unwarrantedly from the order of ideas to that of existence; but this censure is not well founded. Even St. Anselm had observed that the given instance, unique in its kind, fully justified this passage.[22] On their part, Descartes and Leibnitz drew attention to this privileged case: the idea of the divine nature is the only one which formally implies the idea of actual and necessary existence. If we suppose that this idea appears to us as non-contradictory (and this is exactly what the ontological argument does not succeed in showing), we would, conformably to the nature of the intellect, have to conceive the infinite Being as actually and necessarily existing. Hence, if this Being did not exist it would be necessary to conclude from this that there is an irreducible opposition between the intellect and the real, and this in virtue of the laws of thought. But this is impossible, since the formal object of the intellect is being. Consequently, if we legitimately conceive God as having to exist by nature, it is certain that God does exist in reality.

Leibnitz expresses the intelligibility of the idea of infinite being by the word "possible"; if God is possible, He must exist. Evidently, he does not intend to speak of the pure possibility of the being who does not exist de facto, but who could exist. In point of fact, this possibility is precisely that of contingent beings, and Leibnitz' intention is to establish that God is the being who must exist because His nature demands existence. It is just as absurd to conceive God as not existing, as a pure possible, as it is contradictory to think of the contingent as existing necessarily by virtue of its nature. In Leibnitz' argumentation the word "possible" signifies "intelligible," conformable to the laws of thought and therefore to those of being, its formal object.

St. Anselm's argument, therefore, emphasizes the necessity of the existence of God, starting with the definition of the divine nature; but as we have no immediate knowledge of this nature the whole

---

[22] Cf. St. Anselm, *Scriptum contra Gaunilonem respondentem pro insipiente.*

argumentation supposes that the existence of God has been antecedently established by another means, that is, by an a posteriori proof.

3. The Metaphysical Value of the "Five Ways" of St. Thomas

In the Summa Theologica St. Thomas proposed "five ways" to prove the existence of God.[23] Let us examine them briefly in order to bring out their metaphysical orientation. The five ways are constructed on the same plan, a feature quite apparent in the first three; the major indicates a fact of experience, the minor applies the principle of causality to it, and the conclusion deduces from this the existence of God.

The facts of experience are the following: There is motion; there is a series of causes; there are things which do not always exist, they have a beginning and an end; there are degrees of perfection; there is order in nature.[24]

The formula of the principle of causality is adapted to each case: whatever moves, is moved by another thing; it is not possible for a thing to be its own cause. What is necessary finds the reason of its necessity in another, or it possesses it in itself. The greater and the lesser have a reference to a maximum, and the maximum in a genus is the cause of everything which this genus contains. Things not endowed with knowledge are directed towards an end only under the direction of an intelligent being.[25] In the exposition of the first three

---

[23] Summa theol., Ia, q.2, a.3.—In the Summa contra Gentes, I, c.13, St. Thomas sets forth five arguments in which considerations of the cosmological order, notably on the subject of motion, occupy an important place. The Summa Theologica likewise proposes five arguments, but with much more conciseness, and from a more exclusively metaphysical point of view. An historical examination and criticism of these proofs do not enter into the framework of this present work, and so we are confining ourselves to indicating summarily their metaphysical bearing.

[24] "It is certain and it is evident to the senses that some things move in this world. . . . We find that in these sensible things there is an order of efficient causes. . . . We find in reality some things which are possible to be and not to be, since some things are found to be generated and corrupted. . . . Grades or degrees are found in things; for there is found in reality something more and less good, and true and noble. . . . We see that some things which are without knowledge, scil., natural bodies, act for the sake of an end." Summa theol., Ia, q.2, a.3.

[25] "Everything which is moved, is moved by another. . . . It is not possible that any thing should be the efficient cause of itself. . . . A necessary thing has the cause of its necessity in something else, or it does not have such cause. . . .

proofs, it has been remarked that the fundamental cause cannot be found in an infinite series of second causes.[26]

The conclusions of the different proofs are the following: There is a first immovable Mover, a first efficient Cause, a Being, necessary of itself which is the cause of the necessity of the others, a perfect Being which is the cause of the being, the goodness, and the perfection of all reality, an intelligent Being which directs all the things of nature towards their end.[27]

In these five ways we always begin by taking a glance at the world, such as it appears in human experience. We verify there the activity of becoming, and the dependent causality (the first and second ways), of things which begin and which differ among themselves in perfection (the third and fourth ways); and finally we verify the existence of an ordered complexus (the fifth way).

In this way we take notice of five aspects of one and the same reality, which are five indications of limitation. This limitation is revealed in what things do, that is, they change in moving towards a final term, and they act on other things in the measure in which they have yielded to the action of still other things: the first and second ways. This limitation is also revealed in what these things are, namely, things which have a beginning and which possess a certain degree of perfection: the third and fourth ways. Things are, therefore, finite in the dynamic order as well as in the static order. These aspects are undeniable and characteristic; they are verified

More and less are spoken of in reference to a maximum. The maximum in any genus is the cause of all things which are of that genus. . . . Things which are devoid of knowledge, do not tend towards an end unless they are directed by some intelligent being." *loc. cit.*

[26] "But here there cannot be *processus in infinitum*, because thus there would not be some one first moving thing, and consequently there would not be any other moving thing. For secondary moving things do not move, except through this that they have been moved by the first mover. . . . But it is not possible that in efficient causes there should be an infinite process. . . . It is not possible that there should be an infinite process in necessary things which have a cause of their necessity." *loc. cit.*

[27] "Therefore it is necessary that we come to some first mover who is not moved by any one; and this all people understand to be God. . . . Therefore it is necessary to posit some first efficient cause, which all call God. . . . Therefore, it is necessary to posit something which is *per se* necessary, not having the cause of its necessity in something else, but which is the cause of necessity for the others; which all call God. . . . This is, consequently, Being in the fullest sense, . . . which is the cause of the *esse*, the goodness, and every other perfection in all things; and this we say is God. . . . Therefore, there is something intelligent, by which all natural things are ordered to an end; and this we say is God." *loc. cit.*

everywhere in the world. The facts of the dynamic order strike us first of all, and we treat of them in the first place; for by their activity we discover the nature of things. The fifth way begins by emphasizing an aspect of nature, which likewise is quite evident— the order which reigns there and is manifested in the regularity of phenomena. This order bears witness to the fact that things are bound up together in their action as well as in their being.

The first two characteristic notes, becoming and action, are grounded on the active union of things; the movement of one thing is attached to the active intervention of another thing. Similarly, an activity which is turned towards the outside responds to an activity which is undergone and which comes from the outside. In both cases causality comes into play: change and activity in the world depend, the one and the other, on an external cause. Hence, series of causes are formed; and yet these series will never furnish the fundamental reason of the facts, even if the series are infinite. This reason can be found only on an altogether different plane, in an immovable Mover, an independent Cause which is first, in relation to which all the causes of the world are second, since they depend on it completely.[28]

The third way starts from the fact that certain beings are gen- erated and die; they have a beginning and an end. Hence, if we consider them separately, isolated from the rest, we will not find in them the reason of their existence; they are contingent beings. If we suppose that everything is contingent, we should have to admit that at a certain moment nothing whatever existed.[29] But it is impossible that being should proceed from non-being; therefore pure contin-

---

[28] It seems certain to us that St. Thomas does not seek the "first" Cause by passing through a series of causes, of which this cause would be the first term. First of all, he hesitates to declare himself capable of proving that the infinite series is impossible (cf. *supra*, pp. 71–72). Then, he defends the view that the creative action of God produces finite beings directly, without the intervention of a subordinate cause (*Summa theol.*, Ia, q.45, a.5), so that the divine causal influx is not transmitted by intermediary causes but it is exerted immediately on every creature.

[29] As a matter of fact, two hypotheses can be conceived: first, according to which the complexus of things (which are all contingent) has had a beginning. Before this beginning there was nothing; consequently, that which exists is grounded on nothing. A second hypothesis: time did not begin; all the possibilities have had to have occasion to be realized in the course of eternal time, notably that of the simultaneous non-existence of all things. This is possible, since all are equally contingent; but by that token this hypothesis falls to the ground; things have had to begin and they have had to do this by proceeding from nothing.

gency cannot suffice, there must be necessity in being. Hence, what is purely contingent must necessarily rest on another thing which is not contingent, that is, on a necessary cause.

In fact, we see that what is generated depends on what precedes it, just as whatever disintegrates is bound to that which follows; and the being generated must necessarily begin to exist if its parents produce it. Contingent being shares in necessity, but by reason of its immediate causes; its necessity is hypothetical and it does not contain its foundation in itself. If these immediate causes are in the same condition we shall be able to imagine a successive series of similar causes; but if we suppose that the series is without limits and that it does not have a first term, this series cannot explain in any way the necessity which it contains, and so the whole series will remain purely contingent. Now, as we have already observed, it is impossible for reality to be contingent through and through; hence we must conclude to the existence of a Being absolutely necessary, who is the cause of contingent being.[30] The first three proofs are developed in parallel fashion.

The fourth proof considers limitation, as such; it presents it as a "degree," it supposes an order of things all of which participate in one and the same perfection. Perfections are reduced, in the last analysis, to the value of being which is transcendental. The degree or participation implies a deep-seated relativity and a fundamental dependence in reference to the Being which is not relative, which is not a degree, since, being the source, it is complete, perfect.

In this fourth proof mention is made no more of the infinite series of limited causes, in order to determine if it could not contain the sufficient reason of the facts to be explained. The reason is that right from the start we have considered all things as degrees of perfection, and we have understood that their participation in being renders them just as incapable of explaining themselves as of explaining other things. By all their reality all things are related to the cause of their participated being, to the supreme and perfect Being. Here we find the fundamental reason why even the infinite series of second causes (of which there was question in the first three ways) was not in a position to offer a sufficient explanation of any reality. What is en-

---

[30] In this proof three hypotheses are successively envisaged: first of all, the pure contingence of all reality; then, the hypothetical necessity of reality; and lastly, the hypothetical necessity of the contingent and the absolute necessity of its adequate cause. The first hypothesis manifestly implies a contradiction; the second, must be reduced to the first; and so only the third remains.

tirely relative must necessarily rest on the Absolute; the finite can be explained only by the Infinite, which is the adequate cause of its being.

The fifth way endeavors to show that the order of nature is the effect of an intelligent cause. Finality is the fruit of the mind: God is Mind.

This schematic review of the five ways suffices to show that they deepen progressively a way of reasoning which always remains the same substantially. We consider particular being as active (the first and second ways), then particular being without further qualification (third and fourth ways). In the activity of things we study first of all their change or internal evolution (the first way), and we pass from that to the action which they exert on other things (the second way). Being is considered in its contingent origin (the third way), and it is then taken in the totality of its aspects as a degree of being, as limited in all that it comprises (the fourth way). All these ways lead to the affirmation of a First Cause. The fifth way which is bound up with order, and emphasizes especially finality which is an aspect of causality, allows us to take notice explicitly of an essential property of the First Cause, namely, that an intelligent being creates and governs the order of nature.

The argumentation is developed in concentric circles which clinch the proof ever more and more. In the fourth way it gets to the bottom of the problem fully, by taking as the basis of its reasoning participation in the value of being, which is the most universal and the most fundamental reason of the close union of all finite reality with infinite and absolute Being.

St. Thomas contents himself with formulating these proofs in certain concise phrases. The most important points of the reasoning, for example the affirmation that the whole series of finite causes is formed of secondary causes which directly rest on the First Cause (the first three ways), and this other affirmation that all finite beings are directly related to the infinitely perfect Being (the fourth way) —all these points, I say, demand painstaking study which has to do with the most fundamental questions of philosophy. At any rate, St. Thomas has decidedly placed the problem on a metaphysical basis.

The point of departure of every one of the five ways begins with sensible data; the intention is to rivet the argumentation securely to experience. The data here are laid hold of in a human way; they are verified empirically, but in such wise that thought reflects on these data and discloses their metaphysical content.

Evidently, St. Thomas treats the things of the world as so many beings and causes. This rather dogmatic thesis is debatable, but at all events it is certain that man is one being, a person. Thus it suffices to make man the pivot of the various data of experience, of which the five ways make capital, in order to discover there a foundation for an unshakable argument, and likewise to verify the fact that St. Thomas has interpreted the data correctly.

In his activity man undergoes a becoming (the first way) whose immanence is inseparable from material and transient operations; these latter establish an interaction between the ego and the external world (the second way). Inasmuch as he is a personal being man has a beginning in time, but this beginning is a concept which attaches to the operation of other beings, for man is born in the world and into humanity (the third way). By reason of his conscious life man recognizes his nature and his limits, and he sees himself placed face to face with other beings; he understands that there is an order of realities, and he forms for himself an analogous idea of being which includes the degrees of being and implies participation in the value of being (the fourth way). He develops his free and personal actions without bursting the bonds which rivet him to the universe, and in his instinctive tendencies there is manifested the material order of nature (the fifth way).

On the basis of the transcendental idea the proof for the existence of God passes from immediate data to the transcendent Being. The idea of being is transcendental, the idea of good (which lays hold of being under the angle of activity) is likewise transcendental; the argument could be linked in a special way to the one or the other. In both cases it is an ascent from the finite to the Infinite, from the multiple to the One, in such wise that the transcendental idea of the one also comes into play all the time. Further, as this proof is an effort of the mind which is bound up with the transcendental idea of being, it is altogether imperative to make a critique of the relation of the intellect and being. It will likewise be necessary to take into account the transcendental idea of the true.

Emphasis can be placed on one transcendental property rather than on another, and we shall be able to formulate as many arguments as there are transcendentals, expressing ourselves in terms either of being, or unity (order), or goodness (activity), or truth (affinity between being and thought). At bottom these are just so many modifications of one and the same mental process, modifications which differ as much as being differs from its transcendental properties. The one implies the other, and we can no more separate them adequately than we can, strictly speaking, abstract being either from the one, from the true, or from the good.

The transcendental is the formal object of man's spiritual activity. It is one aspect of the problem of which we can likewise avail ourselves in the exposition of the proof for the existence of God, and which is calculated to give this proof warmth and life. By his specific orientation towards being and the good, man tends naturally by his intellect and will towards the possession of all truth and of all goodness. Mind and heart remain unsatiated as long as they do not enjoy the conscious presence of transcendent Being, the source of all existence and of all value. Man is a pilgrim in quest of the Absolute; with all his being he tends towards God. "Our heart is restless, until it rests in Thee." [31]

The proof for God's existence is therefore anchored in man's reality. For knowledge is an immanent activity; its development is none other than that of the knowing subject himself; hence, what knowledge attains to interests the subject, and it ought to correspond to the profound desire of his soul. Thus, we understand that the proof for God is, in a sense, short and easy, since it is limited to traversing a path traced by nature and etched deeply into the heart of man: the relative is related to the Absolute, the finite postulates the Infinite, participated being is bound up with God. This profoundly natural movement of the mind towards the Absolute forms essentially what Newman calls "the fundamental religious experience." Certain moral qualities, recollection, sincerity, humility, are required in order that this experience be developed fully; that man deliberately adopt a personal attitude which corresponds to the natural impulse of his heart, and which bows obediently to the law of the mind. This law is none other than the law of being.

As soon, however, as we have resolved to recognize this profound movement of the soul, and to make a critical examination of it with a view to translating it into philosophical formulae, the task appears as fraught with difficulties. We should be mistaken to be surprised at this. In the study of the foundations of being and of knowledge, we collide inevitably with the mystery of the Absolute. Since the finite

---

[31] St. Augustine, *Confessions,* Bk. I, c. 1.

mind of man can in no wise be disengaged from its limits, how could it ever be given to him to comprehend the Infinite?

4. The Meaning of the Proof "by Creatures"

This impels us to take up again, in a final essay, the proof for the existence of God, so as to determine its importance exactly. This proof is of a very special nature and it could not be otherwise. Creation is an activity unique in its own kind; the relation of the relative and the Absolute nowhere finds its counterpart. Hence, it is not at all surprising that the proof for the existence of God differs fundamentally from every other process of the mind.

This proof is merely a reflection of this twofold datum which always and everywhere forces itself on man's experience: there are many beings, real, subsisting unities which bear witness, all of them, to the absolute value of being. This absolute value, therefore, appears as a diffused, transcendental value, which penetrates to the very core of the reality of beings, and which vouches for their fundamental unity. We might be tempted to conclude to an absolute monism of being, but the individual autonomy of beings contradicts such monism; their subsistence would be merely a word without meaning if all things were confounded in one unique substance. Radical and absolute unity, therefore, must be located more profoundly, in a unique cause, sovereignly independent and infinite, the creative cause. This is the transcendent God who penetrates everything with His power, and whose abiding presence confers on all things participation in His own stability, in His value of being.

For us, creatures are the only way that leads to God. We have no intuition of the divine nature; we can only get to Him by exercising on creatures the powers of our discursive reason. From the real world we must mount up to the creative Cause.

This is not the same as saying that after having started with the created world, we quit it in the course of our reasoning to penetrate into the domain of the Infinite, there to lay hold of the divine Being directly. We are finite and we never cease to be such; we find ourselves inserted in the world: there the field of our experience is located, and we are powerless to disengage ourselves from it. The way which must lead us to God passes through creatures, "per creaturas"; it is located entirely in created territory, "in creaturis." We find God in things, in other words, we succeed in knowing Him by knowing these things here; but we shall never, through our own efforts, succeed in penetrating into God, there to lay hold of Him by an act of knowledge which would have nothing more to do with things. To know God is still to know things, but in a peculiar fashion, that is, in their foundation.

This knowledge takes place as follows: I verify the existence of reality which is solidly, absolutely grounded; I understand that this reality is not identified with its foundation, that it is not the absolute. Hence, I recognize its fundamental relativity, its radical dependence in regard to a foundation from which it is really distinct. Thus, therefore, is God known "in His creatures"; we recognize Him in the orientation of beings towards their Creator. We get to God only in as far as He is Creator; we know Him only in terms of creatures. This is why every idea which we form of God necessarily implies a relation to the knowledge which we have of creatures; our idea of God takes its place in our order of knowledge, and is bound up with the other elements of this order by means of logical relations.[32] For we cannot know God otherwise than relatively, according to our human way, that is, in the limited perspective of our experience of the things of this world. Our knowledge of God, therefore, can never be detached from the knowledge which we have of creatures; it is a conclusion, inseparable from its premises. It is always our knowledge of the Creator.

Through this knowledge, altogether incomplete and relative as it is, we arrive, nevertheless, at truth, because we have consciousness of the imperfection of its human manner. We understand that if finite being participates in the value of being, the Creator is its source and not merely a participation. In other words, we see that this creative source of the order of beings is not itself to be reckoned among the different elements of this order. We understand, therefore, that the Creator is not limited by the creature, that He is not juxtaposed to him, that He is not bound to him by an extrinsic relation. On the contrary, we affirm His liberty without limits, His total independence, His non-relative or absolute perfection. In this sense, while inevitably positing a logical relation between our idea of God and the knowledge which we have of finite beings, we deny every real relation which would bind God to the creature.

I am a being, I am not God; I have consciousness of myself and not of the divine Being. Must I then call God a non-ego? Certainly

---

[32] St. Thomas, *Summa theol.*, Ia, q.45, a.3, ad 1.

not in the sense that external finite beings are a non-ego. These latter are found outside of myself; they do not include my intimate life, my personal decisions. God, however, the creative cause, the total cause, touches me directly in all my being and in all my action. He dominates me more than I can dominate myself; I never succeed in getting to a consciousness of all the reality of my being, and I never exert a complete mastery over all that I am. On the contrary, as God is the unshakable foundation and the full and complete reason of my existence and of my activity, in a word, of everything in me which has the value of being; nothing of all that belongs to me escapes Him, nothing is foreign to Him. Is He, then, my own ego? He is not my ego as I am, but He is such in an infinite creative manner. He is a superior Ego, a transcendent Ego.

In this same sense we must call God the transcendent non-ego, since he is the Creator of everything which is other than the ego. He is not one object of knowledge among others; strictly speaking, I cannot have an impressed species of Him. Still, all that my objective knowledge gets to, rests on the divine foundation; God is in this sense the transcendent Object.

This transcendent Object is identified with the transcendent Ego; He is the transcendent Being, the absolute foundation of every subject and of every object. Precisely in this perspective do I know God, as Creator, namely, of my ego and the non-ego, as the source of all intelligibility and of all value, every time there appears to me the fundamental relativity of the being which I am, and of all that is the object of my knowledge. In the natural order we know things in themselves, and in them we get to the Absolute Being who creates them, and makes them participate in His perfection. "Cognoscimus res in seipsis et Deum in eis": We know things in themselves and God in them.[33]

II. THE NATURE OF THE CREATIVE CAUSE

1. The Method of Transcendence

To make our knowledge of the nature of God precise, there is no other process than the one we made use of in our proof for His

---

[33] In the Christian supernatural order this perspective is reversed: God is revealed to us as He is in Himself, in his "Deity," and we are called to possess Him, to know and to love him in Heaven as He apprehends Himself. Then we shall know God in Himself, and things in Him.

existence, namely, the metaphysical examination of the finite. There would be question then of developing our knowledge of the Infinite, grounding ourselves the while on this metaphysical consideration of beings. God is the adequate cause of particular beings; consequently, He contains all their perfections virtually. In reciting these latter in detail and in referring them to God as their total cause, it becomes possible for us to form a more refined idea of the perfection of God.

Here again we must proceed with circumspection, making the necessary distinctions. There are terms which designate created perfections while signifying formally their limited mode, for example, man, animal, passion, sight, motion. The Scholastics were wont to call these mixed perfections. They are found in God virtually, as in their cause, and eminently, that is, in an infinite manner; but not formally, since the finite mode is formally implied in the meaning of the terms which express these perfections, and since, too, this finite mode cannot be affirmed of the Infinite. Suppose that we wish to use such terms to designate the divine Being, we shall be able to do so only by giving them a metaphorical meaning. Strictly speaking, God is not a man; and it is a figure of rhetoric to speak of the "eye" of God which sees everything, of His piercing "gaze," of His powerful "arm," of His paternal "heart."

On the contrary, the terms which serve to designate perfections which do not necessarily imply a mode of limited being can be applied to God formally. Then there is question of what the Scholastics call simple perfections. Since the proper meaning of these words is not defined by the limited mode of particular things which are responsible for our knowledge of these perfections, this meaning can be isolated from this finite mode, and it can be referred to the Infinite without undergoing any intrinsic change. As soon as we prove the existence of God, there must be simple perfections; otherwise we could not affirm anything of God in the proper sense, and strictly speaking, we should be ignorant of everything concerning Him, even including His existence. The proof for the existence of God rests on the transcendental ideas—being, the one, the true, the good; and these ideas signify simple perfections. Furthermore, by definition a transcendental idea applies to everything without exception, to the Infinite as well as to the finite. Are there other simple perfections? This question must now be examined.

The proof for the existence of God proceeds from the finite to its infinite Cause. As the origin of all our acts of knowledge is bound up with an experience of finite reality, every time we wish to affirm any perfection of God, we must antecedently effect a passage from the finite to its absolute Cause, and elevate ourselves to the plane of the Infinite. In other words, it is indispensable for us to purify the ideas borrowed from particular beings, with a view to making them applicable to the Infinite Being.

This operation presents a threefold aspect: every finite mode must be eliminated (the negative way); the perfection of the finite ought to be affirmed of God as of its cause (the positive way); this perfection must be asserted to be found in God in an infinite manner (the way of eminence).[1] These three aspects are inseparable: the negative way presupposes the positive, just as negation is grounded on affirmation; the positive way is bound up with the negative, for it is always in creatures that we come to know the various perfections. The combination of these two ways implies a third, for a perfection of which every limit is denied, is infinitely eminent; and this third way is not practicable without the first two. For we never arrive at a direct vision of the divine nature, and only in knowing creatures are we able to get to God, their absolute foundation.[2] This method of transcendence, therefore, conduces necessarily towards procuring for us a knowledge of God by means of analogical ideas.

---

[1] "By starting with this order which we discover in all beings . . . we elevate ourselves gradually and by stages, as far as is in our power, up to Him who transcends all being, by denying and then going beyond every attribute, as up to the universal cause of beings." Pseudo-Dionysius, the Areopagite, *De divinis nominibus,* cap. VII, paragraph 3 (869 D–872 A).

"If it is expedient to attribute to Him (the universal cause) and to affirm of Him all that is predicated of beings because He is the cause of all of them, it is all the more expedient to deny of Him all these attributes, because He transcends every being. (This must, however, be) without our believing that the negations contradict the affirmations, but rather that He remains perfectly transcendent to every privation, since He is situated above every position, either negative or positive." *Idem, Mystica Theologia,* Cap. I, paragraph 2 (1000 B).

"God is being not according to this mode, but in an absolute and undefinable way, for He contains in Himself the plenitude of being." *De divinis nominibus,* cap. V, paragraph 4 (817 C).—"Every being participates in Him, and He does not abandon any being. He precedes all, and all pre-exist in Him. To say everything, nothing exists in any way whatsoever, which does not also exist and is not conceived and is not preserved in Him who pre-exists before all." *Ibid.,* paragraph 5 (820 A).

[2] Cf. *supra,* pp. 302–303.

2. The Transcendental Ideas and the Divine Names: the Subsistent One (i.e., the Unique and the Simple: the Pure Act); or Subsistent Being (i.e., the Being of Itself Necessary); the Subsistent True; the Subsistent Good (i.e., Subsistent Action). The Meaning of Absolute Immutability

The fundamental idea to which every other idea is related is that of being. The proof for the existence of God makes us know Him as the subsistent Being, and it furnishes likewise His fundamental definition, the metaphysical definition, to which all the other affirmations concerning the absolute Cause can be reduced. The idea of being is made more precise in the ideas of its transcendental properties. The metaphysical definition of God can be expressed in a more explicit manner by means of the various transcendentals.

First of all, the idea of the transcendental one. It is convertible with that of being: that which is, is one; therefore, subsistent Being is one. He is such in a transcendent way, for He is the Absolute, completely disengaged from all relativity. He cannot enter as an element into any order, into any multiplicity; He is not related to any distinct or opposed term. He is the unique, subsistent Being, the one and only God. His unity is a unity of unicity.

The study of particular being has shown that all that belongs to an order (and thereby it is stamped with relativity and finitude) includes an internal structure, correlations of the principles of potency and act. Unicity, which implies the absence of relativity and finitude, brings in its train, therefore, the negation of such structure. Consequently, the divine unity is a unity of simplicity.

This metaphysical simplicity transcends every structure of potency and act: God is Pure Act. There is an infinite difference between Pure Act and the principle of act which is opposed to the potential principle; the real principle of act is a transcendental relation, it is defined adequately by its relation with the potential principle. It is not a being but merely a constitutive element of a being, and it is conceived only in and by this being which contains it. On the contrary, Pure Act excludes such relativity; it is identified adequately with subsistent Being.

Consequently, we must deny in God all composition of existence and essence. Finite being "has" the perfection of being inasmuch as it has part in being, inasmuch as it participates in being; it is in the act of existing, according to the measure of its essence. On the contrary, subsistent Being "is" the perfection of existence: "God is His own existence." His act of existence is not a principle of a structure which is defined by its relation with a corresponding essence; this act constitutes completely the divine reality. Strictly speaking, God does not "have" an essence, since essence is a metaphysical principle of relativity and finitude, and God is the Absolute. We may attribute a wider sense to the word "essence," and understand by it everything that permits us to recognize a reality and to distinguish it from any other thing. In this case we must say that in God essence and existence are identified: the divine Essence is Existence itself. The two questions: Does God exist? and What is He? can, therefore, give rise to merely one and the same answer: God is, and He is Pure Act. In God the affirmation of self and the affirmation of existence coincide perfectly.

Being and the true are convertible; that which is, is intelligible is ontologically true. Particular being possesses this truth by participation. Its intelligibility is included in that of the whole order of particular beings; it is therefore bound up with the truth of all these beings and it rests on the source of all truth, who is God, the subsistent True, absolute and infinite. Subsistent Being, in as far as it is intelligible, is not defined by an individual nature by reason of which it would be distinguished from the intelligibility of other beings, but uniquely by itself, in an absolute manner, without dependence on any other thing. Its subsistent being is the unique and complete reason of its truth, as it is the adequate source of the intelligibility of everything which participates in the value of being.

As God is defined by His absolute being, we could not conceive Him as not being, as purely possible, for that would be to declare Him to be dependent on a cause for His being, to consider Him as non-absolute. The subsistent Being exists necessarily by Himself; He is not contingent.[3]

Being and the good are convertible. Inasmuch as it is being all reality is bound up with value. In particular being this activity is developed in a becoming, directed towards the complete perfection of the active subject, and it implies a metaphysical structure of

---

[3] Cf. *supra*, p. 286. This is the element of truth contained in the ontological argument. Cf. *supra*, p. 294.

substance (or nature) and of an accidental order, composed of different correlations of potency and act. In the activity of God all relativity and therefore all composition must be denied; divine action transcends the correlation of substance and action. God is pure Action, pure Acting; "Deus est suum agere," just as He is pure Being. There is in Him no mode of individual being, or of essence, and a fortiori there is in Him no mode of individual acting, or of nature. Pure Being is Pure Acting; subsistent Being is subsistent Acting, Goodness, or subsistent Value. Undoubtedly, we can speak of the divine nature, as of the essence of God in the wider sense of the word, to indicate that the divine reality contains in itself the reason of its activity, as it contains the reason of that which allows us to recognize it and to distinguish it from all created reality. This real reason is nothing other than Pure Being.

In defining God as Pure Act we declare that all becoming must be excluded from Him absolutely, that God is perfect and immutable Being. We must, however, give this last term the meaning of a transcendent perfection, under penalty of otherwise not being able to apply it to the Absolute.

We differentiate certain objects which change their place from others which are at rest. Local motion takes place between two points of rest, the point of departure and that of arrival. In our experience other forms of becoming present themselves, notably those of vital evolution. Consciousness bears witness to the fact that the life of the soul follows the graphic curve of personal duration which is unceasingly being enriched, though all the while preserving, under some form of memory, the product of past activity. The points of arrival which we can here distinguish are not points of arrest; for the arrest of life is nothing other than death. They are rather at the same time points of departure towards ulterior terms. And when we admit that our vital evolution is a tendency towards a last end, we conceive this latter not as the cessation of life and of activity, but as the active and permanent possession of our personal worth, expanded into full fruition.

Thus, the immutability of God does not in any way signify immobility, cessation, absence of activity. On the contrary, it must imply the supreme perfection of acting, Pure Acting; it is the adequate and definitive possession of infinite value, of Pure Being. Pure Acting, however, is the Absolute which transcends all multiplicity, all

opposition of relative terms. Consequently, it is not found at the term
of an evolution, it is not the result of a becoming, but rather the sovereign perfection, the active and full possession of Pure Act.

3. Concepts Borrowed from the Material World, and the Divine Names: Metaphorical Names. The Immensity and Omnipresence of God, His Non-Temporality and His Omnipresent Eternity, Properly So-called

If God is subsistent Being, whose simplicity excludes all metaphysical structure in the line of being and in that of acting, a fortiori
He does not contain in the line of essence either hylomorphic structure or that of quality or quantity; He is not a material being. He
has neither body nor soul; His being has no external figure whatever,
any more than it has duration. He does not occupy any corner of
space nor does He fill up any portion of time. We cannot localize Him
by indicating at what distance He could be found from such a point
of spatial or temporal reference; He is not here, nor down there, nor
in any place: He is immense, and we cannot apply any instrument
of spatial measurement to Him. Similarly, the tenses of the verb, the
past, present, future, are not appropriate to express Him, since He
defies all becoming. He is non-temporal; we cannot apply to Him any
instrument of temporal measurement. Strictly speaking, He was not,
He is not (in this moment of time), He will not be; that is, He does
not exist at this moment after having passed through preceding moments and before traversing through those of the future.

This non-temporality is called the divine eternity.[4] It is char-

[4] In speaking of the eternity of the world, we generally have in mind the
absence of a beginning of a world which goes on in time. If we speak of the
eternity of the soul we think in general of a soul which has commenced to exist,
and whose life has been substantially bound up with the temporal existence of
man in this world, but which survives the death of the body, and which will
continue to live without end. When there is question of the eternity of God, we
must think, undoubtedly, of the divine existence which has not begun to exist
and which will never end, but we must insist above all and especially on the
absence of all becoming. For by this the divine Being is transcendent, and His
eternity is fundamentally distinguished from the two preceding. We know the
definition which Boethius gave of the eternity of God: "interminabilis vitae
tota simul et perfecta possessio," (the simultaneously complete and perfect possession of interminable life). *De consolatione philosophiae*, lib. IV, prose 6.

". . . Eternity, a life which persists in its totality, which is not this, then that,
but which is all at once; which is not one thing, then another, but which is one
indivisible perfection. . . . We shall not be able to say of it either that it was,
since there is no past for it; or that it will be, since nothing ought to happen to

acterized by the absence of all evolution, notably of the course of time, and consequently also by the absence of an initial and a final term. "God is" does not signify that He is at this moment in opposition to preceding moments and to those which will follow; it means that He is absolutely, outside of all relativity, peculiar to time and to becoming, and therefore outside of all relations of the past, the present, and the future. "God is": these words express the plenitude of an infinite perfection, subsisting eternally in an absolute instant.

By indicating at what place or at what moment such or such reality is found, we determine the distance which separates it from us in space and in time. If it is here at this moment, it is present to us. In this sense there could be no question of the presence of God, since the categories "ubi" and "quando" cannot be applied to the Absolute. The term "presence" can be used only in the strict sense when we deal with God, if it is possible to disengage it from its ties with the spatio-temporal order and with all relativity. This can be done, if we keep ourselves on the plane of transcendental being.

Presence, in the ordinary sense of the word, indicates a proximity in time and space; it implies a direct and immediate relation between two material beings. Nothing prevents us from using the same word to express an analogous relation which transcends the spatial and temporal order. Now, every particular being is in direct and actual relation of complete dependence in regard to the divine, creative Cause. We can, therefore, affirm in all truth, that God is present to this being. In this sense, God is present to all reality without exception, since He is the universal Creator; or better, He is present in all reality, for He gets to each particular being completely, down to its most intimate and most personal roots. In this respect the creative Cause, the transcendent Cause, is immanent in everything that exists.

From a metaphysical point of view, God is present in every reality always in an identical way; He lays hold of all things in the eternal and immutable instant, which is distinctive of Him. Particular beings

---

it in the future. It remains for it only to be that which it is. 'The being of which we cannot say: it has been or it will be, but only: it is' (as Plato has it in his *Timaeus*, 37e–38a), this is the permanent being which admits no modifications in the future, and which has not changed in the past: behold, this is eternity." Plotinus, *Enneads* II, book 7, chapt. 3, 16–36 (Cf. transl. by Émile Bréhier, Paris, 1925, pp. 129–130).

form an order, and their relations change in various manners; notably in time and in space they are not at equal distances from one another. Thus, from my point of view, certain events are past, others are present; and I distinguish things which are near to me and others which are more remote. These differences exist between the realities which form a part of the order we are considering, and they are measured starting from such or such determined reality. God, however, is not an element of the order of things; He is their source; His being and His action are beyond all relative opposition and all becoming. Consequently, while His creative activity really produces a complexus of realities which succeed each other in time, and which extend through space in a determined order, it is just as certain that this divine activity does not unfold itself in time and in space, that it does not include any succession of terms. God does not act in one place after having acted in another; He does not create one being after having created another: His creative act is absolute and the distinction between the past, the present, and the future does not apply to this act. Therefore, in the eternal instant of His subsistent being the Creator gets at everything that exists, and this all at once; the generations which succeed each other and the many regions which stretch out in the distance: to all these realities He reaches out without any intermediary, in the most immediate and profound fashion. In every being God is present with a radically intimate presence which is absolute.[5] Of this divine presence we can form some idea by referring to the presence of one human person to another; but for this there must be established first of all the role which the spiritual ideas of reality and activity can play in the development of our knowledge of God.

4. Concepts Borrowed from the Human Mind, and the Divine Names: the Subsistent Spirit, Intellect and Will, Idea and Love

We form not merely negative concepts of the immaterial, but we also possess a positive knowledge of it in the measure in which we become conscious of the intellectual and voluntary aspects of our

---

[5] The Scholastics distinguish three kinds of presence: circumscriptive presence, proper to material things juxtaposed in spatial extension; definitive presence, limited to a definite or limited portion of space, which is peculiar to finite spiritual activity in relation to matter; and repletive presence, distinctive of the divine Being who fills all things with His creative, omnipresent activity.

cognitive and appetitive life. Hence, we are fully justified in making use of a positive word to designate immaterial reality; we call it spirit, and by this we designate a perfection of life which is characterized by the intimacy of personal life, by the consciousness of its own distinctive activity, knowledge of and dominion over self, deliberate and free development of the course of one's actions.[6]

This spiritual life unfolds itself formally in the sphere of the transcendental: all intellectual progress is related to being, and the will tends to the good, laid hold of precisely in its value. The bond which rivets spiritual activity to the transcendental, is bound up with the very nature of this activity; this bond constitutes it in its perfection of spiritual activity, since the transcendental is its formal object. On the other hand, the apprehension of the transcendental implies, of itself, the apprehension of the absolute; and consequently, spiritual activity is adequately defined by this natural orientation towards the absolute on the foundation of our apprehension of the transcendental. Consequently, too, just as the transcendental ideas can be applied formally to God, the idea of spirit and that of spiritual activity, intellect and will (whose content is defined by a formal relation to the transcendental), will likewise and in the proper sense be applied to the Pure Act.

And yet the resemblance between the spiritual reality of man and that of God can only be proportional, analogical, for the distance which separates them is infinite. We must take this into account if we wish to avoid misunderstandings. Human thought is based formally on the idea of being, a transcendental idea, but yet obscure and confused; it is developed by making more precise the order of beings, with a view to discovering the adequate cause of all reality, the creative Act. Our will is moved under the light of the transcendental idea of the good, and it tends to guarantee the personal perfection of the subject by its union with the infinite goodness of the divine Being, the source of all value.

Man's activity never ceases to be human and therefore finite, although it is directed towards the divine Absolute; it is capable of getting to God only in a limited measure. By his own natural means man will possess God only by making use of the participated perfection of creatures. On the contrary, God Himself possesses Himself directly in an infinite manner: the simplicity of His act consists in a

---

[6] Cf. Gerard Verbeke, "De wezensbepaling van het spiritueele," *Tijdschrift voor Philosophie,* Vol. VIII, 1946, pp. 435–464.

direct and exhaustive knowledge and in an infinitely beatifying love of His absolute perfection.

Our knowledge is at bottom experiential: we collide with facts both within and outside of ourselves, for they constitute a limit of our knowledge, and they give rise to problems. We must patiently and painfully seek the explanation of data. On the contrary, divine knowledge is infinitely perfect and it is not grounded on any experience; it is neither a consciousness which reveals the existence of the ego, nor can it be an objective knowledge which gets to the fact of the existence of the non-ego. It transcends the one and the other of these modes of knowledge which limit and complete each other mutually. God does not discover reality as a fact to be explained; He possesses it clearly in its absolute foundation; for He possesses Himself completely and in knowing Himself, He encompasses all things in the creative Act which makes them to be and to act.

Our knowledge depends on things since it must verify these latter; it is an imitative knowledge. The knowledge of God, however, is independent of things, since it creates them; it is an exemplary knowledge; hence, we say that every thing corresponds to its idea in God, in as far as it participates in the divine perfection. And yet multiplicity exists only on the side of things; the exemplary idea in God is unique, it is Pure Act itself, in as far as it is imitable in an infinity of modes of participation.

What does God know? He knows Himself perfectly, hence He grasps all things in the measure in which He is their principle, that is, absolutely: "Cognoscit seipsum et omnia in seipso." It would be superfluous to make a detailed list of what God knows; this would come to an enumeration of all things of the past, of the present, and of the future; of things realized and those which remain purely possible, all those things, too, whose development unfolds itself by virtue of a natural determinism, and the other things which are freely decided upon; and every one of these things God knows, considered in itself and in its relations with all the others. Whatever has value of being is known by God: what does not participate in this value, cannot be known, since it is necessarily devoid of intelligibility and of value.

Does God know the futurables? Does He know the free decisions which have not been made, but which could have been, and is He cognizant of the consequences which they could have had? Before all else, we must fix the exact meaning which is attributed to the terms of this problem, and especially to the word "futurable." If the meaning which is given to it, is not nonsensical but expresses a value of being, God must know the futurables; for every participation in being is founded on the divine Being. If the meaning of the word is nonsense, there will be question of contradictions, and there will no longer be any problem.[7]

In treating of God's knowledge we must be on our guard against ascribing the least extrinsic relativity to Him, in particular that of time and space; for this will infallibly involve us in pseudo-problems and in inextricable difficulties. As we have remarked above,[8] divine life unfolds itself neither in time nor place; hence, God does not recall the past, nor yet can He forget it. He does not approach anything nor does He withdraw from it; He does not verify that which is, nor does He foresee the future; He does not deduce the consequences of the natural laws, and He does not wait for free acts to be placed in order to have objective knowledge of them. All these modes of knowing which complement one another mutually, constitute in their complexity the structure of human knowledge which develops in time. God's knowledge, however, transcends all these finite modes and their relative opposition because it transcends all limitation and all relativity, especially those that spring from time and space. In wishing to maintain these modes in God, while affirming the infinite divine properties, such as omniscience and universal providence, we would be led to pose questions which could not be answered, since they are absurd in their very terms. For example, if we suppose that there is a future for God and that therefore He can only know this future by foreseeing it, starting from the present moment, it will be useless to ask how He could know with certitude a free future act.

In reality, for persons whose life and relations are measured by time, the future succeeds the present and it does not exist at the present moment. The free future act is not a datum at this present moment, neither in itself, since it is yet to come, nor in its natural causes, since this act is supposed to be free and therefore not determined by instinctive nature, and hence it cannot be known by way of deduction. To ask how it would be possible for God, under these conditions, to foresee a free future act, is to ask how at this very

---

[7] This question will be taken up later on, pp. 323–325.
[8] Cf. *supra*, pp. 311–312.

moment God could foresee that which by definition is unforeseeable. This would be to pose a pseudo-problem, whose terms are contradictory. In point of fact, divine knowledge is not subject to the course of time; it includes neither the past nor the present nor the future. God does not know at this moment now, since, being eternal, He is not contained in this moment of time. He cannot therefore at this moment now wonder about what the future will be, nor can He foresee in any way free acts or natural phenomena. It is, consequently, altogether senseless thus to ask how God could succeed in knowing such or such decision of man which is yet to be made.

The divine mode of knowledge is infinitely different from the mode of man; by means of an eternal presence, unique and simple, God directly gets at everything which the past, present, and future time contain, just as He gets at all reality which time does not contain. In creating all beings He apprehends them, that is, in completely producing their existence and their activity, in their principles and their effects, in creating them, moreover, by a unique Act which is the absolute instant of the divine Being.[9]

In exactly the same way the willing of God is directed towards all beings, while being directed perfectly towards the divine Being. Creative willing cannot collide with anything since it produces everything; it is not subject to time since it creates time. God does not wait for the realization of His decrees, He does not hesitate, He does not hope for, nor does He fear anything. He has no motions of impatience, no more than He has regrets; inasmuch as these things have relation to the order of time, these expressions can be predicated of God at most in a figurative sense.

In order to be able to use these expressions in their proper meaning, it will first of all be necessary to disengage the spiritual element contained in human activity which they designate, and it is necessary to make them signify this element exclusively. In this way, moreover, we speak of the sovereign will of God, of His love of benevolence, of His prudence, His justice, His mercy, His power and His generosity. In this way, too, we merely bring out in detail the spiritual riches which are concealed in the will and the ineffable love of God, the Creator, who makes all things participate in His perfection.

---

[9] We shall come back later on to certain difficulties concerning the activity and, in particular, the liberty of the Creator.

In treating of presence in time and space [10] we reduced it to proximity, which implies a close relation between two realities. Really, in the language of today the word "presence" is used especially in relation with a being endowed with conscious life. One thing can be near another but we will not say that it is present to it; for example, a table is not present to a chair; on the contrary it could be present to a person. This presence is, therefore, bound up with spiritual activity, the product of the intellect and the will; and as all these terms can be predicated formally of the Pure Act, human presence can help to illustrate the omnipresence of God.

As human activity, considered in as far as it is spiritual has for its formal object the transcendental, which implies the absolute, it is cast on a level which permits it to transcend all relative opposition (among others that of the subject and object), to know them just as they are, and to apprehend their value. In assimilating realities to himself by means of knowledge, man does not suppress their "otherness" for he opposes them to himself in an immanent activity, he renders them present to himself, and he takes in their regard a personal, free, and independent attitude. Presence, properly so-called implies this union of two distinct realities in the immanence of a personal activity; but in human activity this union of presence is always imperfect, because man is a particular, material being, and as such he can never disengage himself entirely from relativity, notably from that of matter, even when he transcends it. This is true because his formal object is not the absolute, subsistent Being, but the transcendental idea of being and of the good, which formally implies everything, the relative and the absolute; and this, moreover, is an idea, conditioned by our senses, and therefore by the conditions of space and time. What is more, material things are quite rebellious to being penetrated by the human mind, which succeeds in defining them only in an abstract way; they remain external to man. Man succeeds in penetrating the more into the personal life of his fellow-men, in as far precisely as this life contains a spiritual element. Men can communicate among themselves and understand one another, because they can put themselves at the same point of view, and this because their spiritual activity has the same formal object. Their concepts, therefore, will be able to meet and to be grounded in one and the same truth; their hearts will be able to throb in unison. In a word, their most personal activities will be able to compenetrate one another

[10] Cf. *supra*, p. 311.

and be united intimately; their lives will be grounded in a mutual sympathy.[11] "Idem velle, idem nolle, ea demum firma amicitia est."[12] There is question here of a genuine presence, of an intimate, profound, personal presence.

Nevertheless, this presence remains imperfect; it collides with limits which it cannot scale. This first of all, because it remains bound up with the activity of the senses, and communication cannot be

[11] The personalism of Max Scheler (1874–1928) places forcible emphasis on the role of activity in the union of persons. According to him, person consists essentially in love, the source of all spiritual activity, and especially of all objective apprehension of values. Person is defined as "ein aktvollziehendes Wesen" (an act-completing being). *Der Formalismus in der Ethik und die materiale Wertethik*, 2nd ed., Halle a.d. S., 1927, pp. 399, 385.

"Person is the concrete, the very essential unity of being of the acts of diverse beings, which in themselves (and therefore not relatively to us) go beyond all essential differences of act. The being of a person 'founds' (grounds) all essentially diverse acts." *Ibid.*, pp. 397–398.

Only in executing them do we know the acts of the person, i.e., spiritual and objective acts, which we must distinguish from the psychical functions which are essentially bound up with the body, as sight and hearing. We know them only as acts, never as objects. "An act is never an object." (*Ibid.*, p. 402). From this it follows that we can know an act of another person only by taking part in it, by executing it with him, "by performing it with him, before him or after him"; spiritual presence is tied up with a union of life of the spiritual order. Scheler applies these ideas to the relations of man to God: we can know God as a person only by participating in the personal activity of God, in executing His acts with Him. Cf. *Vom Ewigen im Menschen*, 3rd ed., Berlin, 1933, p. 350.

Scheler exaggerates the separation between the spiritual element and the organic element in man; but it remains true that human action, in as far as it is spiritual, transcends time and space, and that the acts by which man enters into communication with his neighbor present this same spiritual character (a thing which makes an "intimate" union possible). Furthermore, finite spiritual activity has a formal resemblance with the divine activity, so much so that the human presence, considered under its spiritual aspect, affords an analogy, properly so called, with the creative presence of God.

It is not devoid of interest to compare with certain personalist conceptions of Max Scheler these ideas of Louis Lavelle: "The act, not being a thing, we cannot form any representation of it, even an inadequate one. It has reality only for him who exercises it, and in exercising it possesses it immediately, as he possesses mediately the being which the act gives him. The knowledge of the act is not distinct from its accomplishment. The world ceases henceforth to be for us a spectacle and it becomes an operation in which we collaborate. We will, therefore, make an appeal to internal experience in order to judge if this operation is real or illusory. But we can only judge it by endeavoring to do it. Thus every metaphysical inquiry ceases to be a rational interpretation of reality, in order to become a participation, acquiescing in the work of creation." Louis Lavelle, "De l'insertion du moi dans l'être par la distinction de l'opération et de la donnée," *Tijdschrift voor Philosophie*, III, 1941, pp. 715–716.

[12] "To will the same thing, not to will the same thing: that, in the last analysis, is strong friendship." Sallust, *De Conjuratione Catilinae*, XX.

effected without the assistance of symbols. The intimate life of others is accessible to us only because language and bodily behavior act as interpreters. We cannot penetrate directly into the heart of another, and the intervention of the sensible expression sets up a barrier and keeps us at a distance. Man cannot surrender himself completely; fundamentally, he remains a solitary. Besides, one particular being cannot perfectly grasp the individuality of another, precisely because he carries within himself an incommunicable, irreducible element.

Now these barriers do not exist for the creative Cause, who by His intelligence and will lays hold of the creature completely, since He produces it, wholly and entirely. The being and acting of creatures are always an actual participation in the being and acting of God. Consequently, the divine presence is one of perfect intimacy; it penetrates and envelops particular being with its benevolence and its love in the closest and most fruitful union that could be conceived.

III. THE METAPHYSICAL DUALISM OF THE CREATURE AND THE CREATOR

1. Finite Beings and the Infinite Being

The doctrine of absolute and creative causality has given rise to a goodly number of controversies, notably in what concerns free activity. Evidently, there is a real difficulty in reconciling the liberty of man with the absolute sovereignty of a God who is Creator. If we reflect on it this question supposes another of a more general order, namely, how can we admit any efficient causality whatsoever on the part of creatures if the divine Cause must be conceived as an absolute cause, productive of everything that exists? To solve this question, however, we must enlarge the discussion, for activity belongs to being: "Agere sequitur esse." If God is infinite Being, is He not *all* being? How then can we admit that any thing can exist without being God?

Particular beings, finite beings, exist: this is a fact attested by the experience of everybody. They are explained only by the infinite Being who creates them; this conclusion is forced on whoever observes that particular beings are real only on account of their participation in the value of being. But how does it happen that this dualism of the finite and the Infinite is not contradictory?

320 PHILOSOPHY OF BEING

To be sure, it would be nonsense to wish to complete infinite perfection by means of a finite value. For this reason metaphysical monism is an unacceptable theory, because monism considers all finite reality, which is nevertheless active and always being enriched, as an integral and constitutive part of the unique Being which can exist by itself. On the contrary, if we can show on the one hand that the finite is really distinct from the Infinite, and on the other that we cannot add the one to the other, the contradiction disappears, because then there is question no longer of increasing infinite perfection by adding some other thing to it.

Now precisely this permits us to formulate the doctrine of participation. Finite beings are particular beings, each one having its own individuality. This last is incommunicable: not only is the individuality of the one distinct from that of the other, but it is opposed to it, in this sense that the perfection of the one does not in any way include the perfection of the other; [13] the one is external to the other. Consequently, in order to obtain the complete perfection of particular beings we must take them all together, add them, the one to the other, and make a sum of them.

All these beings, however, considered each in its own complete reality, are nothing other than a participation in the perfection of the infinite Being who creates them. This is the same as saying that they possess absolutely nothing which is not the effect of the activity of this absolute Cause. Their incommunicable individuality, therefore, does not contain anything which is not contained virtually in this infinite Cause. In relation to this total Cause they do not present any new perfection. Consequently, in no sense are we allowed to say that, if we "add" their perfection to that of their infinite Cause, we shall obtain a "sum" of perfection which is greater than that of the divine perfection; for such "addition" would be an absurd operation.

Thanks to participation there are numerous beings, but the total perfection of the value of being is not increased, because this perfection is completely realized in the unique source of beings, in the infinite Being, and this, altogether necessarily.[14] "Dantur plura entia;

---

[13] For this reason, strictly speaking, it is not in the power of a particular being to produce another subsistent being; God alone can do this. We shall say, therefore, that man, who is a subsistent being by reason of his spiritual soul, is in so far created by God. The activity of a finite being is restricted to transforming what already exists.

[14] "For just as a co-numbered part is not something greater than the whole,

non datur plus entis": there exist more beings, but not more *being*. And yet, there is no real identity between finite perfections and infinite perfection; it is not the sum of the first which goes to make up the latter: finite beings are neither modes nor parts of the infinite Being, but rather participations. They have a "part in" the perfection of the Infinite, and this is why they must be distinguished from it. The perfection of finite beings, which are contained virtually in the creative Cause, is realized there "eminently," in an infinitely trans-cendent way, whereas created beings possess their perfection only in the limited mode of their nature.[15]

Consequently, there is no contradiction in the doctrine of the dualism of the Infinite and the finite, at least if we conceive par-ticular beings as participations in the order of being, that is, from the moment that we consider them as creatures, as effects of a total and absolute Cause.

2. Finite Causality and the Creative Act

The problem of the reconciliation of finite activity and creative causality is solved in the same manner. Creation, total causality, in no wise suppresses the activity of particular beings, as occasionalism maintains; on the contrary, it brings this activity into being by mak-ing these particular beings participate in the infinitely active perfec-tion of the Creator.

We cannot confuse the relation which unites one finite cause to another equally finite, with the relation which must exist between

---

because the part itself is included in the whole, so also any good whatsoever, co-numbered with God, does not form any increase of goodness, since it is good only by this that it participates in the divine goodness." St. Thomas, *In I Ethic.*, lect. 9.

[15] A comparison will help to illustrate this idea. The pupils assimilate the theorems which the professor teaches them: the science, such as the professor already possessed is not thus increased, but it is now participated in by a greater number: there are more knowers. "Non datur plus scientiae, sed dantur plures scientes." On the contrary, if any one discovers a new theorem he advances that science.

And yet the comparison is rather lame. For every man is a person distinct from all others, and he has a personal and incommunicable mode of thinking, so much so that every communication of science produces every time a truly new personal value which did not exist antecedently. On the contrary, the creative Cause is a total and adequate cause, and there is nothing in the creature, not even his individuality, which does not come from the Creator, and which is not found already in Him virtually and eminently.

a finite cause and the infinite Cause. Finite beings are distinct and opposed to each other, and it is the same with their operations. Every one of these operations bears the incommunicable trade-mark of the particular being, of the *suppositum* which places the action; and this is why the effect produced depends on them, to the extent of not being able to spring from any other particular cause. The activities of the various finite beings are, therefore, coordinated; they are added, the one to the other, and their effects are added together to produce the total result.[16] Now God, who is not a particular being but rather the source of being and the absolute principle of all participation, cannot be lined up in the series of particular agents. He transcends them; He is not bound by their activity, since He is the creative cause of it. We should precipitate ourselves inextricably into difficulties, were we to commit the fault of "profaning" divine causality by dragging it down to the level of creatures. It is absurd to reduce the Absolute to the relative, the source of the real order to one of the elements of this order, transcendent Perfection to some term which participates in this Perfection.

Thus, every finite cause must be considered in two ways: on the one hand, in the relations which bind it particularly to the other "second" causes, and on the other hand, in the relation of complete subordination which rivets it (at the same time that it binds all the other causes) to the creative or the "first" Cause.[17] If it is true that the activity of every particular cause is "added" to that of the others in order to make up the whole order of secondary causality, it is likewise true that this activity, strictly speaking, is not to be added to creative Activity. This activity could in no wise increase the absolute perfection of the Creator by adding to it anything which would be derived exclusively from itself, since it does not possess any activity which is not a participation in the divine, creative perfection,[18] and which is not already precontained eminently in this absolute Cause.

---

[16] We have already shown that this coordination is maintained even in the case of a hierarchy of particular causes. There is never a pure and total subordination of one finite cause to another finite cause. Cf. *supra*, pp. 276–278.

[17] We have insisted on this distinction in developing the proof for the existence of God and in showing that it is useless to make an appeal to a finite or infinite series of "second causes," in order to furnish a metaphysical explanation of particular being. Cf. *supra*, pp. 287–289.

[18] "No cause gives *esse* (to another) except in as far as it participates in the operation of God." St. Thomas, *Quodlibetum XII*, q.5, a.5.

3. *The Liberty of Creatures and Divine Sovereignty*

The problem of human liberty and the divine sovereignty must be solved in an analogous way. Every finite person has dominion over his free activity, and it is impossible that the reason of his autonomous decisions should be found in any other particular person; his independence in this regard is complete. Finite persons can combine their efforts, they can cooperate towards one and the same end; their operations are coordinated, but the free operation of the one cannot be the result of the decision of any other person. On this point all subordination is excluded.

We should, however, sin by anthropomorphism if we were to juxtapose the free operation of man and God's sovereignly independent activity, so as to make them "concur" towards one and the same end. It would be a mistake to distinguish in a real effect the part which would come from God without being able to come from man, and the part which would come from man without being able to come from God. For there is no reality whatever, which in its entirety and in each of its parts, is not the effect of divine creation, since there is nothing which does not participate in being. The free activity of man is, therefore, not an activity ontologically independent of God, destined to complete the divine work; the divine Cause is never a partial cause, since it is the absolute Cause. All the free causality of a particular being is completely subordinated to God, in the same way that everything that is real is subordinated to Him.

This subordination, therefore, cannot be conceived according to the model of that of instrumental causality. A principal cause directs the instrument by impressing on it a premotion, an instrumental power which is added to the efficacy peculiar to the instrument. Hence, the principal cause and the secondary cause are, both of them, partial causes whose forces are coordinated in an order of subordination; each one does what the other does not do, but the one dominates the other and directs it.[19] God alone is the absolute Cause who does not admit of any coordination with particular causes, but dominates them all completely; with respect to the creative Cause there is only pure subordination. Now this unique relation of complete dependence, far from suppressing the being and the activity

[19] Cf. *supra*, pp. 277–279.

of particular causes, really posits them, since it is nothing other than the relation of participation in creative Being. Similarly, this relation of complete dependence of created persons not only does not suppress their liberty in any way, but it also really establishes it, since it is nothing other than real participation in the sovereign independence of the Creator.

Since the 16th century the scholastic controversies between the Bannezians and Molinists on the Providence of God and the free will of man have been developed, so to speak, without interruption and not without assuming at times very vivid expressions. In his *Commentary on the first part of the Summa Theologica of St. Thomas* (1584) Dominic Bannez, O.P., strives to prove that the free act of man can only be produced under the influence of a "physical premotion" on the part of God, that is, under the influence of a divine action, directly exerted on the human will with a view to moving this will towards a determined act. Undoubtedly, this premotion to a determined act amounts to a predetermination of this act by the divine action; and yet according to Bannez man's freedom would not be suppressed by it, because the omnipotence of God furnishes, at the same time, the mode of origin of this act, namely, the free mode.

The Bannezian doctrine allows us to understand how God possesses knowledge of the free acts of the creature: this knowledge is grounded on the predetermining decree of God which produces every one of these acts. On the other hand, and in spite of all the explanations offered by the Bannezians, the adversaries of this doctrine have never ceased to maintain that it ends logically in the denial of human freedom.

In 1588 Louis Molina, S.J., published a part of a commentary on the *Prima pars* of the *Summa Theologica* of St. Thomas under the title *Concordia liberi arbitrii cum gratiae donis, divina providentia, praedestinatione et reprobatione.* In this work he rejects the theory of the physical premotion to replace it by that of the "divine concursus."

The Molinists do not agree on the nature of this "concursus." Suarez admits a "divine simultaneous concursus," which would be produced at the same time as the act of the human will; the divine action would give "being" to this act, whereas man's free will would determine its "taleity." Others, notably St. Robert Bellarmine, S.J., and Louis Billot, S.J., prefer to admit an "antecedent concursus," since of itself the divine action is antecedently required in order that the creature may be able to pass over into act. And yet this antecedent *concursus* could not be conceived as predetermining, for every predetermination implies a motion "ad unum," that is, determining to one given act, in such wise that it would exclude the free choice of this act.

To explain how God knows the free acts of man the Molinists distinguish the "science of simple intelligence," which has for its object the complexus of the possible realities which could in any way imitate the divine perfection. They also speak of the "science of vision" which has for its object all existing realities, and thirdly, of "scientia media," whose object is the futurables or the future conditionals. The opponents of Molinism stigmatize this doctrine for sacrificing the absolute sovereignty of God to human liberty.

To pass judgment on these different opinions we must keep before our eyes this certain metaphysical conclusion: God, the infinite Being, is the absolute Cause. Divine knowledge which is identified with the Pure and Absolute Act, cannot be founded on any other thing than the divine Being. What is possible but does not exist, God knows as a possible participation in the value of being, on the basis of infinite Being. What really exists, God knows as a real participation in the value of being, on the basis of creative Acting.

Creative activity is absolute and envelops everything in its action. Without doubt, since every particular being participates in the value of being, it subsists in itself and is active, and every finite person is master of his actions. This being, however, is a creature and it does not contain any other thing than created reality, that is, its subsistence and its activity are maintained only by the relation of complete dependence which binds them to the creative Act.

In no finite being is it possible to distinguish two domains, of which one would be entirely subject to the Creator, whereas the other would be less subject or not at all. What is altogether finite is altogether relative to the Absolute. It is likewise impossible to distinguish in God the power which would apprehend such a reality in a sovereign way, and the power which would apprehend such other reality only in an altogether relative manner. For if the relative is absolutely relative, since it rests on the Absolute, in no sense is it true that the absolute Being can be relatively absolute. The absolute cause can be only absolutely independent. Consequently, the Infinite and the finite do not form two adjacent domains either in time or space or knowledge or causality. Strictly speaking, the Infinite is not "along-side" of the finite. The infinity of God, to be sure, places limits on creatures who participate in His perfection without ever being able to equal it; but on the contrary, the active reality of creatures is incapable of placing the least limit on the divine perfection. The Creator and the creature, therefore, have no common frontier where they would be in some way on the same level; for the creature remains always wholly dependent on God, and he cannot therefore in any way limit the divine power. The primacy of the Absolute over the relative is unconditional; the sovereignty of the Infinite over the finite is without limits. And this radical subordination, far from jeopardizing the subsistence, the activity, and autonomy of beings, is on the contrary their one and only guarantee, since the relation of pure dependence is identically that of the effective participation in the infinite perfection and in the absolute independence of the active and creative God.

We shall never be in a position to comprehend fully the divine mode of creation, for it is not given to created nature to enjoy the direct vision of the divine Act. It is only in a human, finite, imperfect way that we succeed in laboriously catching up with the Infinite; it could not be otherwise, since the absolute perfection of God infinitely surpasses the limits of our cognitive faculties. Nor does this imperfection escape us; we are conscious of our limitations, and by that very token we can strive to avoid errors, notably those which an anthropomorphic conception of God would make us commit. This bears witness to nobility of spirit, for this attitude, at once resolute and modest, is grounded on a true knowledge of the infinite Being, and on an exact comprehension of the fundamental relations which unite man with God.

CHAPTER XII

CONCLUSION

1. The Problem: Participation on the Plane of Being; It Is Expressed by the Analogy of the Idea of Being

General metaphysics has as its object the fundamental explanation of all things, considered in the aggregate. Such a study must be grounded at the beginning on a transcendental idea, on knowledge whose content is at once universal and concrete. Its content must be universal, since human experience, perforce limited, could never extend to all that exists. Nevertheless, this content must envisage formally the concrete under penalty of otherwise neglecting the individuality and the existence of things, and of not getting to reality in the fullness of its riches.

The idea of being fulfills these conditions perfectly; it comes to our mind from the least experience, and it is transcendental in the sense we have just defined. By this idea we lay hold of the absolute value which our own existence conceals, just as we lay hold of the value of the objects present to us. At the same time it seems to us that this value of being, in virtue of its absolute character, must envelop and penetrate all things; and this is why we are justified in attributing being to every subject and in attributing it formally.

General metaphysics, therefore, cannot consist in a study of abstract essences, in an essentialism; for the abstract will never give a full account of the concrete. Under the influence of Plato's philosophy of the ideas, ancient philosophers and those of the Middle Ages too often have paid excessive homage to abstraction in this matter; [1] modern philosophy has not succeeded in rising above this current. Again, in our day a good many idealistic systems have done their utmost, but in vain, to "reconstruct" the real by starting out with abstract principles established by reason.

In certain respects present-day existentialism is an energetic reaction against this philosophy of essences or of abstract values. It

---

[1] Cf., for example, what we said about the problem of the possibles, *supra*, p. 91.

would take its departure from existing reality and remain constantly in intimate contact with the concrete, by reason of the consciousness which every man possesses of his own distinctive reality, his life, and his actions. In general, however, the reaction is patently insufficient. Undoubtedly, the existentialists offer phenomenological descriptions of lived reality which are not without interest; still, their observations seem to be related so exclusively to the conscious ego, that we are led to wonder how it is possible to draw from these observations conclusions concerning reality taken in its entirety. As a matter of fact, certain existentialists refuse to do this; they confine themselves to making a record of the typical situations of the existence which we live.[2] Others, on the contrary, labor at the construction of a metaphysics, but we do not see clearly by what means they pass from the existence of man to existence in general.[3]

While the metaphysics of essences neglects concrete existence to immure itself in universal essences, existentialism clings to the concrete at the risk of allowing the universal to slip from its grasp. Essentialism is indeed wrong in considering exclusively essences in themselves, as if they were all finished, fixed wholes; for in as far as they are real, individual, concrete essences, they are, all of them, modes of being, incomplete and open realities, relative to something outside of themselves, that is, to being. We cannot say without qualification that they are identical with being, since they are only concrete modes of being; but precisely for this same reason they can be comprehended only by being to which they are related, and from which in as far as they are concrete essences they cannot be separated, even by reason itself.

On its part existentialism with full right rivets our attention on the concrete and existing ego, while generally forgetting to emphasize the fact that even the ego itself implies a mode of being, which cannot without further qualification be identified with being itself.

---

[2] This is the case with Karl Jaspers' *Philosophy of Existence* (*Existenzphilosophie*).

[3] Martin Heidegger opposes his own existential philosophy to Jaspers' philosophy, in order to assert his pretentions to a metaphysics. A profound critical examination of Heidegger has been made by Alph. De Waelhens, *La philosophie de Martin Heidegger*, Louvain, 1942, pp. 295 ff., 307 ff. In France, R. Le Senne (cf. *supra*, pp. 148, 232), and Gabriel Marcel (cf. *supra*, p. 233) admit the absolute as the fundamental value, a fact which blazes the trail for metaphysics. On the contrary, we do not see how J. P. Sartre can legitimately found a philosophy of being in general on existential data which give us merely something purely contingent. (Cf. *supra*, p. 58.)

Just as the metaphysics of essences erroneously shuts itself up in abstract modes, existentialism is inclined to immure itself in the concrete mode of the ego. Thus it neglects, in its turn, to take account of the essential relativity of this mode of particular being. Driven into this impasse, it finds itself unable to lay down the foundations of a philosophy of existence, as such, which would be applicable to the non-ego as well as to the ego.

Consequently, there is a distinction which real data force upon us right from the start, and which it is imperative for us not to forget: it is that of the value of being and of the modes of being. This value is unique and absolute, whereas the modes are multiple and relative, one to the other. This is a distinction not a separation; the modes lose all meaning outside of the value, and the value manifests itself only in the modes. Now, experience bears witness to the fact that the modes of being are profoundly opposed, to the point of being incommunicable. There exist many beings, subsistent in their being, autonomous and mutually independent in their action. Being, an absolute and unique value, comprises an order of beings.

These beings can have no consistency outside of the value of absolute being; there they are all bound up together. Consequently, their whole reality is stamped through and through with relativity, and they are welded together to form the unique order of beings. Hegel insisted on this fundamental point; he believed that he had to conclude from this that these beings are fixed in the ensemble as parts of a whole.[4] This is a mistake, for if it is true that beings are connected fundamentally with the order which contains them completely, it is just as true that every one of them is subsistent. The autonomy of our activity forces itself upon us, just as the value of absolute being; we cannot reject either one or the other. We do not solve a problem by getting rid of half of the data. Hence, we shall say that beings are wholes and not parts, since they are subsistent; but nevertheless they participate, all of them, in the value of being, since this value is absolute and therefore unique. Every being exists and it truly exists, but it realizes the value of being in a particular fashion, distinct from very many others; it exists according to a mode that is peculiar to it, in the measure of its essence or individual nature. The whole complexus of things is not made up of an arrangement of parts; it is an ensemble, embracing autonomous participations. The ontological order is an order of participation.

---
[4] Cf. *supra*, p. 76.

If the idea of being signifies absolute value [5] it is analogous. On the one hand, this value of being is participable in any number of ways, since there are numerous subsistent beings; on the other hand, being absolute, it cannot be opposed to any external term, and therefore cannot be distinguished from it in any way. Consequently, it must include all, which means that the value of being contains in itself its own proper modes.

It is therefore impossible to abstract being from its modes so as to form a univocal notion of it, as the Scotistic school [6] wished to do; for logically, that would come to relegating the modes of being to the realm of non-being. Besides, it is altogether vain to wish to reduce the value of being to its different particular modes, and to take the word "being" as an equivocal term; for such a thesis would run afoul of the fundamental unity of the value of being. What is more, it is not enough to appeal to an analogy of attribution, the way Aristotle does,[7] in order to explain the grouping of the modes of beings in one and the same synthesis. For by itself alone this analogy can be related only to an order which affects subsistent beings without penetrating down to their fundamental reality. In the last analysis we must always remember that the order of being extends to all things, and that it penetrates them through and through, even in their most autonomous activity and in their most intimate nature. Then, too, because the perfection of being, by reason of its absolute value, can in no wise be abstracted from things, since it extends necessarily to all of them, we must needs admit that the idea of being, which formally signifies this perfection, embraces all things in its content. Consequently, it must be attributed to particular beings in a proportional manner, that is, in proportion to their mode of individual being, or again after allowance is made for their degree of participation in being. The analogy of the idea of being is an analogy of proportionality, because the order of being is grounded altogether on the participation of subsistent beings in the value of absolute being.

All intellectual activity rests on the understanding of being, an

---

[5] We said above (pp. 25 f., 88 f.) that the word "being" is not always used in the same sense. Here we give it a metaphysical signification. The history of philosophy shows that this meaning has been disengaged only progressively, thanks in particular to Neo-Platonism and to St. Thomas Aquinas. It shows, too, that there is a goodly number of philosophers, ancient and modern, who have not noticed its exceptional importance. Cf. *supra*, pp. 50–51; 115–140.

[6] Cf. *supra*, pp. 47–49.

[7] Cf. *supra*, pp. 52–53.

absolute value; this is the formal object of the intellect. Always and only in the light of being do concepts and judgments have any meaning. This foundation is unshakable; whoever understands absolute value, cannot, by that very token, conceive a doubt or be deceived. Starting with this we are justified in extending our investigations to everything which falls under the jurisdiction of being, that is, to everything without exception. Undoubtedly, the human intellect, limited and infirm as it is, is not in a position to raise and to solve all questions. We feel ourselves quite incapable of offering the definition of the majority of particular beings, just as we are unable to establish the exact nature of their activity and their relations. Nevertheless, we are impelled to put certain questions which concern the whole, for we lay hold of beings precisely by their value of absolute being, by the principle of unity in which everything whatsoever is included. Hence, we get to these things also in their concrete and individual essences, in as far precisely as these essences are, completely and altogether necessarily, particular modes of being. On this transcendental knowledge the legitimacy of metaphysics is grounded.

The apprehension of being confronts us right away with a problem: how are we to explain participation on the plane of the absolute? In other words, how are we, first of all, to conceive the reality of a particular being which truly is, since it subsists while not existing absolutely, since it is only one individual among many others? And then, how are we to conceive the absolute unity of being, seeing that the value of being is found truly distributed among multiple beings, relative one to the other? Briefly, the question is: how can the absolute, which implies unicity, be found in an order, which includes a multiplicity? How is the participation of being to be explained? How are we to ground the analogy of the transcendental idea of being? This is the metaphysical problem par excellence; it is the problem of the one and the many on the level of the absolute.

2. The Solution: The Internal Structure of Every Particular Being and the Unconditional Dependence of All in Regard to Absolute Being, the Infinite Source of All Participation, and the Unique Principle of the Ontological Order

Particular being cannot be conceived as a simple reality; it is intrinsically composite, structured.

Evidently, it must contain its essence, its mode of individual being, the measure of its participation in the value of being. But since it acts in an autonomous way, and since it is on that account subsistent; that is, distinct from the others in existence, it must likewise contain in the reality of which it is made up, its own proper *esse*, the intrinsic reason of its own existence. Particular being is made up of this intimate conjunction of two real principles, that of the mode of being, the root of individuality, and that of existence, the root of subsistence, of being a *suppositum*. The one and the other are necessary to enable us to think without contradiction, that being by participation, particular being exists. The two principles could not in any case be founded in a simple reality, unless participation disappeared; no more than they could be separated, for by that very fact they would cease to participate in being and would therefore be annihilated. The two principles are completely relative, one to the other; they are transcendental relations, and their correlation forms the structure which constitutes particular being.

This composition of essence and existence carries another with it, namely, on the plane of action, in the line of essence or concrete quiddity. In fact, the perfection of a being is measured by the plenitude of its subsistence. Particular being, which subsists according to the mode and within the limits of its individual essence, strives to achieve self-mastery, to put forth an autonomous activity, to lead a personal existence, which would be conformed to the exigencies of its nature. The ideal would be, therefore, to have full possession of itself in the clarity of a perfect consciousness; but to yield a distinct account of its nature, particular being must occupy its own proper place in the order of beings. To this end it must needs embrace in the sweep of its vision the totality of reality, with a view to determining its own peculiar attitude in conforming itself to the law of being, which governs the universal order. Particular being, therefore, must assimilate other beings to itself in the intentional order, by an immanent, personal activity, and it must adapt itself to them.

This labor of being ever enriched implies a becoming, but one which does not change in any way the fundamental determination of subsistent being; and more than this, by these operations this being seeks only to affirm itself fully, and always more and more to become stronger, in making more explicit, by all the means at its disposal, the immense riches of perfection which its real participation in the absolute value implies. Hence, along the line of the mode of ontological participation, that is, in that of the quiddity or essence, we must distinguish the real reason of the individual identity of particular being, and the real reason of the evolution which tends to perfect it. These reasons are the principle of substantiality, and the principle of accidental determination. They form a correlation, whose terms are adequately defined by their mutual relation.

The active development of a particular being is a complicated process, which results from putting into play different faculties, each of which we must define by its own formal object. In this accidental order correlations are constantly being multiplied, and this all the more as in the course of its operations particular being unceasingly acquires new determinations, transitory or permanent.

The problem of participation is raised likewise in the matter of essence, of quidditative perfection. In the material world, as experience actually testifies, every quidditative perfection is found in numerous individuals. This permits us to form specific concepts of these perfections which are abstract and absolutely univocal. What metaphysical foundation is required to explain this specific order, to reconcile the one and the many on the level of the species?

The examination of this question leads us to conclude to a hylomorphic composition of the substance of material beings: their mode of substantial being consists in the correlation of a principle of specific determination and of a principle of individuation. This profound quidditative structure reveals itself in the accidental development of these beings, by the correlation of a principle of quality and a principle of quantity, which are the real, immediate reasons of the mixture of activity and passivity which characterizes matter. These structures denote a falling off of spontaneous activity, a diminution of subsistence; in the measure in which a reality is material, it must undergo the action of other things in order itself to pass over into action. It must support itself effectively on the things that surround it, in order to persist in being and in order to act.

The intrinsic structure of particular beings constitutes the metaphysical foundation of their belonging to a real order; internal relativity is reflected in external relativity. The more we go down the pyramid of beings, the more complicated their structure becomes; in the same measure they become more dependent on others, and their autonomy is so much the more diminished.

No particular being no matter how perfect it may be, enjoys an absolute independence, for it is always contained in the order of beings. This is why a fundamental structure is necessarily found in all reality which exists only by participation: the correlation, namely, of the existence and the mode of being; and this structure implies always in this mode of being itself a subsidiary correlation, that of the substantial mode and the accidental modifications of this mode, because every particular being tends to its perfection by a becoming which affects it intrinsically. In material reality this fundamental structure becomes complicated by the hylomorphic composition of the substance, and consequently, by a parallel composition of accidental modifications.

The various elements of this doctrine have always formed the object of numerous controversies; but especially in the modern period has it been exposed to constant attacks. Too often the manner in which it is presented seems to compromise the fundamental unity of subsistent being; and yet if we make the structure of beings a complexus of correlations whose terms correspond as act and potency, as transcendental relations, such structure, far from impairing this unity, on the contrary establishes it solidly. For the union of the terms takes place necessarily and of itself, without necessitating recourse to an extrinsic principle for its realization.

This doctrine does not solve the metaphysical problem, but it defines its terms accurately and promises a solution of the problem. Particular being is a *suppositum*, a subsistent reality, in this precise sense that it possesses existence in its own right; for in its own peculiar structure, and not elsewhere, do we find the real principle of this existence. The *suppositum* is provided with its own proper *esse;* and yet it is only one particular being among others. It is contained in an order larger than itself in virtue of a mode of being, which itself likewise belongs to the internal structure of the *suppositum* and which completely individualizes it. Hence, by its whole structure, including the real principle of being, it belongs to the order of beings and is related to these beings. Hence too, it is impossible for it to contain in itself its absolute foundation, since everything which it comprises, is affected by relativity: particular being is altogether incapable of furnishing the adequate reason of its reality, of the absolute value of being which it manifests.

On the one hand, therefore, one particular being, no matter how autonomous, cannot be explained by itself since it is altogether steeped in relativity; on the other hand, particular beings, all of them together, are not any more in condition to furnish the sufficient reason of what exists. For these beings, while being fundamentally relative, each one to all the others, remain nevertheless truly subsistent *supposita;* and plurality, considered precisely as such, could not possibly constitute the supreme principle of unity. And yet, the absolute foundation of beings exists since these beings are, and since they bear witness to a solidity on every score. If this foundation can in no wise be identified with particular beings, it is because it is altogether distinct from them, without ceasing for all of that to be perfectly real. There exists, therefore, an absolute Being, the adequate reason of these beings. These latter are dependent on it in the most exhaustive way; they are created by it, while it is completely independent of them. It is their absolute Cause.

We must most carefully avoid tampering with the absolute character of this Cause. That is why we cannot consider particular beings as modes of the absolute Being; for this would be to declare that this Cause is infected intrinsically by the relative, and in this case it could not be the foundation of the real.

From the moment that we maintain the fullest respect for the absolute character of the creative Cause, everything is explained. Particular beings are truly independent of one another in as far as they are autonomous in their action, and in the same measure they are subsistent. Moreover, they are altogether dependent on their creative Cause, and they cannot be identified with this Cause, so that this total dependence itself likewise requires their subsistence. Thus, far from jeopardizing the autonomy of particular beings, the creative activity of the absolute Cause is their guarantee. Particular beings form an order necessarily: they are subsistent and nevertheless in an exhaustive way they are relative to one another. The paradox is explained once we admit that these beings are created; for on the one hand the creature must be really distinct from its absolute Cause, so as to form a complete being. On the other hand the activity of this absolute Cause cannot encounter any limit; it must get to everything in the unity of its action, so that all things enter completely into one and the same all-embracing order, that, namely, of creation.

In the last analysis creation answers the problem of participation on the plane of being. Everything which participates in the value of being is fundamentally contingent, and it can be conceived as purely possible; for participation in being does not presuppose any other kind of participation, and it cannot but be total. In other words, it is founded on a total dependence of things, relatively to a Cause which is absolutely independent. The being of the creature is a being completely received, and the solidity which it manifests rests on that of the creative activity actually present in it and maintaining it in being.

This divine cause is therefore the principle of the whole real order, the supreme analogue of the analogy of being. It would not be necessary to understand this in the sense of a principal term, which, while being superior to the analogous terms, would itself be an integral part and by that very fact a dependent part of the order which it governs, no less than the secondary analogues. Quite the contrary—and we can never cease to affirm this truth: creative activity gets to all things, only because it does not depend on anything; it is absolute. Here is the reason why the wholly gratuitous gift which it makes to each creature, is a gift absolutely beneficent; it is the gift of the sovereign value of being.

The general lines of the metaphysical system can be summed up in a few words. Particular beings are subsistent; they possess the value of being, but since they are contained in an all-embracing order they are relative, one to the other, and they are such by their whole reality, and this in an exhaustive manner. Then, too, everyone of them is a structured whole, a pure correlation, a cluster of relations; and even the internal principle of existence, the reason of its subsistence, is reduced to a transcendental relation, a simple element of structure. Complete external relativity serves only to express total internal relativity.

Such a reality is tendency through and through, "desiderium naturae," an appeal to the absolute. If these beings are relative, one to the other in an exhaustive manner, while being multiple and real *supposita*, it is because all of them together in an equally exhaustive manner, are related to the absolute Being by participating in His infinite perfection. Thoroughgoing relativity in the interior of the order of subsistent beings results adequately from the exhaustive relativity of the order in regard to God, the Creator, the unshakable foundation and the absolute source of all perfection. All of this is required by participation in the supreme value, and it is implied by the proportionality signified by the transcendental idea of being.

If it is true that "we measure the significance of a philosophical doctrine by the variety of the ideas which it opens up, and by the simplicity of the principle in which it is summed up," [8] the philosophy of being offers guarantees of power and fecundity. For the transcendental value which the idea of being possesses, makes it branch out into the most expansive and most varied domains, whereas its absolute value and its analogy allow it to penetrate all things, down to their very roots, down to that which is most intimate in them. Consequently, it is capable of drawing all things into a definitive synthesis, the synthesis, namely, of a unique order of participation, whose inexhaustible source is Absolute Perfection.

[8] Preface written by Henri Bergson for the select pages of G. Tarde, published in the collection "Les grands philosophes," Paris, Michaud, 1909. This is cited by Jacques Chevalier, Bergson (coll. *Les maîtres de la Pensée française*), Paris, 1928, p. 68.

INDEX

Absolute
  accidents, 25 note
  being according to Parmenides, 118
    note 38
  being, the metaphysical value of,
    23-25, 26-29, 329-30
  categories, 25 note
  consideration of nature, 124-25
  in the contingent, 24
  and evil, 218-19
  foundation of being, 282-326
  and infinite, 69-74
  in intellectual knowledge, 78-82
  in intrinsic possibility, 89-91
  and the metaphysical problem, 31-
    32
  and non-being, 57-58
  one and being according to Plotinus,
    119
  participation in absolute value of be-
    ing, 29-30
  simpliciter, secundum quid, 25 note
  and the unique, the infinite, 69-70
  and unity, 61
  univocity, 41
  of value according to Lagneau, 232
  of value according to Le Senne, 148,
    232-33
  of value according to Marcel, 233
  value and absolute worth, 230-31
Absolute and relative: in affirmation
    and negation, 56-58; in identity,
    58-60
Absolute Cause; *see* God
Abstraction
  and analogy of attribution, 42-43
  and the concept, 34
  and formation of specific concept,
    156-59
  and the idea of being, 35-37
  meaning of term, 34-35
  and the possibles, 90-91

Abstraction (*continued*)
  and sense knowledge, 34
  and univocity, 41, 44
Accident
  absolute and relative, 25 note
  does not have *esse,* 133-34
  ens entis, 133
  its *esse* is *inesse,* 180
  and the real principle of existence,
    180-81
  substance and accident, 173-202
  substance its final cause, 195
  substance its principle of individua-
    tion, 180
  substance its subject, 194
Accidental act of substance, 175
Accidental order, 194-212
Accidents: order of, 195-97
Act
  accidental, 174-75, 237-39
  and cause, 268
  correlation of act and potency, 239
  esse, the act of essence, 133
  esse, the actuality of all acts, 27
  esse, the first act, 133
  and the good, 216
  internal principle of perfection, 238
  meaning of scholastic term, 160-61
  Pure Act, 284-86
  real principle of existence, 237-39
  substantial form, an act, 161, 238-39
Action: belongs to the *suppositum,*
    241; God is His action, 309; is in
    the patient, 268 note 10; and pas-
    sion, 196-97
Activity
  active evolution of beings, 206-12
  of animals, plants, minerals, 211-12
  being acts according to its nature,
    194-95, 216
  creative and that of creatures, 321-
    25